The Genealogy of Terror *is a book that has been* ⟩
very long time . . .
   Sir David Calvert-Smith QC, former Direc
   former High Court Judge; member of the Parole

I recommend this book for anyone who wishes to understand in exciting breadth and forensic detail the landscape of contemporary Islam.
   Professor Norman Doe, Professor of Law, University of Cardiff

A book of stunning clarity and detail which will be of enormous value to practising criminal lawyers and to the interested 'lay' reader . . . a must-read.
   Max Hill QC, the Independent Reviewer of Terrorism
   Legislation; Head of Red Lion Chambers

This is a terrific book which is highly educational for the non-Muslim reader and the last two chapters in particular are a tour de force . . . Bravo!
   Ms. Jane Haberlin, Consultant Psychoanalytic
   Psychotherapist, The Balint Consultancy

This book is essential reading. Nowhere else have I seen the same clarity and precision in classifying different Muslim behaviors, ranging from highly desirable to downright dangerous. Its approach should be followed by everyone.
   Mohammed Amin MBE, Chairman of the Conservative-Muslim Forum and Co-Chair of the Muslim-Jewish Forum of Greater Manchester

This is a fascinating book which is rich in detail, very interesting to read and should be most helpful to its intended readers.
   James Loudon, Deputy Chairman of the Governors, University of Greenwich; member of the Independent Monitoring Board for HMP
   Swaleside

The Genealogy of Terror is a useful, clear and authoritative guide . . . I found its typology of Islam, Islamism and Non-violent and Violent Islamist Extremism most persuasive.
   Professor Alan Norrie, Professor of Law, University of Warwick;
   President of the International Association of Critical Realism

The Genealogy of Terror

In the first two decades of the twenty-first century, the events of 9/11, 7/7, the War on Terror and the Caliphate and atrocities of the so-called Islamic State have dominated Western consciousness and wreaked havoc in parts of the Muslim-majority world. In their wake, a spate of books has been written explaining the phenomenon of Islamist radicalisation and Jihadism.

Nevertheless, for normal citizens, as well as scholars of religion and legal professionals, the crucial question remains unanswered: how is Mainstream Islam different from both Islamism and the Islamist Extremism that is used to justify terrorist violence? In this highly original book, which draws upon the author's experience as an expert witness in Islamic theology in 27 counter-terrorism trials, the author uses the idea of the Worldview, as well as traditional Islamic theology, to answer this question.

The book explains not only what Mainstream Islam, Ideological Islamism and Islamist Extremism are in their broad philosophical characteristics and theological particulars, but also explains comprehensively how and why they are both superficially related and yet essentially and fundamentally different. In so doing, the book also illuminates the cast of characters and the development of their ideas that constitute Mainstream Islam and Ideological Islamism, and the Non-Violent and Violent Islamist Extremists who constitute the Genealogy of Terror.

Matthew L. N. Wilkinson is Senior Research Fellow at SOAS, University of London, and Associate Research Fellow of the McDonald Centre for Theology, Ethics and Public Life at the University of Oxford. He is Principal Investigator of *Understanding Conversion to Islam in Prison* programme, which researches the causes and consequences of conversion to Islam in prison and how inmates can derive rehabilitative benefit, and avoid any danger, from this religious choice. He has acted as an Expert Witness in Islamic Theology and Law in 27 counter-terrorism trials. His previous book, *A Fresh Look at Islam in a Multi-Faith World: A philosophy for success through education* (Routledge, 2015), was awarded the Cheryl Frank Memorial Prize (2014) as the most creative work of critical realist philosophy.

Photograph ©John Cairns

Law and Religion

The practice of religion by individuals and groups, the rise of religious diversity and the fear of religious extremism raise profound questions for the interaction between law and religion in society. The regulatory systems involved, the religion laws of secular government (national and international) and the religious laws of faith communities are valuable tools for our understanding of the dynamics of mutual accommodation and the analysis and resolution of issues in such areas as: religious freedom; discrimination; the autonomy of religious organisations; doctrine, worship and religious symbols; the property and finances of religion; religion, education and public institutions; and religion, marriage and children. In this series, scholars at the forefront of law and religion contribute to the debates in this area. The books in the series are analytical with a key target audience of scholars and practitioners, including lawyers, religious leaders, and others with an interest in this rapidly developing discipline.

Series Editor: Professor Norman Doe, Director of the Centre for Law and Religion, Cardiff University, UK

Series Board:
Carmen Asiaín, Professor, University of Montevideo
Paul Babie, Professor and Associate Dean (International), Adelaide Law School
Pieter Coertzen, Chairperson, Unit for the Study of Law and Religion, University of Stellenbosch
Alison Mawhinney, Reader, Bangor University
Michael John Perry, Senior Fellow, Center for the Study of Law and Religion, Emory University

Religion, Law and the Constitution
Balancing Beliefs in Britain
Javier García Oliva and Helen Hall

Law, Religion and Love
Seeking Ecumenical Justice for the Other
Paul Babie and Vanja-Ivan Savić

The Genealogy of Terror
How to distinguish between Islam, Islamism and Islamist Extremism
Matthew L. N Wilkinson

For more information about this series, please visit: www.routledge.com/Law-and-Religion/book-series/LAWRELIG

The Genealogy of Terror
How to distinguish between Islam, Islamism and Islamist Extremism

Matthew L. N. Wilkinson

Routledge
Taylor & Francis Group

LONDON AND NEW YORK

First published 2019 by Routledge

2 Park Square, Milton Park, Abingdon, Oxfordshire OX14 4RN
52 Vanderbilt Avenue, New York, NY 10017

Routledge is an imprint of the Taylor & Francis Group, an informa business

First issued in paperback 2019

Copyright © 2019 Matthew L. N. Wilkinson

The right of Matthew L. N. Wilkinson to be identified as author of this work has been asserted by him in accordance with sections 77 and 78 of the Copyright, Designs and Patents Act 1988.

All rights reserved. No part of this book may be reprinted or reproduced or utilised in any form or by any electronic, mechanical, or other means, now known or hereafter invented, including photocopying and recording, or in any information storage or retrieval system, without permission in writing from the publishers.

Notice:
Product or corporate names may be trademarks or registered trademarks, and are used only for identification and explanation without intent to infringe.

British Library Cataloguing-in-Publication Data
A catalogue record for this book is available from the British Library

Library of Congress Cataloging-in-Publication Data
Names: Wilkinson, M. L. N. (Matthew L. N.), author.
Title: The genealogy of terror : how to distinguish between Islam,
  Islamism, and Islamist extremism / by Matthew L. N. Wilkinson.
Description: 1 [edition]. | New York : Routledge, 2018. | Series:
  Law and religion | Includes bibliographical references and index.
Identifiers: LCCN 2018003049 | ISBN 9781138200463 (hardback)
Subjects: LCSH: Islam. | Islamic fundamentalism. | Terrorism—
  Religious aspects—Islam.
Classification: LCC BP161.3 .W5474 2018 | DDC 297.09/051—dc23
LC record available at https://lccn.loc.gov/2018003049

ISBN: 978-1-138-20046-3 (hbk)
ISBN: 978-0-367-37371-9 (pbk)

Typeset in Galliard
by Apex CoVantage, LLC

In the name of God, the Generally Compassionate, the Intensely Merciful

This book is dedicated to Mohammed Amin MBE.

A man whose deep concern for the well-being of British society and humanity in general led him to facilitate this book, graciously and generously, with his time and his money in order to serve the hard and complex work of front-line professionals and scholars in this field.

Contents

Foreword by Professor Norman Doe   xii
Preface   xiii

   The context of this book xiii
   The aims of this book xiv
   A note on the transliteration of Arabic terms xv

Acknowledgments   xvi

1 **Why this book is needed**   1

   A global crisis of misunderstanding: why this book is needed; who its author is; what this book will accomplish 1
   Why? How? What? 2

   Plate section between pages 5 and 6

   Plate 1   Worldviews of Mainstream Islam, Islamism and Islamist Extremism
   Plate 2   Characteristics of the Worldviews of Mainstream Islam, Islamism and Islamist Extremism
   Plate 3   Doctrine of Loyalty & Disavowal (*Al-Wala' wal Bara'*) in the Worldviews of Mainstream Islam, Islamism and Islamist Extremism
   Plate 4   Doctrine of the Unity of God (*Tawhid*) in the Worldviews of Mainstream Islam, Islamism and Islamist Extremism

   My story and credentials 7
   The structure and substance of this book 15

2 **The roots of Islam, Islamism and Islamist Extremism: the historical fault lines of Islam**   17

   Introduction: Islam is shaped by the presence and absence of Muhammad 17
   Political-theological hiatus and split: the Sunni-Shia divide 20

*Institutional hiatus and split: the division of powers between
the Muslim Executive and the religious judiciary 29*
*Intellectual hiatus and split: rationalist vs. literalist intellectual
tension 37*

3 The Worldviews of Islam, Islamism and Islamist Extremism 50

*Islam, Islamism and Islamist Extremism are all internally-
coherent, self-contained Worldviews 50*
The idea of a Worldview 50
Islam, Islamism and Islamist Extremism as Worldviews 52
The Worldview of Mainstream Islam: unity-in-diversity 54
The Worldview of Activist Islam: diversity-in-unity 61
*The Worldview of Islamism: contingent separation
and exaggerated difference 66*
*The Worldview of Non-Violent Islamist Extremism:
absolute Manichean separation 71*
*The Worldview of Violent Islamist Extremism (VIE): absolute,
eternal difference and separation with lethal consequences
for the non-Muslim and wrong-Muslim out-groups 73*

4 Basic beliefs, practices and characteristic themes of Islam, Islamism and Islamist Extremism 78

*The sources of the Worldview of Mainstream Islam:
the Qur'an and the* Sunna *79*
The themes and ethical praxis of Mainstream Islam 94
The themes and ethical praxis of Activist Islam 109
The themes and ethical praxis of Ideological Islamism 114
*The themes and ethical praxis of Non-Violent Islamist
Extremism 117*
The themes and ethical praxis of Violent Islamist Extremism 122

5 Mainstream Islam: the people, texts and contexts 131

*Hermeneutical health warning: people and their ideas
are 'shifters' 131*
Mainstream Islam: the people and the texts 132
The Book of God – Al-Qur'an *(the recitation) 133*
*The Opening Chapter (*Al-Fatiha*) 133*
Other seminal chapters 137
Commentaries on the Qur'an 139
The canonical books of hadith 140
*The great works of Law (*Fiqh*), Jurisprudence (*Usul al-Fiqh*) 140*

The Wahhabi reformation: the Book of Divine Unity
  *(*Kitab al-Tawhid*) 143*
To philosophize or not to philosophize? Al-Ghazali vs. Ibn Rushd 145
Mainstream Islam in the modern and contemporary period 149

6 Islamism: the people, texts and contexts — 154

Maududi, Al-Banna and Khomeini: the Ideological Islamist shift from agency to structure 154
The second phase of Islamism: Sayyid Qutb and the birth of Non-Violent Islamist Extremism 162
Milestones (1964) – the 'ur-' text of Islamist Extremism 166
Ayatollah Khomeini: Shia Islamism succeeds where Sunni Islamism fails 170

7 The Genealogy of Terror: the people, texts and contexts of Violent Islamist Extremism — 174

Violent Islamist Extremism's 'pioneers': Abdullah Azzam and Muhammad Abd as-Salam Faraj 174
Defense of Muslim lands: the first obligation after faith (1979) 177
The glamour of Jihad 179
The ideologues of Al-Qaeda: bin Laden, Al-Awlaki, Al-Zawahiri and As-Suri 179
The impact of the Bosnian War (1991–1995) 181
Al-Zawahiri and As-Suri: Al-Qaeda's backroom boys 187
The ideologues of the Islamic State: Abu Musab Az-Zarqawi, Naji, Abu Bakr Al-Baghdadi and Abu Muhammad Al-Adnani 188
The Arab Spring reaches Syria 191
The state-building of Islamic State 194

8 A second Age of Extremes or a second Age of Enlightenment? — 201

Summary 201
The political conditions of Extremism 202
Why? The root causes of Islamist Extremism 203

Appendix 1: Basic Guides to Mainstream Islam	210
Appendix 2: Digital Islam	211
Glossary of key terms and names	213
References	222
Index	230

Foreword

In the first two decades of the twenty-first century, the events of 9/11, 7/7, the War on Terror and the Caliphate and atrocities of the so-called Islamic State have dominated Western consciousness. In their wake, scores of books have been written explaining the phenomenon of Islamist radicalization and Jihadism, of which recent studies by Gilles Kepel, Peter Neumann, Farhad Khosrokhavar and Shiraz Maher spring to mind.

Here Wilkinson builds on the forensic-style of their analysis from a highly original and illuminating philosophical perspective. Using the idea of the Worldview – an integrated body of belief and practice – as well as traditional Islamic theology, Wilkinson explains not only what Islamist Extremism is in its broad characteristics and doctrinal particular, but also explains comprehensively and convincingly how and why Mainstream Islam and Mainstream Islamic behavior is essentially and fundamentally different from Ideological Islamism and Islamist Extremism. He illuminates the cast of characters and the development of their ideas that constitute Mainstream Islam, Ideological Islamism and Islamist Extremism.

The Genealogy of Terror therefore answers the intuition and hunches that many of us have had – that Mainstream Islam must be different from what terrorists propagate – and explains comprehensively how this is so.

Wilkinson is uniquely well-placed to give us this book: he has acted in 27 counter-terrorism trials related to Islamist Extremism, instructed by both the Prosecution and the Defense and has witnessed the full gamut of the ideology, propaganda and acts perpetrated by the followers and recruiters of Al-Qaeda, the so-called Islamic State and other Islamist groups.

As well as being an academic philosopher and theologian of Islam, he is also a practicing Muslim, and this book is motivated, at least in part, by a love of his faith and a respect for its sincere followers across the ages, as well as a desire to see all types of members of society flourish.

I recommend this book for anyone who wishes to understand in exciting breadth and forensic detail the landscape of contemporary Islam.

Professor Norman Doe
Director of the Centre for Law and Religion,
University of Cardiff
January 2018

Preface

The context of this book

In the first six months of 2017, terrorist atrocities of varying scale have been committed in the name of Islam in Berlin, Paris, Manchester and London, not to mention Istanbul, Kabul and a never-ending spate of suicide attacks by the so-called Islamic State group in Baghdad, Iraq. In response, in his election campaign, the then-candidate for the Presidency of the United States of America, Donald Trump, called for a 'complete shut-down' on Muslims entering the US. In Britain, during his time in office, former UK Prime Minister, David Cameron, and the then Home Secretary, now Prime Minister, Theresa May, repeatedly called on British Muslims to eschew extremism and to embrace the British values of tolerance, the rule of law, democracy and freedom of speech. This gave the impression to many Muslims that Cameron and May believed that there was something inherent to Islam itself which made Muslims more likely to be religiously extreme and less likely to relate to and embrace those British values than other UK citizens. Now-Prime Minister Teresa May is finding the UK Government's Contest of counter-extremism policy and, in particular, its Prevent strategy are under fire for creating a 'suspect' community out of all Muslims rather than being successful in identifying and, where appropriate, prosecuting extremist terrorists.[1]

Yet despite the fact that we have been alerted to the need for a generational struggle against extremism, the measures taken so far seem both to be failing to prevent violent Islamist extremism and succeeding in alienating swathes of the Muslim community.[2] Moreover, the UK Government's efforts both to define and tackle Islamist extremism have so far been both intellectually and practically inadequate. The recent government initiative to set up a Commission on Countering Extremism is evidence that the UK Government itself realizes that there is still a lot of definitional and operational work to be done before it knows properly what it is countering and how to counter it.[3]

---

1 Ross, 'Academics Criticise Anti-Radicalisation Strategy in Open Letter'.
2 The Muslim Community is, of course, comprised of many ethno-cultural communities.
3 Peck, 'Theresa May to Set up Commission for Countering Extremism'.

The Muslim community itself has made little sustained effort to define Islamist extremism carefully at all, so keen has it been, understandably, to promote the message that Islam does not promote or condone extremist violence. Too often the Muslim community has either been in denial that terrorist violence committed in the name of Islam has any connection to religious ideas or even exists at all; or else it has, on occasion, tended to tar great swathes of its own number, quite unfairly and with a degree of hysteria, with the Islamist brush.

What these intractable and polarized situations have in common are failures of thinking. The failure:

1 to recognize *that* and *how* Islam, Islamism and Violent Islamist Extremism are fundamentally different phenomena which are, nevertheless, superficially related; and
2 to recognize sufficiently that the people whose lives are shaped by these different phenomena are likely to have fundamentally different behaviors in the world.

These failures of thinking have led to the failure of governments to create an effective long-term strategy that both identifies and disables terrorists without stigmatizing the entire Muslim community as a whole, a strategy that takes into account and derives benefit from Muslims' faith and their presence in Europe rather than ignoring or trivializing their faith and shutting them out of political and social life.

The aims of this book

Therefore, this book is motivated by three aims to address what threatens to become a highly damaging and deeply entrenched failure of thinking:

1 To provide robust working understandings of what Islam, Islamism and Violent and Non-Violent Islamist Extremism are in their broad characteristics as Worldviews and in their core doctrinal particulars and to describe how and why they are similar superficially but differ fundamentally from each other;
2 To show how these phenomena have emerged from divergent traditions and innovations within the Muslim-majority world and how they are shaped by 'the presence of the past';
3 To show how the attitudes and behaviors engendered by the different Worldviews are also likely to be fundamentally different. The attitudes and behaviors engendered by Islam are likely to benefit society at large; the attitudes and behaviors engendered by Islamism are likely to compromise the individual's ability to flourish in society at large, and the attitudes of Violent Islamist Extremism set out to destroy society at large.

It is an ambitious intellectual agenda, but one of which I believe the world is profoundly in need.

A note on the transliteration of Arabic terms

Throughout the book, my guiding principle is that the text should be as readable to English-speakers and as uncluttered by technical terms as possible. However, since Islam was borne into an Arab environment in Arabic, of necessity the book contains a lot of transliterated Arabic words and some religious technical terms.

In the interests of consistency and clarity, where they exist, I use the Oxford English Dictionary versions of Arabic words and names, e.g. Muhammad, Qur'an, Mecca and Medina. In the interests of readability, I do not use marks for Arabic letters that have no English equivalents, such as an apostrophe for the Arabic letter *'ayn*. For example, Ali is not spelt *'Ali* as it might typically be spelled in an Islamic Studies academic text. The Arabic letter 'Dod' which is a deep 'd', is simply represented by the letter 'd'. The Arabic letter 'dhal', which is pronounced like the English 'th' as in 'that', is represented by 'dh'. There are two Arabic 'h' sounds – one hard, one aspirated – both of which I transliterate using the English letter 'h'.

Whenever I can use an accurate English translation for an Arabic Islamic term, I use it; for example, the Rightly-guided Caliphs rather than Khulafā ar-Rāshidūn. If no adequate English translation exists for a term or an Arabic word has entered English, I stick with the transliterated Arabic; for example, Ulema, rather than either 'legal scholars' or 'religious jurists'.

Arabic words that have entered the English language are not italicized. Arabic words which have not entered the English language are italicized.

I provide a glossary of key Islamic theological terms and people at the end of the book, which briefly explains their meaning and says where they are explained fully in the main text.

Acknowledgments

I would like to acknowledge some important people who gave generously their time and expertise to review drafts of this book and were critical sounding-boards for me of wise and educated advice:

Mohammed Amin MBE, Chairman of the Conservative-Muslim Forum and Co-Chair of the Muslim Jewish Forum of Greater Manchester
Sheikh Salah al-Ansari, former Imam of the Central London Mosque; Lecturer in Islamic Studies, The Muslim College, London
Sir David Calvert-Smith, former Director of Public Prosecutions; former High Court Judge and member of the Parole Board for England & Wales
Ms. Jane Haberlin, Consultant Psychoanalytic Psychotherapist, The Balint Consultancy
Max Hill QC, the Independent Reviewer of Terrorism Legislation; Head of Red Lion Chambers
Mr. James Loudon, Deputy Chairman of the Governors, University of Greenwich; member of the Independent Monitoring Board for HMP Swaleside
Mr. Eoin McLennan-Murray, Chair of the Howard League for Penal Reform; former President of the Prison Governors' Association.
Professor Alan Norrie, Professor of Law, University of Warwick; President of the International Association of Critical Realism
Mr. Richard Wilkinson, former UK Ambassador to Chile and Chair of the Board of Governors of Winchester University

Much of what is of merit in this book is the result of your sage advice; all the mistakes are my own. Thank you all so much.

I would also like to acknowledge the support and kindness of **Professor Muhammad Abdel Haleem** and **Professor Stefan Sperl** at SOAS, University of London, who made me welcome as Research Fellow in Islam in Education and Law. **Sir Anthony Figgis KVCO CMG**, former Marshal of the Queen's Diplomatic Corps and Trustee of Curriculum for Cohesion, and his wife, the sadly late **Lady Mayella Figgis**, have also shown me great kindness over the course of the two years in which I wrote this book.

Finally, my beautiful wife **Lucy** is a constant source of wisdom and strength. I would never have been able to undertake or finish this book without her love and support. And my wonderful son, **Gabriel**, who is a continual joy and inspiration to me and who saw me over the finishing line with scrambled eggs and cups of tea!

1 Why this book is needed

A global crisis of misunderstanding: why this book is needed; who its author is; what this book will accomplish

From April 2015 to January 2016, the Syrian Civil War (2011–present) burst onto the Western European landmass and into the Western European consciousness in the form of three startling and related events, shattering the fragile illusion of separate Muslim Middle Eastern and (post-) Judeo-Christian Western Worlds.

First, the migrant crisis, described by the Economist newspaper in Biblical terms as an 'Exodus', saw hundreds of thousands of Syrians, Iraqis, Afghans, Pakistanis, Somalis, Sudanese and others pouring out of the Muslim-majority world heading inexorably in determined bands, first hazardously across the Mediterranean into Greece and then through the Balkans to Northern Europe and Germany in particular. They were 'pushed' by armed conflict, political instability, corruption and a lack of opportunity and 'pulled' by the open-arms policy of the German Chancellor Angela Merkel.[1]

Second, on Friday 13 November 2015, Europeans experienced first-hand what, amongst other malaises, the refugees were so desperately and determinedly fleeing, as a series of coordinated terrorist attacks, including two suicide bombings outside the French National Football Stadium, ripped through Paris and its northern suburb, Saint-Denis. The terrorists claimed the lives of 130 people, mostly young people out for the night, including 89 rock-concert goers at the Bataclan theatre, where attackers took hostages before engaging in a standoff with police.

---

1 Merkel was both moved humanly by the plight of those in need and politically by the chance to redeem, once and for all, Germany's moral standing on the world stage after the horrors of the twentieth century. Croucher, 'Refugees Crisis'.
  "Germany! Germany!" became the refrain of choice for Syrian migrants who in Berlin were greeted by the German public with cheers and cups of tea. Less stable, prosperous and confident European countries in central Europe responded differently by erecting fences and advocating the need for EU controls and quotas to deal with the overwhelming mass of unregistered foreigners at their gates as gradually the German electorate became more nervous about their leader's humanity and largesse. Stone, 'Germans Worry About Growing Migrant Numbers'.

2 *Why this book is needed*

The attacks were claimed by the so-called Islamic State Group (hereafter known as ISG), saying it was in retaliation against 'the filthy French'[2] for the French airstrikes on ISG targets in Syria and Iraq. The attacks were organized in Belgium and perpetrated with French complicity.[3] They were described by the French President, François Hollande, as "an act of war".[4]

Finally, in the first week of 2016 reports started filtering into and through the European media of coordinated sexual assaults on female revelers[5] at New Year's Eve gatherings in the German city of Cologne by groups of Arab and Asian-looking young men who were immediately assumed to be asylum-seekers from Syria.

These reports were followed-up by further reports of similar attacks in other European cities from Helsinki to Zurich. The reports fueled the fear that the ethics and values that these predominantly male refugees had brought with them from the Islamic Middle East to Europe were fundamentally incompatible with core liberal European values such as respect for the persons and property of women.[6]

Why? How? What?

Intelligence agencies and security forces were not surprised by the Paris terrorist attacks[7] as across Europe many Islamist terrorist plots had been thwarted since the 9/11 attacks by Al-Qaeda on the Twin Towers in New York, both before and after the rise to eminence of ISG in 2013–2014. Nonetheless, French and European publics were faced with three stark questions in the wake of such apparently mindless brutality, which, as they grieved, they asked themselves in this order of incomprehension: Why? How? What?

1   *Why* did a group of young people hate another group of young people so much that they were prepared to slaughter them in cold blood, while at the same time being prepared to exterminate themselves?[8]

---

2   Gardham, 'ISIL Issued Warning to "Filthy French"'.
3   'November 2015 Paris Attacks'.
4   Despite the admirable resilience shown by the French national football team who played a much-lauded friendly match against England at Wembley Stadium, London the following Tuesday, the attacks traumatized northern Europe. As so often with terrorism, in the very short-term, in terms of terrorizing people, the attacks had worked. The City of Brussels, from where the attacks were masterminded, went into 'lockdown' for four days as one of the attackers went on the run. The German open-doors policy for migrants also came under scrutiny as it emerged that one of the terrorists had crossed into Europe from Syria posing as a migrant. Also, the so-called open-border Schengen Agreement within Europe itself was brought into critical relief as the unnerving fact emerged that a car containing assailants with seven Kalashnikov AK47 assault rifles had been driven across the France-Germany border without being apprehended.
5   Eventually around 500 criminal complaints were filed. BBC Europe, 'Cologne Attackers "Were Migrant Men"'.
6   Connolly, 'I've Never Experienced Anything Like That'.
7   Rogin, 'CIA Director'.
8   Pizzi, 'In Wake of Attacks, Parisians Ask, Why Here?'.

2   *How* was it possible that a group of such violent criminals could manage to plan and perpetrate an act of violence on such a scale in the heart of one of the most iconic European capital cities?
3   *What* manner of people were these who could carry out such a sub-human act of butchery, and what were the ideas that were driving and motivating them? This last question provoked a further sub-question driven by understandable fear:

What, if any, were the differences in beliefs and ideas between the killers and other people who also called themselves Muslim who were living in the heart of Europe in great numbers, especially since at least some of these people seemed to espouse outmoded and unethical attitudes towards women as evidenced by the New Year's Eve assaults?

Although it was conceived long before the events related above, this book will address some of these questions head-on.

It will address and answer the 'What ?'[9] question by examining and describing broadly the nature and theological-philosophical characteristics of Mainstream Islam as honed by centuries of integrated religious belief and practice and as manifest in myriad denominational forms by as many as 1.8 billion people. This integrated combination of religious belief and religious practice is central to Islam and is hereafter referred to as 'praxis'.

Comparatively, it will describe how Mainstream Islam differs fundamentally in nature from two different, though related, phenomena, which I, following others, call Islamism and Islamist[10] Extremism.

In so doing, the book will also respond to why these distinct phenomena have come about and begin to suggest how professionals and others charged with a duty of care over young Muslims can respond to enable them to derive maximal benefit from their Islamic faith and avoid the pitfalls and dangers of its skewed, damaging Islamist relations.

It is crucial that all three of these questions are answered thoroughly and properly. The failure to perform a similar diagnostic and follow-up educational exercise after the attacks by Al-Qaeda on New York of 11 September 2001 led to catastrophic failures in understanding that caused fatal flaws in the Bush-Blair 'War on Terror' which have served to alienate, enrage and radicalize swathes of the Muslim-majority world, while palpably not winning the battle against Islamist Extremism. These failures of identification and academic (as opposed to security)

---

9 The so-called ontological/nature of being question.
10 Although to apply the word 'Islamist' to violent extremism is contentious, I think that it is correct since those who perpetrate such acts always do so using language and stating aspirations which they believe are derived from Islam. The charge that, for example, Irish Republican terrorism was never called 'Christianist' is not an apposite one. The IRA, although mostly Catholic, were fighting on the agenda of a united, republican Ireland, not, for example, to establish the Holy Roman Empire of Ireland or a global Catholic State.

4 *Why this book is needed*

intelligence as to the nature of Islamist Extremism are at least partially responsible[11] for the escalation and proliferation of Islamist terror that we are witnessing today.

Rationale: addressing a real, determinate absence

So this book addresses a critical and 'determinate' failure;[12] namely, that British, American and other governments have, for the past 15 years, been drafting legislation and introducing education and preventive national policies targeting Violent and Non-Violent Islamist Extremism without defining in sufficient depth or detail what the natures of Violent Islamist Extremism (VIE) and Non-Violent Islamist Extremism are.

That is to say, governments and think tanks have tended to address the 'How to respond?' question without understanding in sufficient depth or detail what it is that they are addressing. No one has, as yet, provided a systematic and philosophically robust account of the similarities and crucial differences between Mainstream Islam, Ideological Islamism,[13] Non-Violent Islamist Extremism and Violent Islamist Extremism, and such a robust account is what this book intends to provide.

Making clear distinctions between religious/ideological phenomena and their adherents

This book aims to make clear, robust distinctions between the natures of three religious/ideological phenomena, which I will characterize as distinct Worldviews:

1 Mainstream Islam;
2 Islamism (sometimes referred to elsewhere as 'Political Islam'[14]);
3 Islamist Extremism (see Figure 3.1 and Plate 1).

This includes identifying and characterizing some 'grey' areas between these phenomena:

4 'Activist' Islam, which is, broadly, a part of Mainstream Islam but intersects with Islamism;
5 Non-Violent Islamist Extremism, which lies between Islamism and Violent Islamist Extremism and sets up the Worldview of Violent Islamist Extremism without directly encouraging violence (see Figure 1.1 and Plate 1).

These Worldviews are not, in any theological sense, denominational, but rather are supra-denominational. Muslims from different theological denominations or persuasions – Sunni, Shia, Sufi, Salafi, Maliki, Hanafi, Deobandi or

---

11 Burke, *The 9/11 Wars*; Richardson, *What Terrorists Want*.
12 Bhaskar, *Dialectic*.
13 This book will use the term 'Ideological Islamism'. This may seem to some to be a tautology since Islamism is, by its nature, a political ideology. However, I feel that it is important to stress its nature is primarily ideological.
14 Incorrectly in my view for reasons that will be explained in Chapter 3.

Why this book is needed 5

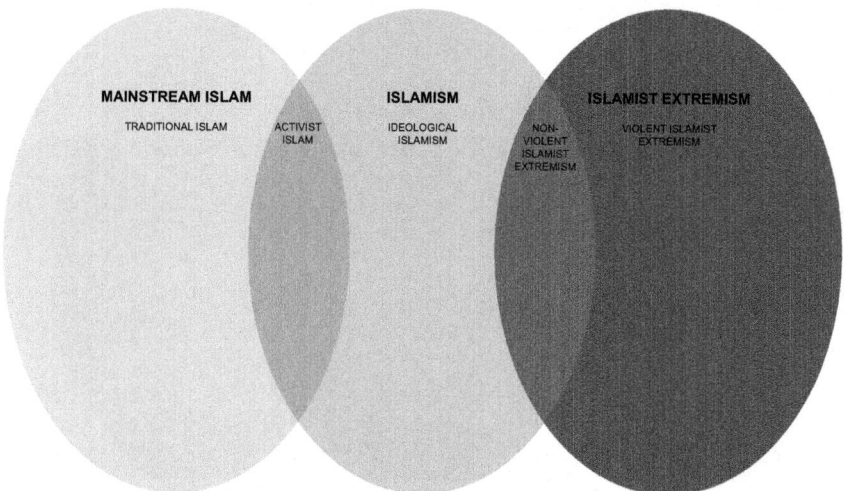

Figure 1.1 Worldviews of Mainstream Islam, Islamism and Islamist Extremism
For full color version please see Color Plate 1 after Page 5.

Barelwi to name but a few – can and do exist in Worldviews that cross the entire spectrum of possibilities.[15]

This definitional task will lead to two further claims. First, the book will claim that these phenomena are often similar in Islamic complexion but are in their basic nature and outcomes-in-the-world foundationally and profoundly different. Color Plates 1–4 deploy a traffic light 'green-amber-red' typology to indicate the significant qualitative differences in outcomes between these Worldviews.

Mainstream Islam, in green, and Activist Islam, in green/amber, both encourage the type of legitimate behavior which is likely to be beneficial both to the individual and society.

Ideological Islamism, in amber, is likely to be damaging to the individual's ability to operate well in mainstream society without usually directly encouraging illegal activity.

Non-violent Islamist Extremism, in amber/red, is likely to be damaging both to the individual and society and, by encouraging hatred of the 'Other', borders on encouraging illegal activities such as Hate Crime.

Violent Islamist Extremism, in red, damages both the individual and society and encourages what is illegal Hate and Terrorist Crime.

In this way, the book is premised on a 'both-and' claim about the relationship between Islam, Islamism and Islamist Extremism that these phenomena are both significantly related in theological-linguistic complexion and profoundly different

---

15 As we will explore in Chapter 2, the Sunni-Shia Split is the major denominational schism in Islam, broadly speaking analogous to the Roman Catholic-Protestant schism in Christianity. The other intra-denominational positions such as Barelwi and Deobandi are broadly analogous in the scale and scope of their differences to the different intra-Protestant Presbyterian, Baptist and Methodist positions in Christianity.

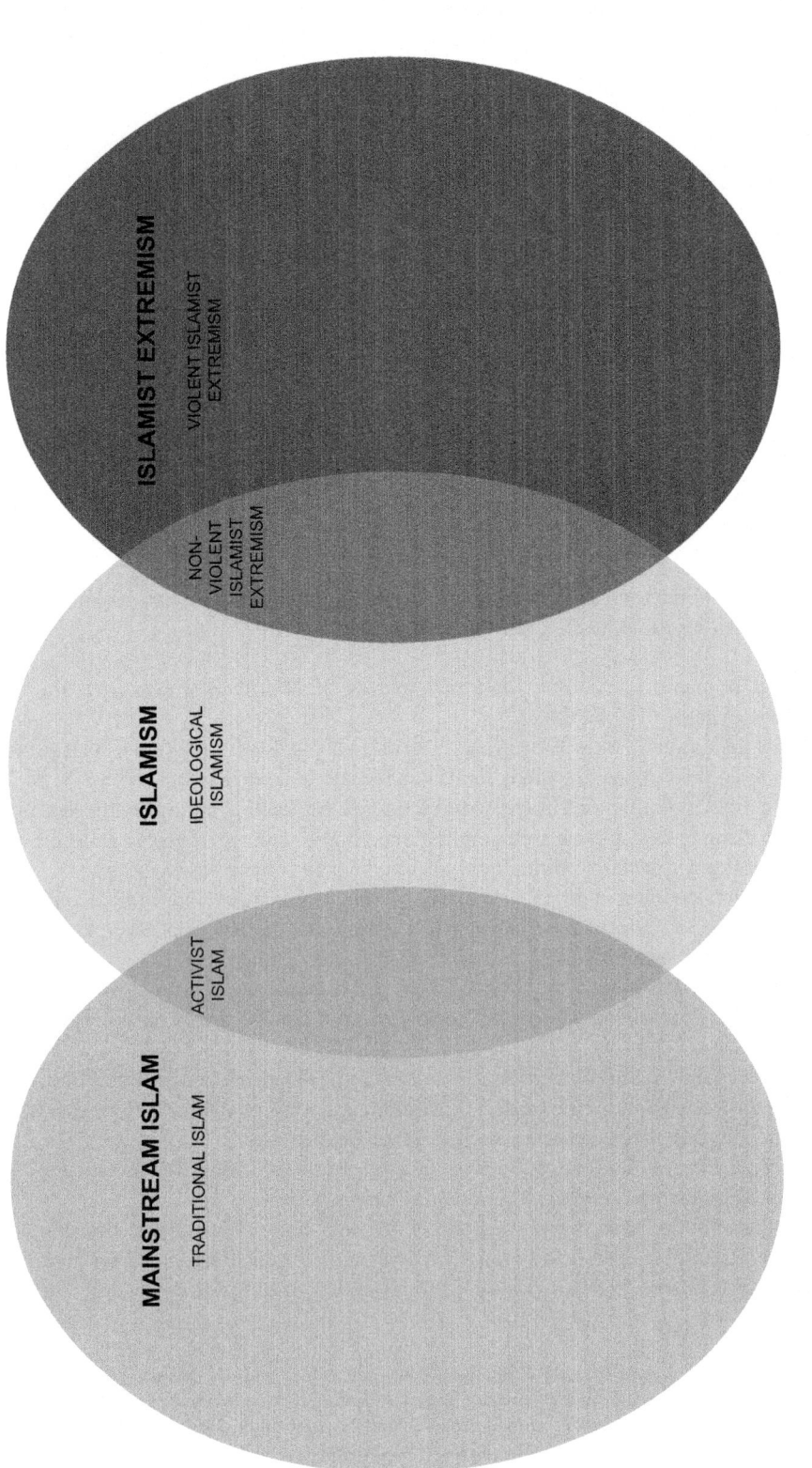

Plate 1 Worldviews of Mainstream Islam, Islamism and Islamist Extremism

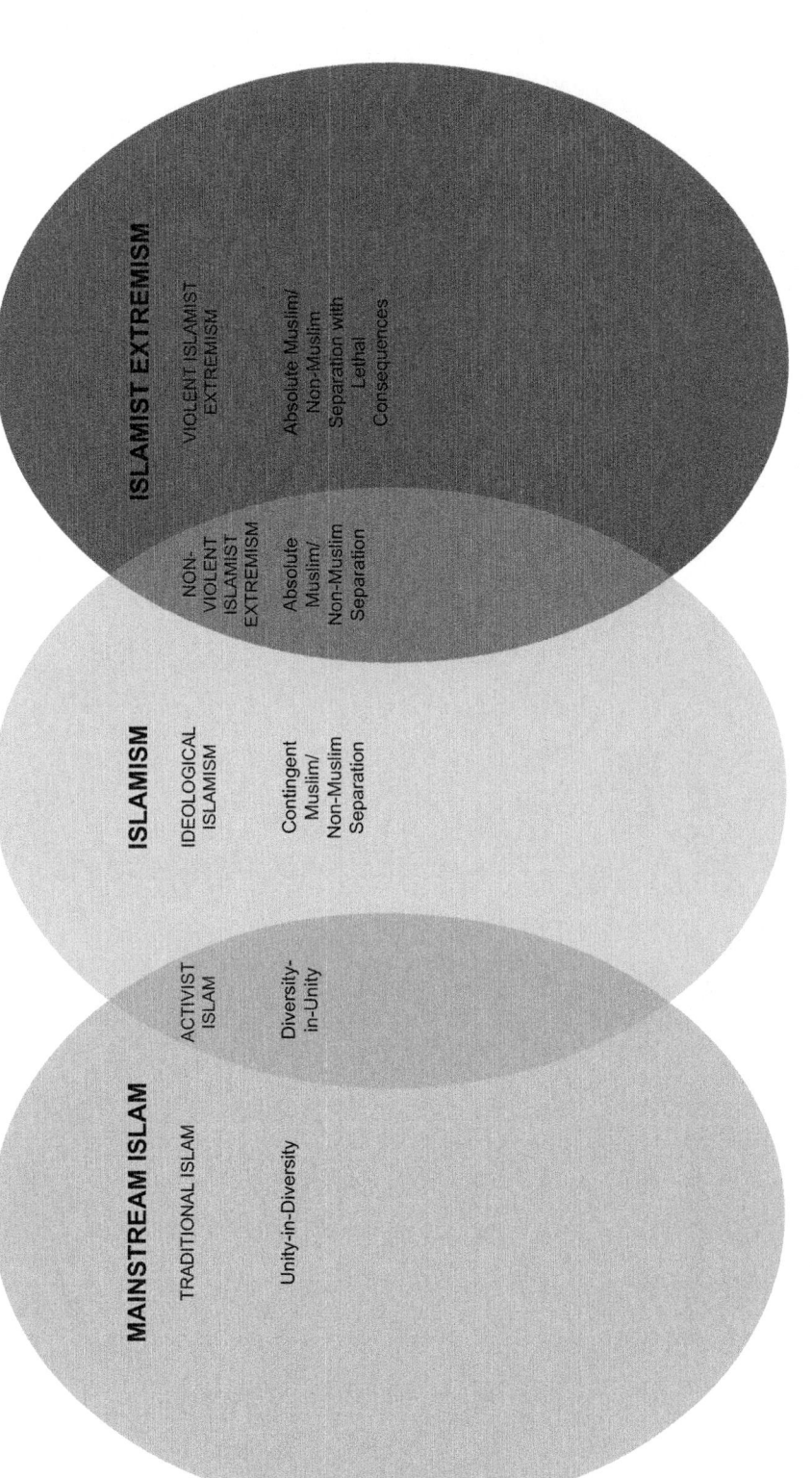

Plate 2 Characteristics of the Worldviews of Mainstream Islam, Islamism and Islamist Extremism

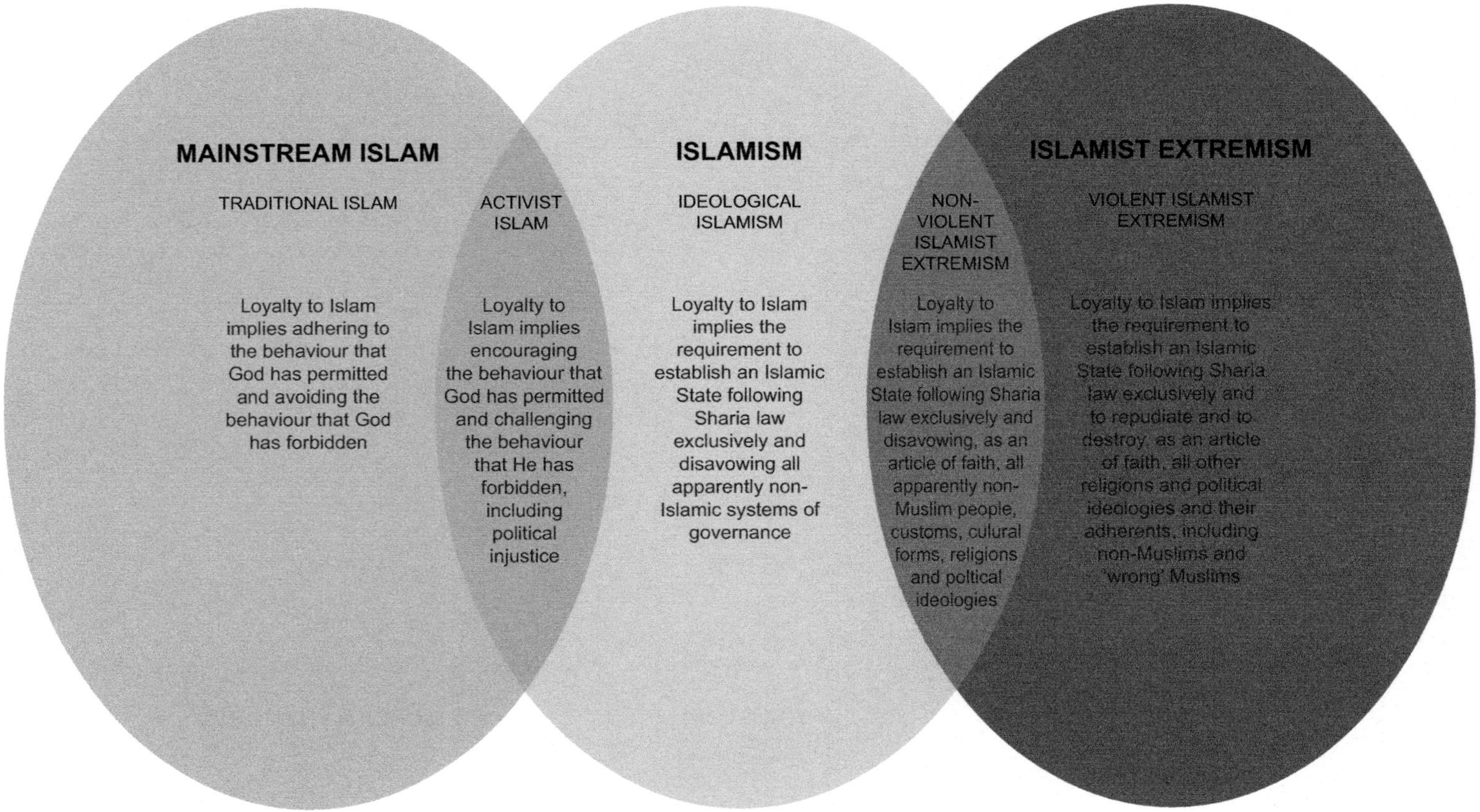

MAINSTREAM ISLAM

TRADITIONAL ISLAM

Loyalty to Islam implies adhering to the behaviour that God has permitted and avoiding the behaviour that God has forbidden

ACTIVIST ISLAM

Loyalty to Islam implies encouraging the behaviour that God has permitted and challenging the behaviour that He has forbidden, including political injustice

ISLAMISM

IDEOLOGICAL ISLAMISM

Loyalty to Islam implies the requirement to establish an Islamic State following Sharia law exclusively and disavowing all apparently non-Islamic systems of governance

ISLAMIST EXTREMISM

NON-VIOLENT ISLAMIST EXTREMISM

Loyalty to Islam implies the requirement to establish an Islamic State following Sharia law exclusively and disavowing, as an article of faith, all apparently non-Muslim people, customs, cultural forms, religions and political ideologies

VIOLENT ISLAMIST EXTREMISM

Loyalty to Islam implies the requirement to establish an Islamic State following Sharia law exclusively and to repudiate and to destroy, as an article of faith, all other religions and political ideologies and their adherents, including non-Muslims and 'wrong' Muslims

Plate 3 Doctrine of Loyalty & Disavowal (*Al-Wala' wal Barra'*) in the Worldviews of Mainstream Islam, Islamism and Islamist Extremism

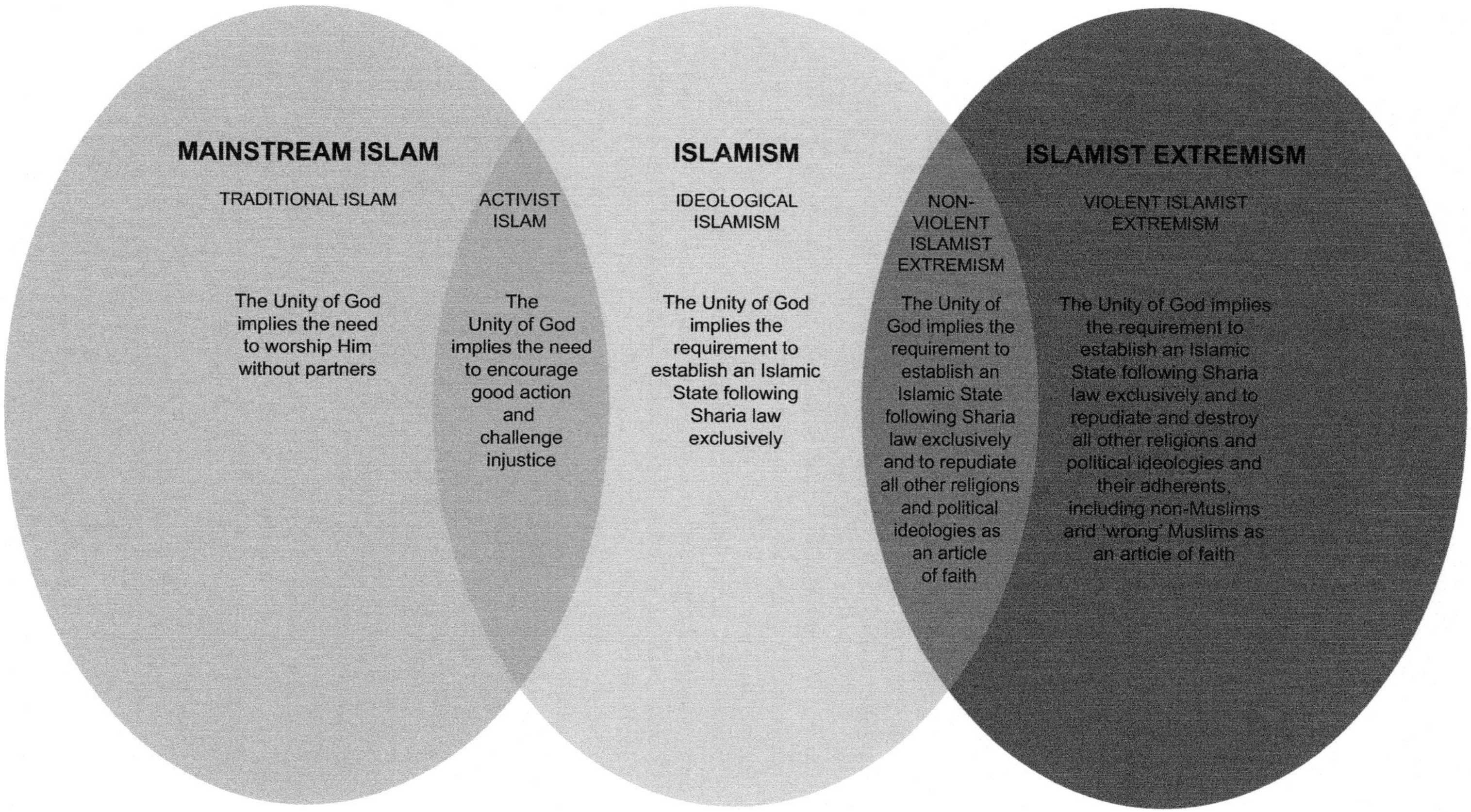

MAINSTREAM ISLAM

TRADITIONAL ISLAM

The Unity of God implies the need to worship Him without partners

ACTIVIST ISLAM

The Unity of God implies the need to encourage good action and challenge injustice

ISLAMISM

IDEOLOGICAL ISLAMISM

The Unity of God implies the requirement to establish an Islamic State following Sharia law exclusively

NON-VIOLENT ISLAMIST EXTREMISM

The Unity of God implies the requirement to establish an Islamic State following Sharia law exclusively and to repudiate all other religions and political ideologies as an article of faith

ISLAMIST EXTREMISM

VIOLENT ISLAMIST EXTREMISM

The Unity of God implies the requirement to establish an Islamic State following Sharia law exclusively and to repudiate and destroy all other religions and political ideologies and their adherents, including non-Muslims and 'wrong' Muslims as an article of faith

Plate 4 Doctrine of the Unity of God (*Tawhid*) in the Worldviews of Mainstream Islam, Islamism and Islamist Extremism

6 *Why this book is needed*

in theological-philosophical essence. As Figure 1.1 and Plate 1 intend to show and as Chapter 3, 4 and 5 explain, there are some links between the Worldviews of Mainstream Islam and Ideological Islamism; there are no essential links between the Worldviews of Mainstream Islam and Islamist Extremism.

Second, and as a corollary of the claim above, the book will claim that it is possible for a Muslim, a person of another faith or no faith[16] or professional who is not necessarily versed in the theology of Islam to distinguish between these phenomena, including recognizing the grey areas between them and the shifting nature of people and their ideas as they move across categories.[17]

Different categories of ideas produce different types of people and different effects in the world

By making these category distinctions, this book will also imply that the people who follow or embrace these phenomena are also likely to be similar in complexion but in essence profoundly different both in outlook and in outcome.

The purpose, therefore, of defining and substantiating these distinctions is to help thinking people across a range of professions – judges, lawyers, teachers, politicians, prison professionals, journalists, as well as scholars of Islam, to make informed distinctions between very different types of people:

1   Citizens who are Muslim whose beliefs and behaviors are far more likely to benefit society in a variety of ways than they are to harm it. These people may (or may not) have an obviously Islamic appearance that is very 'foreign' to the 'West' and hold views about a range of issues that may (or may not) be at odds with some of the majority and normative views in modern democracies.
2   Citizens who are Muslim whose beliefs and behaviors may damage their *own* ability to engage fully and successfully with other people in multi-faith liberal democratic societies, but whose beliefs and behaviors are not in any way illegal and are likely to be only immediately damaging to their own selves and perhaps to their own immediate circle of families and friends.
3   Citizens who are Muslim whose religious beliefs and behaviors may pose an active threat to the well-being of the other members of the societies in which they reside as well as to themselves.[18]

---

16   I will hereafter use the term 'non-Muslim' to denote those of another religious persuasion or of no formal religious faith. It is not intended to suggest any deficiency of faith.
17   This statement also contains the philosophical implication that these phenomena are ontologically and not merely epistemologically different; they are phenomena with different natures and different effects in the world, and these differences cannot merely be reduced to different interpretations and ways of knowing Islam.
18   Quality, not Quantity.
      As far as identifying different broad categories of people is concerned, it is very important to stress that this is primarily a qualitative study and not a quantitative one. I am concerned to make qualitative differentiations and distinctions between different types of theological-ideological phenomena and the types of people who embrace them. When I divide phenomena into three or more categories that appear to be of equal weight, this does not mean that I believe equal numbers of Muslims belong within those categories. My own research and others', e.g. 2016, 'ICM Unlimited | ICM Muslims Survey for Channel 4'

None of these types of people are fixed, monolithic or static; all Muslims can and do shift, to differing degrees, across categories at different times of their life and are prone to change.

My story and credentials

You may be wondering at this juncture how the author can be so presumptuous as to carry out such an ambitious project. Please allow me briefly to explain my background and credentials.

This book therefore represents my engagement with three bodies of experience and the knowledge derived from them:

1   a traditional Islamic education in Andalucia and North Africa and formative experience, as a convert to Islam, of the national British and international Muslim communities;
2   an engagement with academic theological-philosophy and, in particular, an engagement with the philosophy of Critical Realism and its cognate, which I originated, called Islamic Critical Realism;[19]
3   my experience as an expert witness in Islamic theology in 27 contemporary counter-terrorism trials, 15 of which have been in connection with the ongoing Syrian Civil War.

A traditional Islamic education and formative experience of Islam and Islamism as a convert to Islam in the 1990s

I was born into a well-to-do, stable upper-middle class Anglican Christian British family in 1969.

My mother's family is respected 'landed-gentry' whose maternal forebears included my great-grandfather Earl Jellicoe of Scapa Flow who commanded the British Grand Fleet at the Battle of Jutland in the First World War. It includes two former High Sheriffs of Kent, as well as in the nineteenth century a Scots-Dutch Governor-General of the (then) Dutch East Indies.

My father's side is scholarly and clerical. My father, who ended his career as Chairman of the Nature Conservancy Council, and all my paternal uncles were King's Scholars at Eton College where my grandfather, Denys Wilkinson, was a much-loved housemaster and classics teacher. My paternal grandmother, Gillian Wilkinson née Nairn, was the first woman to be awarded the Chancellor's Medal for Classics by the University of Cambridge in the 1930s, although at the time, as a woman, she was not awarded a degree. Before this, my paternal forebears had tended to be, by turns, clergymen or academics.

---

about the attitudes of Muslim young people and experience, suggest to me strongly that the overwhelming proportion of Muslims (upwards of 85%) are broadly to be found within category #1 above, i.e. Mainstream Muslims. A smaller number fall into category #2 (perhaps 10%) of Ideological Islamism and a minute number, by comparison, fall into category #3 of Islamist Extremism (certainly less than 4%, of whom an even smaller proportion will endorse Violent Islamist Extremism).

19   Wilkinson, 'Introducing Islamic Critical Realism'.

Like my father and uncles, I was educated at Eton College where I won a King's Scholarship then became Head Boy and read theology at Trinity College, Cambridge, where I won a scholarship in Theology and Religious Studies after my Part 1 exam in 1989.

However, towards the end of my first year at Cambridge, my hitherto relatively unruffled and privileged, although hardworking, years as a schoolboy and student were severely disturbed by a number of crises.

First, after a botched heart operation, my father, Sir William Wilkinson, went blind. My father was a nature conservationist and Chairman of the then Nature Conservancy Council, and this terrible accident robbed him both of the ability to operate fully as a professional, although he soldiered on bravely, and of beholding the natural world, his greatest pleasure in life.

I was also, with the approach of the world of employment, alienated by the lack of meaning and deeper purpose in the lives of myself and many of my contemporaries. These were often exciting and sometimes brilliant characters, who included, for example, former Prime Minister David Cameron and the former Foreign Secretary Boris Johnson, who had been educated to the nines – only to be siphoned off after university to work as insurance brokers and investment bankers.

I sought meaning in the traditional pursuits of the student and in my first proper relationship with a woman, neither of which brought satisfaction in an ultimate sense.

These feelings of an absence of purpose in myself and others, my father's demise coupled with my fascination for theology and an enduring belief in God, led me to take seriously the approach of an old school friend who himself had converted to Islam a few years before.

I visited the Sufi Muslim group that my friend had joined and was impressed by the presence of the Muslim prayer, which seemed to exist in stark contrast in its seriousness and composure to my own hedonistic and scattered existence. The practical and doctrinal simplicity of Islam, as an uncompromisingly monotheistic faith,[20] also appealed to me as a theology student for whom even the best Christian minds had not been able to convince of the rationale of the doctrine of the Trinity. For me, Islam represented the theological and ethical essence of Christianity stripped of its awkward doctrinal paraphernalia.

After my final exams at Cambridge, I said goodbye to my then-girlfriend and traveled out to Granada in Spain where I embraced Islam at the hand of a Sufi teacher and in the midst of his community. Suffice it to say, therefore, that I am an unusual upper-middle class minority in an unusual minority of English converts to Islam of whom there are now estimated to be c. 90,000 living in the UK.[21,22]

---

20 See Chapter 4 for further details on the core doctrinal characteristics of Islam.
21 Kevin Brice, *A Minority within a Minority*.
22 There have been some notable converts to Islam from the ranks of the British upper classes such as the writer Muhammad Marmaduke Pickthall (1875–1936) whose English translation of the Qur'an remains a much-loved classic.

My first decade (1992–2002) as a Muslim was spent with a Sufi Muslim group, which exhibited – it must be admitted – separatist, slightly Islamist and, in its adulation of its leader, rather cult-like tendencies. It aimed to set up a separate Islamic society within society, including its own Islamic currency, and actively encouraged the practice of polygamy.

Nevertheless, it also drew on the traditional Maliki tradition of Sunni Islam. During this time, when I was not traveling to call people to Islam (*dawa*) or to raise money for various educational projects, I studied and memorized a considerable portion (42 out of 114 chapters) of the Book of Islam, the Qur'an, and studied the Customary Prophetic Behavior of the Prophet Muhammad (God's peace and blessings be upon him[23]), known as the *Sunna*, basic Islamic law and the Arabic language 'at the feet' of some recognized and some less-recognized teachers using traditional techniques such as memorization of Qur'an from a clay-covered writing board (*lawh*).

My main teacher during this formative period was a man called Imam Muhammad Al-Wassani, an Imam and Jurist (*Faqih*) from Melilla in Spanish North Africa who was a *hafidh* of Qur'an (meaning 'Protector' of the Qur'an, i.e. he had memorized the entire Qur'an) and a respected teacher of Qur'an and *Maliki* law.[24] This man, apart from being an erudite teacher, was a humane example of a religion that, contrary to stereotypes, is not a legalistic faith and, in fact, is premised upon respect for what is called *fitra*, or human nature, in all its various dimensions.

Tragically, Imam Al-Wassani was killed in a plane crash in 2001.

1990s: a decade of Muslim self-discovery

The period of 1992–1999 was, therefore, a formative educational period for me as I was exposed to and absorbed the letter and spirit of Islam, partly by instruction and partly through trial and error. The decade of the 1990s was also a tumultuous one for the British and European Muslim community, characterized by its own institutional trial and error. It witnessed and responded to the genocidal assault on the European Bosnian Muslim community by Serb forces and Bosnian-Serb militias in the Bosnian War (1991–1995). This war included iconic episodes of destruction such as the Siege of Sarajevo (1992–1995) and the Srebrenica Genocide (1995). These events were characterized by the persistent failure of politicians and diplomats of the Western Powers first to recognize and then counter Serbian war aims to annex as much of the disintegrating communist

---

23 Believing Muslims normally add this honorific after mentioning the Prophet's name, especially in religious contexts. I include it here to show my respect and love for the Prophet Muhammad as a believing and practicing Muslim. Hereafter, I will omit to use it as this is not a devotional text and since this book is intended for a non-Muslim as well as a Muslim readership.
24 One of the Sunni Muslim Schools of Law whose character and methods will be described in Chapter 2.

10 Why this book is needed

state of Yugoslavia as they were able and to annihilate as many Bosniak Muslims as possible.[25,26]

The combined effects of the Bosnian War and the success of the US-backed Mujahideen in the Afghan Conflict (1981–1989) in apparently single-handedly defeating the might of the Soviet Superpower, as well as domestic events such as the Rushdie (1988) and Honeyford (1984) affairs, had an enormously politicizing impact on the British Muslim community. A community, which had hitherto languished apologetically under the generic ethnic tag of British Asian, now began to assert itself as self-consciously Muslim and develop its own community infrastructure. This was symbolized most obviously by the formation in 1997 of the Muslim Council of Britain, an umbrella organization representing the interests of over 400 disparate local Muslim community centers, mosques and organizations.

However, despite the Muslim community staking claim to a more obvious institutional presence in the UK, the events of the Bosnian War communicated the message to many young British Muslims that European Muslim lives were not as valuable as European Christian lives. By extension, the Afghan Conflict communicated to some Muslims that they were best off taking matters of the pursuit of international justice into their own hands and that, if they did so, God would grant them victory over even the most mighty non-Muslim state.[27] This was especially the case given the backdrop of the gradual undermining of the Oslo Accords during the 1990s by both Islamist and Zionist extremists in the long-term context of the failure of the United Nations and the authorized international community to bring recognition and justice for dispossessed and un-nationed Palestinians.[28]

All three conflicts of the late '80s and '90s – in Afghanistan, in Bosnia and the ongoing Arab-Israel conflict – left devastating ideological, legal and logistical legacies since they seemed to suggest that, in the practice of international politics, politics trumped the law. In other words, since the Western Powers were construed to have played fast and loose with international law to suit their own political ends, some Muslims felt that they were entitled to do the same with the established principles (*maqāsid*) of Islamic Law (Sharia), especially with reference to the strict rules and regulations surrounding the conduct of armed Jihad. The Afghan conflict, in particular, resurrected the notion that armed Jihad fought by Muslims with a pure intention to please God could bring low the mightiest of infidel (*kafir*) superpowers against all the odds and that classical doctrines of armed jihad should be tailored to fit with conditions of insurgency and guerilla warfare rather than authorized, statutory self-defense.

25 Silber and Little, *The Death of Yugoslavia*.
26 The Bosnian War is explored more fully in Chapter 7.
27 Lewis, *The Crisis of Islam*.
28 Rogan, *The Arabs*.

Why this book is needed 11

Of course, the messy and inconvenient geo-political truths that the Afghan Jihad had been sponsored by another 'infidel' power, the United States of America, and that Muslim national Afghan forces fought with the Soviets against the 'Mujahideen' were glossed over in the euphoria of victory, and the feeling that after (in Osama bin Laden's words) "85 years of humiliation" (since the fall of the Ottoman Caliphate in 1924), Muslims fighting religiously as Muslims, rather than Muslims fighting in national armies, had registered a major military success. As we will see in Chapter 7, in the long-term this victory kick-started a prevalent violent Islamist myth that *ad hoc* Muslim insurgency led by charismatic leaders was, in fact, following the true legacy of the armed struggle of the Prophet Muhammad.

I did not go to Afghanistan or Bosnia, but I was present at informal recruiting gatherings of young men who did, and experienced the masculinized, peer-group pressure that was exerted on people to go by recruiters with double-fisted beards and rolled-up trouser legs under shortened Arab-style robes. I also spoke to the recruits on their 'heroic' return from Afghanistan and Bosnia, only to discover later that the brigades of foreign 'mujahideen' in the Bosnian War had been a nuisance for the Bosnian National Army to bring under control and into command and had fed into the Serbian myth that what the Bosnian Serbs were fighting was an international Islamist insurrection rather than a democratically elected, multi-faith, Muslim-led Bosnian government.[29]

My experiences of the Global Community (Umma) of Islam

During this time, I did, however, travel throughout the Muslim-majority world. In 2001, I taught English in Northern Nigeria deep in the countryside near Zaria where the village mosque was a mud hut and the *Maliki*[30] style of Islam had remained largely untouched for a thousand years. In Zaria, astonished, I witnessed joyous street parties to celebrate the attacks on the Twin Towers in New York in September 2001 that was clearly perceived by the common man in Africa to be the 'bloodying of America's nose'. This was in stark contrast to the scenes of disbelief and mourning that prevailed as a result of the same event on my return to England. It was a first-hand lesson in deep theological relativity and of the profound mistrust and often pathological hatred of the United States of America that characterizes swathes of the Muslim-majority world at street-level.[31]

I also went fundraising for school projects in Abu Dhabi and Dubai, studied with Sheikhs (religious teachers) in Melilla and Morocco, and visited the mosques of Istanbul and Bursa, Turkey. Most memorably I went on Hajj to Mecca in Saudi Arabia in 2003 and worshipped in the mosque of the Prophet Muhammad

---

29 Silber and Little, *The Death of Yugoslavia*.
30 One of the five canonical schools whose character will be explained in Chapter 2.
31 Burke, *The 9/11 Wars*.

12 *Why this book is needed*

in Medina. In Saudi Arabia I witnessed the quixotic mix of advanced contemporary statecraft which allows the Saudis to manage the millions of Pilgrims every year with aplomb, as well as the puritanical literalism of the Saudi-Wahhabi prayer police trying to 'correct' other types of Muslims' worship and prayer.

This experience of the Muslim-majority world left me with a strong impression of peoples in whom the education and background of Islam still resonated in their personal habits of hospitality, family-mindedness and personal ethics, but whose formal practice of Islam and social and institutional fabric were often fragile or even shattered. This intuition was corroborated by the events leading up to the Arab Spring and subsequent counter-revolutions across the Arab Muslim world from 2011 to 2014, which showed that much of the Arab-Muslim world was still sustained politically by 'strongmen' and their regimes rather than by enduring political and legal processes that could adapt in the face of radical change. This period of travel also exposed me to some of the extreme poverty that is suffered across the Muslim world, which contrasts brutally with almost unimaginable wealth in the upper echelons of the Saudi Arabian society and some of the Gulf States.

My experiences of the British Muslim community

After this formative period of Islamic education and travel and having been re-introduced to mainstream British life by my sage wife, Lucy, herself a convert to Islam, I qualified as a history teacher on the Graduate Teacher Partnership at Brondesbury College in Brent, London, an Islamic faith school established in 1996 by the former pop star Cat Stevens, now known as Yusuf Islam, and at the then John Kelly Boys' Technology College in the same borough, now the Crest Academy. At Brondesbury College I taught Muslim young people History, Citizenship and Drama for seven years from 2003–2009 where, in a nurturing educational atmosphere and in the presence of usually highly articulate, intelligent and well-mannered Muslim young men, I became aware of the sensibilities, issues and dilemmas facing Muslim young people and males, myself included.

During this time, attacks and planned attacks by British Muslim males on 7 July 2005 and 21 July 2005 thrust young Muslim males into the national British consciousness as never before and led to the supposed securitization[32] of the Muslim community, as the War on Terror continued to rage chaotically and with terrible loss of civilian life in Iraq and Afghanistan. During this tumultuous period (2005–2011), I served on the Education Committee of the Muslim Council of Britain and completed a PhD at King's College London in History curriculum, entitled *History Curriculum, Citizenship and Muslim Boys: Learning to Succeed?* on an ESRC/MCB-funded studentship. Both these experiences further broadened my horizons about life as a young British Muslim and

---

32 Brown, 'Contesting the Securitization of British Muslims'.

exposed me to the strengths of humanity and piety and also to the weaknesses of institutional infrastructure and clear thought that often characterize the British Muslim community. I also studied traditional Shafi[33] Law with two sheikhs qualified from Al-Azhar University at the Central London Mosque in London. Both these Sheikhs were qualified scholars from Al-Azhar University, Cairo (founded in c. 970 AD) which is the chief center of Islamic learning in the world, but, equally importantly, were kind and humane human beings who showed me that God had revealed Islam in the service of humanity more than He had created humanity for the service of Islam.

My engagement with the philosophy of Critical Realism and development of the philosophy of Islamic Critical Realism

With these experiences in the background, in 2008 I found myself at one of very few life-changing academic conferences that I have ever attended. This was the 'Critical Realism and Education' conference at the then Institute of Education, University of London. The principal attraction of this conference was the late Professor Roy Bhaskar (1944–2014), the founding figure of the philosophy of Critical Realism. As Bhaskar expounded his full systematic original, dialectical and spiritual philosophy of Critical Realism, I was struck by its philosophical resonances with some of the underlying basic metaphysical principles of Islam. In particular, Bhaskar's notions of philosophical 'seriousness' (knowledge-practice consistency) and 'under-laboring' (clearing away erroneous ways of thinking), which will be mobilized in this book, seemed to me to have great potential for clearing away the metaphysical debris at the roots of many contemporary expressions of Islam and releasing its innate potential to 'under-labor' successful life in multi-faith society.

This realization became the basis of an entire theological philosophy of Islam in multi-faith society, which I have called Islamic Critical Realism and which I developed in close conversation with Bhaskar as a post-doctoral fellow in Islamic educational philosophy, based first at the Cambridge Muslim College (2011–2013) and then at the UCL Institute of Education (2013–2015). It is expounded and applied to education in full in my book *A Fresh Look at Islam in a Multi-faith World: A Philosophy for Success though Education*. It aims to show that the spiritual rationality inherent in traditional Islamic praxis is fully compatible with and can be accessed through the medium of contemporary dialectical philosophy with sophisticated and nuanced results.

This current book is not intended to be a book of technical theological philosophy as *A Fresh Look at Islam in a Multi-faith World* is. It is intended to help thinking people across a range of professional walks of life – judges, lawyers, teachers, politicians, prison professionals, journalists, as well as scholars and

---

33 Another Sunni Muslim School of Law (*Madhab*) whose character will be explored in Chapter 2.

14 *Why this book is needed*

students of Islam – to make professional decisions in an informed and fair way about the Muslims and the effects of the Islamic faith and its Islamist derivatives that they encounter in their professional lives.

Nevertheless, it is still the result of traditional Islamic theology injected with philosophical coherence by the philosophy of Critical Realism. Moreover, one of the principal insights of *A Fresh Look at Islam in a Multi-faith World* remains: that it is only by examining and bringing clarity to the metaphysical roots of different phenomena that all appear to be Islamic that the true nature of these phenomena will reveal themselves. This can lead, in turn, to the release of those emancipatory and spiritually uplifting forms of authentic Islamic expression that tend towards universal human flourishing.

My experience as an expert witness in 27 counter-terrorism trials

A final and related life-changing experience happened to me in 2011 when I was instructed as an expert witness in Islamic theology in a significant counter-terrorism trial to do with the alleged dissemination of terrorist material. During this trial I was instructed to explain to the court the nature of 19 Islamist and Violent Islamist Extremist texts, some of which were more mainstream Islamic texts that had been doctored and appended with explicitly violent material and others of which were themselves explicitly violent material encouraging Muslims to illegitimate violence, such as the 'martyrdom' videos of suicide bombers in the Iraqi insurgency of 2004–2008.

This experience[34] and my subsequent experience as an expert in Islamic Theology instructed to advise the court by both the Prosecution and the Defense on 27 different occasions has given me a rich and highly contemporary exposure and analytical experience of the ideological material and mechanics of Violent Islamist Extremism, especially in relation to the Syrian Civil War (2012–present) and the ways in which the effects of this war are played out in British lives and in British courts.

This experience as an expert witness has, on the whole, made me more respectful of and more confident in the justice meted out by the British judicial process. Nevertheless, it has also made me aware of a number of other 'determinate absences' of knowledge[35] which this book addresses:

1. an absence in knowledge of some of the basic beliefs and practices of Islam and their sources, even amongst some of the senior judiciary;
2. an absence in knowledge amongst some legal professionals about some of the core features of Violent Islamist Extremism and what distinguishes Islamist derivatives from the 'broad church' of Mainstream Islam;

---

34 . . . together with the often fantastical media and social media coverage that the trial received.
35 Bhaskar, *Dialectic*.

3   an absence in knowledge amongst some young Muslims and their parents and teachers about what constitutes Islam, what constitutes Jihad and how to make authentic distinctions between benign and legal positions in Islamic law and malign, vicious and illegal ones, including those that are politically highly-charged and therefore emotionally (if not legally) seductive.

This book aims to strike these potentially highly damaging gaps in knowledge at their metaphysical roots in the hope that an improvement in the quality of knowledge in this field will contribute to an improvement in the quality of ethical wisdom and practical justice.

The structure and substance of this book

To address this aim, the book is divided into seven further chapters:

> *Chapter 2, The roots of Islam, Islamism and Islamist Extremism* asks why Muslims and Islam find themselves often divided, angry and derided.
> This chapter explores the historical roots of contemporary Islamic and Islamist phenomena by explaining how the 'presence of the past' resonates strongly in the Muslim community through theological-legal fault lines, such as the Sunni-Shia split and divergent theological tendencies towards intellectual rationalism, traditionalism and literalism, which appeared in the early periods of Islamic civilization. The chapter will explain how these early fault lines and tendencies underpin the emergence of Wahhabi-inspired Salafism and are exacerbated by the particular conditions of post-colonial modernity to generate the intellectual and political conditions for Islamist Extremism.
>
> *Chapter 3, The Worldviews of Islam, Islamism and Islamist Extremism* explains how Islam, Islamism and Islamist Extremism are best characterized as Worldviews; that is, integrated bodies of internally coherent practice and belief, and explains what their basic philosophical characteristics as Worldviews are.
>
> *Chapter 4, Basic beliefs, practices and characteristic themes of Islam, Islamism and Islamist Extremism* explains the similarities and differences of these Worldviews expressed and played out in their systems of theological doctrine, their religious practice and their outcomes in the world, including an extensive treatment of how these Worldviews play out in radically different understandings of doctrines of the Struggle in the Path of God (*Jihad fiy sabilillah*).
>
> Chapter 5, *Mainstream Islam: the people, texts and contexts* describes some of the key personalities, texts and contexts that have substantiated the Worldview of Mainstream Islam, including an exposition of the meanings of seminal chapters of the *Qur'an*.
>
> Chapter 6, *Islamism: the people, texts and contexts* describes the key personalities, texts and contexts that have substantiated Worldview of Ideological

Islamism and Non-Violent Islamist Extremism: Maududi, Al-Banna, Khomeini and Qutb.

Chapter 7, *The Genealogy of Terror: the people, texts and contexts of Violent Islamist Extremism* describes the key personalities and texts that have substantiated the Worldview of Violent Islamist Extremism with a focus on VIE 'pioneers', the ideologues of Al-Qaeda and the ideologues of the so-called Islamic State.

Chapter 8, A second Age of Extremes or a second Age of Enlightenment? summarizes the core argument of the book and concludes that Islamist Extremism – and other forms of contemporary extremism such as the Far Right, No-Platforming and the Alt-Right – show that globalized society faces the choice either to surrender to a new Age of Extremes or to stimulate a new Age of Enlightenment. This Age of Enlightenment would create space to enable people to debate contentious issues effectively and moderately and produce a generation of leaders capable of generating real change without resorting to violence.

2 The roots of Islam, Islamism and Islamist Extremism

The historical fault lines of Islam

Introduction: Islam is shaped by the presence and absence of Muhammad

The world of contemporary Islam and Muslims and their Islamist derivatives is characterized by what critical realist philosophers have called 'the presence of past'.[1] Islam, Islamism and Islamist Extremism are all deeply permeated by the spiritual, intellectual and political residue of events that happened centuries ago and fault lines that opened up in the earliest generations of Islam. These fault lines still reverberate, often toxically, down the centuries. Therefore, to understand the roots of Islam, Islamism and Islamist Extremism, we start with the history of early Islam.

Original Islam revolved around the Prophet Muhammad

Original Islam (610–632 CE) was revealed by means of the Book of Islam, Al-Qur'an (which literally means 'the Recitation'), which Muslims believe is the Word of God brought from His Presence by the Archangel Gabriel and delivered to humanity on the tongue of the Prophet Muhammad. The message of the Qur'an, which will be explored in Chapters 3, 4 and 5, was exemplified by the Customary Behavior (as-Sunna) of the Prophet Muhammad (570–632 CE), first in his hometown of Mecca in the Arabian Peninsula (610–622 CE) and then, after his migration (*hijra*) with 100 or so of his Companions from persecution in Mecca, in Medina (622–632 CE).[2]

Original Islam was characterized by, and pivoted around, the presence of the Prophet Muhammad himself in the midst of his Companions (*Sahaba*), providing teaching and guidance in the related beliefs and practices – praxis – of the Muslim faith. Islam means 'submission to the will of God' with the connotations of personal and social peace that this submission entails. Islam was believed by the Prophet Muhammad and the early Muslims, meaning 'those who have surrendered to

---

1 Bhaskar, *Dialectic*.
2 Brown, *Hadith*.

God's will', not to be a new faith, but a renewal of the ancient faith of Abraham, purified of the pagan idolatry and social malpractices, such as female infanticide. These had accrued around worship of God in the Arabian Peninsula in connection with the first place constructed by humans specifically for the worship of God, the Ka'aba (which literally means 'the Cube') in Mecca.[3]

Whilst the Prophet Muhammad was living amongst his companions and teaching them, not only did the verses of the Qur'an itself, as they were revealed, guide Muhammad and his followers at pivotal moments in the conduct of their worship and worldly affairs, but also Muhammad himself fleshed out and exemplified Qur'anic injunctions and was a constant point of ethical reference. For example, while the Qur'an prescribed the Obligatory Prayer at designated moments (e.g. Qur'an 3:103), the Customary Prophetic Behavior (*Sunna*) of the Prophet Muhammad showed the Companions more closely what those moments were, how to make the prescribed ritual ablutions beforehand and how the Prayer itself ought to be performed. The Qur'an revealed the letter of Islamic practice and belief, and the Prophet Muhammad illustrated its modalities and exemplified its spirit.

However, the death of the Prophet Muhammad after a short illness at the age of 63 in 632 CE sent waves of shock and disbelief around the Muslim community, and only the levelheaded leadership of the Companion known as Abu Bakr as-Siddiq in the interregnum between Muhammad and his own Succession (*Caliphate*) prevented the Muslim community from descending into chaos as Muslims came to terms with a loss the had barely dare contemplate. On the death of the Prophet Muhammad, Abu Bakr rallied the Muslim community with a statement of monotheistic consolation: "If anyone amongst you used to worship Muhammad, then Muhammad has passed away, but if anyone of you used to worship God, then God is alive and shall never die."[4]

The absence of the Prophet Muhammad generates the greatness of Islamic civilization

The Qur'an itself (5:3) and the Prophet Muhammad declared the Revelation and Prophetic illustration of Islam complete just before his death. Nevertheless, the renewed faith and its followers now had to work out entirely by themselves, without the continued revelation of Qur'anic verses and in the absence of the person of the Prophet Muhammad, how to apply this completed manifestation of religious faith with its ethos of just governance to new and fast-evolving geo-political, social and ethno-cultural circumstances. This need to work out the implications of the Qur'an, with its light legal and ethical framework, and the Muhammadan example

---

3 This Ka'aba, rather than being the elemental site dedicated to monotheistic worship, had, by the sixth century, become the center and host to hundreds of pagan idols, each with their cult following, which, together with Mecca's strategic position midway between Syria and the Roman Empire in the North and the Yemen and Abyssinia in the South, attracted pilgrims and trade from far and wide.
4 Sahih al-Bukhari, 3667, 3668.

The roots of Islam, Islamism and Islamist Extremism 19

became critical as the Muslim community encountered and began to absorb peoples with established, often ancient social habits and traditions of governance, such as the peoples of Sassanid Persian civilization who lived in what is present-day Iran and Iraq and the peoples of the Byzantine provinces of Syria.

The early Islamic community in the decades following the death of the Prophet Muhammad in 632 CE was, therefore, characterized as much by the absence of its founding, towering figure, the Prophet Muhammad, as by the presence of the religious praxis[5] that he left behind. The absence of the Prophet Muhammad, both as a religious figure and a political leader, and the need to discover legal answers to civilizational issues generated by religious and legal figures and leaders of towering genius in their own right, some of whom we will encounter in Chapter 5. These people took Islam forward into uncharted territory and helped establish one of the world's most successful sacred civilizations.[6] This sacred civilization was a beacon of learning and high culture throughout what is known in Europe as the Dark (c.500–1000 CE) and Middle Ages (c.1000–1500 CE).[7]

The absence of the Prophet Muhammad generates the fault lines of Islamic civilization

Nevertheless, the absence of the unifying figure of the Prophet Muhammad also generated fault lines in the embryonic Muslim community that have expressed themselves in the Muslim majority world down the centuries, sometimes in violent form, and that have spilled out more recently across significant tracts of the rest of the world. These fault lines are most notably:

1   Sunni-Shia split, sometimes known as the Great Divide (*Al-Fitnat al-Kubra*), between Muslims who became known as the *Ahl As-Sunna wal Jama* (the People of Prophetic Practice and Consensus), i.e. Sunni Muslims and the *Shiat'ul Ali* (the Party of Ali ibn Abi Talib), i.e. Shia Muslims.

2   Tensions (both productive and destructive) between the power of the Muslim executive (Caliphs, amirs, sultans and modern leaders) and the power and authority of the religious jurists – the *Ulema*. Throughout Muslim history, this tension between those in political authority and those in religious-legal authority has both created and destroyed (at different moments) the conditions for just governance.

3   Rationalist vs. Literalist tension between those early, later and contemporary Muslim scholars who believed that Islamic doctrine and law was necessarily the product of a rational engagement with the primary sources of Islam in a context-specific way and those who believed that the primary sources of Islam themselves literally contained all the answers.

---

5   'Praxis' throughout the book means the combined, integrated force of religious belief with religious practice.
6   Winter, 'Introduction'.
7   We will refer to its particular achievements later in the Chapter.

These fault lines, as we will see, have been aggravated in the past 300 years by the decline and then collapse and decimation of the last recognizably Islamic polity, the Ottoman Empire, and by the uniquely febrile colonial conditions of modernity (1600–1945) and post-colonial post-modernity (1945–present). During this 300-year period the Muslim-majority world has attempted, with varying degrees of success, to don the alien institutional straitjacket of the modern nation-state[8] and has shifted from being the shaper of global intellectual, political and military activity to being shaped by the intellectual, political and military activity of the rest of the world and particularly the (post-) Christian West.[9]

These historical fault lines, which run across a variety of related and theologically quite unnecessary dichotomies, have accrued enormous historical, religious and political ramifications for the way that Muslims of all types perceive and conduct themselves in the world today.[10]

Political-theological hiatus and split: the Sunni-Shia divide

The united leadership of Muhammad as Prophet and statesman

The early Muslim community operated as a religious community in Mecca for 13 years (610–622 CE) with the Prophet Muhammad in a largely religious function leading the performance of the basic elements of Islamic religious worship such as the Five Daily Prayers and explaining and teaching the meanings of the verses of the Qur'an as they were revealed to him. The meanings of these so-called Meccan verses of the Qur'an had also tended to be overwhelmingly spiritual and ethical, obliging humanity to recognize and worship the One True God, encouraging right action, such as the establishment of prayer, paying of charity, keeping of contracts and respect for parents in the existential context of the inevitable reality of death and the terrors of the subsequent Day of Judgment.

However, after 13 years of rejection and persecution in Mecca, when the Prophet Muhammad was invited in 622 to take up a position of authority in mediating between warring tribal factions in the town of Yathrib (now called Medina), 200 miles North of Mecca, the character of Islam evolved.

After the migration (*hijra*) of Muhammad from persecution in Mecca to Yathrib, the Muslim community increasingly transformed from a group of disciples following a religious leader into a religio-political community built

---

8 Hallaq, *The Impossible State*.
9 Wilkinson, *A Fresh Look at Islam in a Multi-Faith World*.
10 These related historical splits that will be explored in this chapter are what critical realist philosophers have called 'demi-realities'. That is to say, they do not contain or represent any essential Islamic theological truth, and yet they have proved hugely causatively powerful in the empirical world of Islam and Muslims, both in terms of their internal historical relations and in their relations with the rest of the world.

around the presence of a great statesman. This transformation coincided with the (albeit light-touch) legislative guidance of those verses of the Qur'an which Muslims believe were revealed to Muhammad to coincide with his emergence as a political leader of a multi-faith community of tribal alliances and as Islam came to be a governing religious praxis designed to bring justice to the social and legal life of an entire city state. This transformation in both the role of the Prophet Muhammad and the nature of Islam was reflected in the renaming of Yathrib as *Medinat an-Nabawiyya* (known in English as 'Medina'), which means the Place of the Entire Prophetic Transaction with God (*deen*).

It is important to note, therefore, that Islam as a religious practice emerged prior to Islam as a governing political ethos. That is to say that Islam as a religion of witnessing God's reality, with attendant beliefs in other unseen realities, and of Prayer and Fasting came first. The political and institutional apparatus of Islam, such as the payment of the Obligatory Poor-Tax (*zakah*), took shape afterwards in Medina (623–632 CE) and served to protect and preserve the religious elements of Islam, not vice versa.

This relationship between religion and politics with politics serving the ends of religious belief, practice and justice was reflected in the relationship of Muhammad himself to his Companions (*Sahaba*). In matters of religion, revealed through the Revelation of the Qur'an and exemplified by Muhammad himself, Muhammad's word, as Prophet, was law. In matters of political leadership and statecraft, Muhammad governed by taking counsel (*shura*) and operated much more as a first-amongst-equals. In this capacity he is recorded as deferring on many occasions to the advice of his leading Companions, such as the occasion when the companion Hubab ibn al-Mundhir famously contradicted Muhammad before the Battle of Badr by advising Muhammad to station the Muslim army by the wells nearest to his Meccan enemies and to block the others, thus cutting off the Meccan enemies' supply of water.[11]

The death of the Prophet Muhammad and the Succession (Calipha) of the Rightly-guided Successors (Caliphs)

Although the manner in which the Prophet Muhammad exercised his religious authority and his political power were different, he had been the early Muslim community's unrivalled political and religious leader. To draw a not-entirely-inappropriate analogy from the early European Middle Ages, as Prophet he had been both Holy Roman Emperor and Pope. His presence had been so pivotal to the early Muslim community that, as we have seen, when he died, some of the senior Companions initially refused to believe that he was actually dead. His death left a vacuum of both political power and religious authority.

---

11 Ibn Ishaq, *The Life of Muhammad*.

Divisions over the Successor (Caliph) to the Prophet Muhammad

Moreover, for reasons hotly disputed for centuries, Muhammad had not made it unambiguously clear who should be his Successor (*Caliph*) as leader of the Muslim community or, indeed, how the Muslim community should govern itself on his death, beyond following the injunctions of the Qur'an and the example of his Customary Prophetic Behavior (*Sunna*).

This absence of an appointed Successor left a power-vacuum after Muhammad's death, and while Medina was reeling in grief and disbelief at their loss, three factions quickly asserted their rights to lead the community of Medina.[12] The first to assert its claims were the so-called *Ansar* – the Helpers – who were the original inhabitants of Medina and who had welcomed the Meccan migrants with the Prophet Muhammad to Mecca. The second was called the *Muhajirun* – the Migrants – who were Muhammad's original followers from the Meccan tribe of Quraysh, and this group included his Senior Companions. The third group was the Prophet Muhammad's immediate family, the so-called *Ahl Al-Bayt*, the People of the Prophetic House, foremost of whom was Muhammad's cousin and son-in-law, Ali ibn Abi Talib, who was married to Muhammad's daughter Fatima.

The Migrants (*Muhajirun*) believed and convinced the Helpers (*Ansar*) that Muhammad had clearly indicated that the Companion Abu Bakr as-Siddiq would be the worthiest candidate by asking him to lead the collective prayer during his final illness. Abu Bakr as-Siddiq, which means Abu Bakr the Confirmer of the Truth, had, like the Prophet Muhammad, dedicated almost his entire adult life and entire fortune to the cause of Islam and had crucially, as far as the *Muhajirun* were concerned, been the Prophet Muhammad's intimate at such events as the Migration (*Hijra*) from Mecca itself in July 622 CE.

Moreover, the Migrants (*Muhajirun*) believed that Customary Prophetic Behavior (*Sunna*) for deciding such significant issues was the process of simple, informal tribal consultation called *Shura*. This *Shura* was, broadly speaking, a refined version of the means of political succession to tribal authority that had existed in pre-Islamic Arabia, by which authority was passed to the most suitable of a range of candidates who were connected to the right families and had the right personal attributes and credentials for leadership.

Muslims who believed that Customary Prophetic Behavior (*Sunna*) required the election or appointment of the Caliph by consensus were gradually, in the first century of Islam, to become formalized as the *Ahl as-Sunna wal Jama* – the People of the *Sunna* and Consensus – or Sunni Muslims.

Other Companions were angry that, due to the speed of events following the Prophet Muhammad's death, the People of the Prophetic House (*Ahl Al-Bayt*) had effectively been excluded from the critical *Shura* because they were making the funeral arrangements for the washing of Muhammad's body for burial and, in general, plunged into grief.

12 Kennedy, *The Caliphate*.

The People of the Prophetic House (*Ahl Al-Bayt*) largely believed that the Prophet Muhammad's cousin and son-in-law, Ali ibn Abi Talib – the father of the Prophet Muhammad's grandsons, Hasan ibn Ali and Hussain ibn Ali, and the first male convert to Islam after Muhammad himself – was ordained to be the Successor to the Prophet Muhammad by the command of God and the clear indication of Muhammad himself. They also believed that the Prophet Muhammad had transmitted the greater portion of his spiritual wisdom and insight to Ali. They believed Ali and, thereafter, Ali's direct descendants had both the hereditary right and the necessary spiritual and temporal qualities to be the Prophet Muhammad's true Successor (*Caliph*).

Those early Muslims who believed in the claims to leadership of Ali, the daughter of the Prophet Muhammad, Fatima, and their descendants were later to become formalized and categorized as Shia Muslims. Shia is short for *Shiat' ul Ali* which means the 'Party of Ali'. However, in the era immediately subsequent to the Prophet Muhammad's death, there was no sense that the supporters of Ali's claims to succeed him were in any sense part of a separate community, let alone a different branch of the faith. There merely existed the simmering of political discontent that their champion's claims to the Succession had not received, in their eyes, a fair hearing.[13]

The Rightly-guided Caliphs

In the early Muslim community, therefore, the Sunni argument for appointing or electing the Caliph won out due to the simple fact that it represented most closely existing Arab tribal custom. The early Muslim community chose by a simple, rough-and-ready consensus the first four Caliphs (Successors to Muhammad) who ruled after the death of the Prophet Muhammad. These so-called Rightly-guided Successors (*Khulafā ar-Rāshidūn*) were:

1 Abu Bakr as-Siddiq (632–634 CE),
2 Umar ibn al-Khattab (634–644 CE),
3 Uthman ibn Affan (644–656 CE), and
4 Ali ibn Abi Talib (656–661 CE).

This period of the Rightly-guided Caliphs is remembered as a 'Golden Age'; as the period of the preservation and expansion of the religious and political integrity of Islam and because the Four 'Rightly-guided' Caliphs were seen to govern after the pattern of excellence and justice established by the Prophet Muhammad himself.

The period of the Rightly-guided Caliphs included the so-called Wars of Apostasy (633–634 CE) prosecuted by the Caliph Abu Bakr that were fought to quell multiple tribal rebellions around Medina and ensured the survival of

---

13 Hawting, *The First Dynasty of Islam*.

Islam and, in particular, the retention of the connection between the Obligatory Prayer (*Salah*) and the Obligatory Poor Tax (*Zakah*). This ensured the continuance of just governance according to Islamic principles. This period saw the exponential expansion of the sphere of governance by Muslims into Syria and Persia after wars to protect the integrity of Islam led to conquest and the implementation of far-sighted measures in taxation and statecraft, such as the establishment by the Caliph Umar of a registered pension for the old and veterans of military campaigns. It also witnessed the final codification and writing down of an authorized, standardized Qur'an under the auspices of the Caliph Uthman, which Muslims still recite and read to this day.

Moreover, the Four Rightly-guided Caliphs represent the first and last time that the entire Muslim community (*Umma*) was united under one Ruler. Thereafter, both what became the Sunni-dominated and Shia-dominated Muslim worlds were ruled by a series of monarchic dynasties who called themselves Caliphs (or Imams) in order to claim the religious legitimacy of the Prophet Muhammad but who were, in reality, dynastic monarchs. The Umayyad and Abbasid dynastic rulers, therefore, began to style themselves not so much as Successor to the Messenger of God (*khalifa rasul Allah*), but as Deputies of God (*Khalifat Allah*),[14] monarchs by divine right, who increasingly delegated the religious elements of the role of the Rightly-guided Caliphs to the fast-growing class of religious jurists – the *Ulema*.

However, even this period of leadership of these great and spiritually enlightened men, who ensured the very survival and integrity of Islam, was not devoid of crisis and did not please everybody. In some Muslims' eyes, no ruler could ever live up to the example of religious piety, political acumen and judicial impartiality set by the Prophet Muhammad himself. Also, peoples who had formerly been themselves the beneficiaries of imperial status, such as the Sassanid Persians, resented the Arab-Muslim ascendency. For example, a Persian captive, resentful at his newly conquered status, murdered the Caliph Umar ibn Al-Khattab in 644 CE. The Caliph Uthman ibn Affan, Umar's Successor from the powerful Umayyad clan and an early Companion of Muhammad, was murdered in his house, undefended, as he recited the Qur'an. Uthman's murder was the culmination of a 12-year reign characterized by civic unrest and charges of political nepotism, with the next Caliph, Ali ibn Abi Talib, 'waiting in the wings'. Ali was backed by a party of supporters who were increasingly frustrated that Ali had three times been overlooked for the 'top job'.

Divisions lead to rebellion

Ali ibn Abi Talib himself, therefore, succeeded Uthman ibn Affan as Caliph, and his wisdom and eloquence is widely regarded by Sunni and Shia Muslims as constituting an apex of early Islamic spirituality and wisdom. His religious

---

14 Crone and Hinds, *God's Caliph*.

aphorisms such as, "The one who is hindered by his actions cannot be helped by his lineage", have provided spiritual sustenance and guidance for Muslims for 1,400 years. Ali was and is revered by Sunni and Shia Muslims alike as the second (after the Prophet Muhammad's wife, Khadija bint Khuwaylid (555 CE to 619 CE)) convert to Islam and as the Prophet Muhammad's cousin and son-in-law, who was married to his daughter, Fatima, and was the father of the Prophet Muhammad's grandchildren, Hassan and Hussain. Ali, who on at least three occasions volunteered himself for single-combat before major military engagements, is celebrated for his bravery in combat which, for many, epitomize the traditions of Islamic chivalry that later found their way into Europe through the actions of Saladin (*Salah Uddin al-Ayyubi*) during the Third Crusade (1189–1192 CE).

Nevertheless, in this account of the *political* schism which is at the root of the Sunni-Shia split, Ali was suspected by the supporters of Uthman in the powerful Qurayshi Umayyad clan, at best, of not acting to prevent the murder of their kinsman, since he had been present in Medina with forces when Uthman was murdered, and, at worst, of encouraging it. Muawiya ibn Abi Sufyan (602–April 680 CE), the son of the former ruler of Mecca – who had, for a time, been an implacable enemy of the Prophet Muhammad, though latterly his secretary – came out in open rebellion against Ali, seeking revenge for the murder of his kinsman Uthman and raised an army from his powerbase in Damascus, Syria, where the Caliph Umar ibn al-Khattab had appointed him governor.

After a stalemate at the Battle of Siffin (657 CE), during which his opponents impaled copies of the Qur'an on their spears in a gesture to remind the Caliph that they were Muslims and that it would be best to sue for peace, the Caliph Ali entered into negotiations with Muawiya. However, at this apparent sign of political and military weakness, Ali was abandoned by a significant out-group of his supporters who set up a rival militarized faction to his rule.

This out-group of rebels became known as the *Kharijites* (pl. *khawarij*), literally meaning 'the ones who departed' from the Caliph's forces.[15] They gathered under the de-contextualized Qur'anic slogan (6:57), "Judgment belongs to God alone", by which they meant that no human being was fit to govern in the name of Islam. Although the Kharijites were eventually defeated by Ali's forces at the Battle of Nahrawan (659 CE), Ali himself was murdered by one of their number in the mosque of Kufa, Iraq in 661 CE. Even more significantly than the murder of the Prophet Muhammad's cousin, the Kharijites set a highly damaging precedent of violent political rebellion against a legitimate, Muslim authority on the grounds that this authority was not, in their opinion, Muslim-enough.

---

15 Kennedy (2016) supports an alternative view that Kharijite means the 'the ones who departed on armed Jihad'. I do not think that this is likely since almost all the early male Muslims departed on armed Jihad to defend the integrity of Islam at some point.

The idea that rulers who do not rule strictly or according to Islamic precepts enough can be deposed by force and killed – which, as we shall see in Chapter 7, has no basis in the Qur'an[16] and *Sunna*, which mandates just governance by humans on behalf of God, even if that governance is far from perfect[17] – has been highly toxic throughout the centuries of Islam. In the contemporary period, for example, this has manifested as the violently extreme doctrines of *takfir* – declaring a confessing Muslim to be a non-Muslim who can be fought – and *irtidād* – declaring apostasy. By means of these two doctrines, Violent Islamist Extremists such as Al-Qaeda have deemed Muslim-majority regimes to be 'Infidel' because these regimes either do not apply Islamic Law strictly enough or because they enter into alliances with non-Muslims powers. We will explore this violent legacy of the *Kharijites* further in Chapters 3, 4, and 7.

After the Rightly-guided Caliphs: the irrevocable split

On the death of Ali, Muawiya ibn Abi Sufyan himself was appointed to succeed Ali as Caliph in 661 CE. Muawiya, who already controlled both Syria and Egypt, moved the capital of the emerging Arab-Muslim Empire from Medina, where the Prophet Muhammad had established the full breadth of Islamic praxis, to Damascus in Syria, which was territory recently annexed from the Byzantine Empire by the expanding Muslim polity.

Not only did Muawiya relocate the hub of the newly empowered faith to Syria, but also, in a break with the precedent of a simple election/appointment of the Caliph, he maneuvered to have his son Yazid appointed as Caliph, ignoring the claims of the descendants of Ali – the Prophet Muhammad's grandsons, Hassan ibn Ali and Hussain ibn Ali. Thus, at a blow, Muawiya departed from one of the core practices of early Islam that the Caliph was, as the Successor to Muhammad, to be chosen in a simple form of election. In the process he created the first Muslim so-called 'Umayyad' dynasty and alienating, once and for all, the Supporters of Ali and those who thought that political leadership ought to have been transferred to the family of Muhammad right from the start.

The overlooking of Hassan and Hussain and the establishment of the Umayyad dynasty proved intolerable for the Party of Ali (*Shia't ul 'Ali*), who rebelled in Kufa and raised an army in order to further the claims of the grandson of the Prophet Muhammad, Hussain ibn Ali. In the dynastic struggles that followed, Hussain ibn Ali was killed at the Battle of Karbala in Iraq by the armies of Muawiya's son, the Umayyad Caliph Yazid I in 680 CE and Hassan ibn Ali was placed under house arrest.

Although no one realized it at the time,[18] the Battle of Karbala marked the irrevocable theological and political split between Sunni and Shia Islam, which thereafter gradually became two distinct branches of the Islamic faith with distinctive doctrinal and political claims and geographical spheres of influence.

16 Qur'an 16:90; 42:15; 5:8.
17 Sahih Muslim, 4528, 4532.
18 Hawting, *The First Dynasty of Islam*.

Sunni Islam, in the form of the Umayyad and then the Abbasid dynasties, gained influence and conquered territories in the areas of Arabia and North Africa formerly dominated by the Eastern and Western Roman Empires, as well as the rest of the Arabian Peninsula. It was characterized by the dynastic claims of families due to their descent from the tribe of Quraysh and the increasing authority of a semi-autonomous religious judiciary – the *Ulema* – who developed *Sharia* law (see next sections).

The Party of Ali, and then Shia Islam, gained influence in eastern Iraq and Yemen with outposts in North Africa, where eventually, by dynastic twists and turns of dizzying complexity and some genealogical imagination,[19] it gave rise to the great Fatimid Ismaili Dynasty based in Cairo in the tenth and eleventh centuries. Shia Islam also gradually took root in Persia, which was always at a distance, both culturally and intellectually, from Sunni centers of authority in Damascus and Baghdad. It became the official faith of the Safavid dynasty of Persia in the sixteenth century and has subsequently become an inseparable component of Iranian national identity.[20] The Shias came to believe that religious and true political authority of the Muslim Community[21] belonged to a series of Imams descended directly from Ali and his wife Fatima, who at times were manifest and known and at other times hidden.

Shia Muslims celebrate and lament the Battle of Karbala as marking both the founding moment of their faith and the death of the grandson of the Prophet Muhammad, Hussain ibn Ali. Sunni Muslims often lament the Battle of Karbala as the moment when a grandson of the Prophet Muhammad was killed and a united faith community became two sectarian positions, both closer in reality to hereditary monarchy than to Succession (Caliphate) to the Prophet Muhammad.

This period of political civil war also saw the emergence of theological divisions with groups using theology and its deduction from the Qur'an to justify their political allegiances and actions. Prominent amongst these were the so-called *Qadarites* (from *qadara*, meaning 'determining') and the *Jabarites* (from *jabara*, meaning 'determined'). The *Qadarites* supported the Party of Ali and asserted that the Qur'an stated that human beings determined their own actions, destiny and mistakes and, therefore, the Umayyad dynasty had been responsible for great crimes against the People of Muhammad's House (*Ahl al-Bayt*) by usurping the claims to the authority of Ali.

The *Jabarites*, by contrast, asserted that the Qur'an asserts that human actions are both created and pre-determined by God and, therefore, that the ascent to authority of the Umayyad dynasty, at the expense of the Party of Ali, however it happened, was an inevitable part of God's Plan. These two initially fluid theological positions were, like the Sunni and Shia positions

---

19 Kennedy, *The Caliphate*.
20 It is one of the ironies of history that the center of contemporary Sunni orthodoxy – Al-Azhar University in Cairo – was founded by this Ismaili Shia dynasty in 970 CE.
21 Umma.

themselves, to harden, as we shall see, into two or even three distinct theological traditions in Islam.

Thus, the Great Fitna (division) was not only responsible for the rupture and then gradual growing apart of two distinct branches of the Islamic faith, but was also responsible for the emergence of a third group, the Kharijites, whose spiritual and political legacies have been felt in some form or other throughout the centuries of Islam until the present day:

1. *Sunni* Muslims, who have often looked nostalgically to the period of the Rightly-guided Caliphs and of the first three generations after the Prophet Muhammad as a period of pristine 'Salafi' Islam when Muslims followed the *Salaf as-Salih* (the Righteous Predecessors) and Islam had neither been 'contaminated' politically by the nepotism of hereditary monarchy nor religiously by the accretions of foreign Zoroastrian (Persian) and Christian (Byzantine) influences. Also, for many Sunni Muslims, Greater Syria (*Shām*) and its capital Damascus, the capital of the Umayyad dynasty, came to represent the historic, and therefore symbolic, epicenter of distinctively Sunni, as opposed to Shia, Islam. Sunnis today represent c.90% of the global Muslim population.

2. *Shia* Muslims, who over the centuries have both felt that the injustices suffered by the family of the Propet Muhammad have never been righted and that the true spiritual and political status of the Propet's family has never been recognized by the main body of the Islamic tradition. For many Shia Muslims, the Umayyad Sunni dynasty based in Syria and Damascus came to represent the party that had opposed Ali and then murdered Muhammad's grandson Hussain at Karbala. In the absence of temporal authority in the early centuries of Islam, Shia Muslims also developed a distinctively millennial eschatology that looked to the End of Time for the righting by the Guided One (*Al-Mahdi*) of the evils perpetrated on the family of Muhammad. They believe that, until then, Muhammad's spirit and teaching would be kept alive through a succession of spiritual leaders – Imams – related to his line. *Shias* today represent c.10% of the global Muslim population.

3. *Kharijite* Muslims, those who depart from the ideas of both these groups, for whom no Muslim is ever pious enough and no political system ever sufficiently untainted by corruption or sufficiently Godly as to command their allegiance. Kharijite Muslims in their abandonment and rebellion against the Caliph, their violent rejection of legitimate Muslim authority and their use of decontextualized Qur'anic verses as political ideology set a precedent and established a trend that has existed throughout Islamic history.

This Kharijite-like 'departure' from the theological and political mainstream of Islam has characterized Muslim sects and groups as disparate in time as the Assassins of the eleventh-century Middle Ages, whose stock in trade was political assassinations of Sunni Abbasid officials, to Al-Qaeda and ISG[22] in our own times, whose beliefs that all Muslims, apart from themselves, especially those Muslim regimes and their functionaries in positions of authority, are prone to apostasy (*irtidad*) and fit for murder, are both highly reminiscent of this early Kharijite group.[23]

As I explained in the introduction, for the majority of Muslims these tendencies merely flavor a benign commitment to the religion of Islam broadly construed within mainstream doctrinal and practical religious parameters that, as we will see, both Sunni and Shia Muslims accept by consensus. Nevertheless, these characterizations are also tendencies that, as we will see, sharpen under certain circumstances into antagonistic violent extremes, as has been the case recently in the Syrian Civil War (2011–present).

In circumstances of conflict, often after centuries of coexistence, for Sunni Muslims Shia Muslims become the *Rāfidha* – Rejectors – who reject the authority of the first three Rightly-guided Caliphs, and thus reject the true spiritual and political legacy of Muhammad. For Shia Muslims, Sunnis become the successors to the murderers of the grandson of the Prophet, Hussain, who have for centuries unjustly thwarted the true claims to spiritual and temporal leadership of the People of the Prophetic House (*Ahl al-Bayt*).

Institutional hiatus and split: the division of powers between the Muslim Executive and the religious judiciary

The gradual division of the early Muslim community into recognizably different theological-political denominations was not the only division that resulted from the absence of Muhammad in the early period of Islamic expansion, consolidation and Civil War.

The first two centuries of post-Muhammadan Islam (632–832 CE) also saw the unified religio-political powers of the Caliph divide into those of the executive power of dynastic rulers in tension with the emergence of a new class of religious jurist – the *Ulema*, which means 'the ones who learn.'

The idea of Caliphate evokes memories of Muslim greatness

While the Four Rightly-guided Caliphs probably represent the only phase of Muslim history when the type of Islamic governance as practiced and envisioned by the Prophet Muhammad existed in a recognizably Muhammadan form under the united religious-political leadership of one person, in practice Islamic civilization was

---

22 Al-Yaqoubi, *Refuting ISIS*.
23 Those with Kharijite leanings come from both Sunni and Shia groups. For example, the Assassin sect alluded to above was Ismaili Shias and both Al-Qaeda and Islamic State are, nominally at least, Sunni.

quick to make effective, pragmatic and legal accommodations with the new 'dynastic' state of affairs. This meant that the intellectual, cultural and military vitality that had characterized earliest Islam continued unabated for centuries, arguably until the fall of the Abbasid[24] dynasty in 1252 CE.

From the eighth to thirteenth centuries, Muslim scholars, often motivated by the demands of their faith, protected by religious (*Sharia*) law derived from the Qur'an and Customary Prophetic Behavior (*Sunna*), and living under the governance and with the patronage of the Umayyad and then Abbasid Caliphs, created a sacred civilization that left the rest of the Western world looking to Islamic civilization for intellectual and technological guidance.[25] During this period, Muslims, Christians and Jews living within Islam-inspired and ordered civilizations:

1. adapted the Hindu and Babylonian number systems for the advanced arithmetic we use today, including the use of the advanced concept of zero, thus liberating mathematics from Latin and Greek numerals;[26]
2. adapted and developed ancient Greek and Persian geometry and trigonometry and invented algebra for both religious and civic purposes, such as the legal calculation of inheritance;[27]
3. made the earliest studies of the circulation of the blood and infection and established hospitals based on scientific principles of hygiene;[28]
4. re-initiated the study of scientific history and sociology according to systematic conceptual precepts, categories and principles;[29]
5. developed astronomical models of the universe which were to contribute directly to the heliocentric models of Copernicus;[30]
6. contributed to the development of the systems of sonic harmony that in the fullness of time and together with Christian ecclesiastical traditions became the basis of Western classical music;[31] and
7. preserved and developed both Platonic and, especially, Aristotelian philosophy, in the latter case laying the foundations of Western, empirical scientific method, without which Aristotle and Plato would have been lost to the world.

---

24 So-called because it traced its lineage to an uncle of Muhammad called Al-Abbas ibn Abdal Mutallib and thus justified its claims to leadership.
25 Al-Hassani, *1001 Inventions*.
26 Al-Khalili, *Pathfinders*.
27 Ibid.
28 Ibid.
29 Ibn Khaldun, *Al Muqaddimah*.
30 Al-Khalili, *Pathfinders*.
31 This includes, quite possibly, developing the solfège syllables (do, re, mi, fa, sol, la, ti) of music, which are likely to have been derived from the syllables of the Arabic solmization system Durr-i-Mufassal ("Separated Pearls") from the Arabic letters – dal, ra, mim, fa, sad, lam, ta – to which the solfège syllables bear a striking ressemblance.

Moreover, during this 'Golden Age' of Islamic Enlightenment, Caliphal societies made pioneering and lasting contributions to generating a social ethos that would now be considered to bear the hallmarks of a flourishing democracy, including features such as:

a   the protection of women's rights to property and to lead autonomous, fulfilling lives;
b   high levels of civic justice which included civic, criminal and administrative law; and
c   the institutionalized tolerance of different faiths which astounded European visitors to Ottoman Istanbul in the seventeenth century, who were used to small doctrinal differences in Christian sects being the cause of executions on charges of heresy and wars within and between states.[32]

This period of intellectual leadership of the civilized world and of great intellectual and commercial success means that many Muslims have a strong folk memory of Islam under the Caliphate as a dominant and respected faith[33] and often equate spiritual and political unity with intellectual greatness.

The separation of powers between the Executive and the religious judiciary

Nevertheless, this development of Islamic civilization under the Abbasid Caliphs from their capital in Baghdad was sustained, inter alia, by the division of powers between the Executive with the state administration of services through taxation and an independent class of religious jurists who were responsible for the administration of *Sharia* law and its courts. These religious jurists were called the Ulema – meaning 'the ones who learn' – i.e. the ones who learned how to derive Islamic Law (*Sharia*) from the Qur'an and the Customary Prophetic Behavior (*Sunna*) of Muhammad.

The religious judiciary – the Ulema

These early *Ulema* were initially a far cry from trained expert jurists, and the jurisprudence that they developed emerged slowly and organically. In the first century after Muhammad, the *Ulema* were often craftsmen or tradesmen who gained a reputation for sound proto-legal judgments and methods for understanding and applying the Qur'an and the Customary Prophetic Behavior (*Sunna*) in a convincing and fair way and who had sat with those who had learned from the Companions of the Prophet Muhammad himself.

---

32   Norton, 'Blurring the Boundaries.'
33   Kennedy, *The Court of the Caliphs*; Lyons, *The House of Wisdom*.

In their derivation of legal precepts from the Sunna of Muhammad and the way that he applied the teachings of the Qur'an in Medina, the early Ulema showed great and innovative jurisprudential acumen and were usually characterized by both the humanity and legal sensitivity and flexibility that had characterized Muhammad himself. The greatest of these people and their followers gradually became canonized as the Five Schools of Islamic Law (four Sunni, one Shia), each one named after its eponymous founder with the jurisprudential methods reflecting the needs of the environments in which they were teaching.

The *Ulema* developed a whole range of jurisprudential apparatus, such as analogy (*quiyas*), consensus (*ijma'*), public benefit (*maslaha*), respect for custom (*'urf*) and legal precedent (*taqlid*), in order to effect the principles (*maqasid*) of Divine Law, such as the sanctity of intellect, lineage, property, religion and honor, that they deduced from the Revelation itself. These jurisprudential tools and principles mitigated the post-Qur'anic divine silence and the absence of the Prophet Muhammad from matters of daily legal guidance, as Islam and Muslims encountered novel legal and social circumstances and yet still needed and wanted to remain true to the spirit, and indeed the letter, of the Qur'an and the Prophetic *Sunna*.

The character of the traditional Schools of Law (Madhahib)

In Medina – the town in which Islam took institutional shape and where, as we have seen, the Prophet Muhammad lived for ten years of increasing empowerment and political success amongst 10,000 Companions (*Sahaba*) – the school of Malik ibn Anas (711–795 CE), the Maliki School, gradually took shape. Malik's school gave primacy to the recorded habitual behavior of Muhammad and his Companions and those who followed them, called the Behavior of the People of Medina (*amal ahl al-Medina*), over individual prophetic sayings (*hadith*). In support of this position, Malik repeated his teacher, Rabiah ibn Abdurrahman's, view that "One thousand following one thousand are better than one taking from one" – meaning that the general customary practice (*amal*) of the People of Medina provided a stronger legal precedent than one Prophetic saying passed down to/through one transmitter.[34] Malik and his followers gave priority to public interest (*masalih mursala*) in his legal opinions and was famous for replying, "I do not know" when the Qur'an and the *Sunna* provided no definitive judgment over a matter. Thus, Malik indicated that it was up to the questioner to make up his or her own mind according to the dictates of his/her conscience and understanding.

In Kufa, Iraq, at this time a dusty 'Wild West' garrison town, there neither resided significant numbers of Companions of the Prophet or their immediate successors (*tabi'in*), and the general customary practice (*amal*) of the People of Medina was less visible and less easy to establish. Here the great Imam Abu

---

34 Abu Zahra, *The Four Imans Their Lives, Works and Their Schools of Thought*.

Hanifa al-Numan ibn Thabit (699–767 CE), who was also a notable merchant, and his followers developed the process of using analogy (*quiyas*) to establish legal rulings on matters on which the Qur'an and the Sunna were silent using the principle of public benefit (*istishan*). This marked a significant development of Islamic jurisprudence (*usul al-fiqh*) away from its place of origin in Mecca and Medina where the Prophet had lived and is characteristically traditionalist in its application of reason to bring the Revelation and the Prophetic tradition to bear in new unforeseen circumstances.

A different approach to the relationship between reason and Prophetic sayings is found in the work of Muhammad bin Idris Ash-Shafi' (767–820 CE), a Gazzan legal scholar, who, unlike Malik and Abu Hanifa, was widely traveling for study with Malik himself in Medina and serving as judge in Najran in the Yemen. Unlike Malik and Abu Hanifa who defended jurisprudential diversity, Ash-Shafi' argued for the need for universal interpretative legal principles for Islam rather than localized practices and jurisprudential traditions. In this quest for a consistent, universal legal response, Ash-Shafi' argued that the principles of analogy, consensus and public benefit only applied in the clear absence of the Prophetic sayings (*ahadith*) as identified and recognized through authenticated chains of transmission.

The tendency of Muhammad Idris Ash-Shafi' to pin religious and legal interpretation exclusively on the primary texts continued in a more pronounced form in the *Hanbali* School of Law, established by the pupils of Ahmad ibn Hanbal (780–855 CE). Partly in response to the sponsorship of rationalist theology by the Abbasid Executive, which we will explore in greater detail below, Ahmad ibn Hanbal largely discounted emerging *Shafi'* and *Maliki* jurisprudential tools as potential sources of deviation and innovation from the Original Islam of Muhammad and his Companions. For ibn Hanbal, only what the Qur'an ordained and what the Prophet and his Companions did or said could ever provide an authoritative legal precedent for Islamic law, and thus he was responsible for the compendious collection and authentication of hadiths.

By contrast to ibn Hanbal's exclusion of both reason (*'aql*) and consensus amongst the Muslim community (*'ijma*) beyond the Companions as legitimate tools for determining religious and legal practice, the School of Imam Jafar as-Sadiq in Medina (d.748 CE) explicitly recognized both Consensus and Reason as legitimate jurisprudential tools as well as the centrality of the jurist himself in making legal judgments. The Jafarite School was to become the School of Shia Islam which explicitly recognizes both the objective universal, and the subjective and particular character of law-making.

This separation of executive and judicial powers between the Caliphs and the *Ulema* was achieved by the strong relationship of mutual interest between the two. The *Ulema* embodied the living institution and juridical tradition of Islamic Law (*Sharia*[35]), and the Caliph embodied the legitimate succession to the Prophet Muhammad

---

35 Detailed explanation of what the Sharia is provided in Chapter 4.

who, although the holder of executive authority, was required to uphold the *Sharia* and whose position required the legitimacy of the Religious Juridical class.[36]

However, in this separation of powers, the Executive often did not come off well. Since Islamic Law was believed by Muslims to be derived from the Book of God and the *Sunna* of His Prophet, it was the *Ulema* and not the Executive who came to be regarded by Muslims to be the inheritors of the mantle of Prophetic wisdom according to the famous Prophetic saying, "Scholars are the inheritors of the Prophets."[37]

This meant that throughout the period of classical Islam, and despite Islam not officially having a religious priestly class, the *Ulema* performed the crucial social and religious functions of both legitimizing and restraining the role of the Executive (the Caliphs) and of administering daily justice by issuing formal and semi-formal religio-legal judgments (*fatawa*). This restraining of the powers of the Executive was often achieved with considerable popular success.

When the Executive did try and enforce a religious doctrine without the consensus of the *Ulema*, they found themselves opposed and risked losing the support of the Muslim community. For example, when in the eighth century the governor of Medina, Jafar ibn Sulayman, thought (incorrectly) that Imam Malik ibn Anas (711–795 CE), the eponymous founder of the *Maliki* School of Law, had issued a legal judgment (*fatwa*) that an oath to the Abbasid Caliph al-Mansur was not binding because it was given under coercion, basing his opinion on a saying of the Prophet Muhammad, "The divorce of the coerced does not take effect," he had Malik publicly flogged and racked.[38] Far from denting Malik's popular appeal, his torture by the Executive was regarded as part of the proof of Malik's religious authenticity and integrity.

This was also the case when the Abbasid Caliph Al-Ma'mun tried to enforce the so-called *Mu'tazilite* (see next section) rationalist doctrine that the Qur'an was created and time-bound (see next section) as official state dogma in a process called *Al-Mihna* (the Inquisition). He was opposed by the aforementioned Ahmad ibn Hanbal (780–855 CE), founder of the eponymous Hanbali School of Law, who, in the process of opposing what he considered to be the Caliph's heterodox position, brought imprisonment and torture upon himself, but also great credence and kudos with the masses.

Of course, the sanctification of religious authorities by dint of their opposition to civic ones is far from exclusive to Islam to wit; for example, the sanctification of Archbishop Thomas à Becket following his murder as a result of his opposition to the English Angevin King Henry II. What marks out the Islamic experience is that both this tension between the Executive and the *Ulema* and the appeal of religious authorities who oppose political authority in the name of Islam marked, and continues to mark, a consistent trend throughout the

---

36 Feldman, *The Fall and Rise of the Islamic State*.
37 Related by Tirmidhi, Abu Dawud, Ahmad, Ibn Hibban and others.
38 Abu Zahra, *The Four Imams Their Lives, Works and Their Schools of Thought*.

ages of Islam to the present day, whereby resistance to authority is often seen by everyday Muslims as an essential hallmark of religious authenticity.

This relationship of tension between the Executive and the *Ulema* was, by and large, a *creative* tension that sustained the possibility of civilization subject consistently to the rule of law.[39] However, in the early nineteenth century the necessary bureaucratization of the Ottoman State, following the French legislative model, first brought the *Ulema* fully within the orbit of the State and then did away with the need for the scholarly *Ulema* class altogether with the Ottoman Tanzimat ('reorganization') Reforms that lead to the Meccelle – a European-style constitution – in 1876. This disintegration of the *Ulema* as an empowered, autonomous legal class and the assumption of law-making into the State fractured and ended a key institutional relationship that had sustained Islam for 13 centuries and set up the conditions for post-Islamic twentieth-century dictatorship by reducing and then eliminating the traditional checks and balances on executive Muslim power.

The disintegration of the class of the *Ulema* in the Ottoman Empire was mirrored in the Indian sub-continent by the gradual waning of the authority of the organic tradition of Islamic Law administered by *Ulema* from the Hanafi School of Law and its replacement under British colonial rule by Anglo-Muhammadan Law. Anglo-Muhammadan Law, like the Meccelle, was a European-style legal code administered by civil servants. It was not an organic tradition of religious law that depended on a trained independent class of religious lawyers. Islamic Law under colonial rule thus morphed from a dynamic, living process of applying eternal principles of justice to contingent circumstances into rigid, unchanging content and fixed rulings that were either followed inflexibly (*taqlid*) and/or administered by non-Muslim colonial authorities. Either this became the new legal model or, as in the Deobandi Movement, the *Sharia* was mobilized and then fixed to preserve Islam from the influences of Western rule, and in so doing it further distanced traditional Muslim scholarship from the type of thinking that might enable Muslims to embrace the modern age.

The unfettered, unchecked and unaccountable authority of the regimes of the likes of Saddam Hussain in Iraq, Muammar Qadafi in Libya, Hafiz and Bashar al-Assad in Syria and Hosni Mubarak in Egypt is directly the result of the demise of the class of educated *Ulema* in the Ottoman Empire and colonial India and Egypt.[40] By the end of the colonial period in the twentieth century, the traditional Maliki, Hanafi, Shafi'i, Jafari and Hanbali Schools of Law, once the vibrant institutions that had for centuries acted as the heartbeat of Islamic civilization in its different forms, were all but moribund in terms of active institutional participation in governance.[41]

---

39 Rogan, *The Arabs*.
40 Moreover, where the *Ulema* as a class do exist, e.g. in contemporary Iran and Saudi Arabia, far from being independent, they have been reconstituted as part of the State.
41 Feldman, *After Jihad*.

36   The roots of Islam, Islamism and Islamist Extremism

The relative decline of the Muslim world is often attributed incorrectly[42] to the supposed closing of the doors of independent legal reasoning (*ijtihad*) by the Religious Jurists of the Islamic Middle Ages. In fact, quite the opposite is the case. The collapse of the intellectual vibrancy of Islam can be attributed in no small part to the collapse of the organic traditions of teaching, education and judgments of the *Ulema* and the reduction of Islamic scholarship to the harsh literalism of an elite of scholars who, far from being independent, began to be implicated in the excesses of various dictatorial regimes.

The product of the elimination of the *Ulema* as an independent but highly trained jurist class is that today there exists a great absence of genuine, independent religious authority across the Muslim-majority world, together with a proliferation of semi-authorized individuals making legal pronouncements (*fatawa*) about Islamic affairs. The tradition and folk memory of the greatness of the *Ulema* also means that these semi-authorized, populist jurists hold disproportionate sway among the Muslim masses as "the inheritors of the Prophets" and retain the power to mobilize huge numbers of people, either for or against the Muslim executive.

This has been evidenced recently, for example, in the Second Iraq War (2003–2010) in the machinations and insurgency orchestrated by the Shia Muslim cleric Muqtadar al-Sadr[43] and, more recently (2013–2014), in the calls of prominent Sunni religio-jurists, such as Yusuf al-Qaradawi, for 'Jihad' against the regime of President Bashar al-Assad in Syria. It also accounts for the enduring appeal of clerical 'outlaws' such as the late Osama bin Laden and Ayman Al-Zawahiri, the former and current leaders of Al-Qaeda, who by taking on the power of the 'infidel' (*kafir*) United States and apostate (*murtad*) Arab-Muslim regimes, however nefariously, re-enacted for some Muslims the early travails of the jurists such as Malik and ibn Hanbal as they were hounded by an unjust executive.

This tension between the Executive and the *Ulema* is also seen residually in the modern Islamist belief that Muslim-majority states can be undermined from within if they are not believed to be implementing Islamic Law (*Sharia*) correctly or fully enough. It is no accident that both opposition to Muslim-majority states that are widely regarded as unjust (or even to use Islamist language 'apostate') and Muslim opposition to foreign, 'infidel' intervention in Muslim affairs has come from a (self-appointed) modernist *Ulema* class.

In a mirror image of the repressive, often despotic actions of the contemporary Muslim Executive, this class of self-appointed, often self-trained *Ulema* such as Hassan al-Banna (1906–1949 CE), Sayyid Qutb (1906–1966 CE), Muhammad Abd as-Salam Faraj(1954–1982 CE), Ayman Al-Zawahiri (born 1951 CE), to whom we will return, and others have taken on the mantle of (often violent) opposition to authority, often without understanding the traditional Islamic ethos of critical

---

42 Reilly, *The Closing of the Muslim Mind*.
43 Burke, *The 9/11 Wars*.

respect for political authority, except in extremis[44] (e.g. Qur'an 4:59), or the fact that Islamic civilization was sustained by a creative (rather than a destructive) tension between the *Ulema* and the Executive.[45] This tension also feeds into the Manichean Islamist narrative – which is explored in depth in Chapters 3, 4 and 5 – that Muslims must choose either between obedience to compromised, Western-loving Muslim authority or pristine, pure, inward-facing Islam.

Intellectual hiatus and split: rationalist vs. literalist intellectual tension

As well as the fault-lines between Sunni, Shia (and Kharijite) Muslims, the Executive and the *Ulema*, a third fault line, that still generates division today, opened up in the first three centuries of Islam between three different types of intellectual-spiritual points of view on the relationship of human reason with the divine Revelation of the Qur'an and guidance of the Customary Prophetic Behavior Practice (Sunna) of the Prophet Muhammad. These points of view are still all highly influential in the Muslim-majority and Muslim-minority worlds today. I will call them, for want of more precise terms, Rationalist, Traditionalist and Literalist.

Rationalists

The rationalists were those who believed that human reason and divine revelation played a mutually complementary role in the determination of correct, Islamic ethical practice but who tended, nevertheless, to give primacy to reason over revelation and primacy to reason over both literal textual meaning and, sometimes, even over the consensus of the community (*ijma*) in interpreting the Customary Prophetic Behavior (*Sunna*) of Muhammad.

Islamic rationalists also tended to believe both that ethical values had an *objective* existence that was not entirely dependent on the injunctions of the Qur'an, and that human accountability before God, one of the basic tenets

---

44 I explore the full terms and conditions for opposition, including armed opposition, to authority in Islam in chapters 4 and 5.
45 It is, of course, a cruel irony of history that a number of the religio-jurists who are adduced by contemporary violent Islamist '*Ulema*' to justify violent action 'from within' what are regarded as corrupt states, such as the fourteenth century Damascene jurist Ibn Taymiyya who risked life and limb to uphold legitimate Muslim authority in the face of violent, unauthorized Muslim attack (Rapoport and Ahmed, *Ibn Taymiyya and His Times*.) Moreover, contemporary scholarship has shown that, far from being bigoted, inflexible ideologues arrogantly carving-up the world into spurious religiously defined spaces, the greatest classical *Ulema* such as Ibn Taymiyya and the Andalusian Ibn Rushd (known to the West as Averroes) were usually characterized by a nuanced and flexible legal pragmatism (Michot, *Muslims Under Non-Muslim Rule Ibn Taymiyya*.) in recognition of the fact that Law, even law based on divinely revealed principles, must always cater for the needs of concrete people in the ever-changing circumstances of time and place.

of Islamic belief, was dependent on the existence and exercise of human free will if the Justice of God was to be maintained. In the period of early Islam, rationalists were known first as *Qadarites* (see page 27) and then as *Mutazilites*, and their types of beliefs also later characterized the work of the great Muslim philosophers such as Ibn Sina (c.980–1037 CE) (known as Avicenna in the Latin West) and Ibn Rushd (1126–1198 CE) (known as Averroes in the Latin West).

The word 'rationalist' has tended to refer to the philosophers and natural scientists of the European Enlightenment, and, in spirit, the rationalists of early and classical Islam were not completely dissimilar from their later European counterparts. Like Descartes, Spinoza and Liebniz, the classical Islamic rationalists believed that the exercise of reason to determine the logical necessity for the existence of God was a necessary prior step to acceptance of the injunctions of Scripture.

Also, like the thinkers of the European Enlightenment, which coincided with the relative demise of the intellectual hegemony of the Church and the birth of nationalism, Islamic rationalism was born in and of particular political circumstances. Under the perceived iniquities of the Umayyad regime of the Caliph Abdal Malik (ruled 685–705 CE) towards the Party of Ali, an early ascetic scholar called Hasan of Basra (*Hasan al-Basri*) (642–728 CE) claimed that only if human beings had the freedom to commit their own acts, independent of the will of God, could they also be accountable for their acts before the Justice of God.

The rationalist *Mutazilites* – meaning 'those who have withdrawn' – were a group of scholars, so-called because they withdrew from the circle of Hasan al-Basri, and formed new schools of theology (*kalam*). From these schools they asserted, simply put, that the starting point for understanding the relationship between humans and God was not Revelation and Prophetic tradition – although these were things the *Mutazilites*, as Muslims, held as Articles of Faith – but rather that the starting point was reason (*aql*). Rather than belief in Revelation being a necessary first step for a relationship with God, for these rationalists the obligatory exercise of reason was a necessary first step to gaining knowledge of God through Revelation and Prophetic guidance.

As the late Mutazilite theological Qadi Abdal Jabbar (935-1025 CE) noted in his *Book of the Five Fundamentals*:[46]

> *If it is asked: What is the first duty that God imposes upon you? Say to him: Speculative reasoning which leads to knowledge of God, because He is not known intuitively or by the senses. Thus, He must be known by reflection and speculation.*

The *Mutazilites* believed in the primary exercise of speculative reason because they also held that the whole of Creation was subject to the principles of reason

---

46 Qadi 'Abdal Jabbar cited in Martin et al. (1997: 90).

and that it was the custom (*ada*) of God to act according to these principles. Indeed, they limited their belief in miracles to the miracles performed by God at the behest of Prophets since they believed that a Just God acted as much as possible according the dictates of a reasonable and predictable universe that He had created.[47] As well as championing the exercise of 'pure reason', the *Mutazilites* attacked traditionalist scriptural literalism, which they believed led to an anthropomorphic notion of God that compromised His Absolute Difference from Creation as described by the Qur'an (112).

The Islamic rationalist belief that ethical values had an existence independent of Revelation led the *Mutazilites* to conclusions that sound startlingly contemporary in their theological flavor. For example, the *Mutazilite* Master Abu Ali al-Jubba'i (died c.915 CE) asserted that a person living outside *Dar al-Islam* (the Territory of Islam) who had never been introduced to the Qur'anic Revelation and who had never been called to Islam could, through the exercise of reason, lead an ethical life and therefore be saved and achieve Paradise.[48] This belief stemmed from the idea that Justice and Goodness existed as part of the nature of God's Created Order and, although Divine Revelation and Law was the most effective way to access this justice and goodness, it was not the only way to access the Mercy of God.[49]

As part of this belief in the rational, predictable nature of the created universe, the *Mutazilites* championed a belief that was classed by many of the *Ulema* as heretical: that of the created nature of the Qur'an as one expression in time of the Eternal Word of God. This doctrine became state policy under the Abbasid Caliphate of Al-Ma'mun (786–833 CE) who saw in it the means to reduce the power and influence of those *Ulema* who had been loyal to the previous and recently deposed Umayyad regime and who instigated an Inquisition (*Al-Mihna*) against jurists who opposed it.[50] In the long run, this political patronage did the *Mutazilites* no favors as the doctrine, which was not their most important contribution to the development of Islamic theology, was opposed, as we have seen, by the popular and resilient traditionalist jurist Ahmad ibn Hanbal and led to a powerful and concerted traditionalist backlash against this doctrine. This ultimately proved their political and intellectual undoing as the successor to Al-Ma'mun, his brother Al-Mutasim (795–842 CE), backed traditionalist theological Asharism rather than *Mutazilism* (see below).

In this episode of the Inquisition and its aftermath we see the emergence of a phenomenon that has bedeviled the world of Islam until the present day: that of the entanglement of religious dogma with the political aspirations of different dynasties, groups and regimes.

---

47 In this belief, as well, one can detect the type of Worldview held by the philosophers and natural scientists of the European Enlightenment such as Sir Isaac Newton.
48 Martin et al., *Defenders of Reason in Islam*.
49 Hourani, *Reason and Tradition in Islamic Ethics*.
50 Reilly, *The Closing of the Muslim Mind*.

Islamic Rationalist Hellenism

The first *Mutazilite* principle of the primacy of reason for gaining knowledge of God has clear resonances with principles of Hellenistic Christianity such as expressed in the first verse of John's Gospel (1:1): "In the beginning was the Word (*Ho Logos* or Reason) and the Word was with God and the Word was God." And the same environment of Abbasid Baghdad that had patronized theological reasoning with respect to Qur'anic doctrine nurtured the rationalist assimilation and thought from a variety of ancient 'pagan' cultures, including Ancient Greece, India, Persia and (to a lesser degree) Rome into the intellectual milieu of Islam.

This Abrahamic-Hellenistic synthesis was also occasioned by the exposure of Muslims to the texts contained in the libraries and scholars of Alexandria and Persia, as those territories came under Muslim influence and rule, and by the need for Muslim rulers, scholars and jurisprudents to convince the intellectuals of newly annexed territories of the intellectual vitality and sophistication of Islam in centers of ancient metropolitan culture such as Damascus. These were a far cry from the tribal Arabian society in which Islam had first been revealed and taken root.

This synergy between rationalist Islam and the empirical and philosophical naturalism of the ancients, and particularly Aristotle through the work of the Neoplatonists such as Empedocles (490–c.430 BCE) and Pythagoras (c.570–c.495 BCE), produced one of the greatest flowerings of philosophical and natural scientific thought that the world has ever witnessed and is rightly remembered as Islamic civilization's 'Golden Age'.[51]

The instigation of Islamic rationalist philosophy (in Arabic, *falsāfa*) is usually credited to Abu Yusuf al-Kindi who worked in the Caliph Al-Ma'mun's polyglot, multi-faith proto-university – the House of Wisdom (*Bayt al-Hikma*)[52] – and benefitted from the copious translations of Galen, Euclid, Ptolemy and the Neoplatonists made by the so-called Translation Movement sponsored by the Abbasid Caliphate. In his treatise *On the Definition and Description of Things*, Al-Kindi set out to render Greek philosophical terms in Arabic such as 'the efficient cause' (*fā'il*), and in *On First Philosophy* he specifically justified philosophy in terms of the study of the truth of The First Truth, i.e. God, which is sanctioned by the

---

51 It is, indeed, made even more golden and remarkable by its temporal juxtaposition to the European Dark Ages and early Middle Ages in which Western Christendom suffered severe intellectual atrophy and political hiatus in the aftermath of the collapse of the Western Roman Empire. During the period of the relatively unified consolidation and flowering of Islamic civilization (c.800–1000 CE), Frankish and Germanic tribes vied to establish and consolidate their power in proto-kingdoms on the European landmass, usually seeking the political patronage of the Roman Catholic Church to validate their claims.

52 Kennedy (2016) argues that the Bayt al-Hikma was really no more than a big library. Most scholars believe that it was a much more proactive and organized center of learning than that.

Qur'an. Al-Kindi made the crucial contribution of reconciling conceptions of God from three different spiritual traditions:

1. The God of Aristotle as the 'First Cause', the pure immaterial intellect, and the Unmoved Mover;
2. The God of the Neoplatonists Neo-Platonists for whom God was both the first and efficient cause of the world, which emanates from the being of God as an "overflowing of generosity and power, mediated by Intellect";[53]
3. The creating God of Revelation and the theistic traditions, including Judaism, Christianity and Islam.[54]

Islamic Rationalism was both theistic and original

This act of intellectual integration by Al-Kindi gives us a clue as to the nature of Islamic Rationalist philosophy and the opportunity to dispel myths that frequently attach themselves to it.

First, Islamic Rationalism was always set within the context of belief in and acceptance of the reality of God, Prophethood and Revelation and was never undertaken to refute the realities of faith, but rather to explicate philosophically the relationship of God to His creation.

Second, the Islamic rationalist achievement was not simply the reconstitution and translation of Ancient Greek, Babylonian, Persian and Indian thought. This process of translation and reconstitution, to which Christians, Jews and Hindus were important contributors, was one significant impetus for the Islamic rationalist achievement.[55] It was also the development of the thought of the ancients in novel and highly creative new theistic directions inspired, primarily, by the mandate of the Qur'an and the Sunna to seek knowledge of all types.

Al-Kindi was followed by Al-Farabi (872–c.950 CE). Al-Farabi systematically developed Neo-Platonist and Neo-Aristotelean ideas of emanation of causes and of logic into an elaborate metaphysical and physical system that governed an entire cosmology. Al-Farabi blazed a trail for Ibn Sina, known to the West as Avicenna, who, amongst a vast array of intellectual achievements in philosophy and natural science, commented on and developed Aristotelian theories of the relationship of the soul to the body and the nature of the God, the Necessary Existent, as "the only being which, by virtue of itself, necessarily exists, in contrast to all other beings, which necessarily exist only by virtue of another, namely their cause, God."

The Islamic rationalists also tended to believe in what the great Andalusian philosopher, Ibn Rushd (Averroes) called the Unity of Truth – that is to say in the lack of contradiction between God and the Universe as described by religious scripture and God and the Universe as understood upon philosophical principles

---

53 Adamson, *Al-Kindi*.
54 Ibid.
55 Al-Khalili, *Pathfinders*.

or syllogisms or as understood (at a more lowly level) by natural science.[56] This profound recognition of the holistic complementarity between different intellectual disciplines was the mainspring of the diverse intellectual achievements of Islamic civilization listed in the previous section. Moreover, it resulted in the creation of a culture of Muslim polymaths who brought the idea of the University to Europe, as an educational site where the young person was to be inducted by means of a holistic and interconnected range of sciences into a sophisticated understanding of both the Unity of God and the multi-dimensional and comprehensible unity of His Creation.

Traditionalists

However, for all the intellectual brilliance of the classical rationalist contribution of Islam, Islamic Rationalist Hellenism was not without its own internal contradictions and intellectual problems. Not least of these were that some of the key Aristotelian ideas about God and the world – such as the eternity of creation – which had been absorbed into aspects of Islamic rationalism seemed to many others in the *Ulema* class to contradict some of the basic teachings of the Qur'an.

The ideas and politics of the Islamic rationalist theologians (*mutakallimun*) and the Islamic Rationalist philosophers (*faylasuf*) tended to be opposed by a group of thinkers who have come to be known as traditionalist.

Traditionalists were those who believed, like the rationalists, that human reason and divine revelation played a complementary role in the determination of correct, Islamic ethical practice and for understanding the nature of reality, but, unlike the rationalists, traditionalists tended to give primacy to Revelation over reason. In interpreting the Customary Prophetic Behavior (*Sunna*) or Traditions (hence traditionalist) of Muhammad, they looked to the literal meaning of the text and the received wisdom of the community (*'ijma*) before looking for the reasons (*illa*) behind the *Sunna*, including its context.

Early traditionalists who opposed the doctrines of the *Mutazilites* feared that by proposing a doctrine of human free will in order to preserve the Justice of God, rationalists had limited the Omnipotence and Omniscience of God as described in the Qur'an. Later traditionalists such as the great mystic (*Sufi*) and jurist Al-Ghazali (c.1058–1111 CE) were concerned that over and above what they regarded as the doctrinal innovations and heresies of the rationalist philosophers, such as Ibn Sina's doctrine of the eternal universe,[57] the rationalist philosophers had also relegated the role of God to a philosophical bystander in His own creation, who had been left with nothing to do in a continuous emanation of a first and efficient cause. We might say Al-Ghazali feared that the Islamic rationalist philosophers had created a deistic God who wound up the clock of Creation and let it run through

---

56 Taylor, 'Averroes'.
57 See Chapter 4 for further details about core Muslim beliefs.

an emanation of cause and effect, whereas Al-Ghazali, in his famous *Incoherence of the Philosophers*, re-asserted a theistic God who was actively involved in the affairs of His creatures.

As well as re-asserting the primacy of Revelation over reason, Traditionalists also re-affirmed the subordination of human reason to the Will and Revelation of God who was uniquely the creator of all human actions, which were predestined by Him. Acknowledging that human accountability before God on the Day of Reckoning (one of six core elements of belief in Islam) was indeed dependent upon at least a limited exercise of human free will if God was to be deemed just, Traditionalist theologians reasoned how to reconcile the exercise of human free will within the overall framework of Divine Predestination. They came up with often-ingenious theological-philosophical solutions.

For example, Abu al-Hasan al-Ashari (d. 936 CE), the eponymous founder of the Asharite School of Belief (*aqeeda*) that eventually became normative across the Arab Sunni Muslim world, who was himself a renegade *Mutazilite* theologian, came up with a highly rational solution to the apparent tension between human free will and Divine pre-ordination: that humans chose to perform actions that God has already preordained and created. Thus he opted for a dual and simultaneous sphere of willed activity, one divine and the other human, in which the human will was different in nature to the divine will and, therefore, in some senses still free.

Another Traditionalist theologian, Muhammad Abu Mansur al-Māturīdī (853–944 CE) of Samarqand, whose views became orthodox in the Indian subcontinent and in the Ottoman Empire, worked out a solution whereby man really does choose to act and then God creates the action for him.[58] The systems of belief of the *Ashari* and *Maturidi* Schools of Belief that acknowledge the primacy of Divine Predestiny over human will, and indeed of Divine Will over Divine Knowledge, eventually became orthodox in the Sunni Muslim world. They preserved the primacy of Revelation and Divine Will but constrained the independent function of the human reason to operate within the parameters of what was perceived by traditionalist *Ulema* to be Divine Writ.

Literalists

We have seen that the traditionalist paradigm allowed for the exercise of reason only within the parameters squarely suggested by the primacy of the Revelation (of Qur'an) and Traditions (of the Prophet Muhammad). However, the trend towards scriptural literalism and exclusivism that we noted earlier was a logical characteristic of the School (*Madhab*) of Muhammad Idris Ash-Shafi that continued in a more pronounced form in the School of Law established by Ahmad ibn Hanbal, the eponymous founder of the *Hanbali* School of Law.

---

58 Hourani, *Reason and Tradition in Islamic Ethics.*

Ahmad ibn Hanbal's thought was forged in the conflict between the so-called People of Hadith (*Ahl al-Hadith*), those scholars and proto-jurists who thought that Islamic doctrine should only be derived by a literal, prima facie understanding of the Qur'an and the hadith material, and the rationalists who were known at the time as the People of Opinion (*Ahl al-Rayi*). This was in response to the then *Mutazilite* orthodoxy of the Caliph Al-Ma'mun. Indeed, as we have seen, Ahmad ibn Hanbal was imprisoned for his refusal to accept the *Mutazilite* doctrine of the created Qur'an.

The *Ahl Al-hadith* placed the use of the sayings of the Prophet Muhammad, even ones that were of doubtful reliability (though usually not proven false or fabricated), above the use of Accepted Practice of the People of Medina (*amal*), Consensus or Analogy in the derivation of law or the interpretation of the Qur'an. This practice of the literal application of Prophetic sayings was tenable for a man of ibn Hanbal's immense personal integrity, prodigious memory and attested and sensitive intellectual abilities.[59] Nevertheless, it opened a path to literalism in the *Hanbali* School of thought, including anthropomorphist ideas of God and the belief that every answer to every question – be it religious or other – was to be found either within the text of the Qur'an itself or in the Prophetic traditions, as well as to the notion that Islam could only be kept pristine and free from un-Islamic influences, such as rationalist Hellenistic thought, by literal adherence to the text.

In other words, Hanbalism opened a path to the type of textual literalism that characterizes young-Earth creationists and others who believe that sacred texts provide the literal answer to every question under the sun, including those that are by nature the preserve of and speak the language of natural science.[60]

This trend to seek ontological, legal and doctrinal certainty in the compendious and literalist collection and interpretation of *hadiths* was (and is) not unique to Sunni Islam. Within Shia Islam, after many centuries of a more rationalist approach to the use of Prophetic sayings and the sayings of the Imams for the derivation of law, in the seventeenth century the School of Authentic Reports (*akhbari*) also called for the return of a literalist and compendious approach to the original Notebooks (*usul*) of the students of the sixth Imam Jafar as-Sadiq. This was despite the fact that a highly scholarly tradition of hadith criticism within the Shia tradition had shown a number of these Notebooks to be forgeries.

---

59 Abu Zahra, *The Four Imans Their Lives, Works and Their Schools of Thought*.
60 This tendency towards literalism in the Ahl al-Hadith and the Hanbali School is not to be confused with the fact that Muslims of all types believe that the Qur'an is literally the Word of God. Rationalists and Traditionalists both believe this to be the case but also believe that the literal Word of God (the ontology of its text) requires a flexible interpretative epistemology to apply it to novel contexts.

Hanbalism gives birth to Wahhabism

The *Hanbali* school remained centered on the Hijaz region of Central Arabia (now Saudi Arabia and Yemen) and became the official School of Law (*madhab*) of the Wahhabi intellectual movement and the House and then regime of the Ibn Saud family, as they engaged in a partnership formed in 1734 first in opposition to the Ottoman Empire and then against the Hashemite regime after the fall of the Ottoman Empire in 1923.

The Wahhabi movement, so-called after its eponymous founder Muhammad ibn Abdal Wahhab (1703–1792 CE) (see Chapter 5 for further details), took Hanbalism to its logical extreme by declaring that all religious practices that were not ordained and practiced by the Prophet Muhammad and his companions and the early righteous Muslim generations – the *Salaf al-Salih* – such as the spiritual practices of various Sufi movements that proliferated under Ottoman sponsorship, were religious innovations (*bida*) and needed purging from the body of orthodox Islamic praxis. Second, the early Wahhabis declared that people who practiced such innovations were not merely 'bad' or wrong-acting Muslims, but *kuffar*, i.e. infidels, who could be fought and killed. On this basis, the early Wahhabi armies fought and killed 'Muslim infidels' on the fringes of the Ottoman Empire with terrifying savagery, including the massacre of 5,000 Shia Muslims at Karbala in modern Iraq in 1802.[61]

The modern Kingdom of Saudi Arabia, together with its clerical hierarchy, has, after two centuries of sometimes painful trial and error, achieved both an accommodation with the diversity of the rest of the Muslim world as the Guardians of the Two Protected Places – Mecca and Medina – and has clearly worked out an, often uncomfortable, accommodation with the highly rationalized (and now secularized) environment of post-modernity. Nevertheless, Hanbali-Wahhabi traits, when taken to extremes, persist as the intellectual backdrop of some Islamist Extremism:

1. textual literalism and the belief that all life's answers can be found literally in the text of the Qur'an and the Hadith material applied *prima facie* to contemporary circumstances;
2. belief that practices – both the obviously religious and the less obviously so – that were not performed by the Salaf (the earliest generations of Islam) are religious innovations which cast those who perform them beyond the pale of Islam, making them infidels through excommunication (*takfir*) who, in the most extreme interpretations, are fit to be fought and killed.[62]

---

61 Rogan, *The Arabs*.
62 People who sign up to this set of beliefs have been labeled 'Islamic fundamentalists', although this is a misnomer carried over into Islam from evangelical Protestant Christianity. Almost all types of practicing Muslim are fundamentalists in that they believe and aim to practice the foundational elements of Islam as revealed in the Qur'an, explained by the *Sunna*, agreed by consensus ('*ijma*') and generations of inherited practice (*amal*).

How rationalist, traditionalist and literalist tensions play out in modernity

Moreover, while the tensions between Muslim rationalists, traditionalists and literalists do not (usually) erupt into state-sponsored violence as they did in the Caliphate of Al-Ma'mun, these trends in Islam have persisted throughout the centuries of Islamic society. They can be seen clearly in three sets of intellectual-political responses of contemporary Muslims to modernity.

Modernity (1860–present) has been characterized by relative Muslim decline at the end of the Ottoman period (1850–1924), which led to the disastrous alliance of the Ottoman Empire with the Germany of Kaiser Wilhelm II (1888–1918 CE). This, in turn, presaged the colonial carve-up and mandate of Arab Muslim lands after the First World War. The three sets of responses to modernity are those of:

1 Rationalist Modernists

   These are Muslims who believe that the application of human reason to the Islamic primary sources is the key to re-establishing Muslim justice and global dignity.

   The rationalist Modernists – represented quintessentially by the quixotic Jamaal al-Deen Al-Afghani (1838/1839–1897 CE),[63] and the influential Egyptian theologian and jurist Muhammad Abduh (1849–1905 CE), whose work we will revisit in Chapter 5 – pointed to gaps and obstacles in the interpretative infrastructure of Islam which they believed had prevented Islam and Muslims from adapting to the challenges of modernity. Contemporary Rationalist Modernists such as Mohammed Talbi (1921–2017) hold that a shift in the interpretation of Islam and the exercise of personal and legal reasoning (*ijtihād*), rather than jettisoning Islam entirely, is what is required to bring the Islamic world effectively into the modern age. For this shift, much as the Hellenist rationalists engaged with the non-Muslim scholars of antiquity, the rationalist modernists have advocated the application of Western-style technologies of reason, such as the modern disciplines of economics, politics, and sociology, to reinvigorate Islam and to restore it to its basic guiding principles (*maqasid*).[64]

   Rationalist modernists claim that a productive engagement with the best of an ascendant Judaeo-Christiana legal and intellectual culture in modernity will release the innate qualities of Islam of mercy and rationality in line with the Qur'anic principle that Islam pertains to all times and all places. But they are likely to be viewed with suspicion by other more traditional Muslims as overly accommodating to Western secular rationalism and potentially compromising with the traditions of Islam.

---

63 Who was Iranian, not Afghan!
64 Razeq, *Islam and the Foundations of Political Power.*

2   Madhabist Traditionalists

These are Muslims who adhere closely and strictly to the rulings and what remains of the jurisprudential traditions of the Five Canonical Schools of Law mentioned above, as well as, typically, Asharite or Maturidite traditionalist theology. The influential Deobandi and Barelwi movements that are prominent in Britain and which are traditionally associated with the Hanafi School of Law fall, broadly speaking, within this category.

Madhabist traditionalists gain their strength from referring back to identifiable religious and legal traditions which have survived centuries of geopolitical flux in the Muslim-majority world and which can lay claim to great historical authenticity. They suffer from the fact that the fabric of the Schools of Law as functioning, organic, responsive institutions of law-making have all but been destroyed and, therefore, traditionalists are often reduced to precedence (*taqlid*) in the establishment of legal rulings and are slow to respond to contextual-legal changes in the world.

Muslims of this nature tend to see the influence of Western and non-Muslim thought and politics as a necessary evil with which Muslims need to find an accommodation to coexist peacefully, if not creatively and productively. This means that the most rigid forms of Madhabist traditionalism can, on occasion, create the separatist environment in which Western-style rationalism, such as natural science, is viewed with suspicion, as it is in certain sections of the Deobandi Hanafi movement, and in which, occasionally, Non-Violent and Violent Islamist Extremism can go unchallenged and thrive, as it does in the so-called Blasphemy, anti-Ahmadi Movement in Pakistan.[65]

3   Salafi Literalists

Salafist Literalists, deriving their approach from the compendious hadith-ism of Ahmed ibn Hanbal, tend to brook no accommodation either with Traditionalism or with Rationalism and are typically[66] suspicious of the intellectual traditions and cultural habits of the West, which are often regarded as alien to the civilization of Islam.[67]

Salafis of all types call for a return to what they saw as the 'pure' Islam of the first three Muslim Pious Generations – *Salaf as-Salih* – before what they tend to regard as the religious innovations (*bida*) of the jurisprudential tools developed by the Canonical Schools of Law. As we have seen, the ideas of Salafi Literalists were presaged in the eighteenth century by extreme interpretations of Hanbalism in the particular form of Muhammad ibn Abdal Wahhab (1703–1792), the founder of the eponymous Wahhabi

---

[65] We will explore this further in Chapter 7.
[66] Although not necessarily, as there exist many different types of Salafi Muslim from the quietist and traditional to the violently extreme.
[67] This is, of course, highly ironic since many of the customs of the West were borrowed from Islamic civilization.

religious ideology, whose pact with Muhammad ibn Saud (d. 1765) provided the founding pillar of the Saudi Arabian state. This original Salafism called for the stripping away all of the accretions to the monotheistic purity of Islam (*Tawhid*), both Sunni and Shia, that had been allowed to develop under the pluralist Ottoman Empire.

In the second half of the twentieth and twenty-first centuries, the enormous oil-wealth of the Kingdom of Saudi Arabia has also extended the influence of Salafism, developed in its institutions such as the University of Medina, around the globe and has given much of the Muslim-majority world that traditionally manifests highly localized legal Islamic cultures based quite loosely on the Canonical Schools of Law a more homogenously Salafi feel.

As we shall see in Chapters 3, 4 and 5, most forms of Salafism clearly form part of Mainstream Islam and cannot be regarded as Islamist or extreme, and certainly not Violently Extreme. Many pious and highly regarded Muslims are self-declared Salafis and, indeed, the aspiration to follow the example of the *Salaf* – the first pious generations of Muslims – is one that is in principle shared by a range of observant Muslims. However, in the tendency to apply Qur'anic verses and Prophetic hadith literalistically, often without sufficient regard for the context of the Revelation (*asbab un-Nuzul*), the aims of Islamic Law (*maqasid as-sharia*) and in their tendency to frame all *cultural* customs and habits that are not overtly 'Islamic' as *religious* innovation (*bida*) some Salafis have created an intellectual culture in which both Non-Violent Islamist Extremism and Violent Islamist Extremism can take root and thrive. This is because extremists of both a non-violent and a violent nature can justify their attitudes and actions with apparent Islamic legitimacy using the methods, though not the outcomes, of Salafism. This has caused regimes such as that of Saudi Arabia a degree of religious and existential crisis, since the doctrinal language of Violent Islamist Extremists such as Osama bin Laden, including various extreme forms of the doctrine of Divine Unity (*Tawhid*) and extreme anti-Shia Muslim rhetoric, are often uncomfortably similar to their own.

Summary

In summary, Islam as a faith and civilization is to an unusually large degree inscribed, inspired and burdened by the presence of its past. In particular, we have looked at the genesis and lasting effects in the contemporary world of tensions between Sunni, Shia and *Kharijite* Muslims; the *Ulema* and the Executive; and rationalist, traditionalist and literalist theological tendencies for understanding the relationship of the Divine Revelation and Prophetic Traditions of Islam to human reason.

It is important to bear in mind as we consider contemporary manifestations of Islam and its Islamist derivatives as complete Worldviews in the following chapter, that the roots of the contemporary dilemmas and struggles that face

Muslims today tap into debates and feelings that have delineated Muslim society, thought and culture for centuries. The contemporary crises of Muslim belief, practice and identity are to some degree innate to existential tensions that lie within perfectly normal Islamic intellectual attitudes to life and in other ways are particular to the acutely disempowered and fragmented political and economic position of many Muslims today. These tensions are exacerbated by the difficulties faced by an essentially sacred civilization,[68] after centuries of debilitating European colonialism, in forging an authentic and consistent response to a secular-dominated world.

---

68 Winter, 'Introduction'.

3 The Worldviews of Islam, Islamism and Islamist Extremism

Islam, Islamism and Islamist Extremism are all internally-coherent, self-contained Worldviews

In the previous chapters, we looked at how the 'presence of the past' is formative of the Islamic attitudes and values that are shaping the world today.

The contention of this chapter is that Islam-derived theologies and Islamist ideologies, which are the contemporary product of the historical and theological processes outlined in the previous chapter, form identifiably different 'Worldviews'. That is to say, they are unified ways-of-being in the world[1] together with ways-of-knowing the world,[2] "in which knowledge and action are knit-up together, and organized into a single view of life and the nature of the universe."[3]

Contemporary Islam-derived theologies and ideologies are internally coherent Worldviews, which cohere internally by the logic of their whole even if they by no means cohere according to external intellectual and social criteria. In philosophical language, they are 'totalities' which require commitment from the Muslim believer in his/her attempt to believe, think and act in a coherent, unified way. Each Worldview has its own theoretical perspectives and suggests a particular way of being-in-the-world. These ways-of-being in the world will range from the personally and socially benign to the personally and socially malign and yet, crucially, they will serve and substantiate and reinforce the Worldview from which this behavior is derived.

The idea of a Worldview

The philosophical idea of a Worldview – Weltanschauung – is derived from nineteenth-century German theological-philosophy and became a feature of the thought of luminaries such as GWF Hegel (1770–1831 CE), Søren Kierkegaard (1813–1855 CE) and Friedrich Nietzsche (1844–1900 CE). According to Orr (1893), a person's Worldview has a theoretical and practical aspect. Theologically, philosophically and psychologically, the human

---

1 Known academically as 'ontologies'.
2 Known academically as 'epistemologies'.
3 Orr, *The Christian View of God and the World*, p. 15.

mind is unsatisfied by un-integrated, fractured, piecemeal knowledge, but seeks coherence and integrity in its understanding of reality.

> *Worldviews are generated by the mind's aspiration to a unified comprehension of the universe, drawing together facts, laws, generalisations and answers to ultimate questions.*[4]

Practically, Worldviews are generated by the need of humans to live according to a (relatively) consistent response to the world around them, including nature, other people and the transcendent dimensions, if they are to sustain a believable and coherent idea of the Self.

The second key aspect of Worldview theory is that, while each individual must of necessity live and act according to their Worldview to sustain their sense of Self, even if at times with a knowing inconsistency or tension, Worldviews are also shared by collectives such as families and nations. In his explication of Worldview in the thought of Hegel, Vincent McCarthy states:[5]

> *Thus a Worldview is a general shared view which one acquires automatically by participation in the times and society which one forms with one's fellows . . . a worldview is the understanding from apprehending the unfolding of Spirit in the exterior world.*

Critically, in this notion of collective Worldview, a particular Worldview can be absorbed unconsciously by an individual-as-part-of-a collective and indeed the collective quality of a Worldview is essential to its nature as a Worldview – Weltanschauung – rather than merely a view-of-the-world. Thus, for example, the majority of citizens recognize and obey the law, usually not due to an analytical decision about the law's innate justice, but because we are enculturated unquestioningly into a law-abiding Worldview, together with an awareness of the penalties involved in breaking the law.

Embedded within this Hegelian notion of Worldview is the notion that Worldviews have an often unarticulated philosophical substratum that makes all Worldviews, to some extent, philosophical Worldviews.[6] Thus, according to the Belgian philosopher Leo Apostel (1925–1995), a Worldview is a descriptive model of the nature of the world[7] which is comprised of these six elements:[8]

1. An ontological explanation of the nature of the world
2. A futurology, answering the question "Where are we heading?" both in and after this life

---

4 Naugle, *Worldview*, p. 9.
5 McCarthy, *The Phenomenology of Moods in Kierkegaard*, p. 136.
6 Vidal, 'What Is a Worldview?'.
7 I.e. an ontology.
8 Vidal, 'What Is a Worldview?'.

52 *The Worldviews of Islam, Islamism and Islamist Extremism*

3   An ethical framework: "How should we behave?"
4   A praxeology or theory of action: "How should we attain our goals?"
5   An epistemology, or theory of knowledge: "What is true and false?"
6   An etiology: a Worldview should contain an account of its own 'building blocks', of its origins and construction.

These combined 'Worldview components'[9] allow us to integrate as many elements of our experience as possible into a unified understanding of the universe.

Islam, Islamism and Islamist Extremism as Worldviews

This model of the Worldview that draws together facts (and factions), laws, norms, generalizations, answers to ultimate questions and suggests particular behaviors provides the philosophical framework for understanding the differences between different religious phenomena which, on the surface, all look and sound Islamic and yet, in reality, are very different and have their own distinguishing characteristics. I will delineate and refer to these different phenomena as (see Figure 3.1 and Color Plate 1):

1   **Traditional Islam,** which falls within the general category of **Mainstream Islam.**

    This is the Worldview of unity-in-diversity (see page 54) generated by the religious practice of those who accept and follow, to the best of their ability,[10] the basic injunctions of the Qur'an and the Customary Prophetic Behavior (*Sunna*) of the Prophet Muhammad, in a way that is appropriate to their circumstances without their aspiring to effect change in the political space.

2   **Activist Islam,** which falls at the intersection of **Mainstream Islam** and **Islamism.**

    This is Mainstream Islam as characterized by diversity-in-unity, practiced at least, in part, to effect both transformative personal change and transformative structural change in the public space according to Islamic principles. It is a type of Islamic Worldview that has existed since the Prophet Muhammad as an integral part of the experience of Islam but has never, to my knowledge, been formally categorized.

3   **Ideological Islamism,** which falls within the category of **Islamism.**

    This is the first major category shift from Islam as *religious praxis*[11] to Islam as *revolutionary political ideology* directed at overthrowing, rather than transforming, existing political structures and replacing them with an Islamic State governed by what Islamists regard as Islamic Law (*Sharia*).[12] It is

---

9   Ibid.
10 And notwithstanding the limitless ability of human beings throughout history to make moral and intellectual mistakes and to fall well short of our aspirations and ideals.
11 Praxis, as we have seen in the previous two chapters, is the combined force of belief and practice.
12 Islamism is sometimes called political Islam, which I believe fails the capture the essentially modern ideological nature of Islamism. Islamism is also sometimes called political Islamism,

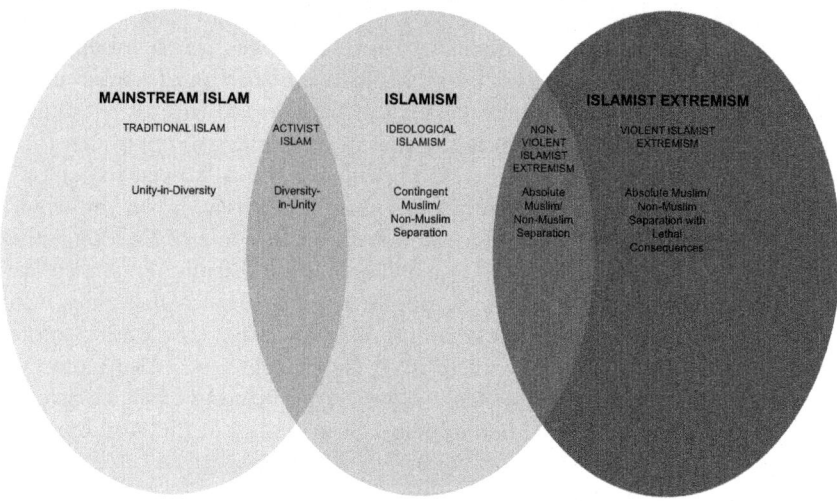

Figure 3.1 Characteristics of the Worldviews of Mainstream Islam, Islamism and Islamist Extremism

For full color version please see Color Plate 2 after Page 5.

characterized by exaggerated separation between Muslim and non-Muslim peoples and ideals, including in the political space.

4 **Non-Violent Islamist Extremism,** which falls at the intersection of **Islamism** and **Islamist Extremism**.

This is Islamist ideology as it sharpens antagonistically into an absolutely divided, Manichean Us vs. Them Worldview that stresses the absolute difference between the 'true' ideological Muslim 'in-group' and the non-Muslim and 'wrong' Muslim 'out-groups', who are afforded a less human or sub-human status.[13] This is the extremist Worldview that begins to suggest that the Islamic State (or equivalent) should be fought into existence.

5 **Violent Islamist Extremism (VIE),** which falls within the category of **Islamist Extremism.**

This is the extreme Manichean Islamist ideology by which the cosmos is constructed as a manifestation of the Eternal Struggle between Islam and Unbelief (*Kufr*). The non-Muslim and 'wrong' Muslim, who do not struggle violently to establish a global Islamic state, are construed as eternal enemies of 'true' Islam and therefore fit to be exterminated.[14]

---

which, to my mind, is tautologous and, again, fails to capture the ideological – not political – nature of Islamism.

13 It is sometimes referred to after its principal protagonist Sayyid Qutb as Qutbism.

14 Violent Islamist Extremism is also known popularly as Jihadism or, more academically, as Salafi-Jihadism. The former term runs the risk of conflating what Islamist terrorists do with

Figure 3.1 and Plate 1 suggests that there exist clear qualitative differences – of World-view, including praxis (integrated belief-action) and outcomes in the world – between Mainstream Islam, Islamism and Islamist Extremism. There are also overlapping grey areas between Mainstream Islam and Islamism giving rise to Activist Islam and between Ideological Islamism and Islamist Extremism, giving rise to Non-Violent Islamist Extremism. The reader will note that there are no overlaps, however, between Mainstream Islam and Islamist Extremism.

This does not mean that those people whose Worldview is, on the whole, characterized by Islamist Extremism do not do or say some of the things that Mainstream Muslims do and say – for example, most Islamist Extremists will perform the Obligatory Prayer. Nor does this schema mean that those who follow Islamist Extremist ideologies are not Muslim. They are Muslim insofar as they believe and declare that there is no God except God (Allah) and that Muhammad is the Messenger of God. However, contained within this schema is the strong contention that the outlooks and outcomes of the Worldviews of Mainstream Islam and Islamist Extremism in terms of their effects on Self, Other and on the World bear nothing essentially in common.[15]

The Worldview of Mainstream Islam: unity-in-diversity

The fundamental philosophical nature that characterizes the Worldview of Mainstream Islam (in both its Traditional and Activist forms, within the Sunni and Shia traditions) is one of unity-in-diversity. In Mainstream Islam the contingent and apparent difference of the created universe is trumped by its essential unity in its Source: God (Arabic: Allah, the One Worthy of Worship). In the Mainstream Islamic Worldview, differences between objects, people and things are real. Yet

---

the noble doctrines of struggling to please God (*Jihad fiy sabilillah*). The latter suggests that Jihadism is connected at the hip to Salafi Islam, which does a grave injustice to the Islam of Mainstream Salafi Muslims.

15 Nor does this schema mean that those who follow extreme Islamist ideologies are not Muslim. They are Muslim in that, and insofar as, they declare that there is no God except God (Allah) and that Muhammad is the Messenger of God. They are Muslims insofar as they are sincere in that declaration, but what they follow is not Mainstream.

In this contention that these phenomena are essentially different, this book also makes a normative claim that is itself not normative to typical academic Islamic Studies: that the beliefs and actions that constitute Mainstream Islam – both Traditional and Activist – Islam are more truly Islamic than those that constitute Ideological Islamism which are, in turn, more truly Islamic than those that constitute Non-Violent Islamist Extremism and Violent Islamist extremism, which barely contain any vestige of true Islam at all beyond, perhaps, a basic belief in One God and that Muhammad is the Final Messenger of God.

In this process of making distinctions, the analogy of the relationship of traditional Labour Party socialism to National Socialism (Nazism) is germane. Both political Worldviews advocate the state taking control of some of the collective means of production, but only Nazism does so on the basis of a racialized Worldview with genocidal tendencies and a war economy. In terms of the outcomes in the world, the outcomes of Labour Party socialism are, amongst other things, the UK National Health Service; the outcome of National Socialism (Nazism) is the Holocaust.

underlying this difference is a more essential unity of being with its source in the Unity of Divine Being.

Essential unity in the Qur'an

Therefore, the most basic principle underlying the Mainstream Islamic Worldview is that the whole universe, as the Creation of God, is essentially one inter-related reality created by One God. This is the most basic Islamic understanding of reality articulated in the Qur'an (e.g. Qur'an 112) and formalized theologically as the doctrine of Divine Unity (*Tawhid*, lit. Things made as One).

The Doctrine of Divine Unity in Mainstream, Traditional Islam

The doctrine of Divine Unity (*Tawhid*) states that God is the unique, sole god of the whole created universe, including every human being who is destined to return to Him to account for his/her actions (e.g. Qur'an 2:156). The fact that the whole of creation has God as its Source and Creator is the determining feature of life on Earth and the unifying fact that underlies the whole of existence. The apparent duality of the universe in, for example, the creation and alternation of night and day and the 'opposition' of the sexes are themselves, in their necessary and intrinsic relationship, signs of the underlying Unity of their Divine Source (Qur'an 3:190). Adam and Eve, for example, are cited by the Qur'an as the father and mother of the whole of humanity which God created "out of clay" (3:59) who, taken together, represent the whole human being.

The primordial unity of humankind is a fundamental philosophical-theological premise of the Qur'an as the Qur'an was sent to all humankind to call us all to belief in One God and to right action. A large part of the Qur'an, for example Qur'an 56:57–74 or 10:45–46, is directed at humankind in general without any distinction being made between believer or non-believer, Muslim or non-Muslim. These General (*'am*) Verses directed at the whole of humanity generally start with the oration, "Oh humanity . . . " and indicate the essential I–Thou relationship that every human being[16] shares with their Creator, God. Furthermore, the essential spiritual covenant that all human beings share with God by dint of being human is specifically alluded to (Qur'an 7:172) as existing even before the existence of created matter.

This is the brother/sisterhood that all human beings share by dint of being from the tribe of Adam (*Banu Adam*). All of us are creatures of God and all of us are accountable before God on the Day of Judgment. In the sense of our essential properties as humans, we all share an essential first-order equality before God regardless of wealth, race, faith or gender (Qur'an 4:1). To exemplify this essential first-order equality, a supplication made by the Prophet Muhammad after every prayer included the statement, "I testify that all your servants are brothers".[17]

---

16 Recognized or unrecognized.
17 Al-Qaradawi, *General Characteristics of Islam*.

56 *The Worldviews of Islam, Islamism and Islamist Extremism*

Although Muslim theologians, philosophers and jurists have differed throughout the centuries of Islam, in the degree to which the Independent Unity of God is differentiated and separated from the dependent unity of His Creation, ranging from the near-monism of some scholars, such as Ibn al-Arabi (1164–1240 CE), to the near-dualism of others, such as Ibn Taymiyya (1263–1328 CE), on this aspect of the essential unity of God and humanity they are all, following the General Verses of the Qur'an and the spirit of the *Sunna*, of the Prophet Muhammad agreed.

Real diversity in the Qur'an

Within this essential, first-order unity, Mainstream Islam (Traditional and Activist), following the Qur'an, recognizes natural and necessary diversity:

> *Humanity! We created you from a single man and a single woman and then divided you into races and tribes that you should get to know one another. In God's eyes, the most honoured of you are the ones most mindful of Him: God is all knowing, all aware.*
>
> Qur'an 49:13[18]

Thus, the underlying essential unity of existence is also characterized by real, second-order contingent differences. Men and women are different; different nations, countries and tribes exist in the realm of real duality and difference; there exists a plurality of different religions – not everyone is intended by God to be a Muslim (Qur'an 5:48).[19] Nevertheless, these differences are intended by God to be the source of greater mutual understanding and cultural enrichment and as a test to see who is best in action (Qur'an 67:1–2).

Essential unity and real diversity in the Sunna

As the verse above indicates, within this essential created unity it is not our essential properties, e.g. race and sex-gender, that are ultimately our crucial distinguishing features but the moral quality of our behavior. Thus, the Prophet Muhammad's famous last sermon explicitly declared the essential unity and equality of humanity in the eyes of God:

> *Someone who heard the sermon of the Messenger of God in the middle of the days of at-Tashriq narrated to me that he said, "O people! Indeed, your Lord is one and your father [Adam] is one. Indeed, there is no superiority of an Arab over*

---

18 My translation of Qur'an is closely based on the M.A.S Abdel Haleem translation (OUP, 2010), which is authorized by Al-Azhar University, Cairo, Egypt. Occasionally, I make my own translation of some words if I think that they can be rendered more felicitously in contemporary English.

19 The Qur'an (22:40) explicitly recognizes that churches, synagogues and mosques are all places in which God is legitimately worshipped.

a non-Arab, nor of a non-Arab over an Arab, nor of a white over a black, nor a black over a white, except by awareness of God. Have I conveyed the message?" They replied, "You have conveyed it, Messenger of God!"[20]

In this sermon the Prophet Muhammad was clear that second-order difference is real but morally neutral, and the quality of ethical behavior is what distinguishes people from each other in the Reality of God.

Mainstream Islamic praxis: the marriage of belief and practice

If the Worldview of Mainstream, Traditional Islam in its myriad denominational manifestations is characterized philosophically by unity-in-diversity, it is also characterized in practice by a necessary unity and consistency of practice and belief. I have termed this unity and consistency of belief and practice as religious seriousness.[21]

Religious seriousness in Mainstream Islam

Mainstream Islam has, from its earliest manifestation by the Prophet Muhammad and his Companions, been characterized, as a Worldview, by religious seriousness in the connection between religion and outcomes in the world generated by the balanced and inseparable partnership of practice and belief.[22]

In the Qur'an belief and practice are united in intrinsic and inseparable partnership. The phrase used to characterize believers, "Those who believe and do right acts" (e.g. Qur'an, 2: 82–83) is the most repeated of all Qur'anic refrains.[23] The Arabic pronoun for 'and' (*wa*) in this Qur'anic motif indicates an intrinsic partnership, like father-son, not an extrinsic relationship.[24] That is to say, belief and right action in the Qur'an exist in a relationship of essential mutual interdependence where right action is the necessary and natural corollary of sound belief, and sound belief is necessarily reinforced by right action.

Religious seriousness in the Sunna of the Prophet Muhammad

The literature recording the actions and words of the Prophet Muhammad is also replete with sayings that show how religious seriousness – a united praxis of belief and action – is an essential characteristic of the Mainstream, Traditional Islamic Worldview in practice.

---

20 Sahih Al-Bukhari 1623, 1626, 6361; Hadith no. 19774, Masnud of Imam Ahmed ibn Hanbal.
21 Religious seriousness – seriousness (r) – is modeled on the type of philosophical seriousness – seriousness (p) – advocated by the contemporary philosophy of Critical Realism.
  'Serious' in the Critical Realist and philosophical sense means that your practices and behavior are consistent with your knowledge and belief.
22 There exist multiple occasions, of course, throughout the history of Islam when this balance has not been maintained.
23 Sherif, *A Guide to the Contents of the Qur'an*.
24 'Iyad, *Foundations of Islam*.

For example, the companion of Muhammad, Abu Hurairah (may God be pleased with him) narrated that the Prophet Muhammad said:

> *Let him who believes in God and the Last day, either speak good or keep silent, and let him who believes in God and the Last Day be generous to his neighbour, and let him who believes in God and the Last Day be generous to his guest.*[25]

In each phrase the connection between belief and sound action is seamless; right action is the inevitable outcome, corollary and proof of sound belief. Conversely, wrong action, such as an absence of practical compassion, is proof enough that the beliefs underpinning it are flawed and unreal, as shown by the famous Prophetic saying:

> *He is not one of us [i.e. a believer] who does not show tenderness to the young and who does not show respect to the elderly.*[26]

The determining feature of human relationships

Thus, in the Worldview of Mainstream, Traditional Islam, the quality of Islam as a religious faith is determined by the subjective quality of Muslims' inter-human relationships.

> *Goodness does not consist in turning your face towards East or West. Those who are righteous are those who believe in God and the Last Day, in the Angels, the Scriptures, and the Prophets; who give away some of their wealth, however much they cherish it, to their relatives, to orphans, the needy, travellers, and beggars, and to liberate those in bondage; those who keep up the prayer and pay the prescribed alms; who keep pledges whenever they make them; who are steadfast in misfortune, adversity, and in times of danger. Those are the ones who are true, and it is they who are aware of God.*
>
> (Qur'an, 2:177)

In this passage sound belief and ethical behavior constitute a united 'praxis' – that is a unity of practice and belief – that is both the product of and indicative of true awareness of God.

Similarly, in Chapter 23 of the Qur'an, The Believers, those who believe are characterized as those who *do* or who abstain from *doing* certain actions rather than as those who know or believe certain things:

> *The believers are successful, those who pray humbly; those who avoid idle gossip; those who pay the prescribed alms; those who guard their chastity except with spouses. . . Those who faithfully observe their trusts and their contracts, and who keep up their prayers. They will be the heirs of Paradise.*
>
> (Qur'an, 23: 1–11)

---

25 Narrated in Sahih al-Bukhari 6136.
26 Narrated in at-Tirmidhi.

Likewise, Unbelief or false belief is shown, Qur'anically speaking, within the Mainstream Islamic Worldview to be unserious precisely because it tends to be manifest as faulty, unkind and anti-social outcomes in the world.

This idea is shown in exemplary fashion in the Chapter of Small Kindnesses (*Surat al-Ma'un*):

> *Have you considered the person who denies the Covenant with God (deen); this the person who pushes aside the orphan and does not encourage the feeding of the destitute. So woe to those who pray, but are heedless of their their prayer; those who are all show and yet who refuse common kindnesses.*
>
> (Qur'an 107: 1–7)

This beautiful and much-loved Meccan chapter describes the outcomes and proof of an unserious relationship with God – both an outright rejection of Him and a hypocritical relationship – as malign social behavior in the rejection of the claims of the most vulnerable in society to compassion and support. The defining quality of false belief is the neglect of the small acts of kindness that lubricate the social mechanics of civilized life.

Mainstream, Traditional Islamic ethics: balance between worship and well-being

When beliefs are uncoupled from social responsibility and right action, they become religiously 'unserious'. They also undermine a core aim within the Mainstream Islamic Worldview to achieve multi-faceted balance and to strike the median position between opposites that exist on a continuum.[27] The Qur'anic verses and Prophetic sayings cited previously as examples of religious seriousness indicate that there exists in Mainstream Islam an essential balance between two basic related core purposes:

1 Worship: God Almighty is worshipped and obeyed.
2 Human well-being: human life is protected and flourishes.

The Religion of Islam is called in Arabic *Deen al-Islam*. The word *Deen* means 'a life transaction' between the Creator and the created. The Worldview of Mainstream Islam as *deen* is structured around unified pairs of concepts, duties and ideas in the Qur'an that reflect these core related purposes of worship and well-being:

Therefore, the entirety of Islam as a Worldview represents a balance of these elements. The Qur'an is clear:

> *Thus We have made you a middle community.*
>
> (Qur'an, 2:143)

---

27 Michot, *Ibn Taymiyya*.

Table 3.1 Worship and Well-Being

Worship		Well-Being
God	and	His Prophet(s)
Allah		*Rusul*
Next World	and	This World
Akhira		*Dunya*
Belief	and	Right Action
Iman		*Amal salih*
Prayer	and	Poor Tax
Salah		*Zakah*
Rules of Worship	and	Rules of Social Life
'Ibadat		*Mu'amalat*

'Middle' in this verse, according to traditional commentators, means a nation that represents the center point-of-view between extremes.[28] And this center-point includes, according to the primary sources of Islam and its derivative legal infrastructure, the avoidance of extremes, even in acts of goodness and worship according to Prophetic sayings such as:

> *Never be extreme regarding religion. Many nations have been destroyed before you only because of going to extremes in religion.*[29]

> *Abu Hurairah, may God be pleased with him, relates that the Prophet, peace be upon him, said, "This religion is easy. No one becomes harsh and strict in the religion without it overwhelming him. So fulfill your duties as best you can and rejoice. Rely upon the efforts of the morning and the evening and a little at night and you will reach your goal."*[30]

Mainstream Islam, as a Worldview characterized by unity-in-diversity, is representative of a balance between the realities and rights of God, of humanity and of nature, of this Life and the Next Life, of the individual and the collective, including family and society. Extremes of anything, even of the actions that please God, let alone acts that may harm others, do not fit into the Mainstream Islamic Worldview as revealed to the Prophet Muhammad, honed and preserved by centuries of Islamic praxis and scholarship and as understood by millions of Muslims of different theological denominational colors today.

---

28 Ibid.
29 Narrated in Sunan Ibn Majah.
30 Narrated in Sahih al-Bukhari.

The Worldview of Activist Islam: diversity-in-unity

This understanding of the nature of Being as unity-in-diversity, together with a praxis of religious seriousness and an ethic of moderation and balance that characterizes the Traditional Islamic Worldview, also characterizes the Worldview of Mainstream, Activist Islam. In addition, in Mainstream, Activist Islam there is acknowledgement, derived from the primary sources of the Qur'an and reflected in its jurisprudential derivatives in the Schools of Law, that imbalance, inequality and injustice also exist as a component of created duality in the world and that these things sometimes demand change.

Indeed, there is no doubt that a commitment to personal and structural change can form a key component of a Mainstream Islamic Worldview. The Qur'an (13:11) advocates transformative (rather than revolutionary) change in a way that explicitly gives primacy to personal/agentic change over structural/institutional change in the cause of changing the status quo:

> *God does not change the state of a people until they change what is in themselves.*

Change of the world in the Qur'anic message begins with transformation of the Self.

Moreover, the Prophet Muhammad advocated challenging and changing wrongdoing in the famous hadith:

> *On the authority of Abu Sa'eed al-Khudri (may God be pleased with him) who said: "I heard the Messenger of God (God's peace and blessing be upon him) say,*
> *"Whosoever of you sees an evil, let him change it with his hand; and if he is not able to do so, then [let him change it] with his tongue; and if he is not able to do so, then with his heart – and that is the weakest of faith."*[31]

It is this Mainstream Islamic Worldview, when it is imbued with the ethos of change, which I delineate as 'Activist Islam'. It is a recognized feature of the Worldview of Mainstream Islam that when wrongdoing, imbalances of wealth and power, or absences of peace and justice exist,[32] it is a corollary of the same Worldview of unity-in-diversity, seriousness and balance as outlined previously that the believer should be the agent of necessary change.

Activist Muslims, such as many of the groups representing the Muslim community in the UK – e.g. TellMama, The Muslim Women's Network UK and

---

31 Narrated in Sahih Muslim.
32 At the levels of the embodied self, interpersonal relations, institutional relations and in human transaction with nature.

the Muslim Council of Britain, – also operate on the premise of the essential unity of humanity as stipulated by the primary sources of Islam: the Qur'an and the sayings (*hadith*) of the Prophet Muhammad. This Mainstream Worldview of unity-in-diversity, religious seriousness and a commitment to transformative change can be seen, for example, in the press releases of the Muslim Council of Britain[33] in the advocacy of Muslim participation on religious grounds in causes, such as combating climate change, in which the well-being of all are implicated.

Muslims Make Joint Declaration to Fight Climate Change

18th August 2015

The Islamic Climate Declaration released today calls on 1.6 billion Muslims to work towards phasing out fossil fuel use, as a religious duty to fight climate change. It also calls on all leaders and politicians to do their part for a better future for all.

In common with all the Abrahamic faiths, Islam considers mankind to be stewards of resources endowed by Allah. This implies responsible stewardship of these resources. In particular this leads to the avoidance of asraf (abuse) of God-given resources.

In this context Islamic investments and activities have to have a moral and ethical framework. This clearly lays the foundation of protection of the environment as a key requirement.

Given Islam's emphasis on equality and justice, the present order of predatory capture of global ecological capital would be challenged. Although climate impacts in the UK dwarf those of countries on the front lines, greater heat wave related mortality, flood-induced pauperization and drought are realities for which we will all be preparing.

British Muslims can respond to climate change in a countless number of ways. We would urge caution over public relations-orientated work in this sector, as it is seldom sustainable and recommend genuine grass roots dialogue, creativity and negotiation. Citizens might be moved to become supporters of the community energy agenda and neighborhood-led climate-safeguarding activity.

Dr. Shuja Shafi, Secretary General of the MCB said, "We are encouraged by the Pope's recent encyclical on climate justice and look forward to joining hands and hearts with our sisters and brothers in different faiths to explore each other's ecological traditions and challenge the systems of inequality that endanger humans and non-humans on our common home."

---

33 Muslim Council of Britain, 'Muslims Make Joint Declaration to Fight Climate Change | Muslim Council of Britain (MCB)'.

Nevertheless, it is in the nature of community representation and of highlighting the particular contribution that Muslims can make to general causes that Activist Muslims tend to emphasize and justify second-order cultural-religious difference between Muslim and non-Muslim as a difference that is worthy of recognition and respect.

For this reason, I have characterized the Worldview of Activist Islam as one of **diversity-in-unity**. According to this Activist Islamic Worldview, heedlessness of God and the arrogance and prejudices of the human ego, when it is out of line with the spirit, cause political and social injustices that need addressing through peaceful, active engagement with political structures and agencies.

This Worldview characterized by diversity-in-unity in which the particular characteristics and needs of the Muslim community are thematized and given prominence can also be observed, for example, in a press release on the burkini ban by the Mayor of Cannes issued by the Muslim Women's Network UK.[34]

---

24 August 2016

Media statement

Banning of Burkinis on Beaches – standing against patriarchy in all its forms

We at Muslim Women's Network UK (MWNUK) are deeply disturbed about the continued banning of the Burkini – an item of clothing some women are choosing to wear on the beach and whilst swimming. The banning sadly highlights the increasing anti-Muslim sentiment across Europe which is clearly at the core of these ludicrous decisions.

While it is true that many countries are at risk of terror attacks, how can the enforcement of dress code, specifically women's dress, lessen such risk? Instead, what it does do is further marginalise minority Muslim communities and works against community integration and cohesion.

To be clear, the Mayor of Cannes' ruling states:

- "Access to beaches and for swimming is banned to any person wearing improper clothes that are not respectful of good morals and secularism."
- "Beachwear which ostentatiously displays religious affiliation, when France and places of worship are currently the target of terrorist attacks, is liable to create risks of disrupting public order."

---

34 Muslim Women's Network UK, 'Banning of Burkinis on Beaches – Standing Against Patriarchy in all its Forms'.

- The infringement is punishable with a fine of €38 (£33).
- The ban remains in place until 31 August 2016.

MWNUK Executive Director, Faeeza Vaid said: "Just as the mayor of Cannes described the Burkini as 'a uniform that is the symbol of Islamist extremism', I argue that his ban is secular extremism, and actually gives ammunition to Islamists. As a women's rights activist, I question how can it be okay in 2016 to dictate to women what they wear? Let's be clear: it is NOT okay – and is an abuse of current French laws."

Historically, a number of factors have influenced dress code including: class, ethnicity, work, country of origin and residency, climate, religious interpretations, politics and of course fashion. And as we can see in the photograph above [not included], in many contexts there have existed self-appointed enforcers (most often male) of such dress codes, who validate their patriarchal thinking through law and/or threats of actions, like monetary fines. At the core of these decisions is the control of women's autonomy.

MWNUK urge all human rights activists to stand equally against this direct discrimination of Muslim women, as we would stand for the rights of all women to wear what they choose.

If you, or anyone you know, is being subjected to anti-Muslim hatred, bullying and intimidation, you can call the MWN Helpline for advice on 0800 999 5786. Anyone who fears for their safety should contact the police immediately.

A similar appeal to human rights on the Mainstream Islamic principle of essential human equality and the need for equal treatment can be seen in this article of the Anti Hate Crime charity TellMama:[35]

How could Bob Blackman MP host an anti-Muslim extremist in Parliament?

by TellMAMA | Oct 25, 2017 | News, Opinions |

Serious questions have to be asked! In today's world, due diligence around people, organisations and what they have previously said, are the norm, to ensure that extremists have no platform or legitimisation in the eyes of the public. Yet, on October 18th in Committee Room 12, Bob Blackman hosted Tapan Ghosh, a well-known anti-Muslim extremist in the mother of democratic structures.

---

35 TellMAMA. 'How Could Bob Blackman MP Host an Anti-Muslim Extremist in Parliament?'.

How Bob Blackman hosted, and thereby validated Mr. Ghosh, is yet to be looked into, though what makes matters even more unpalatable is that Blackman is a member of the Department of Communities and Local Government (DCLG) committee. One of the functions of DCLG is to ensure the integration of communities and to ensure that British values of tolerance are protected, maintained and built upon. How Blackman, who sits on this Committee, could not be aware of Ghosh's anti-Muslim hatred is deeply concerning. For example, Ghosh has spoken about controlling the birth rate of Muslims, praised the genocide of the Rohingya Muslims in Myanmar and even suggested that Muslims should be forced to leave their religion if they come to a western country. Simply put, would the latter view then apply to other faiths or just to Muslims? It is pretty clear that Mr. Ghosh was the 'intolerant' in an event called 'Tolerating the Intolerant'.

Mr. Ghosh's militancy based on his skewed views of Muslims also extended to the creation of a 'Hindu Defence Force' which he allegedly set up in response to 'Muslim violence'. In a Twitter post that the *Times* reported on, Ghosh even stated that,

> "Backwardness is the most powerful 'weapon' of Islam. Rohingyas are glaring example."

This is who Bob Blackman MP hosted and, in doing so, legitimised.
What Do We Call For?
We are calling for the following:

- That Parliament's Sergeant-at-Arms open up a formal investigation into how Ghosh came to be in Parliament and that some serious questions be asked of Bob Blackman MP. The investigation should then be published as a learning tool for other MPs.
- That Blackman be removed from the DCLG Committee that he sits on, until he can explain his actions and apologise for hosting an anti-Muslim extremist in our country's Parliament.
- That all MPs and their offices receive a notice from the Sergeant-at-Arms regarding undertaking due diligence checks on speakers whom they invite in.
- That Blackman contact us and meet with a Rohingya refugee, to listen first hand at the appalling genocide that has been conducted against this defenceless people by Burma's military junta, which itself has been legitimised by Aung Saan Su Kyi.

We leave you with this thought. Just imagine if an Islamist extremist had been hosted in Parliament by an MP. Today's newspapers would, rightly, splash the story all over their front pages. Exactly how is this different?

Essential to the Worldview of Activist Islam is the fact that – in alignment with the model of the Prophet Muhammad and the early Muslim community – religious commitment and the necessary requirements of Islam *qua* a serious religious praxis are a necessary predicate for sound political engagement. Politics serves the religious rights of Muslim believers and not vice versa. Political structures, *whatever their complexion*, according to an Activist Islamic Worldview, are benign insofar as they create, enable or at least permit the institutional and social conditions for the core purposes of Islam, namely worship of God and human well-being, to take place. Thus, Islamic principles of essential human equality and freedom of religious expression are often mobilized by Activist Muslims within the overarching aim to serve the Common Good.

Thus, Activist Muslim groups, such as the TellMama and the MCB, have unequivocally and consistently condemned acts of terror perpetrated in the name of Islam not only as criminal and profoundly un-Islamic but, moreover, as detrimental to the interests of the Muslim community, since after every act of Islamist terror in the UK and Europe there has been a marked spike in hate crime attacks on Muslims and a less tangible Muslim/non-Muslim polarizing of society.[36]

Insofar as worship of God and, relatedly, human well-being and justice are significantly compromised, Activist Muslims operating within the Worldview of Mainstream Islam will advocate the necessity for change according to Islamic principles in the furtherance of common justice. We will return to some of these principles of Activist Islam, such as reform (*islah*), advice to rulers (*nasiha*) and the idea of theological Deputizing for God (*Khilafa*) in Chapter 3 and the advocates who can best be delineated by the term 'Activist Islam', including Muhammad Abduh (1849–1905 CE), Mohammad Hashim Kamali (born 1944 CE) and Salman al-Awda (born 1956 CE) in Chapter 5.

The Worldview of Islamism: contingent separation and exaggerated difference

So far we have seen that the Worldview of Mainstream Islam in its Traditional and Activist forms is a religious praxis that is premised upon a first-order and essential identity, unity and equality between human beings of different ethnicities, classes and creeds and posits real second-order, contingent duality and difference between, for example, different nations and faiths that is worthy of both recognition and respect.

By contrast, in the first major paradigm/category shift of my typology, Islamism, as an '-ism', is a political ideology rather than a religious praxis, which, as such, significantly departs from Mainstream Islam. As such Islamism – both

---

36 TellMAMA, 'Anti-Muslim Hatred, Terrorism, Media Sources, Far Right Networks & Spike Points'.

Ideological Islamism and Non-Violent Islamist Extremism – invert the first-order unity and second-order difference of Mainstream Islam to suggest the first-order, *essential difference* between the Muslim and the non-Muslim and second-order, accidental similarity between them as human beings. Both these Islamist Worldviews also invert the Mainstream Islamic primacy of agency over structure and transformation over revolution by advocating the revolutionary overthrow of the existing geo-political world-order and the establishment of an Islamic State.

Ideological Islamism: the inversion of religion and politics

The first of the two Islamisms that I identify – Ideological Islamism – also referred to as Political Islam, inverts the relationship of religion and politics that characterizes the Worldview of Mainstream Islam. In Ideological Islamism, religion serves political aspiration and the desire for the wholesale governance of society by Islamic Law (*Sharia*), whether or not just governance according to the *Sharia* or any other just process already exists in a particular jurisdiction or not.

In other words, theologically speaking, Ideological Islamism inverts the ontological and chronological relationship of Mecca and Medina in the Islamic process. As an ideology, it puts the structural and constitutional changes that served the totality of Islamic flourishing in Medina before (rather than after) the necessary religious and ethical changes that preceded it in Mecca. This inversion of the natural dialectical order of Islamic implementation is one reason (out of many) why Islamism is an ideology and not a religious praxis and why it has singularly failed in its core project to establish a viable Islamic polity or state in the modern age.

This inversion of religion-politics and agency-structure and the ideologization of Islam is epitomized, for example, by the motto of the Egyptian and now global Muslim Brotherhood:

> *God is our objective. The Prophet is our leader. The Qur'an is our constitution. Jihad is our way. Dying in the way of God is our highest hope. God is greater!*

As an ideological rather than a religious Worldview, Ideological Islamism is, ironically, given its declared rejection of the values and aspirations, e.g. materialism, of the West, often characterized by the technologies and aspirations of Western ideologies, e.g. the political party and manifesto, borrowings from Marxist and Fascist ideology interwoven with the texts of the primary sources of Islam (see Chapter 5). As such Ideological Islamism, while superficially and overtly derivative of Islam, is in its nature and spirit as 'Western' as it is Muslim. Ideological Islamists have typically decried the moral decadence and corruption of the 'West' while affirming and aspiring to the basic Western political form – the bureaucratic nation state.

68 *The Worldviews of Islam, Islamism and Islamist Extremism*

Ideological Islamism is also imbued with the Western spirit of utopianism in that it advocates the deal that the City of God (according to pure, Islamic principles) can be built in this world. This is unsurprising given that Islamism is a direct reaction to Western, Western-inspired and Western-backed political hegemony. It is also due to the fact that its leading exponents, such as the founder of the Muslim Brotherhood, a charismatic schoolteacher called Hassan Al-Banna (1906–1949 CE)(see Chapter 6), have often not been religiously-trained *Ulema*, but European-style intellectuals whose discourse was born in the intellectual environment, not of classical or even Ottoman Islam, but the colonized or UN mandated contemporary Middle East.[37]

Ideological Islamism: the inversion of agency and structure

As well as the Islamist inversion of religion and politics in its attitude to change, Ideological Islamism is characterized by the inversion of the Mainstream Islamic primacy of and individual over structural and institutional change by giving primacy to structure over agency. In other words, Islamists aim to *overturn* states and the institutions of states so that they become constitutionally and politically Islamic before/instead of attending to change in the behavior and attitudes of religious individuals that would set up the conditions for a more just and righteous society for everybody, which, as we have seen, is the accent of change in Activist Islam.

In Mainstream Islam, the locus of Islamic implementation is primarily the individual, which then has collective implications for the family and for mechanisms of governance. For Ideological Islamists, the locus of Islamic implementation is the State (e.g. Maududi, 1939/1975), which then has implications (often profound ones) for the individual and the way that s/he chooses to lead his/her individual life. Moreover, the Islamic character of that state is deemed by Ideological Islamists to be comprehensive and explicitly ideological:

> An [Islamic] state is . . . universal and all-embracing. Its sphere of activity is coextensive with the whole of human life. It seeks to mould every aspect of life and activity in consonance with its moral norms and programme of social

---

37 Thus, Islamism is in many senses a post-Islamic ideological construct. It is an ideological response to the crushing disappointments felt in particular by the intellectual elites in the Arab Middle East after the broken promises of independence of the Arabs' wartime European partners after the First World War and the failure of Arab nationalism and pan-Arab nationalism to rekindle Arab political and intellectual glory after the Second World War, which include the humiliation (from an Arab Muslim point of view) of the creation and consolidation of the State of Israel (1947–1948) out of British-mandated Palestine (1918–1948). Thus, unlike Mainstream Islam which was born out of circumstances of spiritual and political flourishing, transformation and the pulse of expansive freedom, which has since suffered periods of crisis, stagnation and decline, Islamism was born out of circumstances of spiritual and political frustration and betrayal, underscored by highly ambiguous admiration-rejection attitudes to Western intellectual and institutional hegemony.

reform. In such a state no one can regard any field of his affairs as personal and private. Considered from this aspect the Islamic State bears a kind of resemblance to the Fascist and Communist States . . .[38]

In order to achieve this utopian purity, the goal of Ideological Islamism is to establish either a national or global Islamic State or Caliphate. In this, again, Islamists embrace (implicitly) the realities of the modern nation-state. The means of achieving this end, if they are specified at all, are usually non-violent. Thus, theocratic statism is usually regarded by Islamists as intrinsically better than and superseding democracy. Nevertheless, Ideological Islamists such as activists from the Muslim Brotherhood and the Jamat e-Islami have tended to recognize that an engagement with the political status quo, pluralist democracy in particular, may be a necessary preliminary (evil) to what is regarded as full Islamic governance.[39]

Thus, as we have seen in the quote above, Islamists have tended to suggest the essential incompatibility of Islam with democratic political models because democracies allow for the possibility that governance according to *Sharia* law may not be the outcome of the democratic political process. This incompatibility also exists in Islamist eyes because democratic states, in particular Britain and the United States of America, are perceived as being responsible for the demise of the political integrity – real, inflated and imagined – of Islam, such as the fall of the Ottoman Caliphate in 1924. Democracy for Islamists such as Maududi, Al-Banna and, particularly, Sayyid Qutb is synonymous with Westernism and Westernism is synonymous with not-Islam.[40]

The Worldview of separation and exaggerated difference

To bolster this notion of the political incompatibility of Islam as a governing ethos with other forms of governance, Islamists tend to point to those Qur'anic texts that stress the difference and separation of humanity into different groups e.g. Qur'an 109. In particular, they begin to emphasize an exaggerated separation between Muslims and non-Muslims who are characterized wholesale as Infidels, (*kafir*, pl. *kuffar*), as indicative of an ontology of the world that is necessarily and contingently, if not essentially and eternally, divided. This impulse to exaggerated contingent difference is exemplified by the writings – for example, Abu Ala Maududi:[41]

> *Islam, speaking from the point of view of political philosophy, is the very antithesis of secular Western democracy [. . .] Islam has no trace of Western*

---

38 Maududi, 'Political Theory of Islam', p. 166.
39 The famous joke about Islamists' attitude to democracy, "One person, one vote, one time!"
40 A view shared by the extreme Right and extreme secularists.
41 Maududi, 'Political Theory of Islam'.

democracy. Islam, as already explained, repudiates the philosophy of popular sovereignty and rears its polity on the sovereignty of God and the viceregency of man.

A more apt name for the Islamic polity would be 'kingdom of God' which is described in English as a 'theocracy'. But Islamic theocracy is something altogether different from the theocracy of which Europe has had bitter experience.[42]

Ideological Islamists begin to stress the need for 'pure' Muslims to avoid contact with the society, habits and beliefs of the infidel (*kuffar* or *kafirun*) in a way that is more redolent of Marxist rejection of 'the Bourgeoisie' than Qur'anic injunctions about the just treatment of non-Muslim faith communities. In other words, Ideological Islamism opens the pathways to 'Us' and 'Them' mentalities exaggerated beyond the warrant of second-order difference mandated by Mainstream Islam.

The 'wrong' or deficient Muslim

As well as the introduction of the Worldview of separation and exaggerated difference between the Muslims and the non-Muslim, Ideological Islamism introduces the notion, which will find its most extreme form in Non-Violent Islamist Extremism and Violent Islamist Extremism, of the deficient and 'wrong'-Muslim. This is the idea that the Muslim who is not politically engaged in the establishment of the Islamic State is *religiously* deficient as we will see further illustrated in Chapter 6 in the writings of Maududi.

In this rejection of Western-style democracy, the sharpened division between 'Us' and 'Them' and the identification of the ideologically-deficient Muslim, Ideological Islamism betrays its historical roots as the inheritor of communist-inspired Nasserism and pan-Arabism as the ideological vehicle intended to galvanize the Arab Muslim world.[43]

As would be expected, therefore, Worldview of Ideological Islamism has tended to manifest itself as political parties. The Society of Muslim Brothers (a.k.a the Muslim Brotherhood or *Ikhwan al-Muslimin*), *Jamat e-Islami* in Pakistan and the trans-national *Hisb ut-Tahrir* (the Party of Liberation) are three obvious examples of Ideological Islamist groups whose goal is the national (and if possible) global implementation of a purified Islamic State as a *replacement* for other existing political settlements, usually, although not always, by peaceful means. The texts characterizing these groups and their pivotal figures will be examined more fully in Chapter 6.

---

42 Maududi, 'Political Theory of Islam', p. 160.
43 Rogan, *The Arabs*.

The Worldview of Non-Violent Islamist Extremism: absolute Manichean separation

This tendency of Ideological Islamists to emphasize contingent separation and division between different Muslim and non-Muslim groups sharpens antagonistically among Non-Violent Islamist Extremists into a Worldview con-structed on positions of absolute, first-order eternal and irreconcilable difference between Islam and Unbelief (*kufr*), which includes everything and everyone who is not overtly a Muslim with a politicized agenda to establish a pure Islamic polity.

> *Thus, this struggle [between Islam and Unbelief] is not a temporary phase but an eternal state – an eternal state as truth and falsehood cannot co-exist on this earth.*[44]

In other words, for Non-Violent Islamist Extremists, such as Sayyid Qutb, those Muslims who are not committed to the establishment of an Islamic State or Caliphate are not just 'deficient' Muslims as they are for Ideological Islamists, but are taken beyond the pale of Islam itself into pre-Islamic Ignorance (*jahiliyya*), Apostasy (*irtidad*) or Unbelief (*kufr*).

This means that in this extreme manifestation of ideologized religious difference not only are Christians and Jews no longer respected, as in Mainstream Islam, as People of the Book (*Ahl al-Kitab*), but instead are branded as Infidel (*kafir*), but Muslims are also liable to be described, not just as 'wrong', 'deficient' or 'partial' as in Ideological Islamism, but rather as apostate (*murtad*) by collaboration and association with non-Muslim people and powers. This association (by implication) takes them beyond the pale and rights of the protection of Islam.

In setting up its core characteristic of the absolute Manichean separation of the religious and moral universe into two opposed groups – the 'pure', 'blessed' camp of political Muslims and the 'impure', 'damned' camp of the infidel (*kuffar*) who include the 'apostate', 'collaborating' Muslims – Non-Violent Islamist Extremism is closer to Manichaeism, which gave an ontological and creative status to Evil that was independent of God's active goodness than it is to Mainstream Islam. Non-Violent Islamist Extremism, like ancient Manicheanism, excludes the 'impure' and 'damned' group from the Mercy and Goodness of God and construes the history of the Cosmos as the eternal working out of the absolute struggle between these two opposing camps.

Dehumanizing of the 'other' as characteristic of extremism

In its Manichean Worldview, Non-Violent Islamist Extremism is characterized by its mobilization of dichotomies of 'purity' and 'impurity', and the 'pure'

---

44 Qutb, 'Milestones', p. 7.

Muslim in-group and the 'impure', even 'poisonous' (Qutb, 1964) non-Muslim out-group, with whom contact by Muslims acts as a dirty infection to the pristine, purity of Islam.

This, of course, quite apart from giving historical lie to the fact that Islamic civilizations have been at their most productive and vibrant when Muslims were absorbing and processing non-Muslim ideas and cultures, creates the characteristically *extremist* dynamic, whereby the 'Other' is stripped of its humanity and demonized, monolithically, as the cause of all the wrongs and injustices suffered by the in-group.[45] It is in this demonizing and de-humanizing of the non-Muslim and wrong-Muslim out-group that Non-Violent Islamist Extremism is appropriately to be identified as extremism rather than merely exaggeratedly ideologized Islam.

As a corollary of this absolutely divided and Manichean Worldview, Non-Violent Islamist Extremism departs radically from Mainstream Islam by suggesting that the ties of a purified, politicized version of the Muslim faith negate and supersede all other natural ties, such as those of family, kinship and nation.

This encouragement to separation even goes so far as to encourage separation from kith and kin:

> *A Muslim has no relationship with his mother, father, brother, wife and other family members except through their relationship with the Creator, and then they are also joined through blood.*[46]

This, as will be explained in detail in the next chapter, is in blatant contradiction of both Qur'anic teaching and the Normative Prophetic Behavior (Sunna), both of which enjoin the maintenance of ties of kith and kin even in extremis. It betrays the obvious character of Non-Violent Islamist Extremism as an extreme political ideology masquerading as religious praxis.

By establishing the intellectual conditions of the absolute, eternal separation and difference between Islam and Unbelief (*kufr*) and in the demonization and sub-humanization of everything connected with people that are not Muslim, Non-Violent Islamist Extremism sets up a Worldview that begins to suggest that the use of violence against non-Muslims and wrong-Muslims is the necessary practical outcome of the God-given nature of the world.

This theme of the necessary annihilation of Unbelief (*kufr*) as a corollary of the very God-given nature of the Universe is pursued with vigor and internally-coherent rigor as a component within the final category identified by my typology – Violent Islamist Extremism (VIE).

---

45 Richardson, *What Terrorists Want*.
46 Qutb, *Milestones*, p. 133.

The Worldview of Violent Islamist Extremism (VIE): absolute, eternal difference and separation with lethal consequences for the non-Muslim and wrong-Muslim out-groups

A shared basic Worldview with Non-Violent Islamist Extremism

Violent Islamist Extremism is, like its philosophical premise in Non-Violent Islamist Extremism, grounded in a Worldview of a total, eternal Manichean separation of the Universe into Islam and Unbelief.

It divides the Universe absolutely into those who are 'blessed' or 'saved' (i.e., the 'right kind' of politicized Muslim) and those who are damned for eternity (i.e., everyone else). In this absolutely divided Manichean Worldview, those who are either non-Muslims or 'wrong'-Muslims have abdicated facets and attendant rights of their basic humanity. The difference between Non-Violent and Violent Islamist Extremism is that, for Violent Islamist Extremists, this absolute and eternal division has, by 'natural necessity', lethal consequences for the 'wrong' and 'damned' out-groups.

Like Non-Violent Islamist Extremists, Violent Islamist Extremists also postulate that the maintenance and manifestation of this absolute Muslim vs. Infidel (*Kafir*) dichotomy is the divinely ordained mechanism that has organized the entirety of human history. In other words, according to Violent Islamist Extremists, everything that happens does so in order to differentiate and manifest the distinction between the Blessed and the Damned and God's plan to elevate the former and eradicate the latter.

The praxeology of Violent Islamist Extremism: absolute separation with lethal consequences for the out-group

While their basic Worldviews are similar, the principal difference between Non-Violent Islamist Extremism and Violent Islamist Extremism (VIE) is practical. For Violent Islamist Extremists, e.g. Abdullah Azzam (1941–1989 CE), Osama bin Laden (1957–2011 CE), Anwar al-Awlaki (1971–2011 CE), etc.,[47] the violent eradication, or at least the violent subjugation, of the non-Muslim and 'wrong'-Muslim out-groups to a puritanical literalist version of Islam, and to those Muslims who espouse it, is the inevitable and logical practical corollary of the very nature of the world as set up by God.

Thus, it is the duty of the Muslim, according to VIE ideologues, not only to identify the salvation of God in the separation of the Blessed from the Damned, but also to be the *agents* of that Divine destiny by bringing about the eradication of the Damned from the Earth as a prelude to their eternal castigation in Hell-Fire. This, again, is an extreme doctrinal departure between

---

47 See Chapter 7 for further details of the people, texts and contexts that constitute The Genealogy of Terror.

74 *The Worldviews of Islam, Islamism and Islamist Extremism*

from Mainstream Islam which, following the Qur'an and a body of the hadith literature, affirms that the Cosmos will come to an end, but also that it is the duty of humans to carry on with their business as usual rather than to look out for it.

Violent Islamist Extremist apocalyptic eschatology

This is why Violent Islamist Extremist groups have tended to be both apocalyptic and eschatological. They believe that their actions are ushering the Final Showdown between Belief and Unbelief that will be the prelude to the coming of the Guided One (*Al-Mahdi*), Jesus[48] and the End of Time. The chaotic and spiraling violence meted out unrelentingly during the Syrian Civil War (2011–present) is due in no small measure to the fact that both so-called 'Sunni' VIE groups, such as ISG and the Al-Qaeda affiliate, Jabhat al-Nusra, and 'Shia' VIE groups such as the Zainabiyoun Brigade and the military wing of Hezbollah have all set out to convince their followers that their own actions have been both fulfilling and enacting the prophecies of the End of Time. This call for Muslims to become agents of the Apocalypse has been both a powerful means for justifying acts of brutality against those who are on the wrong side of history and makes for a powerful recruiting tool.[49]

Both the spokesman of Al-Qaeda, the late Anwar Al-Awlaki, (1971–2011 CE), and the late spokesman of ISG, Abu Muhammad Al-Adnani (1977–2016 CE), gave their messages both of urgency and theological authenticity by framing the actions of violent insurgency as part and parcel of the Divine Plan for the pending Armageddon.

> *So within a short period of time of twenty years, all of this is happening. Does this not tell us that victory is soon? Does it not show us that these areas that Rasoolullah (sallallahu 'alayhi wassallam)* [the Messenger of God, peace and blessings be upon him] *emphasised and talked about in the ahadith are being prepared by Allah 'Azza wa Jall* [May He be exalted and glorified] *for the next stage? Al-'Iraq, Khurasaan,*[50] *Yemen and al-Shaam*[51] *are being prepared for what is coming next. And what is coming next is al-Malhama*

---

48 Like in some forms of Christianity, belief in the Second Coming of Jesus is part of Islamic eschatology.

49 In VIE Shia discourse, this apocalypticism has been especially focused around the coming of the Rightly-Guided Messiah (*al-Mahdi*), who is believed in strands of Shia Islam to be the unveiled Occult Twelfth Imam. In VIE Sunni discourse, it tends to revolve around a final military showdown between the cosmic forces of Belief (Iman) and Unbelief (Kufr).

50 Khurasaan or Khorasan was an ancient Islamic territory in and to the northeast of Iran. It comprised principally of the cities of Balkh and Herat (now in Afghanistan), Mashhad and Nishapur (now in northeastern Iran), Merv and Nisa (now in southern Turkmenistan), Bukhara and Samarkand (now in Uzbekistan), and Balochistan and Khyber Pakhtunkhuwa, touching certain parts of Northwestern Punjab (now in Pakistan).

51 Sham means Greater Syria and is the preferred Islamist name for the Levant. Using the names of ancient Islamic terrorities by Islamists both evokes the days of Islamic glory and suggests the illegitimacy of the modern nation-states that have replaced them.

[Armaggedon] *because Rasoolullah (sallallahu 'alayhi wa salam)* [the Messenger of God, peace and blessings be upon him] *talks about these places in reference to al-Mahdi* [the Messiah] *and al-Malhama.*

Al-Malhama is this epic battle that will occur between the Muslim nation and ar-Room and that will be followed by the global Khilafah [Caliphate]. *We are not living in a local Khilafah, we are living in a global village, therefore you either win it all or lose it all; it's not like you can win over localised small area and they will leave you alone – no, the long arm of American injustice will get you wherever you are. So you either win it all or lose it all.*[52]

The Abode of Islam (Dar al-Islam) vs. The Abode of Unbelief (Dar al-Kufr)

In order to make their Manichean, apocalyptic Worldview concrete in the lived world and by abuse of a medieval Islamic geo-political construction, Violent Islamist Extremist (VIE) ideologues have tended to divide the world strictly, inflexibly and absolutely into the Abode of Islam (*Dar al-Islam*), the Abode of Unbelief (*Dar al-Kufr*) and the Abode of War (*Dar al-Harb*), with the last two Abodes interchangeable. The Abode of Unbelief (*Dar al-Kufr*) and the Abode of War (*Dar al-Harb*) are *not*, according to VIE ideologues, such as Abdullah El-Feisal (born 1963 CE), places or countries that have declared an actual military war against Islam, Muslims or a recognized Muslim-majority State. For VIE ideologues, these Abodes can be anywhere (including Muslim-majority countries) where a purified, literalist version of Sharia law is not established without any 'impurities' from Western political and legal systems.

There can only be two possible responses for a Muslim who finds him/herself in the Abode of Unbelief or War: either migration to an Islamic State, which recently has meant the territory controlled by the ISG or the effort to eradicate the people and institutions of Dar al-Kufr.[53]

Violent Islamist Extremists are also committed without wavering or any grey-areas to the fact that the noxious out-group who must be eradicated not only includes all non-Muslims, including those protected by Qur'anic injunction, e.g. Jews and Christians (and in some readings Hindus), but also the 'wrong kind of Muslim' including moderate Sunni Muslims, all Shia Muslims and anyone who associates or 'collaborates' with them and the governments that represent

---

52 Awlaki, *Allah Is Preparing Us for Victory.*
53 These constructs are applied without any of the nuance of the classical Islamic jurists who created them and in geo-political circumstances that no longer give any warrant to this geo-political construction, given the nexus of international treaties and declarations of rights of which (almost) all Muslim-majority, Organization of Islamic Cooperation states are signatories.

76 *The Worldviews of Islam, Islamism and Islamist Extremism*

them. According to Violent Islamist Extremist ideologues, those collaborating Muslims in their refusal to bear arms to establish an Islamic State have apostatized from their Islam. Collaborating apostates include Muslims who in VIE discourse are 'used' as human shields, i.e. civilians, by collaborating Muslim regimes and who are, therefore, the legitimate collateral damage in suicide attacks.[54]

The VIE vilification of Shia Muslims

This core ideological commitment to the eradication of a wrong-Muslim out-group means in the context of the Syrian Civil War and the Islamic State Group (ISG), the special commitment to eradicate Shia Muslims. In this commitment to eradicate an out-group, Violent Islamist Extremism is highly redolent of Nazi racialized ideology in its commitment to eradicate the Jews, by which the cohesion of the extreme 'in-group' is maintained by violent demonization and repudiation of a particularly vilified out-group. The commitment of the ISG to eradicate the 'heresy' of Shia Islam and its out-group adherents was manifest in the Syrian Civil War at such genocidal episodes as the execution of 1,700 Shia air force cadets at the Camp Speicher massacre near Mosul, Iraq on 12 June 2014. At this massacre, Shia recruits were separated out from Sunni recruits and then slaughtered by ISG *en masse*.[55]

In a similar manner to the way that Nazi ideologues pinned the blame for the travails of the Great Depression Germans on 'the Jews', sometimes justifying their anti-Semitism by quoting out-of-context texts from the Christian Gospels such as Matthew 21:12–13,[56] VIE 'Sunni' ideologues blame the travails of the post-colonial Middle East on Shia Muslims working in collaboration with the Infidel powers (*kuffar*) (or in the case of Shia violent Islamist extremism, vice versa). This is done without any nuance or taking of responsibility by the 'in-group' for any of the events of the past or applying any forensic historical or economic analysis.

This is why, on the understanding of Hannah Arendt (1906–1975 CE) of ideologies as "isms which to the satisfaction of their adherents can explain every occurrence by deducing it to a single premise,"[57] Violent Islamist Extremism is an archetypical extremist ideology in which the meaning of every historical and contemporary occurrence is deduced from the premise of the Manichean and eternal 'Muslim vs. non-Muslim and wrong-Muslim' separation of the Cosmos.

The nihilism of Violent Islamist Extremism

In practice, despite Violent Islamist Extremism sharing the rhetoric of Ideological Islamism regarding the establishment of a global Islamic polity, state or

---

54 Maher, *Salafi-Jihadism*.
55 Cockburn, 'We Visited the Site of Isis's Worst-Ever Atrocity'.
56 Lovat, *Saving Islam from Jihadism*.
57 Arendt, *The Origins of Totalitarianism*, p. 457.

Caliphate, Violent Islamist Extremist groups, e.g. Al-Qaeda, Al-Shabab and Boko Haram, have tended to be in practical terms nihilist and nurtured by an ethos of extreme persecution and victimhood leveled (not always without some justification) at the West. VIE militants have tended to be more interested in laying the conditions for a Global Caliphate by ridding the world of *kuffar* and 'wrong' Muslims[58] and annihilating the Abode of Unbelief (*Dar al-Kufr*) than they have been in establishing a governed 'Muslim' territory, their ultimate agenda being the overthrow of democratic states, often in a millennial prelude to Armageddon.[59]

ISG has mobilized its nihilistic praxis more 'creatively' in the stated aim to establish a functioning state or Caliphate ruled by what they consider to be Islamic law. The ideological appeal of ISG has resided both in its throwing off the shackles of the relative 'moderation' of Al-Qaeda in its mobilization of choreographed and managed savagery (see Chapter 7), amplified through social media, and in its claims to statehood in a way that has never been convincingly achieved by previous Violent Islamist Extremist groups, including Al-Qaeda. Of course, the enduring statism and apocalyptic tendencies of ISG generated a fundamental ideological tension in its Worldview: on the one hand, ISG ideologues are keen to be seen to be ushering in the End of Time and on the other they aim to establish an 'expanding and enduring' Islamist Caliphate. However, ISG ideologues manage these tensions because both the discourse of the Apocalypse[60] and of establishing the Global Caliphate have been effective and necessary for gathering recruits.

---

58 McCants, *The ISIS Apocalypse*.
59 Ibid.
60 It is likely that with the territorial demise of ISG (2017–2018) in Syria and Iraq, the nihilistic discourse of the Apocalypse will gain ascendency over that of Global Caliphate in ISG propaganda.

4 Basic beliefs, practices and characteristic themes of Islam, Islamism and Islamist Extremism

In the previous chapter, I explained how Islam, Islamism and Islamist Extremism are Worldviews characterized by superficially related but essentially different understandings of the nature of the Cosmos.

I explained that the Worldview of Mainstream Islam – both Traditional Islam and Activist Islam – is one of unity-in-difference, including the essential Unity of God and unity of humankind despite being differentiated by accidental[1] properties of sex-gender, race, faith and class, in which essential unity trumps contingent difference.

I explained that the Worldview of Ideological Islamism is one of contingent separation tending to absolute difference between the 'true' Muslim in-group,[2] who are defined as those committed to establish an Islamic State, the 'partial' Muslim and the non-Muslim out-groups, in which contingent ideological difference tends to trump the general Qur'anic ethos of essential unity and the interconnectedness of Creation.

I explained that in the Worldview of Non-Violent Islamist Extremism this contingent Islamist difference sharpens antagonistically into a Worldview of absolute Manichean separation and difference between an absolutely and eternally divided 'pure' and politically-committed Muslim and the 'wrong'-Muslim and 'sub-human' Infidel (*kafir*).

In the Worldview of Violent Islamist Extremism, this eternal separation has lethal consequences for the different non-Muslim and 'wrong'-Muslim outgroup(s) since the logical consequence of their sub-human and damned status is that they should be annihilated as a corollary of the way that God has set up this world and the Next.

This Chapter will describe how these different Worldviews are enacted characteristically as:

1   Praxis – the interpenetration of religious belief and practice;
2   Legal-ethical bodies of themes and behaviors, including attitudes to non-Muslim 'others' and living in non-Muslim countries, and attitudes to struggle in the path of God (*jihad fiy sabilillah*) and fighting (*Qital*).

---

1   In the philosophical sense of non-essential.
2   Tajfel, *Human Groups & Social Categories*.

The sources of the Worldview of Mainstream Islam: the Qur'an and the *Sunna*

In Chapter 1, we saw that there are two primary sources from which all Mainstream Islamic praxis is ultimately derived. These are:

1. the Qur'an – the Revelation, literally 'Recitation', from God; and
2. the *Sunna* – the Normative Example of the Prophet Muhammad.[3]

> As the Prophet Muhammad himself said, "I have left two things among you. You shall not go astray as long as you hold to them: the Book of God and my Normative Example (Sunnaty)."[4]

The Qur'an and the *Sunna* are considered unanimously by scholars of the Five Schools of Islamic Law (Maliki, Shafi', Hanafi, Hanbali [Sunni Schools] and Jafari [Shia School]) following the Qur'an (e.g. 4:58–59; 4:80) to be the primary sources of Islamic belief and practice of equal merit which need to be taken together.[5]

> Oh you who believe, obey God and His Messenger and those in authority among you. If you are in dispute refer it to God and His Messenger, if you truly believe in God and the Last Day: that is better and fairer in the end.
> (Qur'an 4:58–59)

The nature of the Qur'an

The first of the primary sources of Islam and its Legal Framework (*Sharia*) – the Qur'an, literally means 'the Recitation', a fact that betrays its oral rather than textual origins. The Qur'an is believed by Mainstream Muslims to be the inimitable, uncreated word of God brought from the presence of God by the Archangel Gabriel, in stages, to be delivered on the tongue of the Prophet Muhammad to humanity to guide the God-fearing (Qur'an 2:2) in God-aware ways in all times and places.

---

3   The Sunna is itself derived from three further sources (Kamali, 2003):

   1. the hadith material – authenticated collections of what the Prophet Muhammad said and did with his Companions;
   2. the behavior of the earliest generations of his followers in Medina and
   3. the biography of the Prophet Muhammad in narrative form.

4   Al-Muwatta of Imam Malik, 1601.
5   If the Qur'an and Sunna clash, as they occasionally do with some hadiths of doubtful authenticity, the Qur'an takes legal precedent. Nevertheless, usually the Qur'an provides the religious-legal principle and the Sunna provides the exemplar. This includes, importantly, examples in the hadith literature where particular exemptions to the injunctions of the Qur'an and the *Sunna* prove the general rule, as in the many reported examples of financial reparations, e.g. for the breaking the fast of Ramadan, which the Prophet Muhammad waived if the offender pleaded poverty.

80 *Basic beliefs, practices and characteristic themes*

Muslims believe that the Qur'an was revealed to the Prophet Muhammad over a period of 23 years from 610 CE to 632 CE. It is made up of 114 chapters (*Surahs*) and 6,236 verses (*Ayats*). The word *ayat* – verse – literally means 'a sign', so while the verses of the Qur'an are conceived of as part of a coherent internally-related whole, each verse is considered in and of itself a sign of God's Power, Will and Knowledge. Eighty-five chapters of the Qur'an were revealed in the main while the Prophet Muhammad and the early Muslim community were resident in Mecca, and 29 chapters were revealed in the main after the Prophet Muhammad's migration (*Hijra*) to Medina in 622 CE.[6]

Receiving verses of Revelation is reported to have had an extreme effect on the Prophet Muhammad, bringing upon him a trance-like state and sometimes preceded by what sounded to him like the clanging of a bell. At other times he is reported to have broken out into a cold sweat.[7]

The written record of the Qur'an

Initially, the verses of the Qur'an were recorded by the Prophet Muhammad's Companions (*Sahaba*) orally and/or written down on pieces of stone, leaf and leather that came to hand – we need to be mindful that early medieval Arabia was a predominantly oral society and that the Prophet Muhammad himself was illiterate. The Prophet Muhammad is believed by Muslims to have rehearsed his recitation of the Qur'an with the Archangel Gabriel every month of Ramadan[8] in the canonical order in which it was eventually compiled during the Caliphates of Abu Bakr, Umar and definitively in an authorized form in the Caliphate of Uthman (see Chapter 1). This means that all copies of the Qur'an today reflect the authorized Uthmani version of which there are seven major extant styles of recitation with a few very minor differences between them.[9] An early and much-revered copy of the Qur'an authorized by Uthman that is believed to show the stains of his blood after his stabbing to death (see Chapter 1) still exists in the Topkapi Palace in Istanbul.

The content of the Qur'an

The Qur'anic verses (*ayats*) that were revealed in Mecca tend to deal with Divine Unity, the need for worship and social responsibility, the trials of the Day of

---

6 Both cities are in the western part of what is now Saudi Arabia, in a region known as the Hejaz.
7 Ibn Ishaq, *The Life of Muhammad*.
8 The ninth month of the Islamic lunar calendar.
9 As an example of how minor these differences are, the most significant one is the difference in pronunciation of *Maliki yawmidin* from Surat al-Fatiha in the *warsh* and the *hafs* recitations. The *hafs* recitation there is a long alif 'aa' sound as in *Māliki yawmidin*, which means 'Owner of the Day of Reckoning'; the warsh 'a' sound being short as in *Maliki yawmidin*, which means 'King of the Day of Reckoning'.

Resurrection, the delights of Heaven and the terrors of Hell in the After-Life and Stories of the Prophets.

The verses (*ayats*) that were revealed in Medina, after the migration (*hijra*) of the Muslim community in 622 CE into circumstances of nascent state-craft, tend to deal more with legislation, or the principles of legislation, about matters such as marriage, divorce, inheritance, trade and war.

Therefore, the Qur'an reflects the context and proto-legal circumstances of the time and place into which it was revealed. This was a society characterized, for example, by the complete absence of all the modern technologies of reformative and punitive justice – the absence of legislature, criminal justice system and police force. It was only in Medina that Islam came to govern the legal and political life of an entire community of 10,000 souls that included Muslims, Jews, Christians and Pagan non-believers. Despite its modern reputation as a legalistic book, only one tenth of the Qur'an deals with legal matters.[10]

The interpretation of the Qur'an

The Qur'an describes itself as "guidance for those who are mindful of God" (2:2), and thus by its own injunctions is intended to be recited and studied by the ordinary Muslim believer to guide him/her in the ways that are pleasing to God and as a means by which the believer can create a covenantal narrative for interpreting the meaning of his/her life (Qur'an 67:2).[11]

For centuries, since the days of the Prophet Muhammad himself, Muslims have committed the Qur'an to memory, delighted in its sound and rhythmical cadences and celebrated its verses in beautiful calligraphic inscriptions. Muslims regard the Qur'an as the quintessential miracle of the Prophet Muhammad and the crowning glory of Islam. Every Muslim is expected to read, reflect and derive meaning from the Qur'an.[12]

As a rule, anyone may, and indeed is encouraged, to reflect on the meanings of the Qur'an and draw his or her personal conclusions from it and share them as a source of wisdom and guidance for others. At a higher threshold of jurisprudential training and knowledge, *muftis*, who are those entitled to pass religious-legal judgment (*fatwa*), can issue judgments on a whole range of issues, usually from a position within one of the canonical Schools of law usually on a take-it-or-leave-it basis.[13] However, only trained scholars, called mujtahid, may make legally-binding judgments that must be accepted by all after a process of intense engagement with the Islamic primary sources and legal precedence, called *ijtihad*.

---

10 Kamali, *Principles of Islamic Jurisprudence*.
11 Ibid.
12 Sardar, *Reading the Qur'an*.
13 Baderin, 'Sharia Law and Secular Democracy'.

The requirements in Mainstream Islam for a person to make legally binding judgments from the Qur'an and the *Sunna* are stringent. The qualities demanded of the *mujtahid* include a compendious and detailed knowledge of Arabic grammar and morphology and a rigorous training in Qur'anic exegesis.[14] They also include, critically, an ability to derive legal meaning from the Qur'an taken as a whole, i.e. the Qur'an as a spiritual totality. This means that a *mujtahid* requires an in-depth understanding of the spirit of Islam as a whole, as well as an in-depth knowledge of the social and cultural circumstances to which the legal ruling would apply in order to make a legal ruling. Such an expert needs to be versed in a variety of jurisprudential principles. These tools have typically included:

1. **Knowledge of the Context of the Revelation** (*Asbab an-Nuzul*) – The Qur'an was revealed in response to specific, time-bound circumstances. Therefore it is vital for the legal interpreter to understand what these were to know whether a Qur'anic injunction is General (*amm*) and applicable to all times and places or Particular (*khass*) to that instance. This is of particular relevance, as we will see, to verses of the Qur'an that authorize and stipulate the conditions for armed struggle (*Qital*) for which it is vital to separate the General principles regulating the conditions for the conduct of warfare from the particular circumstances of the Prophet Muhammad which the Qur'anic verses address.

2. **Abrogating or Abrogated Verses** (*Nasikh* and *Mansukh*) – Some Qur'anic verses abrogate – either replacing or building upon – others. For example, verses that give qualified permission to the consumption of intoxicants are abrogated by later ones that prohibit intoxicants in a process of 'gradual prohibition'. Many Muslims believe this process of 'gradual prohibition' reflects Divine Wisdom in allowing early Muslims realistically to respond to Qur'anic injunction and to absorb the full force of the *Sharia* by degrees.[15,16,17]

---

14 Milani, *The Core of Islam*.
15 Al-Qaradawi, *General Characteristics of Islam*.
16 The first revealed verse concerning alcohol reads (2:219):

> *They ask you (O Muhammad) concerning alcoholic drinks and gambling. Say: "In them is a great harm and (some) benefit for men, but the harm is greater than their benefit."*

This verse is not so much normative as a descriptive – alcohol may damage one's health but the verse does not prohibit its consumption.

Then verse 4:43 strengthens the normative-moral force of the previous verse and prohibits drunkenness in the Obligatory Prayer:

> *O you who believe! Approach not the Obligatory Prayer when you are in a drunken state until you know (the meaning) of what you utter . . .*

Finally, verse 5:90 prohibits all intoxicants, including drugs and alcohol:

> *O you who believe! Intoxicants, gambling, idolatry, and diving arrows are an abomination of Satan's doing. So avoid them in order that you may be successful.*

The imperative 'avoid' in this verse, according to Muslim jurists, bearing the force of a full prohibition (Nasr et al., *The Study Qur'an*).

17 A significant strand of modernist rationalist Islamic thought led by the Egyptian exegete Muhammad Abu Zahra (1898–1974) has questioned the process of abrogation for determining Qur'anic meaning.

3. **Obvious (*Qati'*) and Obscure (*Zanni*)** – Some verses give a clear, unambiguous legal ruling; others require or may be open to interpretation. Unambiguous verses include those stipulating the performance of the Obligatory Prayer at prescribed times of day, the prescription of the Fast of Ramadan and the payment of the Poor Tax (*Zakah*). Ambiguous verses include such things as the level of penalty for certain crimes such as banditry and the spiritual meanings of more esoteric verses such as the famous Verse of Light (24:35).[18]

Principles such as these have enabled *Ulema* throughout the centuries of Islam to determine the meanings and injunctions of the Qur'an that were particular (*khass*) to the circumstances of the Prophet Muhammad and his Companions, such as certain circumstances under which the Qur'an encouraged the Prophet Muhammad to forge treaties with his enemies or to defend himself through force of arms, and those injunctions which contain principles that are applicable to all times and all places (*amm*). This is to say, in Mainstream Islam the fact that every verse of the Qur'an is believed to have its source in the One, Eternal God does not mean that every verse is eternally and literalistically applicable. These, and other principles, have also enabled Muslims to derive authoritative Qur'anic meaning, often in the absence of a centralized religious authority.

Normative Prophetic Example (Sunna)

Together with the Qur'an, the Normative Prophetic Example (*Sunna*) of the Prophet Muhammad is absolutely central to the praxis of the Worldview of Mainstream Islam. It exists in inseparable connection to the Qur'an as the primary source of Islam, which are the Qur'an *and* the *Sunna*. As a Companion of Muhammad, Imran ibn Husayn is supposed to have said about Obligatory Prayer and fasting Ramadan, "The Qur'an ordains this; the *Sunna* explains it".[19] An illustration of this intrinsic partnership between the Qur'an and the Normative Prophetic Example is the Obligatory Prayer. The Qur'an (4:103) declares the fact that the Prayer must be performed at certain times; the *Sunna* informs us what these times are, how they are calculated and how the actions, such as Standing, Bowing, Prostrating must be performed in order to complete a valid Obligatory Prayer.

The *Ulema* are agreed on the point that the *Sunna* is a source of the Law (*Sharia*) in that in its rulings with regard to the permitted (*halal*) and the forbidden (*haram*), the *Sunna* stands on an equal legal (though not ontological) footing as the Qur'an. This is why the Muslim Declaration of Faith in Islam (*Shahada*) is not simply "there is no god but the one God (Allah)" but rather the double declaration that "there is no God but the one God (Allah) and Muhammad is the Messenger of God". In this sense, more often than not it takes both the Qur'an and the *Sunna* to understand a Qur'anic injunction completely. For

---

18 Kamali, 2003.
19 Brown, *Hadith*, p. 150.

example, the Qur'an forbids the eating of carrion (see below) and permits eating everything that comes from sea. The *Sunna* shows that when the carrion comes from the sea (and is still edible) the latter permission takes precedent over the former, prohibition and the carrion can be eaten.

The person and *Sunna* of Muhammad is for Mainstream Muslims – Sunni and Shia – both the vessel and the proof of the religion of Islam. The Qur'an describes the Prophet Muhammad as an "Excellent Example" (*Uswa Hasana*) (33:21) and the *Sunna* as "Wisdom" (*Hikmah*) (62:2). Put bluntly: without Muhammad's Prophetic *Sunna* as a means to substantiate and exemplify the meanings and the spirit of the Qur'an, there would be no Islam.[20]

Derivation of the Sunna

The *Sunna* is derived from a vast corpus of recorded sayings and actions[21] of the Prophet Muhammad with his Companions called *hadiths*, which literally means 'happenings'. The *hadiths* record Prophetic events that usually both include words and actions and are of their very nature contextual. *Hadiths* were recorded and committed to memory by the Prophet Muhammad's Companions during his life and immediately after his death. The procedural collection of *hadiths* gathered momentum in the generations afterwards.

This process of memorization and collection resulted in the retention of an unprecedented amount of reliable, first-hand information about the founding figure of Islam gathered from those who knew him best. It also resulted in an unprecedented amount of invented fabrication about his life, deeds and sayings which were propagated in the circumstances of Civil War (see Chapter 1) and then Islamic dynastic expansion by those who either wanted to abuse his revered status to bolster their own political ambitions or to justify or prohibit the actions of the cultures into which Islam expanded. The dire need to distinguish between authentic and inauthentic reports about the life and teachings of the Prophet Muhammad led to the emergence of a process of authenticating chains (*isnad*) of narrators of this process of oral transmission.

This process of gathering and authenticating the sayings and actions of the Prophet Muhammad created an industry of *hadith* collection with scholars of *hadith* traveling the length and breadth of the Islamic world to hear (*sama*) *hadiths* narrated from reliable narrators together with their full chains of transmission that were included as part of the *hadiths*.

This impulse to authenticate Prophetic hadith also meant the emergence of specialist scholars of *hadith* (*muhadith*) who gathered formalized collections of

---

20 The centrality of the *Sunna* to Islam, together with the amplification of identity-politics and Muslims' resentment at a global imbalance of power and resources, explains why Muslims take insults to the Prophet Muhammad so seriously and occasionally to extremes.
21 Hadith is often incorrectly translated as prophetic 'saying'. The word is more correctly translated as 'event' or 'happening' and refers both to what Muhammad said and what he did.

them. In the emerging Sunni tradition, these formalized collections emerged between the years 700 CE, when the first relatively informal so-called *musanad* ('with chain') collections[22] to the eleventh century when the task of verifying the authenticity of the major collections of hadiths and agreement on their canonical (*sahih/sunan*) status was finalized.[23]

In the Twelver Shia tradition, sayings of the Prophet Muhammad and Ali, and usually only those Companions who were considered to be Supporters of Ali (*Shia tul Ali*), were transmitted in the first two centuries of Islam by the first six Imams descended from Ali and Fatima, whom the Party of Ali, as we have seen, considered to be the rightful heirs to the Prophet Muhammad. These sayings, which included voluminous accounts of the wisdom and spiritual teachings of Ali himself, were eventually gathered into four canonical books, mainly by means of collection and codification of the Notebooks (*'usul*) of the students of the great Imam Jafar as-Sadiq (702–765 CE).[24,25]

These canonical collections of *hadith* and, in particular, the so-called Two Authentic Collections (*Sahihayn*) of Bukhari and Muslim for Sunni Muslims, can be considered analogous to the Christian Gospels in that these Authentic

---

22 Such as Al-Muwatta (The Well-Trodden Path) of Malik ibn Anas (See Chapter 2).
23 These Six Canonical Books of Sunni hadith (*Kutub as-Sittah*) are: (numbers of hadith in these collections are approximate as they are disputed due to repetitions)

   1 Sahih Bukhari, collected by Imam Bukhari (d.870 CE), which includes 7,275 *hadiths*.
   2 Sahih Muslim, collected by Muslim b. al-Hajjaj (d.875 CE), which includes 9,200 *hadiths*.
   3 Sunan Abu Daud, collected by Abu Daud (d.888 CE), which includes 4,800 *hadiths*.
   4 Jami al-Tirmidhi, collected by al-Tirmidhi (d.892 CE), which includes 3,956 *hadiths*.
   5 Sunan al-Sughra, collected by al-Nasa'i (d. 915 CE), which includes 5,270 *hadiths*.
   6 Al-Muwatta, collected by Imam Malik (795 CE), which includes 1,720 *hadiths*.

24 1 *Kitab al-Kafi* (The Book that is Sufficient) by Muhammad ibn Ya'qub al-Kulayni al-Razi (329 AH) contains 16,199 hadiths.
   2 *Man La Yahdhuruhu al-Faqih* (For Whoever Lacks a Jurist) by Muhammad ibn Babawayh contains 9,044 hadith.
   3 *Tahdhib al-Ahkam* (The Refinement of Judgments) by Shaykh Muhammad Tusi contains 13,590 hadith.
   4 *Al-Istisbar fima ukhtulifa fihi al-akhbar* (Seeking Clarity on Matters on which Reports Differ) by Shaykh Muhammad Tusi contains 5,511 hadith.

25 Despite the emergence of these relatively distinct Sunni and Shia traditions of *hadith*, it should be noted that a high proportion of both the sayings and the transmitters of the sayings in the Sunni and Shia Canonical Works are the same. For example, *hadiths* that extol the virtues and spiritual status of Ali are certainly not exclusive to the Shia *hadith* tradition. Both canonical traditions also contain sayings which clearly reinforce the emergent politically partisan nature of two distinct denominations. Therefore, as Brown has pointed out, despite a rigorous tradition of *hadith* authentication based on both the quality and quantity of transmission, to say a *hadith* collection is canonical does not mean to say that it is infallible.

Collections were authenticated as providing canonical accounts of what the Prophet Muhammad said and did by a gradual process of elimination of rivals. Also, like the Christian Gospels, after they were granted canonical status, no further collections were subsequently validated. Together they lay claim to c. 40,000 *hadith*. Thereafter, the industry of *hadith* collection, although not interpretation or criticism, withered by the end of the eleventh century in both Sunni and Shia Islam.[26]

The same basic principle of interpretation of the Qur'an, therefore, applies with the *Sunna*. Anyone may read the hadith material and the life of the Prophet Muhammad, his Companions and family (*Ahl al-Bayt*) and be inspired and nurtured spiritually as regards their faith and the conduct of their own daily lives. Only those with a specific training may make binding legal judgments and issue legal rulings (*fatwa*) about what is *Sunna* derived from *hadith* having taken into careful consideration the context and the purpose of the Prophetic utterance or action, as well as the quality and quantity of the transmission of the *hadith(s)* that form its basis.

The Sharia of Islam is a pathway to God's pleasure

The legal injunctions (*ahkam*), such as the legal categories of what is permitted (*halal*) and forbidden (*haram*) in Islam, and also the methods by which the legal injunctions are derived from the combination of the Qur'an and the *Sunna* are collectively called the *Sharia* (legal path) of Islam.

Sharia is an Arabic word of pre-Qur'anic origin that means a 'pathway to a spring of pure water'. Therefore, the word 'law' only very partially represents what the *Sharia* means to Mainstream Muslims. It is much more closely conceived and enacted by Muslims in their daily lives as a religiously serious route from birth to death by which the human can be assured to be traveling through life according to God's Mercy, and not in ways that may incur His Anger.[27] Mainstream Muslims believe that the former route, following the *Sharia*, tends to health and happiness; travelling through life without following the *Sharia* leads to disappointment and failure. This concept is encapsulated in the well-known saying of the Prophet Muhammad:

> O God, I seek refuge in Your pleasure from Your anger, and in Your forgiveness from Your punishment, and I seek refuge in You from You. I cannot count Your praises, You are as You have praised Yourself.[28]

It is important to note, however, that the judgments of the *Sharia* derived from the primary sources of Islam are in the vast majority of cases human legal derivatives of Divine and Prophetic principles. In other words, they are context-bound and fallible. In philosophical-legal terms, the *Sharia* of Islam

---

26 Brown, Hadith.
27 Wilkinson, 'The Metaphysics of a Contemporary Islamic Sharia'.
28 Sahih Muslim, 4: 986

is a legal epistemology – it is regarded by observant Mainstream Muslims as the most efficient and God-aligned route to access Divine pleasure, guidance and justice; it is not, in itself, the reality of Revelation, Justice or God. Muslims believe that God, the reality of Divine Justice, and the texts (*matan*) of the Revelation are fixed, eternal, perfect and unchanging. The corollary of the eternal and infallible status of these Divine realities is that all interpretations of the same by humans are fallible, contingent and geo-politically bound and prone to revision and change.[29]

Basic Obligatory practices in Islam: the Five Pillars of Islam

For Mainstream Muslims, the *Sharia* of Islam is most obviously made manifest as the so-called Five Pillars of Islam. These are the Five Individual Religious Obligations (*Fara'id al 'Ayn*) that every adult, sane Muslim agrees to fulfill as his/her basic Covenant (*Deen*) with God.

The Prophet Muhammad said in an authentic hadith related by Al-Bukhari and Muslim about the practice of Islam:

> *Islam has been built upon five [elements]: testifying that there is no god but God and that Muhammad is the Messenger of God, establishing the Obligatory Prayer, paying the Poor Tax, making pilgrimage to the House of Allah, and fasting the month of Ramadan.*[30]

These so-called Five Pillars of Islam[31] are:

1 **The Witnessing** (*Shahada*) – This is the Declaration of Faith that there is no god but God (*Allah*) and that Muhammad is the Messenger of God. On this declaration, made in front of two Muslim witnesses, a person enters Islam. This Declaration of Faith means that he or she agrees to perform:

2 **The Prayer** (*Salah*) – Five daily Obligatory Prayers that are performed at prescribed times of day that move according to the position of the sun. The Prophet said, "The Prayer is the basis of the Life-transaction."[32] Traditionally speaking, failure to perform it is an act of Unbelief (*Kufr*). It is comprised of rotations of standing, bowing and prostrating before God together with the recitation of certain phrases and verses of the Qur'an. The word *Salah* is derived from the Arabic word *Silat*, meaning 'a connection'. Thus, Obligatory Prayer is the means by which the believer connects with and accounts

---

29 Conflation of the status of ontology with epistemology has been called by critical realist thinkers such as Roy Bhaskar 'the epistemic fallacy' (Wilkinson, 2015: 51–56). It is prevalent across swathes of modernist and post-modernist ideological thought, including Islam-isms.
30 Nawawi, 40 Hadith, 3.
31 Although the hadith does not actually use the word 'pillars' which has been implied in translation from its general meaning.
32 Narrated in Sunan Al-Sughra.

for himself or herself before God five times a day, recognizing the Lordship of the Almighty Creator and the servanthood of the created human being.

3 **The Poor Tax** (*Zakah*) – This is a tax on 2.5% of a believer's unused savings which is paid to a religious authority or directly to the recipient for the maintenance of the poor and a variety of other categories of needy people. It is paid once someone's unused wealth has reached a certain threshold (*nisab*). Within the Worldview of Mainstream Islam of unity-in-diversity, the Poor Tax is intended both as an act of individual purification and to enact the essential solidarity and unity of humankind and the fact that all wealth is a Gift from God, as well as catering materially for the most vulnerable in society.

4 **The Fast** (*Sawm*) – This is to abstain from all food, drink and sexual relations from dawn to sunset during the month of Ramadan. The purpose of the Fast is to teach self-restraint and moderation of the appetites, gratitude to God for His provision and empathy with the poor.

(Qur'an 2:183–185)[33]

5 **The Pilgrimage** (Hajj) – The believer agrees to perform the rites of Hajj at the first place dedicated to the worship of God, the *Ka'aba* in Mecca and surrounding areas, once in a lifetime if she/he is able to afford it while still fulfilling his/her duties to provide for his/her family. The Hajj is performed by all men in two pieces of white shroud called an *Ihram* and by women in white modest clothing without covering the face. The *Hajj* is a reminder, again, of the Worldview of the essential unity and equality of humankind before God and that death and accounting for ourselves before God is our shared human Destiny.

These so-called Five Pillars of Islam, while they may appear to be comprehensive, are the only obligatory tenets of worship in Islam. The performance of them is believed by Mainstream Muslims to guarantee the believer (God willing) the promise of Paradise. According to Mainstream Muslim scholars, this is shown by the authentic *hadith* (saying) of the Prophet Muhammad narrated by Muslim:

> *Jabir bin Abdullah Al-Ansari narrated that:*
>
> > *A man asked the Messenger of God (may the blessings and peace of God be upon him): Do you think that if I perform the obligatory prayers, fast in Ramadan, treat as lawful that which is lawful and treat as forbidden that which is forbidden, and do nothing further, I shall enter Paradise? He (Muhammad) said: Yes.*

In other words, fulfillment of these Individual Religious Obligations (*fara'id al-'ayn*), together with observance of the permitted (*halal*) and the

---

33 There is great flexibility as to the timings of the Fast for Muslims living at extreme latitudes or living under unusual circumstances. Those who are travelling may choose not to fast and make the days up later; those who are ill or pregnant women should not fast and pay a small compensation.

prohibited (*haram*), makes the believer the complete item, the Total Believer – there is nothing that need be added to this and nothing must be taken away from this for the believer to have fulfilled his/her covenantal contract (*deen*) with God completely. By observing the Five Pillars of Islam, the believer fulfils the Qur'anic injunction to enter into Islam completely (Qur'an 2: 208). This *hadith* also leads us to consider what is permitted (*halal*) and prohibited (*haram*) according to the *Sharia* of Islam.

The permitted (halal) and prohibited (haram) in Islam

Contrary to the popular stereotypes, the *Sharia* of Islam is not a prohibitive, ascetic Pathway. Very little behavior is explicitly prohibited in the Qur'an and the *Sunna*. Moreover, the supposed prohibition of many practices in Islam, e.g. figurative art and instrumental music, find their source in the necessary distancing of early Islamic culture from the culture of pagan idolatry and the actions that were culturally associated with these activities, e.g. alcohol with music, rather than any direct prohibition that is to be found in the primary sources of Islam.

Indeed, it is a core principle of the *Sharia* that it is *just* as illegal and immoral to prohibit what God has permitted as it is to permit what God has prohibited.

> *Oh you who believe, do not forbid the good things which God has made lawful to you – do not exceed the limits; indeed, God does not love those who go to excess. And eat lawful and good things that God provides for you, and be mindful of God, in whom you believe.*
>
> (Qur'an 5: 87–88)

It is within a broad understanding of the Worldview of Mainstream Islam as unity-in-diversity and as a balance of worship and social responsibility, which excludes excesses, as articulated in Chapter 3, that we can understand why Muslims believe that God and His Messenger have permitted (made *halal*) some activities and prohibited (made *haram*) other facets of human life.

The permitted in Islam is believed to be conducive to the good of social unity and individual human health and flourishing. In Islam, the traditionally permitted includes:

1. just government;[34]
2. knowledge and learning of all types that we would term both secular and sacred;[35]
3. trade;[36]

---

[34] Qur'an 5:8; 42:38; 3:159. The Hanbali jurist Ibn Taymiyya famously stated the God prefers just, non-Muslim government to unjust government by Muslims.
[35] Qur'an 20:114; 39:9; 35:28.
[36] Qur'an 2:275.

90 *Basic beliefs, practices and characteristic themes*

4   productive work of all types that does not involve the manufacture or sale of things that are forbidden;[37]
5   consumption of all foods that are both good and permitted;[38]
6   fully expressed sexual relations within the legal parameters of contractually-binding marriage;[39]
7   friendly relationships and affection between groups of all types;[40]
8   artistic expression, so long as is it does not celebrate what is forbidden;[41] and
9   under very strict conditions, war, because it is a part of the natural way (*fitra*) by which human beings must occasionally protect themselves from greater harm and by which worship of God is sometimes necessarily protected.[42]

The traditionally forbidden includes in a rough order of religious-legal severity:

1   overt worship of other-than-God (*shirk*);[43]
2   political oppression, rebellion, injustice and anarchy (*fitnah*);[44]
3   gratuitous violence, terrorism (*hiraba*) and unjust war;[45]
4   murder;[46]
5   suicide;[47]
6   theft;[48]
7   sexual acts outside legally-binding, heterosexual marriage;[49]
8   breaking of contracts;[50]
9   usury/charging interest (*riba*) and other forms of financial malpractice;[51]
10 slander;[52]

---

37 Imam Ja'far as-Sadiq reports the Prophet Muhammad as saying: "It is necessary for the believer to work hard even if he feels the scorching heat of the sun." Also, taking charity unnecessarily or begging unnecessarily if one can work is disliked in Islam. The performance of good deeds (*amal salih*), including earning a living, is an idea repeated multiple times in the Qur'an.
38 Qur'an 2:168; 5:4.
39 Qur'an 2:223.
40 Qur'an 60:8–9.
41 Qur'an 7:32. Also, the Psalms of David in which Muslims are required to believe mandate singing to God.
42 Qur'an 22:39–40.
43 Qur'an 4:48; 5:72; 31:13.
44 Qur'an 2:191.
45 Qur'an 2:190; 5:33–34.
46 Qur'an 4:93; 5:32.
47 Qur'an 4:29–30 and numerous authentic *hadith*.
48 Qur'an 5:38–39, numerous authentic *hadith* and the additional fact that Muslims accept Mosaic Law, which forbids theft.
49 Qur'an 17:32; 24:2 and numerous authentic *hadith*. These forbidden acts include fornication, adultery and homosexuality.
50 Qur'an 16:91.
51 Qur'an 2:275.
52 Qur'an 49:12.

11 gambling;[53]
12 intoxicants, including alcohol and drugs;[54] and
13 the meat of pigs, carrion and animals consecrated to other-than-God[55] and the consumption of uncooked blood.

These are forbidden because they are believed by Muslims to disrupt or destroy the conditions under which the two basic purposes of Islam – worship of God and human well-being – can be pursued. In these prohibitions, Islam reflects the Abrahamic heritage of the Torah, the Psalms, and the Gospels as well as the Qur'an. This Abrahamic tradition, as well as in Sharia law,[56] find its most obvious contemporary expression in contemporary common law legal traditions, which, despite popular notions, are far from secular and have deep-seated religious assumptions.[57]

---

53 Qur'an 5:3, 5:90–92.
54 Qur'an 5:90–92.
55 Qur'an 5:3; 5:90–92. What does and does not constitute so-called 'halal' meat is a debate in Mainstream Islam which is beyond the remit of this book to rehearse.
56 The Islamic Penal Code (*hudud*)
    The so-called hadd (corporal and capital) penal code connected with the gravest of these religious-legal crimes, such as stoning for adultery, cutting-off fingers of the hand for theft and 100 lashes for fornication is, of course, a matter of great national and international controversy. For some, these penalties seem to belong to a bygone age and have no place in an age of international human rights and rehabilitative justice. For others, they are further evidence of the Clash of Civilizations between Islam and the West.
    A number of points should be made about the Islamic Penal Code, however.
    First, it was first brought into a criminological environment of the seventh century, i.e. at the time of high Anglo-Saxon England, when none of the technocratic infrastructure of modern justice – police force, criminal justice systems, corrective prisons – existed or feasibly could exist.
    Second, the evidence threshold for many religious crimes, such as adultery, is/was so high, i.e. four adult male witnesses to the sexual act itself, that, except in cases of four repeated confessions, the penalties were rarely enacted and served as deterrents that indicated the severity of the misdeed. Moreover, the Prophet Muhammad encouraged people to cover their sin-crimes and repent to God rather than confess to him, as only once a confession had been made in front of him four times was he obliged to exact the penalty.
    Third, in the age of technocratic, rehabilitative justice, many Mainstream Muslim scholars have called for the spirit of the penalties to be enacted rather than the letter, which has, indeed, taken place in many Muslim-majority states with some notable exceptions, e.g. Saudi Arabia.
    Notwithstanding, the fact that some of these actions, e.g. acts of sexual impropriety, are forbidden at all shows that Mainstream Islam exists ethically in some ways at an angle from majority secular-liberal culture.
57 We only have to reflect upon the British experience of riots in August 2011 and the financial meltdown of 2008–2009 in whose aftermath we still live to become aware of the relevance of the first two prohibitions: political oppression, rebellion, injustice, anarchy and financial malpractice even if one is not a Muslim believer. These riots showed us that no society can exist for even the remotest length of time in a state of civil disobedience and violent protest. The financial meltdown taught us that the speculative, futures-based casino economy is liable to be a grave threat to an economy based on savings and real investments.

The basic beliefs of Islam: the six articles of faith

Under the rubric of the authority of both the Qur'an and the *Sunna* as the primary sources of Islam and as the basis of the *Sharia* by which certain actions are forbidden by God, Mainstream Muslims are also required to believe in Six Tenets of Faith. These tenets are traditionally called aqeeda and according to Mainstream Islam constitute true belief (*iman*):

1. **God** (*Allah*, meaning 'The One who is Worthy of Worship') –

    the One who is uniquely God without partners: Creator, Sustainer and Lord of the entire created Universe and other Worlds that we do not know about. Islam, like Judaism, is an uncompromisingly monotheistic faith. There ultimately exist no creating powers apart from God who is, ultimately, both Creator of human beings and their actions. He is the Independent Power upon which everything else is dependent. In the words of the Qur'an (112:1–4):

    > Say [Muhammad]: He is God is the One and Only! God, the Eternal, Absolute; He does not give birth nor was He begotten. And there is nothing like Him.

2. **The Angels** –

    Angels in the Islamic Worldview are beings of pure light that exist in the Unseen and are dedicated exclusively to the worship of God.[58] They relay the commands of God from the Divine Presence to Earth and carry them out. They also record the actions of humankind. The most important of them perform vital cosmological functions.

    i. Gabriel (*Jibra'il*) is the Archangel responsible for human-Divine communication. Gabriel was responsible for revealing the Qur'an to the Prophet Muhammad, verse by verse, and was responsible for announcing the miraculous birth of Jesus to Mary.

    ii. Raphael (*Israfil*) is the Archangel who will blow the trumpet twice at the End of Time. The first blow will end all life, while the second blow will bring all human beings back to life again to meet their Lord on the Day of Reckoning.

    iii. Michael (*Mika'il*) is the Archangel charged with the distribution of material provision and natural resources. Michael is often depicted as the Archangel of mercy who is responsible for bringing rain and thunder to Earth. He is also responsible for the rewards given to good people in this life.

    iv. Azrael ('*Azrail*) also known as *Malak al-Maut*, the Angel of Death. He is responsible for removing the Spirit (*ruh*) from the body upon death (Qur'an, 79:1–2).

3. **God's Books** – the Books of Revelation given to the Prophets Abraham, Moses, David, Jesus and Muhammad (peace be upon them all). These books are the Torah,

---

58 Qur'an 21:20; 41:38.

the Psalms, the Gospels and the Qur'an. Muslims believe that only the Qur'an is still known to us in its pristine revealed form, but are required to believe in the message of all of the Books and in the reality of all of the Prophets who have transmitted them.

4   **His Messengers** – the Qur'an refers to 25 known Prophets. Prophets in Islam are divided into two categories: (1) those who are given divinely revealed/inspired books, who are called Messengers (*Rusul*) and (2) those who are sent to remind their peoples of the message of Divine Unity (*Tawhid*), who are called Prophets (*anbiyyā*). The Messengers who were given Books of Revelation are: Abraham, Moses, David, Jesus and Muhammad (peace be upon them all). As well as the Prophet Muhammad, other renowned Prophets of Islam include: Adam, Noah, Aaron, Lot, Ismael, Isaac, Jacob, Joseph, Solomon and John (the Baptist).

Other Prophets who are less well known include: Enoch, Shiloh, Eber, Job, Zachariah, Jethro, Ezekiel, Elijah, Elisha and Jonah. The Qur'an requires believers to make no distinction between the Prophets (2:136) in that they all deliver the message of Divine Unity without partners and the need to worship and obey Him. All Prophets in Islam are fully human, although God often works miracles through them, e.g. Jesus healed the sick and raised the dead, as a sign of the truth of their message and their status with God.

5   **The Day of Resurrection and Judgment** – the Day of Reckoning when every human being will stand before God to account for his or her life. It is axiomatic to Mainstream Islam that every human being is individually accountable before God Almighty for his or her actions and their intentions without an intermediary or the need for a priest.

6   **The Decree** – God Almighty has destined and has power over the good and the bad of everything that happens. Islam differs from Christianity in that Christian belief has tended to stress the Goodness of God and His Love to the exclusion of other Divine attributes. Islam is aligned with these Divine aspects of Goodness and Love, but also teaches that God may manifest himself through His Names of Majesty, Restriction and Anger. However, God Almighty has also said in a Holy Saying of the Prophet Muhammad, "My Mercy prevails over my Anger". In other words, it is Mercy that is the defining attribute of God Almighty with regards to His creation.[59,60]

---

59   The apparent tensions between these last two articles of faith – Divine Predestination and human accountability before God on the Day of Resurrection – played strongly into the early debates and political struggles between the Qadirites and the Jabarites as we have seen in Chapter 2. Most Traditional Muslims today take a 'both-and' attitude to these articles of faith and do not find any contradiction of them in the conduct of their lives in the Presence of a Merciful, Living God.
60   In addition, Shia Muslims hold The Justice of God (*'Adala*) and the infallibility of the Imams from the family of Muhammad (*Imama*) to be Articles of Faith.

A religiously 'enchanted' Worldview

All the Schools of Law, Thought and Traditions of Mainstream Islam, with the possible exception of a few highly esoteric sects, are agreed on the previously listed core elements of Islamic belief (*Aqeeda*). Thus, Mainstream Islam can be said to offer a religiously 'enchanted' Worldview.[61] The Worldview of Mainstream Islam attributes real existence and causal powers to Unseen realities (Qur'an 2:3) that tend not to be given credence in standard Western, post-Enlightenment secular Worldviews.[62] Indeed, belief in the Unseen is cited by the Qur'an as one of the essential characteristics of the believer (Qur'an 2:3). In this, as in its ethical code, Mainstream Islam can be said to exist at an angle with majority Western secular rationalist mindsets.

The themes and ethical praxis of Mainstream Islam[63]

Mercy and compassion

If Mainstream Islam is characterized as a Worldview by unity-in-diversity, and theologically by the inseparable partnership of the Qur'an and the *Sunna*, it is characterized ethically by the overarching principle of Mercy. Every chapter of the Qur'an (except Surah 9: Repentance) starts with the phrase, "In the name of God, the Generally Compassionate, the Intensely Merciful" (*Bismillahi Ar-Rahman, ir-Raheem*).

Apart from the 113 times these Names of Mercy – *Ar-Rahman, ir-Raheem* – are used in the Qur'an, God also describes himself 84 times in the Qur'an as the "oft-Forgiving, most Merciful" (*al-Ghafur, ar-Raheem*).[64] This makes 'Mercy' by far the most referenced attribute of God in the Qur'an. Some commentators have said that the name "the Compassionate" (*Ar-Rahman*) refers to God's Mercy in showering blessings on the whole of Creation and "the Merciful" (*Ar-Raheem*) refers to God's specific mercy in granting those who believe in and obey Him the reward of Paradise.[65]

Whatever the case, the two names by which God has chosen to identify Himself are both intensive forms of the verb *rahima* – to be merciful. This is

---

61 Taylor, *A Secular Age*; Ipgrave, 'Multiculturalism, Communitarianism, Cohesion, and Security'.
62 It is worth noting that these are the absolutely standard Muslim beliefs that, for example, Muslim children are likely to bring into the Religious Education classroom and can be both a source of enrichment and/or confusion in an educational context depending on the attitude of teachers. Ipgrave, 'Multiculturalism, Communitarianism, Cohesion, and Security'; Wilkinson, *A Fresh Look at Islam in a Multi-Faith World*.
63 To claim that the Worldview of Mainstream Islam is characterised by certain ethical themes and tropes is not the same as claiming that mainstream Muslims always live up to these ethical aspirations. In common with those of all religious (and non-religious) worldviews, Muslims, including the author, often fall short of our stated ideals.
64 Sherif, *A Guide to the Contents of the Qur'an*.
65 Nasr et al., *The Study Qur'an*.

the word that in another form also describes the mother's womb. In other words, in the Mainstream Islamic Worldview God is believed to be intensely Merciful in a way that is analogous to the place of security and total provision that is the mother's womb. Similarly, the Qur'an repeatedly encourages people to be kind and merciful to each other, even suggesting, for example, that it is better for people who have been the victim of great injustices to forgive the perpetrators if they are able rather than to turn to the retribution of the Law (Qur'an 42:43).

The *Sunna* of the Prophet Muhammad was a living exemplar of a life lived according to God's Names of Mercy. He forgave those who persecuted him, even, for example, a woman who poisoned his food on account of the fact that her husband had been killed in battle against the Muslims. When the Prophet Muhammad conquered Mecca at the head of a 10,000-strong army, barely a drop of blood was spilled and all his former enemies were spared punishment, even those who had killed members of his family.[66]

The Prophet Muhammad is described in the Qur'an as sent as a "Mercy to all the Worlds" (Qur'an 21:107), and he encouraged his Companions always to show kindness and compassion saying, "He who shows no mercy to his fellow man will not be shown mercy by God".[67]

Justice and excellent conduct

On the basis of a human-Divine covenant (*deen*) grounded in the quality of Mercy, the Qur'an encourages people to act throughout life with justice (*adl*) and excellence (*ihsan*) (16:90) with a verse which is repeated in the formulaic introduction to the Friday sermon every week:

> *Indeed, God orders justice and excellent conduct and giving to relatives and forbids immorality and bad conduct and oppression. He admonishes you that perhaps you will be reminded.*
>
> (Qur'an 16:90)

Justice and excellent conduct can be considered basic guiding principles (*maqasid*) of the Islamic covenant with God (*deen*).

Similarly, the Prophet Muhammad explained that the core purpose of his mission was to engender noble behavior:

> *Malik reported: The Messenger of God, peace and blessings be upon him, said, "I have been sent to perfect good character."*[68]

---

66 Ibn Ishaq, *The Life of Muhammad*.
67 Sahih al-Bukhari 6941, Sahih Muslim 2319.
68 Al-Muwatta 1614.

The Prophet Muhammad encouraged his Companions to excel in everything that they did saying, "God loves the servant who perfects his task".[69] Justice and excellence are fundamental Islamic aspirations and natural corollaries of a Universe created with both justice (*adl*) and balance (*qist*) in which moderation aligns the person with the very nature of Reality.

> *O you who believe, be steadfast in your devotion to God and bear witness impartially, and do not let hatred of other people prevent you from being just. Be just; that is closer to awareness of God. Be mindful of God; God is well-aware of what you do.*
>
> (Qur'an 5:8)

The fair treatment and equal status of women

An important component part of a commitment to justice and excellent conduct in the Worldview of Mainstream Islam includes the fair treatment of women as equal partners in the human project.

Original Islam emerged into a society in which the basic inferiority of women was endemic and taken for granted. In pagan, pre-Islamic Arabia, men could and did marry as many as 40 wives, took female slaves as concubines, married off their daughters without their consent, denied women basic rights to self-determination, education and property, and, most abhorrently of all, condoned the live burial of unwanted female infants, since females were expected to marry with a dowry and hence often constituted an unwanted expense to their families.

In respect of the status and treatment of women, Original Islam was revolutionary in:

1. declaring the basic ontological and spiritual parity of men and women;[70]
2. outlawing female infanticide;[71]
3. giving women full property rights,[72] including the rights to take part in business and trade;
4. obliging that both male and female parties enter into marriage by consent;[73]
5. *limiting* men to taking four wives on the stringent condition that they were all treated equally,[74,75] and if this condition could not be met then only monogamy was allowed;
6. insisting that men paid women a dowry on marriage;[76]

---

69 Reported by Bahhaqi.
70 Qur'an 4:1; 7:189; 42:11.
71 Qur'an 17:31; 6:151.
72 Qur'an 4:32.
73 Qur'an 4:2.
74 Ibid.
75 In the contemporary age, many Muslim commentators, have argued that monogamy is the fairest and most appropriate marital option for Muslims and the vast majority of Muslims are monogamous.
76 Qur'an 4:2.

Basic beliefs, practices and characteristic themes 97

7 encouraging the manumission of slaves at a time when slavery was an inherent part of societies across the globe;[77] and
8 encouraging women to take a lead in religious scholarship and education, as in the exemplary case of Muhammad's wife Aisha bint Abi Bakr, who transmitted and taught thousands of Prophetic sayings.

Not only this but the Prophet Muhammad's first wife, Khadija bint Khuwaylid (555–620 CE), was the first convert to Islam who believed in the Prophetic mission even when the Prophet Muhammad himself was plunged into a crisis of self-doubt. Khadija had previously employed Muhammad, was the owner of a trading empire in her own right and shared her entire wealth with the Prophet Muhammad in support of the new faith.

Given the pivotal role of women in Original Islam, it is not surprising that the *Sunna* of the Prophet Muhammad is replete with actions and injunctions that make the fair treatment of wives, daughters and women generally a basic, *sine qua non*, feature of Muslim piety. By sharing housework with his wives, including cooking, cleaning and mending his own clothes, the Prophet Muhammad showed the deep religious value both of the traditional home-making of women *and* the value of liberating women to take an active part in society. He also insisted on the education of women and girls, starting with his own wives and daughters. Importantly, in the *Sunna* domestic duties that women choose to perform are not obligatory, they are designated as acts of charity. In other words, if a wife choose to do housework, this is added to her reckoning of good deeds. If she chooses not to, it is not a sin.

It should be obvious, therefore, from even a cursory understanding of the *Sunna* how far regimes and groups such as the Taliban and male chauvinist individuals who deny women and girls basic rights to education and self-determination, in the name of Islam, have strayed from the foundational principles of Mainstream Islam.

Moreover, not only do the Qur'an and the *Sunna* demand the fair and equitable treatment of women in general, but also they highlight the uniquely important status and role of mothers which remains a feature of Mainstream Islam today: For example, when a man consulted the Prophet Muhammad about taking part in a military campaign, the Prophet Muhammad asked the man if his mother was still alive. When told that she was alive, the Prophet Muhammad said: "Stay with her, for Paradise is under her feet."[78]

On another occasion, the Prophet Muhammad said: "God has forbidden for you to be undutiful to your mothers."[79]

The Prophet Muhammad was once asked to whom a person should show the most respect. Muhammad replied: "Your mother, next your mother, next your mother, and then your father."[80,81]

---

77 The role that the sharia-minded abolitionists played in the international abolition of slavery has often gone un-mentioned. Clarence-Smith, *Islam and the Abolition of Slavery*.
78 Narrated by At-Tirmidhi.
79 Sahih Al-Bukhari.
80 Sunan, Abu Daud.
81 Brockwell and CAIR, 'What's the Role of Mothers in Islam?'.

Of course, to say that Mainstream Islam encourages the equal treatment of women does not necessarily mean that Islam and Muslims are inclined to ape secular models of gender equality. In Mainstream Islam, gender equality does not mean gender same-ness. Given the significance and status of maternity in Islam, and despite the relentless policy direction of Western states to take women out of the home and into the workplace, Muslim women often *choose* to be homemakers and full-time mothers.[82] Thus large female sectors of the Muslim community are often branded by governments as 'economically inactive' when these stay-at-home wives and mothers, who dedicate themselves to bringing up a family, are very far from inactive!

The Hijab

Similarly, commentators – both male and female – often fail to understand that many Muslim women choose, quite independently of men, to wear the Islamic headscarf – the *hijab* – which covers the hair and the neck, which are regarded in Islam as part of a woman's private parts (*awra*),[83] in accordance with the Qur'an and the *Sunna*. The idea of a modern woman covering herself up to please God seems to many commentators to be counterintuitive in an age when women are routinely expected to exploit their 'erotic power'[84] in order to get on in the world. This is even the case when, as is increasingly being shown in the wake of the Harvey Weinstein affair, it is now obvious that sexualized dynamics between men and women in the public space often have tragic consequences, usually for women.

It should be noted that from a Mainstream Muslim perspective, far from being a mechanism of confinement and restriction, the wearing of the *hijab* is viewed as *enabling* women to operate in the public space while signaling to men that they are in that space on a strictly professional basis. This is because since its inception and following the example of Muhammad's wife Khadija, who was herself a successful businesswoman, Mainstream Muslims have recognized that women often have great talent for business, trade and work in society more generally that needs to be deployed respectfully and appropriately.

Misogyny and crimes against women

Therefore, given the Muhammadan exemplar, it is tragic that in the field of the treatment of women, Islam and male Muslims have often become synonymous with misogyny, inflexible patriarchy and the excessive control of women that lies at the heart of crimes such as forced marriages, grooming rings, female genital mutilation and so-called 'honor killings'. These crimes reveal the darkest side of human behavior and give proof that with Islam and Muslims, as with those of other faiths and none, the actual often falls way short of the ideal.

---

82 Lewis, *Islamic Britain*.
83 Men's private parts consist of everything from the navel to the knee (inclusive). According to Mainstream Islam, neither men nor women should wear figure-hugging clothing that is explicitly designed to be sexually attractive. This is certainly not to say that Muslim women or men should dress dowdily or all in black!
84 Hakim, *Honey Money*.

While misogynist crimes such as the above are often conflated with and justified by the perpetrators by faulty recourse to Islamic teaching, they are more often than not fueled precisely by the residual forms of tribal patriarchy that Islam came to eliminate in the ways listed previously. Moreover, these crimes, which are illegal both in Islamic Law as they are in Common Law traditions, are often rooted in the 'Us vs. Them' Islamist Extremist Worldview by which non-Muslim women are afforded a sub-human status and therefore believed to be prone to sub-human treatment.

Not only these extremist crimes, but also, more anodynely, the fact that in some Islamic School of Law the testimony of women appears to be worth half of that of men suggests to some a basic misogynist discrimination at the core of Mainstream Islam.

In this respect, classical commentators of Qur'anic verses such as 2:282 sometimes explained the unequal treatment of the legal testimony of men and women by asserting that women's nature made them more prone to error than men. However, more sophisticated and credible commentators, e.g. ibn Taymiyya (1263–1328 CE) and ibn Qayyim Al-Jawziyya (1292–1350 CE), explained that, due to their centrality to the life of the home, women were simply less accustomed to being witnesses to business transactions and the like and hence more of them were needed to ensure reliability.

Following this line of thinking, Activist Muslim thinkers have followed the Egyptian reformer Muhammad Abduh (1849–1905 CE) in viewing the passages of the Qur'an that deal with the testimony of women as particular (*Khass*) and contingent upon the different gender roles and life experiences that prevailed in the early seventh century at the time of the Revelation. This makes the Qur'anic rule not generally applicable in all times and places and open to contemporary reform in line with the role and status of women today.

Therefore, whether one's understanding is of more reformist or literalist flavor, the fair and good treatment of women is a necessary hallmark of the Mainstream Islamic Worldview in recognition of the fact that women are equal partners with men in the Mainstream Islamic project of worship of God and human well-being. If either men or women are unfairly treated, all humanity suffers. Anything that falls short of this understanding, as regrettably Muslims often do, is to fall short of the most basic Mainstream Islamic teaching.

Solidarity with family, kith and kin and society

For Mainstream Muslims, the primary ethical expression of the essential unity of the Created Universe is to show concrete, practical solidarity with family, kith and kin and society.

Many Prophets prior to Muhammad, such as Jesus, brought the Message of Divine Unity into marginal social circumstances, preached to a small band of followers, were shunned by majority society of the day and often did not marry. By contrast, the Prophet Muhammad's message was delivered in and for civic circumstances first, in the town of Mecca and then in the town of Medina – the Place of the Transaction – where it was witnessed and enacted by 10,000 citizen Companions (*Sahaba*), protected and united by constitutional rights. Civility and the nurture of civic responsibility are at the very heart of the Mainstream Islamic Worldview, and this ethos of civic responsibility begins in Mainstream, Traditional Islam with the family and the extended family of kith and kin.

For example, respect for parents is specifically connected in the Qur'an to worship of God as part of the religiously serious character of the true believer.

> *Your Lord has commanded that you worship none but Him, and that you treat your parents well. If either or both of them reach old age with you, say no word that shows impatience with them and do not be harsh with them, but speak respectfully and lower your wing in humility towards them in kindness and say, 'Lord, have mercy on them, just as they cared for me when I was little.'*
>
> (Qur'an 17: 23)

> *We have commanded people to be good to their parents. Their mother carried them, with strain upon strain, and it takes two years to wean them. Be grateful to Me and to your parents – all will return to Me.*
>
> (Qur'an 31:14)

Moreover, it should be noted that no distinction is made in the Qur'an and the *Sunna* between the good treatment of believing and non-believing parents, unless they actively aim to prevent the believer from worship of God.

Following on from parents, the Qur'an and the *Sunna* specifically require the good treatment and the nurturing of relations between kith and kin as an intrinsic element of worship of God.

Two hadith collected by Al-Bukhari indicate the centrality of the ties of blood to the *Sunna*:

> "*The person who severs the bond of kinship will not enter Paradise.*"[85]

> *I heard* God's Messenger *saying,* "*Whoever* wants to *be* wealthy and healthy, should keep good relations with his kith and kin.*"*[86]

Beyond the immediate concern for family and the extended concern for kith and kin, civic cohesion was central to the Prophet Muhammad's message. It was also central to the very survival of the multi-faith community of Medina and enshrined constitutionally in the Constitution of Medina which gave a wide range of faith and tribal communities full legal rights. The Prophet Muhammad himself maintained his family ties throughout the period of his mission, even with those who did not believe in his Prophetic calling such as his beloved uncle, Abu Talib. Mainstream Islam is a Worldview of healthy social relations in which the

---

85 Narrated by Jubair bin Mut'im.
86 Narrated by Abu Huraira.

fulfillment of the believer can only happen in the context of the fulfillment of one's fellow man. This is encapsulated in the famous Prophetic saying:

> *None of you truly believes until you desire for your brother what you desire for yourself.*[87]

In his commentary on this saying, the classical Damascene scholar of hadith, Imam An-Nawawi (1234–1277 CE), states that 'brother' refers to fellow human beings and is not restricted to the brotherhood of Islam. Mainstream Islam is built upon an ethic of transcendental solidarity with the needs and happiness of all humankind, starting with the material, emotional and spiritual needs of one's dependents at home and moving out in concentric circles through the provision of both the compulsory Poor Tax (*Zakah*) and Voluntary Acts of Charity (*Sadaqa*)[88] to attend to the needs of society at large.[89]

The sanctity of life

At the core of this ethic of transcendental solidarity expressed in the Poor Tax (*Zakah*) and other acts of voluntary charity (*Sadaqa*), the sanctity of all life and especially human life, is a fundamental value in Mainstream Islam (for example Qur'an, 5:32 and Qur'an, 6:151) – the most fundamental value, since without the Right to Life none of the other values pertain.

> We decreed to the Children of Israel that if anyone kills a person – unless in retribution for murder or spreading corruption in the land – it is as if he had murdered mankind entirely. And whoever saves a life – it is as if he had saved the lives of all humankind.
>
> (Qur'an, 5:32)

Notable in this verse is that the sanctity of each individual human life is comparable to the sanctity of an entire community. This is a complete departure from the tribal ethos that was prevalent at the time of the Prophet Muhammad when individuals only enjoyed rights as part of protective tribal groups. This Islamic ethic is closely aligned with the modern ethos of human rights in which the basic locus of the Right to Life is the individual.

In addition to this general principle, the Qur'an specifically abolished the practice of female infanticide that was rife in pre-Islamic Arabia (Qur'an, 81:8–9). Thus, at a blow, the sanctity of human life was extended by the Prophet Muhammad to

---

87 An-Nawawi: 13.
88 Qur'an 2:245.
89 It should come as no surprise, therefore, that Muslims are the most charitable religious community in the UK. Madden,Imran. 'Why Muslims Donate So Much To Charity, Particularly During Ramadan.' HuffPost UK. May 17, 2018.

mean all human life. The Prophet Muhammad also mandated the excellent treatment of animals at a time when they were routinely ill-treated. He forbade the beating and branding of beasts of burden and on one occasion, is recorded as preventing a man from destroying a colony of ants. He even expressed the view that a prostitute, i.e. someone who had routinely engaged in sexual acts that are forbidden in Islam, would inherit Paradise on account of her good treatment of a dog.

> *Abu Huraira reported: The Prophet, peace and blessings be upon him, said, "God had once forgiven a prostitute. She passed by a dog panting near a well. Seeing that thirst had nearly killed him, she took off her shoe, tied it to her scarf, and drew up some water. God forgave her on account of that."*[90]

This principle of the Sanctity of Life is given full expression during the rites of *Hajj* when a pilgrim may kill no living creature, not even a mosquito.

Freedom of religion

To realize the sanctity of life meaningfully, Mainstream Islam, following the Qur'an and the *Sunna*, stipulates the inalienable right of people to decide for themselves how to conduct their religious lives and choose their ultimate values.

In articulation of this fundamental principle of Freedom of Religious Conscience, the Qur'anic Verse of the Throne (2:256) states:

> *There is no compulsion in religion: true guidance has become distinct from error, so whoever rejects false gods and believes in God has grasped the firmest hand-hold, one that will never break. And God is all hearing and all knowing.*

This verse has been taken by both historical and contemporary commentators of Mainstream Islam as a Qur'anic mandate for Freedom of Religion as a fundamental human right and value in Islamic Law.

This traditional Qur'anic value was one of the most highly treasured in the early Islamic expansion as exemplified famously by the Second Successor to the Prophet Muhammad, the Caliph Umar, who refused to pray in the Church of the Holy Sepulchre in Jerusalem for fear that his followers might convert it into a mosque and thus deny Christians the right to practice their own faith. In illustration of the strict adherence of this principle in early Islam, it has been estimated that for the first two hundred years of the post-Muhammadan Muslim settlement in the Middle East, North Africa and Andalucía in Spain, Muslims were in the religious minority in the territories that they governed.[91] Moreover, even after 1,200 years of Muslim rule, places such as Egypt, Morocco, Syria and Iraq had large Christian and Jewish minorities who could not have survived over

---

90 Sahih al-Bukhari 3143, Sahih Muslim 2245.
91 Hourani, *A History of the Arab Peoples*.

that extended period if Muslims had sought to suppress their religions by force. This makes the contemporary repression of non-Muslim minorities by both state and extra-state Muslim actors in the Middle East such a tragic and un-Islamic theological and historical anomaly.

This principle of Freedom of Religion, like so many other basic Islamic purposes (*maqasid*), reflects realities of human nature that when people decide their values and beliefs *for themselves* they are likely to adhere to them sincerely and meaningfully.

Struggle in the path of God (Jihad fisabilillah)

It is in the general context of the Sanctity of Life that we must also understand the Doctrines of Struggle in the Path of God (*Jihad fiy sabilillah*) in Mainstream Islam. The word Jihad has the linguistic meaning of 'struggling', 'exerting oneself' or 'striving'. It is the nominal participle from the Arabic root j-h-d. By extension, it has a religious meaning in Islam following its use in the Qur'an which is 'struggling in the cause of God', *Jihad fiy sabilillah*. When Jihad is used with this religious sense, the words 'in the cause of God' (*fiy sabilillah*) are understood.

None of the 41 verses of the Qur'an that mention *Jihad* explicitly mention *Jihad* as an armed struggle, although 12 of them are mentioned in contextual relationship to armed combat in defense of Islam (*Qital* – see below). According to the commentators[92], this explicitly shows that in Islam struggling in the path of God – *Jihad* – is absolutely *not synonymous* with *Qital* – fighting (lit. killing) to defend Islam. As we will see below, *Qital* was authorized, under very particular conditions, by the Qur'an for the defense of Muslim lives, faith and property and was merely one branch of a multitude of forms of Jihad. At-Tabari, for example, mentions 32 forms of Jihad of which only one was *Qital*.[93]

According to al-Dawoody,[94] 17 derivatives of Jihad occur in the Qur'an altogether 41 times with the following five meanings:

1   striving generally because of religious belief (21 citations);
2   armed combat (*qital*) (12 citations);
3   non-Muslim parents exerting pressure, that is, Jihad, to make their children abandon Islam (2 citations);
4   solemn oaths (5 citations); and
5   physical strength (1 citation).

In the earliest collection of hadith used to derive the *Sunna* of the Prophet Muhammad and the practices of the early Muslim community in Medina, which

---

92 Afsaruddin, *Striving in the Path of God*.
93 Ibid.
94 Al-Dawoody, *The Islamic Law of War*.

104 Basic beliefs, practices and characteristic themes

is the '*Al-Muwatta*' (The Well-Trodden Path) by Imam Malik ibn Al-Anas, of the eponymous Maliki School, the topic of armed struggle takes up:

- only 11 of 424 pages of Prophetic *Sunna* and rulings (2.6%) ... compared with
- 73 pages dedicated to the Prayer (17.2%),
- 50 dedicated to the correct conduct of business and trade (11.8%) and
- 37 dedicated to marriage and divorce (8.7%)

This is why classical jurists of all the Schools of Islamic Law tended to regard the daily struggle of the believer to live correctly according to Islamic precepts and the struggle against inner evil of the Self as the Greater Struggle (*Jihad al-akbar*), and armed struggle (*Jihad al-asghar*) as the Lesser Struggle. It was the believer's normal actions in daily life that made up the substance of their Reckoning with God, not the abnormal situation of war.[95]

Following Qur'anic usage, for the early Muslim community *Jihad* came to mean the struggle to establish or preserve the religion of Islam in one's own life and the life of the Muslim community. Occasionally, if there was no other way open, it meant the defense of Islam by force of arms. In other words, more often than not, the very act of being and remaining a Muslim for the early Muslim community contained an on-going element of *Jihad*. It was, indeed, inevitable that the 'purified' Abrahamic faith should tackle the need and the conditions for armed defensive struggle since in early medieval Arabia fighting for survival was endemic. Indeed, it was such a feature of their way of life that the Arab tribes had instituted a Sacred Seventh Month of the Lunar Calendar in which fighting was forbidden and in which families and tribes could recover.

Types of struggle (Jihad) in Islam

Following the lead of the Qur'an and the *Sunna*, classical jurists, such as the famous Maliki jurist Ibn Rushd (1126–1198 CE) (Averrroes), classified *Jihad* into four main categories:

1 **Jihad of the heart** (*jihad bil qalb/nafs*)

   This is concerned with combating the evil insinuations of the ego and the devil. This type of *Jihad*, as we have seen, was regarded classically as the Greater Struggle (*al-jihad al-akbar*) as it concerns the daily business of training the rebellious ego to obey God's injunctions.

---

[95] The authenticity of the particular (*ahad*) *hadith* that reports the Prophet Muhammad saying that we have come from the Lesser Struggle (*Jihad al-asghar*) to the Greater Struggle (*Jihad al-akbar*) – in other words, from the battlefield to the battle with the ego – has in some quarters been cast into doubt. However, there is no doubt that the behavior (*amal*) of the community of Medina as recorded by the early jurists operated on the principle articulated in this *hadith*, hence its enduring appeal.

2 **Jihad by the tongue** (*jihad bil lisan*)

   This is concerned with speaking the truth and spreading the word of Islam.

3 **Jihad by the hand** (*jihad bil yad*)

   This refers to choosing to do what is right and combating injustice and what is wrong with action. We might call this 'activism'.

4 **Jihad by the sword** (*jihad bis saif*)

   This refers to armed fighting in the way of God, or holy war (*Qital fi sabilillah*), the final resort if other types of Jihad fail and the integrity of the Islamic religion and safety of the Muslim community are threatened.[96]

According to such classical and contemporary typologies of the Struggle in the Path of God, in the Mainstream Islamic Worldview any legal struggle or exertion that is made with the intention to please God either by the establishment and preservation of Islam or by God-fearing acts of self-restraint can been described as 'religious Jihad in Islam'.[97]

The authorization of fighting (Qital) in the Qur'an

In relation to the Struggle with the Sword (*jihad bis saif*), the Prophet Muhammad himself was initially extremely reluctant to fight against his enemies with anything other than the verses of the Revelation and considered debate. This was in part due to his own peaceable inclinations and partly because he had not been authorized to do so by the Qur'an. However, in the face of the repeated theft of Muslim property and the persecution of Muslims left behind in Mecca after the Emigration to Medina, Muslims believe that the Prophet Muhammad was authorized by God to fight (Qur'an, 2:190–193).

All of the verses of the Qur'an that authorize and then encourage the conduct of armed struggle (*Qital*) were revealed after the Emigration of the Prophet Muhammad and his Companions from Mecca to Medina (*Hijra*) when they were no longer a part of Qurayshi Meccan society.

During this ten-year phase of the Prophet Muhammad's mission, the fledgling Muslim community in Medina and its non-Muslim fellow citizens were engaged in a life or death struggle for survival with hostile, bellicose tribes led by the pagans of Mecca. These tribes desired nothing other than the total annihilation

---

[96] It has been said in this regard that classical jurists can be divided into those who encouraged or even instituted armed Jihad through, for example, an annual campaign against non-Muslim neighbors and those for whom armed Jihad was purely defensive. I do not regard this division as either necessary or accurate. Since during the medieval period, the borders of the Territories of Islam (*Dar al-Islam*) were always under threat of attack, even those, e.g. Ibn Rushd, who enjoined the institution of an annual armed Jihad can be said to be responding to the persistent threat of attack by neighboring regimes. In these circumstances, on occasion, attack was the only form of defense, and jurists responded accordingly.

[97] Shaltut, 'The Qur'an and Combat'.

of the new religion and its followers which threatened, as they saw it, the very existence of the polytheist, tribal way of life. In these circumstances, the permission to fight was a reasonable and necessary response to the need for physical and spiritual survival in a broader early medieval cultural environment in which claims to spiritual authenticity and political authority were routinely settled at the point of the sword.

The General (Am) and the Particular (Khass) Verses that permit fighting (Qital)

These Qur'anic verses that permit fighting sometimes articulate the General (*Am*) conditions and ethical principles of armed Jihad (*Qital*) as just warfare, such as the first of the so-called Verses of the Sword:

> *Those who have been attacked are permitted to take up arms because they have been wronged – God has the power to help them . . .*
>
> (Qur'an 22:39)

In this verse, the word 'fighting' is used and not '*Jihad*', and the clear General conditions for the fighting are articulated:

1 that those who fight are already under attack, i.e. the action of fighting back is defensive;
2 those who fight have been wronged, i.e. are the victims of a prior injustice.

The Qur'an continues by way of elaboration and clarification of the nature of the injustice that constitutes an act of war:

> *. . . those who have been driven unjustly from their homes only for saying, "Our Lord is God." If God did not repel some by means of others, many monasteries, churches, synagogues, and mosques where God's name is much invoked, would have been destroyed. God is sure to help those who help His cause – God is strong and mighty . . .*
>
> (Qur'an 22:39)

In other words, the prior wrong that has been inflicted is the expulsion of people without cause from their homes and the purpose of fighting back is so that the conditions in which God is worshipped *in diverse religious traditions* are protected and maintained. In all the Qur'anic verses permitting war, the cessation of hostilities is mentioned in conjunction with the authorization for war as articulated by the Qur'an as the preferred state of affairs. In other words, the purpose of war: is to return to the conditions of a worshipful peace.

At other times, Particular (*Khass*) verses refer to the particular circumstances in which the Prophet Muhammad and his Companions found themselves. Most famously, (and infamously to counterterrorism officials), these include the much-misunderstood and abused verses:

> *Kill them wherever you encounter them, and drive them out from where they drove you out, for persecution is more serious than killing. Do not fight them at the Sacred Mosque unless they fight you there. If they do fight you, kill them – this is what such disbelievers deserve – but if they stop, then God is most forgiving and merciful.*
> (Qur'an 2:191–192)

These verses refer to the particular circumstances when the Prophet Muhammad and his Companions feared that they would come under attack under conditions of Pilgrimage in the Sacred precincts of Mecca. If they did, they were authorized by the Qur'an to respond with lethal force to ensure their survival. It needs to be noted that, as with all Particular verses that authorize fighting, these particular verses are bookended by the General Principles of regulated, defensive warfare:

> *Fight in God's cause those who fight you, but do not overstep the limits: God does not love those who overstep the limits . . . but if they stop, [then you stop] . . .*
> (Qur'an 2: 190–192)

Particular verses such as these were never understood by the Prophet Muhammad and his Companions as a General permission to kill non-Muslims, with whom, in circumstances of peace, the Qur'an enjoins cooperative co-existence[98] combined with the call made with "wisdom and beauty"[99] for them to recognize and worship the One God Almighty.

The legal conditions of Qital in the Sunna

As with other matters in the *Sharia*, the nature of regulated, self-defensive warfare authorized by the Qur'an was established by the Prophet Muhammad's *Sunna*. During his life, the Prophet Muhammad gave various injunctions to his forces and adopted established ethical practices toward the conduct of war, some of which, such as his humane treatment of prisoners of war, became the source of much conversion to Islam.[100] The most important of the ethical principles for the conduct of Qital were summarized by the Prophet Muhammad's Companion and first Caliph, Abu Bakr, in the form of Rules for the Muslim Army:

> "People! I charge you with these rules; learn them well!
>
> 1   Do not betray or misappropriate any part of the booty.

---

98 Qur'an 109.
99 Qur'an 16:125.
100 As we noted in Chapter 2, the ethical-religious conduct of warfare was a matter for the adjudication of the Prophetic *Sunna*; the tactical-strategic side of warfare was agreed by consultation (*shura*).

2   Do not practice treachery or mutilation.
3   Do not kill a young child, an old man or a woman.
4   Do not uproot or burn palms or cut down fruitful trees.
5   Do not slaughter a sheep or a cow or a camel, except for food.
6   You will meet people who have set themselves apart in hermitages; leave them to accomplish the purpose for which they have done this.
7   You will come upon people who will bring you dishes with various kinds of foods. If you partake of them, pronounce God's name over what you eat.
8   You will meet people who have shaved the crown of their heads, leaving a band of hair around it. Go in God's name, and may God protect you from sword and pestilence."[101]

Following the above Rules for the Muslim Army and other rulings, jurists of the emerging Schools of Islamic Law, for example Sahnun of the Maliki School in 'The Compendium' (*al-Mudawwana*), drew up 'Five Basic Legal Conditions of Armed Struggle' (*Jihad*), which, for the early medieval period, were astonishing in their stringency and restraint:

1   Armed struggle must be declared and fought under recognized Muslim leadership, an Amir, Imam or a Caliph or a modern Leader. This is because an authentic armed struggle is fought for the public good of the Muslim community and the preservation of the faith and not for private gain.
2   Armed struggle must be openly declared to the enemy who must first be invited to embrace Islam before fighting or to pay the Poll Tax (*Jizya*). This is to prevent killing people who might potentially be Muslim believers and who are protected People of the Book (Christians and Jews).
3   In armed struggle, non-combatant men, women and children may not be harmed.
4   In armed struggle, the agricultural and architectural infrastructure of the enemy must not be destroyed or damaged nor may civilian property be pillaged.
5   In armed struggle, one fifth of all booty must be given to the Amir, Imam or a Caliph for the upkeep of the Islamic polity.[102]

---

101 At-Tabari cited in Lewis (2004).
102 There is no evidence whatsoever in the accounts of the early Muslim defence and expansion (*futuh*) of suicide as a means of warfare, even when there are accounts of Muslims fighting against incredible odds such as, most notably, when a force of approximately 300 Muslims took on and defeated a force of 1300 pagan Quraysh at the Battle of Badr.
   Suicide is not only expressly forbidden in the Qur'an (4:29) and the *Sunna*, but also defeated the point of armed struggle which was to see human life protected within the parameters of a divinely revealed religious and social dispensation. This is why the twenty-first century 'cult of martyrdom', and especially suicide 'martyrdom', has nothing to do with the Islamic doctrine of armed struggle and everything to do with a nihilistic violent ideology.

In the Mainstream Islamic Worldview, from these earliest ethical principles for the praxis of Just War, the conditions for the declaration of armed defensive combat in the contemporary period have been authoritatively adduced by leading Mainstream Muslim legal scholars from around the Muslim world as follows:[103]

1. all peaceful avenues for the avoidance of armed defensive combat, such as international diplomacy, must have been explored and exhausted before war is declared;
2. armed defensive combat must be declared against a direct, open and known armed aggressor and this would never include, for example, civilian populations;
3. armed defensive combat must be declared by the appointed/elected and recognized leader of a Muslim political entity against a declared and clear aggressor, except in direct self-defense by ambush;
4. armed defensive combat must be declared to protect the religion, persons and property of those who have been wronged and not for personal gain;
5. international peace treaties and agreements must not be breached.[104]

This means that there is a long and strong ethical tradition in Mainstream Islam for the necessary, humane and regulated conduct of armed struggle and combat stretching back to the times of the Prophet Muhammad (570–633 CE) until the present day. This tradition can be characterized as a realistic, humane and regulated response to a world characterized by unity-in-diversity in which human wrong-doing, thirst for power, corruption, greed and propensity for oppression sometimes give rise to situations in which self-defensive[105] combat is the only remaining option for the preservation of civilized life.

The themes and ethical praxis of Activist Islam

The praxis, themes and ethics of the Mainstream, Traditional Islamic Worldview also substantiate the Worldview of Mainstream, Activist Islam. What gives Activist

---

103 Kamali, 'Introduction'; Gomaa, 'A Fatwa on Jihad'.
104 Kamali, 'Introduction'.
105 Adjudicating what constitutes self-defense is, of course, not always ethically simple. For example, the early expansion of Islam and Muslim rule (633–670 CE) into the crumbling Sassanid Persian (205–637 CE) and the Byzantine Roman Empires (330–1453) came as the result of initial Muslim resistance to the incursion or threat of incursion of those powers into Muslim territory which was followed up by expansion and conquest so that these considerable forces could not reassemble to further threaten Muslim lives and property. An analogy to this is the D-Day Landings in June 1944 when Allied forces needed and were, almost all would agree, ethically entitled both to repel Nazi Germany from occupied France and to press on for the conquest of Nazi Germany to prevent that power from reconstituting its aggressive forces.

Islam its distinctive edge is the dynamic to transform both wrong-acting individual agency and iniquitous political structure.[106]

Indeed, the principle of knowledgeable and civic non-violent resistance to injustice and social malpractice is as old as Islam itself and is enshrined in the Qur'an and the *Sunna*. The Qur'an requires believers to "enjoin what is recognized to be right and forbid what is recognized to be wrong" (Qur'an 3:110). The *Sunna* of the Prophet Muhammad was both to persevere, respectfully, in the performance and explication of the core tenets of Islam in the face of determined and malign opposition and to condemn openly social malpractices of his day such as the murder of female infants. The principle of non-violent resistance to the iniquities both of unjust authority in the cases, for example, of Malik ibn Anas and Ahmad ibn Hanbal, as we saw in Chapter 2, and of anarchy, e.g. in the case of Ahmad ibn Taymiyya, both protected some of the core principles of Islamic jurisprudence and cemented the reputations of the greatest of Islam's legal scholars.

Theological Caliphate

In the Activist Islamic Worldview, this principle of resistance and commitment to transform injustice is carried out neither with the quasi-Kharijite notion (see Chapter 1) that no human authority is worthy of the office of governance nor with the Qadirite notion that the exercise of injustice is itself ordained by God. It is carried out in the spirit of a *theological*[107] Caliphate – which means deputizing for God in the place of the apparent absence of God, which is a Qur'anic notion that has been developed by thinkers such as the Egyptian reformer Muhammad Abduh (1849–1905 CE).

Typically, therefore, Activist Muslims would live actively (either knowingly or unknowingly) according to the *theological* doctrine of Caliphate, which necessitates some explanation of the notion of Caliphate (*Khalifa*) in Islam.

The word Caliph (Khalifa)

The word Caliph is derived from the Arabic word *Khalifa* which has two basic meanings in the Arabic:

1. one who *deputizes for* someone else in a position of authority; and
2. one who *succeeds to* someone else to a position of authority.

---

106 By wrong-acting human agency is meant individual behavior that is radically non-aligned with the principles of the Qur'an and the *Sunna*. What is meant by iniquitous political structure is political processes and institutions that either prevent or outlaw the establishment of the basic tenets of Islam or that create general conditions of unacceptable inequality in which the basic human needs of large sectors of society for food, shelter and the prospect of meaningful human relationships such as marriage and employment go unfulfilled.
107 To be clearly distinguished from political Caliphate, as we will see in the next section.

The word Caliph appears in the Qur'an primarily with the first of these two meanings and in particular in the famous verse early in the Qur'an which delineates the primordial status of humanity – represented by the Prophet Adam – in relation to God and the rest of the Creation:

> *When your Lord told the angels: "I am going to place a deputy [Caliph] on earth," they said: "How can you place someone who will cause damage and bloodshed when we celebrate Your praise and proclaim Your holiness?" But He said: "I know things that you do not know." He taught Adam the names of all things and showed them to the angels and said: "Tell me the names of these things if you truly [think that you can]."*
>
> (Qur'an 2:30–31)

In these verses, the human race is described as 'a deputy of God' because God has delegated to humankind the power to control and dominate the Creation and entrusted humanity with a duty to look after it through the exercise of reason ("the names of all things") in the apparent absence of God.[108]

This idea of taking responsibility for the Creation on behalf of God puts into practice the Worldview of diversity-in-unity of Activist Islam. Therefore, Activist Muslims, as an act of faith, are likely to enter the public domain,; for example, to address homelessness, champion the environment or to struggle for the more obviously Muslim causes such as prayer spaces, respect for traditional female dress codes and Palestinian nationhood. This is undertaken *within* the legal process of established internationally recognized jurisdictions and by encouraging Muslims to take an active part in the processes of democracy as a means to ensuring that distinctively Muslim points of view are heard.

Some Activist Muslims campaign for the right for domestic and civil elements of *Sharia* law to find a place in non-Muslim legal processes,[109] while others may challenge this idea on the Islamic principle of equality before the Law. Nevertheless, what unites both these Activist Muslim groups is belief in the essential unity and freedom of humankind and the belief that Islamic principles (*maqasid ash-sharia*) can further that essential unity and enhance and deepen an ethos of universal human rights.

Sincere Counsel (nasiha)

As part of the role of deputizing for God in advocating positive transformative change at individual, social, institutional and natural levels, Activist Muslims, such as the Saudi-leader of the *Sahwa* (Islamic Awakening) Movement Salman al-Awda (born 1956 CE) (in his latest manifestation) have formalized the Qur'anic principle of "enjoining what is recognized to be right and forbidding the reprehensible"

---

108 Yusuf Ali, *The Holy Qur'an*.
109 Nichols, *Marriage and Divorce in a Multi-Cultural Context*.

112 *Basic beliefs, practices and characteristic themes*

(Qur'an 3:110) and the Prophetic injunction to offer sincere Counsel and Advice according to the hadith:

> *The Messenger of God said, "Religion is sound advice (nasiha)." They asked, "To whom, Messenger of God?" He said, "To God and His Book and His Messenger and the leaders of the Muslims and the common people."*[110]

This *nasiha* includes the process of formally advising and, as necessary, criticizing political figures and regimes, both Muslim and non-Muslims ones, insofar as they act as obstacles to the conditions of human flourishing and do not bring about the protection of life, lineage, intellect, property and Freedom of Religion and Freedom of Expression and property as required in Islamic law.

Famously, for example, Salman Al-Awda and Nasser al-Omar drafted and gained support for proposals for a raft of civic reforms, such as anti-corruption measures for state officials, that were presented by powerful delegations of religious scholars to the Saudi Government in two documents 'The Letter of the Scholars' (*Kitab al-'Ulama*) and 'A Memorandum of Advice' (*Mudhakkiat al-Nasiha*) in 2014.[111] Furthermore, Al-Awda has developed an extensive *nasiha* theology which balances the Islamic obligations of respect and compliance with legitimate authority (Qur'an 4:59) with the Islamic ethos to establish justice for all citizens in the spirit of equality before the law.

*Reform (*islah*)*

This dynamic of transformation toward conditions of greater universal justice and the implementation of human rights driven by the ethos of Islamic activism is typically called 'reform' (*islah*) and can refer to both reforming the legal and political structures of Islam, or reforming the political conditions in Muslim and non-Muslim states, to bring about either human emancipation or greater protection of the natural world.

In particular, the goal of reform has been championed by a group of Muslim scholars led by the Afghan scholar and former Professor of Law at the International Islamic University of Malaysia Mohammad Hashim Kamali (born 1944 CE). Kamali advocates mobilizing and developing the fundamental objectives (*maqasid ash-sharia*) of *Sharia* Law – protection of life, lineage, intellect, property and freedom of religion, freedom of expression and property – in order to free up the essence of *Sharia* Law to respond with the legal flexibility to the challenges of globalized modernity and to effect civilizational Islamic renewal.[112]

Also, there is a movement amongst Twelver Shia scholars such as Ayatollahs Khumayni, Fadlallah, Sanei and Mohagheg Damad to revive the extensive use of exegetical

---

110 Related by Muslim in An-Nawawi's Forty Hadith.
111 Maher, *Salafi-Jihadism*.
112 Kamali, M. H., *Maqasid Al-Sharia'ah Made Simple*.

reason to avoid literalism in Qur'anic interpretation to re-discover the *rationale* of law derived from the Qur'an rather than following its time and place-bound rulings.[113]

This type of scholarly reforming impetus is driven by the conviction of Activist Muslims both that the core principles of Islam are eternally true and that the way that they need to be lived legally and culturally need to be responsive *to* and the agents *of* purposive change in each particular age.[114]

The call for reform of the general social circumstances experienced by Muslims is exemplified in countries such as Britain and Australia by Muslim community-group opposition to, and protest against, the types of anti-terrorism legislation that is viewed by many (both Muslim and non-Muslim)[115] as either excessively or exclusively targeting Islam as the cause and Muslims as the source of contemporary extremism and that is deemed to violate human privacy rights.[116]

Both Sincere Counsel (*nasiha*) and Reform (*islah*) are but two necessarily peaceful and transformative doctrinal tools by which Mainstream Muslims can and do legitimately and authentically exercise the activist role as the deputy of God in the name of Islam and to further less-obviously Muslim causes, such as combating Climate Change, in which the well-being of humanity more generally is implicated.

*Struggle (*Jihad fiy sabilillah*) in activist Islam*

This type of faith-based activism to see the conditions of greater equality, Freedom of Religion and of intellect established in both Muslim-majority and non-Muslim majority society, often at the peril of the activist, certainly fits legitimately under the Qur'anic rubric of Struggle in the Path of God (*Jihad fiy sabilillah*) according to the two types of struggle outlined in the previous section:

1 **Jihad by the tongue** (*jihad bil lisan*)

    This is concerned with speaking the truth and struggling for Freedom of Religion.
2 **Jihad by the hand** (*jihad bil yad*)

    This refers to choosing to do what is right and combating civic injustice with acts of protest.

In certain exceptional circumstances, when Muslims' lives, property and ability to perform the Obligations of Islam are directly and violently targeted by a regime – Muslim or other – and the means of migration (*Hijra*) from the conditions of oppression are cut off, it may be legitimate for Muslims to take up arms in Jihad by the sword (*jihad bis Saif*) as an act of defensive, Activist Jihad.

For example, the Bosnian Muslim-majority defense of Sarajevo (1992–1995) can undoubtedly be classed as a legitimate act of defensive, Activist armed *Jihad*

---

113 Takim, '*Maqasid ash-Sharia* in Contemporary Shi'i Jurisprudence.
114 Johnston, 'Yusuf al-Qaraḋawi's Purposive Fiqh'.
115 Whether rightly or wrongly.
116 These rights also exist in Islam and were strongly adhered to by Muhammad and his companions. Islamic Law is particularly concerned with the protection of the public whereas acts undertaken in private are a matter between the believer and God.

114   *Basic beliefs, practices and characteristic themes*

(although the Bosnian government never, in fact, called it as such partly because it was always a multi-faith, multi-ethnic body). However, the conditions of this type of authentic armed Jihad, in which both the conditions and the rules of armed combat (*Qital*) can be observed, are few and far between and include the exhaustion of all peaceful, activist means to avert bloodshed.[117]

In short, the themes and doctrines of Activist Islam and the actions of those Muslims inspired by them over the centuries of Islam, shows clearly that the struggle (*Jihad*) to see the individual and social conditions of worship and well-being more thoroughly realized, according to God's Word and Law, and in legal ways is an intrinsic, ancient and vital part of the Mainstream Islamic Worldview.

The themes and ethical praxis of Ideological Islamism

Political Caliphate

The Worldview of Islam identifies with and is informed by the spirit of theological Caliphate (*Khilafa*) – deputizing for God in His apparent absence. The classic theme that gives substance to the Worldview of Ideological Islamism is that of political Caliphate (*Khilafa*). This is the doctrine of the political establishment of the united political Global Community (*Umma*) of Islam to govern either the nation-state or, more usually, the entire world by Islamic Law *in place* of all other political ideologies and systems of governance. Thus, the accent of change shifts critically from 'reform' of structure in Activist Islam to 'replacement' of structure in Ideological Islamism.

Ideological Islamists such as Abu Ala Maududi (1903–1979 CE) and Hassan al-Banna (1906–1949 CE) have understood Caliphate and/or the Islamic State as superseding and taking precedence over democratic processes and states. They have tended to aspire to governance according to a limited understanding of *Sharia* Law, whereby *Sharia* is not understood as the full legal and moral engagement of Muslims with the law through organic traditions of jurisprudence, but the literalist application of Qur'anic injunctions into contemporary circumstances according to an ideological blueprint or manifesto. This political literalism is in turn premised, as we have seen, on a Worldview of exaggerated separation and difference between the Muslim and the non-Muslim.

Without political Caliphate, the Muslim is deficient

For Ideological Islamists, the need to establish an overtly Islamic political system becomes the basic premise and goal of Islam without which the Muslim believer is an incomplete, deficient Muslim. Thus, for Ideological Islamism, governance

---

117   Gomaa, 'A Fatwa on Jihad'.

according to *Sharia* under Muslim leadership becomes, in theory at least, an essential requirement for the believer to be properly, fully Muslim.

This idea can be exemplified, for example, in the writings of Abul Ala Maududi (1903–1979), a highly influential Indian-Pakistani journalist, politician and political theorist to whom we will return more fully in the next chapter:

> *Everyone who desires to remain a Muslim is under an obligation to follow the Qur'an and the Sunnah which must constitute the basic law of an Islamic State [. . .] The object of the state is not merely to prevent people from exploiting each other, to safeguard their liberty, and to protect its subjects from foreign invasion[. . .] its object is to eradicate evil and to encourage all types of virtue and excellence expressly mentioned by God in the Holy Qur'an.*[118]

This idea of the establishment of Islamic State as an Obligatory Act of Faith is also a keystone of the ideological writing of the founder of the Muslim Brotherhood organization, Hassan al-Banna (1906–1949 CE):

> *. . . as long as this* [Islamic] *state does not emerge, the Muslims in their totality are committing a sin, and are responsible before God the Exalted, the Great, for their failure to establish it and for their slackness in creating it.*[119]

The Islamist manifesto of Hizb ut-Tahrir

These themes of political Caliphate, premised on a Worldview of exaggerated Muslim-non-Muslim difference have been traduced (often vulgarly and simplistically) into the manifesto material of contemporary global political Islamist Parties such as Hizb ut-Tahrir (the Party of Liberation):

The aim of Hizb ut-Tahrir

> *Its aim is to resume the Islamic way of life and to convey the Islamic da'wah* [call to Islam] *to the world. This objective means bringing the Muslims back to living an Islamic way of life in Dar al-Islam and in an Islamic society such that all of life's affairs in society are administered according to the Shariah rules, and the viewpoint in it is the halal and the haram under the shade of the Islamic State, which is the Khilafah "Caliphate" State. That state is the one in which Muslims appoint a Khalifah* [Caliph] *and give him the bay'ah* [Oath of Allegiance] *to listen and obey on condition that he rules according to the Book of Allah (swt) and the Sunnah of the Messenger of Allah (saw) and on condition that he conveys Islam as a message to the world through da'wah* [calling to Islam] *and jihad* [striving in the path of God].

---

118 Maududi, Political Theory of Islam, p. 165.
119 Al-Banna, *Five Tracts of Hassan Al-Banna (1906–1949) a Selection from the Majmu'at Rasa'il Al-Imam Al-Shahid Hasan Al-Banna*, pp. 31–32.

The Party, as well, aims at the correct revival of the Ummah through enlightened thought. It also strives to bring her back to her previous might and glory such that she wrests the reins of initiative away from other states and nations, and returns to her rightful place as the first state in the world, as she was in the past, when she governs the world according to the laws of Islam.

It also aims to bring back the Islamic guidance for mankind and to lead the Ummah into a struggle with Kufr, its systems and its thoughts so that Islam encapsulates the world.[120]

The key themes of Ideological Islamism

This 'manifesto' is characterized by the basic Worldview and all the key themes of Ideological Islamism:

1   Islam is manifest not primarily as an individual and collective religious praxis but as a "revolutionary" political party;
2   Being a complete Muslim is only possible in a 'Khilafah State' under a 'Caliph';
3   this involves an 'Oath of Allegiance' to the said Caliph which trumps other political allegiances, e.g. to the governments of nation-states;
4   the purpose of the establishment of this 'Khilafah State' is the revival of the Global Community (Ummah) of Muslims;
5   which is set against a background of a global struggle with Unbelief (*kufr*) which is conceived of as a complete, integrated system (*milla*) that encompasses the whole world and which is set in diametric opposition to the governing principles of an Islamic State.

This core Islamist notion that 'other' systems of governance apart from Caliphate are intrinsically 'un-Islamic' is also neatly encapsulated on the same website:

Bismillahi Al-Rahman Al-Raheem

Voting on the 7th June Elections is Forbidden by Shariah and It Serves the Survival of the Secular System (Translated)

The meaning of the word 'election' is to outweigh, it is permissible in Islam if it is not related to something forbidden. In the era of the Righteous Khaleefs, the Khalifs took their post as leaders of the believers by election. Although the reality of election is permissible, but not all elections are permissible. Because the elections these days are "democratic elections" and it is used to make democracy which is a Kufr system a legitimate project. This type of election therefore falls from the permissible elections.

Democracy is a system contrary to Islam, and it considers man to be more capable than Allah The Exalted Almighty in legislating. Sovereignty in it is unconditional and without limit to humans. And thus it does not recognize the sovereignty and legislation of Allah. Because the members of Parliament

---

120 Hizb ut-Tahrir, 'Hizb Ut Tahrir', 2016.

who are chosen as representatives for the people do not give value to many of the rulings of Allah (swt) and His Messenger (saw), and they issue new rules in its place instead. Matters prohibited by Allah and His Messenger such as alcohol, adultery, usury, gambling and others are considered legitimate by members of parliament in democratic systems.[121]

In this piece of Islamist text, *political* democracy is specifically characterized as *religious* Unbelief (*Kufr*) on the grounds that democratically elected officials do not legislate according to *Sharia* law.

In this, we see the characteristic way that Islamism inverts the relationship between politics and religion seen earlier in the Mainstream Islamic Worldview. In Mainstream Islam, political structures are subservient to the establishment of the basic principles of worship of God and human well-being; in Ideological Islamism the religious praxis of the individual believer is subservient to the establishment of an Islamic State.

Despite their often shared ethic of political change, we can also observe that the political ethic of Ideological Islamism is diametrically opposed to that of Activist Islam. Activist Islam, by contrast to Ideological Islamism, endorses and encourages Muslim engagement with the democratic political process precisely because this is one of a range of possible legitimate ways in which Muslims can ensure the conditions in which the principles of worship and well-being can be furthered and protected. This shift from Activist Islam to Ideological Islamism is a shift from serious, realizable religious, social and political gains aimed at universal benefits to utopian political fantasy which is intended only to benefit the idealized (and therefore non-existent) Muslim.

Ideological Islamism defines this ideal Muslim, for the first time in our model, as significantly different from other non-Muslim human beings, and defines Muslim governance as essentially different from 'non-Muslim' systems of government to the degree that participation in 'non-Muslim' systems is deemed to be forbidden (*haram*).

The themes and ethical praxis of Non-Violent Islamist Extremism

In the previous chapter, we noted how the relative and contingent separation of the Ideological Islamist Worldview between Muslims and non-Muslims sharpens to an absolute and eternal Manichean separation in Non-Violent Islamist Extremism in which Islam (submission to God) and Unbelief (*Kufr*)[122] as Worldviews are set up as diametrically, essentially and eternally opposed.

In the praxis of Non-Violent Islamist Extremism, the Ideological Islamist themes of the obligation for political Caliphate and the need for the structure of an entire Islamic State persist. This includes the understanding that allegiance to a Muslim leader supersedes or bypasses the need for the Muslim believer to be a law-abiding citizen of a modern nation-state.[123] Nevertheless, in distinction from Ideological

---

121 Hizb ut-Tahrir, 'Hizb Ut Tahrir', 2015.
122 Or equivalents such as 'Jahiliyya' – pre-Islamic Ignorance.
123 In other words, the Islamic Oath of Allegiance (*baya*) makes the social contract of democratic citizenship between the governed and governing null and void.

118 Basic beliefs, practices and characteristic themes

Islamism, Non-Violent Islamist Extremism introduces a set of religious-ideological 'doctrines' that formalize religiously the extreme Manichean Worldview of absolute and eternal separation of *Islam* (Submission to God) and *Kufr* (Unbelief) and the absolute irreconcilable hostility between Muslims and those of other faiths.

These doctrines include, most characteristically and foundationally:

The Doctrine of Loyalty and Disavowal (Al-Wala' wal-Bara')

The Doctrine of Loyalty and Disavowal (*Al-Wala' wal-Bara'*) means absolute loyalty (*Al-Wala'*) to the doctrines, principles and peoples of Islam in a binary with the absolute rejection (*al-Bara'*) – Disavowal – of anything – belief, practice, behavior or people – that are deemed to fall outside Islam.

As Bin Ali has shown,[124] mild strains of this doctrine percolate throughout Wahhabi-Salafi Islam, in Mainstream and Activist forms, in the notion that part of loving what God likes and has permitted, e.g. monotheistic worship and marriage, entails distancing oneself from what God does not like and has prohibited, e.g. polytheist worship and adultery, to give the binary opposites of the two examples given above.

However, as a basis for the Manichean Worldview underpinning all Islamist extremism, this element of Disavowal (*al-Bara'*) takes on totalitarian proportions and becomes the necessary proof of true belief. In the Islamist Extremist Worldview, the aspects of the infidel (*kafir*) life to be disavowed include all supposedly and overtly non-Muslim political systems, especially democracy, 'non-Muslim' cultural habits, national belonging(s), intellectual ideas, education and social relations, including those of kith and kin.

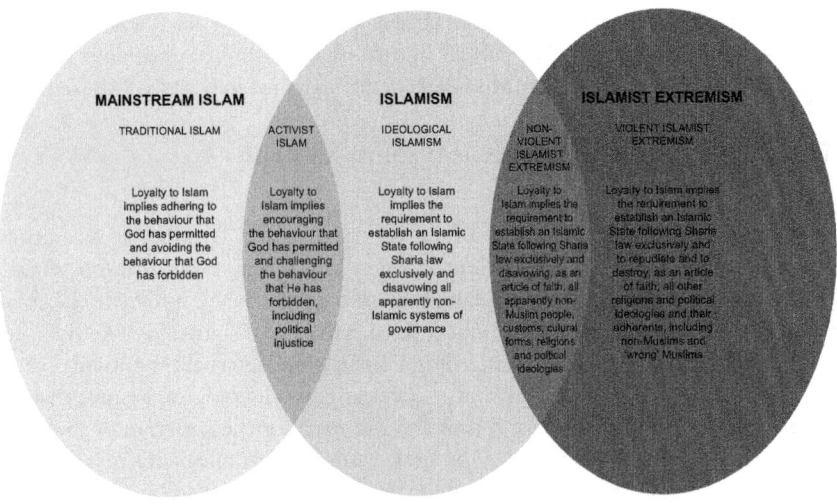

Figure 4.1 Doctrine of Loyalty & Disavowal (*Al-Wala' wal Bara'*) in the Worldviews of Mainstream Islam, Islamism and Islamist Extremism

For full color version please see Color Plate 3 after Page 5.

124 Bin Ali, *The Roots of Religious Extremism.*

Basic beliefs, practices and characteristic themes 119

In other words, in Non-Violent Islamist Extremism, this Doctrine of Loyalty and Disavowal (*Al-Wala' wal-Bara'*) means the absolute privileging of the overtly Islamic identity at the obliteration of every other human association or statement of belonging as being emblematic of the True Believer.

> ... *Islam's main foundations, namely the qualities of al-wala' wa'l-bara'* [Loyalty and Disavowal], *which are two major prerequisites of true faith: al-wala'* [Loyalty] *is a manifestation of sincere love for Allah, His prophets and the believers; al-bara'* [Disavowal], *on the other hand, is an expression of enmity and hatred towards falsehood and its adherents. Both are evidence of iman* [belief].[125]

Loyalty and Disavowal becomes the basis of Tawhid

In the Non-Violent Islamist Extremist Worldview, this twin act of Loyalty to Islam and Muslims and Disavowal of everything and everyone else becomes the basis for true belief in the Unity of God – the Doctrine of Divine Unity (*Tawhid*).

> *The doctrine of al-Wala' wal Bara'* [Loyalty and Disavowal] *is the real image for the actual practice of this faith. It has a tremendous significance in the mind of the Muslim, as much as the greatness and significance of the faith. Therefore, Tawhid will never be achieved on earth until we apply the doctrine of al-Wala' wal Bara'. Some people think that the principle of faith is a matter of secondary importance, but in reality it is the opposite.*[126]

In this passage one of the founding figures of the doctrine of Loyalty and Disavowal, the Saudi ideologue, Mohammed Saeed Al-Qahtaani (born 1957 CE)

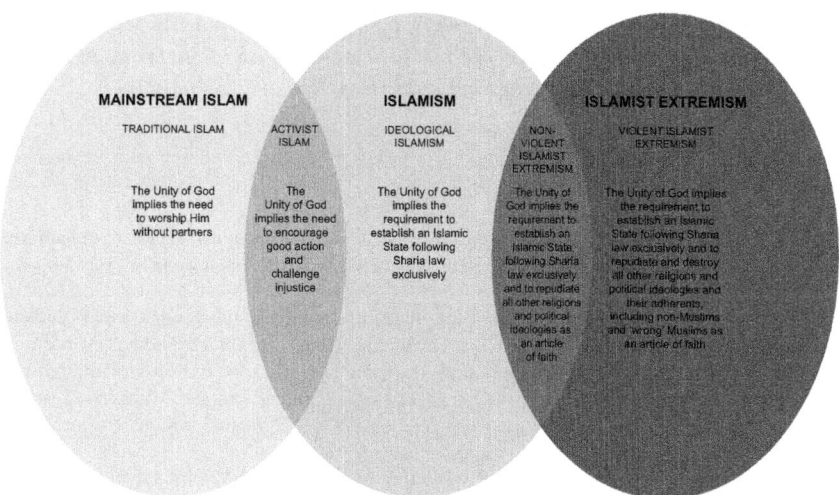

Figure 4.2 Doctrine of the Unity of God (*Tawhid*) in the Worldviews of Mainstream Islam, Islamism and Islamist Extremism
For full color version please see Color Plate 4 after Page 5.

125 Al-Qahtaani, *Al-Wala' Wa-l Bara'*, p. 1.
126 Ibid.

120 *Basic beliefs, practices and characteristic themes*

by Al-Qahtaani, the Doctrine of Divine Unity (*Tawhid*), which we saw in Chapter 3 is doctrinally emblematic in Mainstream Islam both of the Absolute Singularity of God and the essential unity of His Creation; it transforms to become, under the strictures of the Doctrine of Loyalty and Disavowal, emblematic of the absolute difference and separation of created existence into the camps of Islamic Belief (*iman*) and Unbelief (*kufr*) in all spheres of life. In other words, recognition of the Unity of God becomes dependent on acceptance of the essential difference of different types of humans and the systems that they use to govern themselves. This setting up of the cosmos as an absolute, eternal, irreconcilable Believer-Infidel binary is at the core of the radicalist departure from Mainstream Islam into Islamist Extremism (see Figure 4.2 and Plate 4).

Salafist, which is different from Salafi, means decontextualized literalism

In creating the intellectual environment of this doctrinal expression of an absolutely divided Worldview, Non-Violent Islamist Extremism is often Salafist (rather than Salafi[127]) in its literalist and decontextualized use of the Qur'an. For example, in the same volume Al-Qahtaani cites the following Qur'an verses in support of his position:

> It [Loyalty and Disavowal] *is a matter of belief and disbelief, as Allah says:* "O You who believe! Do not take your fathers or your brothers as protectors if they prefer disbelief to faith. Whoever among you takes them for protectors will only be wrongdoers. Say, If your fathers, your sons, your brothers, your wives, your kinsmen, the wealth which you have acquired, the commerce in which you fear a decline, or the houses you love – if these are dearer to you than Allah and His Messenger, and striving hard and fighting in His cause, then wait until Allah brings about His Decision (torment). Allah does not guide those who are Al-Faasiqun."
>
> (Surat at-Tawba: Verses 23–24)

---

127 Salafi Islam refers to the Islam practised by the Companions of the Prophet Muhammad and the two generations who followed them, known as the 'Salaf as-Salih', meaning the 'Righteous Predecessors'.

In practice, Salafi Islam, which is sub-divided into myriad sub-groups, often tends to scriptural literalism and is inclined to ignore the contextual understandings of Islam as developed by the four Sunni Canonical Schools of Islamic Law and often, although not always, cherry picks verses of the Qur'an and sayings of the Prophet Muhammad (peace and blessings be upon him) to form religious-legal judgments without the necessary contextual reasoning (*Asbab an-Nuzul*).

It should be stated, however, that while the majority of Non-Violent Islamist Extremists and Violent Islamist Extremists will claim to be Salafi Muslims, the vast majority of Salafi Muslims who may look and dress and sound similar to them are neither Non-Violent Islamist Extremists nor Violent Islamist Extremists and are indeed Mainstream observant Muslims.

Hence, in this book I use the word Salafist rather than Salafi to denote the extreme textual literalism of Non-Violent Islamist Extremism and Violent Islamist Extremism.

The aspiration to be a Salafi Muslim by following the early generation of Muslims as closely as possible is certainly an authentic Mainstream Muslim aspiration.

> *Allah says: "O you who believe! Take not the Jews and the Christians as Awliya' (friends, protectors), they are but Awliya' to one another. And if any amongst you takes them as Awliya', then surely he is one of them. Verily, Allah guides not those people who are the Zaalimun (polytheists, wrong-doers)."*
> (Surat al-Ma'idah: Verse 51)

Both these Qur'anic verses are quoted by Al-Qahtaani as proof of the General eternal and transfactual reality of the enmity of Muslims and non-Muslims outside of the Particular conditions of war between the Muslims and the pagan Quraysh into which the verses were revealed in which 'friends and protectors' really means 'allies' in the particular circumstances of conflict.[128] As we have seen, this distinction between the General and the Particular verses of the Qur'an is especially important in connection with relations between Muslims and non-Muslims.

In this sense, while Non-Violent Islamist Extremism can often appear to be a highly conservative and traditional form of Islam, and indeed is often described as such in the mainstream non-Muslim media, in its abandonment of the tools of Islamic exegesis it, in fact, represents the undermining of tradition.[129] Ironically, in its literalist abandonment of context, Islamist Extremism, in common with other types of religious extremism, can co-opt the primary texts of Islam – the Qur'an and the canonical *hadith* – to justify almost anything. In the next chapter, I will provide a more detailed analytical account of Non-Violent Islamist Extremism with a critique of its 'ur-' text, *Milestones* (1964) by Sayyid Qutb.

This undermining of the Qur'anic message is perhaps best exemplified by the fact that, in Non-Violent Islamist Extremism, those whom the 'true believer' is required to disavow and reject, include, contrary to the most basic Islamic ethical framework family, kith and kin, neighbors, fellow citizens and all those co-religionists who associate with the disavowed groups.

> *A Muslim has no relationship with his mother, father, brother, wife and other family members except through their relationship with the Creator, and then they are also joined through blood.*[130]

Thus, the Doctrine of Loyalty and Disavowal sets up the intellectual conditions for its adherents to think only of the 'right kind of Muslim' as 'blessed' and to think of non-Muslims and 'wrong-Muslims' as less than fully human and 'beyond the pale' of those whom God has destined for Paradise.

Jihad in Non-Violent Islamist Extremism

In the Worldview of Non-Violent Islamist Extremism it is axiomatic that, as diametrically opposed 'blessed' and 'damned' ways of life (*deen*), Islam and Unbelief (*Kufr*), cannot co-exist within families, within communities and within nations. This is because, according to Non-Violent Islamist Extremists, e.g. Qutb

---

128 See translation and commentary of M.A.S Haleem on Qur'an 5:51 and Qur'an 9:23–24.
129 Lumbard, *Islam, Fundamentalism, and the Betrayal of Tradition, Revised and Expanded.*
130 Qutb, *Milestones*, p. 133.

(1906–1966), Islam and *Kufr* (Muslims and non-Muslims) are eternally at war and eternally committed to each other's ideological eradication.

In this ethic of mutual destruction which belies, for example, the contemporary realities of intense Muslim-non-Muslim connectedness and cooperation, Non-Violent Islamist Extremism allows for the possibility that armed violence,[131] which it calls Jihad, will be necessary to accomplish this eradication, but does not foreground its accomplishment.

This task of justifying and giving prominence to the cosmic eradication of Unbelief (*Kufr*) and Infidels (*kāfirun*; *kuffar*) by Islam and Muslims, as an apocalyptic prelude to the establishment of a Global Islamic State, is left to the Worldview and exponents of Violent Islamist Extremism.

The themes and ethical praxis of Violent Islamist Extremism

If Non-Violent Islamist Extremism sets up the Worldview of total, eternal opposition and absolute Disavowal by Muslims of Unbelief (*Kufr*) as a complete, all-encompassing system (*milla*), Violent Islamist Extremism generates and applies the doctrinal tools to justify and accomplish the annihilation of Unbelief (*Kufr*).

*The doctrine of Loyalty and Disavowal revisited: the domain of Islam vs. the domains of Unbelief and War (*Dar al-Islam vs. Dar al-Kufr wal Harb*) and the 'wrong' Muslim*

Violent Islamist Extremism builds on the doctrine of Loyalty and Disavowal (*Al-Wala' wal-Bara'*) as established in Non-Violent Islamist Extremism to formalize the world into a strictly divided Place of Islam (*Dar al-Islam*) and Place of Unbelief (*Dar al-Kufr*), which is also a Place of War (*Dar al-Harb*). Thus, Violent Islamist Extremists rework a medieval geo-political construction of the world[132] into contemporary geo-political circumstances. VIE exponents add the politicized twist that wherever a state, be it Muslim or other, does not govern according to what Violent Islamist Extremists regard as *Sharia* law; that state and its Muslim rulers and peoples are deemed to be either apostate (*murtad*) or polytheist (*mushrik*), i.e. beyond the pale of the sanctity of Islam, and therefore rightly fit to be killed.[133]

In this, as we will see in detail in the next chapter, Violent Islamist Extremists, in particular those who were opposed to the secular nationalist regime of Gamal Abdul Nasser in the 1960s and 1970s, took the notion of *Jahiliyya* – pre-Islamic Ignorance – developed fulsomely by Sayyid Qutb and gave it a radical twist.

---

131 Maududi, *Jihad in Islam*.
132 Michot, *Muslims Under Non-Muslim Rule Ibn Taymiyya*.
133 Faraj, *The Absent Obligation*.

Whereas in the early and classical periods, 'Disavowal', such as it was, had been directed at non-Muslim beliefs, habits and regimes as a means of garnering political loyalty to a *Muslim* regime; disavowal for this modernist strain of Violent Islamist Extremists became the tool of claiming the loyalty of a group of 'true' Muslims *within* and *against* a Muslim regime on the grounds that that regime was not Muslim enough. As we will see in Chapter 7, this move was, in particular, the contribution of the Egyptian ideologue Muhammad Abd as-Salam Faraj (1954–1982 CE). Thus, for Violent Islamist Extremists, 'Disavowal' not only entails rejection of *Kufr* (Unbelief) and every political, social, intellectual and cultural form that is believed to emanate from *Kufr*, but it also entails Disavowal of the 'Wrong Muslim' and every political, social, intellectual and cultural form that is believed to emanate from 'wrong, deficient Islam'.

Moreover, in Violent Islamist Extremist tracts, e.g. Ayman Al-Zawahiri's infamous tract on Loyalty and Disavowal (2013), the Doctrine of Loyalty and Disavowal transmogrifies effectively into the even more nihilistic Doctrine of Disavowal and Loyalty. By this logic, the adherent of Violent Islamist Extremism proves his/her[134] commitment to the Unity of God (*Tawhid*) by the strength and absolute nature of the Disavowal of Unbelief (*Kufr*), the Infidel (the *kuffar*) and the apostate (*murtad*) and the degree to which s/he is prepared to sacrifice him/her-self to the cause of this Disavowal.[135]

Excommunication of the 'wrong Muslim' (takfir)

This act of Disavowal and the move to eradicate the 'Wrong' Muslims is called by Violent Islamist Extremists *takfir*, meaning 'to declare as an infidel'.

The identification of the 'wrong Muslim' through *takfir* and the preparedness of Violent Islamist Extremists to kill other Muslims whom they have 'excommunicated' is one of the most distinctive contributions of Violent Islamist Extremism. The doctrine of *takfir* is, for example, the ideological cause of the persistence of the internecine Muslim violence of the Syrian Civil War (2011–present). It is the tool of choice in the long-running battle between Al-Qaeda and ISG in their competing claims to pre-eminence over Jihadist militias, such

---

134 It is often assumed that Violent Islamist Extremism is an almost exclusively male preserve. Regrettably, the persistence and recruiting power of VIE can be in no small part attributed to the commitment of large numbers of prominent women to its cause, e.g. the Glaswegian Aqsa Mahmood, who is believed to have recruited the Tower Hamlets trio Shamima Begum, 15, Kadiza Sultana, 16, and Amira Abase, 15, to the so-called Islamic State group in 2015.

135 This dynamic of the Disavowal of the Wrong-Muslim as well as the non-Muslim has a long, tragic history, from Khaled Al-Islambuli's declaration on the assassination of Anwar Sadat in 1981, "I have shot Pharaoh", to British Muslim recruits to so-called Islamic State in the Syrian Civil War strapping themselves up with sticks of dynamite before being sent to "slaughter the Rejectors (Rafidha)", i.e. to slaughter Shia 'Wrong-Muslims', so-called because of their rejection of the authority of the Rightly-Guided Caliphs of early Islam (see Chapter 1).

as the Al-Nusra Front, and the justification given for the seemingly endless inter-militia assassinations, such as the murder of the Al-Qaeda 'representative' to Syria Abu Khalid as-Suri by so-called Islamic State in February 2014.

Takfir is the means by which Violent Islamist Extremists undermine the ancient Mainstream Islamic injunctions about the sanctity of another Muslim's blood, property and honor according to the *Sunna* of the Prophet Muhammad. Mainstream Muslims often refer to Violent Islamist Extremists as *takfiris* – excommunicators – precisely because of their willingness to declare all other Muslims as *kafir* as a prelude to fighting them. For example, the charge of *takfir* was one of the principal complaints of Muslims fighting in Iraq in the second Iraq War (2003–2011) against the group Al-Qaeda in Iraq (AQI) led by the notoriously bloodthirsty Abu Musab Az-Zarqawi. This loosely aligned offshoot of Al-Qaeda was to become the basis for the so-called Islamic State for whom *takfir* is a standard ideological device to justify their slaughter of Shia and Sunni Muslims alike.

Millennialism

This tool of excommunication (*takfir*) of other Muslims, including other Violent Islamist Extremists, is given an added dynamism and momentum by the millennialism of Violent Islamist Extremism. This to say that Violent Islamist Extremists tend to believe not only that the contemporary world is in a state of cosmic pre-Armageddon before the End of Time, but also that they are themselves the *agents* of the End of Time and that their violent acts both against the Christian and Jewish Infidel and against other 'wrong' Muslims are the Divine Tool of Armageddon.

To give one of many possible examples, ISG named their in-house magazine after a small village near the Syrian-Turkish border in Northern Syria called Dabiq because in one reading of one Prophetic hadith the site of the Battle of Armageddon between Christian and Muslim forces is narrated as taking place in Dabiq.[136] On this basis, the so-called Islamic State group spent a disproportionate amount of men and firepower assaulting the village of Dabiq in August 2014 in the attempt to accomplish this apocalyptic Prophecy at a site of little or no strategic value but redolent in apocalyptic symbolism.

In this fact, we can observe not only how Violent Islamist Extremism is fueled by an extreme apocalypticism, but also how a single (*ahad*) Prophetic saying can be used in a literalist, decontextualized way to build an entire military policy and campaign. In this militarized religious literalism, no regard is given for either the conditions or regulations of armed Jihad in Islam, such as the sanctity of civilian life. This brings us to the core of Violent Islamist Extremist praxis – the rewriting and abuse of the Islamic Doctrines of Jihad.

---

[136] Narrated in Sahih Muslim:
"The Last Hour would not come until the Romans would land at al-A'maq or in Dabiq."

The revisions of Jihad in Violent Islamist Extremism

The Particular made General and the General made Particular

If the Doctrine of Disavowal and Loyalty is a core component part of Violent Islamist Extremism's distinctive and violently skewed version of the Doctrine of Divine Unity (Tawhid), at the doctrinal heart of the absolutely divided Worldview of Violent Islamist Extremism, is a complete revision of Mainstream Islamic Doctrines of Jihad.

Earlier in this chapter, we explored how in Mainstream Islam, the word and concept of Jihad means 'struggling in the path of God' (*Jihad fiy sabilillah*). We saw how this refers traditionally to any struggle or exertion by a believing Muslim undertaken legally with the intention to please and obey God, including preserving and protecting the integrity of Islam. It is a multifarious doctrine built theologically in the first and second centuries of Islam to include multiple strands, for example 'struggle with the heart' – opposing evil thoughts and deeds – 'struggle with the tongue' – speaking the truth – 'struggle with the hand' – opposing political injustice peacefully – and 'struggle with the sword' – armed combat (*Qital*) under very stringent conditions of declaration and prosecution as a means of preserving Islam and Muslim life.

Violent Islamist Extremism is built upon some subtle, but game-changing, revisions of this multi-faceted and regulated set of doctrines of Jihad.

The reduction of struggling (Jihad) to fighting (Qital)

The first of these Violent Islamist Extremist moves is to misconstrue and reduce the Qur'anic multivarious idea of *Jihad* as meaning 'struggling in the path of God' (*Jihad fiy sabilillah*) to 'fighting' (*Qital*) in a move which both eradicates the entire range of peaceful means to strive in the path of God rehearsed on pages 103–105 and pages 113–114.

Typically, for example, Violent Islamist Extremists will deny or belittle the validity of non-violent struggle by denying the authenticity of the *hadith* material that narrates it, and then will characteristically deem armed Jihad (*Qital*) as the *only* type of struggle that is rewarded by God. This effectively reverses the Muhammadan Sunna by turning the Greater Jihad of opposing the evil of the self into the Lesser Jihad, and turning the Lesser Jihad of fighting (*Qital*) into the Greater, if not the only, acceptable form of Struggle.

This move of the contemporary monopolization of the meaning of the word *Jihad* as 'fighting' began with Abdullah Azzam (1941–1989 CE) during the Afghan Jihad against the Soviet Union (Azzam 2001/1981).

> *The word Jihad . . . only means combat with weapons[. . .] and upon this the four Imams have agreed.*[137]

[137] Azzam, Join *the Caravan*, p. 51.

The monopolization of the meaning of *Jihad* as fighting has been so successfully accomplished that the ubiquitous word for someone who fights in what they believe is the cause of Islam is now a 'Jihadist'. This is in spite of the fact, as we have seen, since the earliest days in the classical centuries of Islam, *Jihad* had a wide variety of forms, only one of which was '*Qital*' – fighting.[138]

Qital as an Individual Religious Obligation (Fard al-Ayn) *and a sixth Pillar of Islam*

Once *Jihad* (Struggle for God) has been monopolized by *Qital* (fighting), the second Violent Islamist Extremist move has been to declare armed *Jihad* as an Individual Religious Obligation (*Fard al-Ayn*) in order:

a   to defend Muslim lands from 'Infidels' (*kuffar*)[139]
b   to expel 'apostate' Muslim rulers (the Near Jihad)
c   to propagate Islam by force (the Far Jihad) and[140]
d   to fight the supposed enemies of Islam in their own territories.

In some Violent Islamist Extremist accounts, armed Jihad even takes precedence over the Five Pillars of Islam and is termed "the first obligation after faith".[141] More regularly Violent Islamist Extremists refer to armed Jihad as the Sixth Pillar of Islam.[142]

By declaring armed Jihad as an Individual Religious Obligation, Violent Islamist Extremists designate it legally as an Islamic activity that must be prosecuted by *every* adult Muslim in every time and place on a legal par with the Five Pillars of Witnessing (*Shahada*), the Obligatory Prayer (*Salah*), the Poor Tax (*Zakah*), the Fast (*Sawm*) and the Pilgrimage (*Hajj*).

In so doing, VIE ideologues will routinely cover up Jihad's traditional position in Islamic Law as a Collective Obligation (*Fard al-Kifaya*) (Qur'an 9:122): that is a Collective Obligation which, in the right conditions, one part of the Muslim community must take on in order to fulfill the whole community's obligation. In other words, if a Muslim state is attacked, an army, for example, must take on the communal obligation to fight.[143]

> *Jihad (armed combat) is currently an Individual Religious Obligation – in person and by wealth, in every place that the disbelievers have occupied. It remains Individual Religious Obligation continuously until every piece of land that was once Islamic is regained.*

---

138 Afsaruddin, *Striving in the Path of God*.
139 Azzam, *Defence of Muslim Lands*.
140 Faraj, *The Absent Obligation*.
141 Azzam (2001).
142 Thus, turning a rhetorical device of some jurists for describing the fact that struggling to please God is embedded within all Islamic praxis into a legal prescription to fight.
143 Azzam, Join *the Caravan*, p. 51.

In the Worldview of Al-Qaeda, for example, "every piece of land that was once Islamic" referred to in the quote above includes the whole of India, most of China, almost all of Spain, Sicily and large tracts of Eastern Europe, as well as the more obvious historical boundaries of what was the territory of Palestine.

The suspension of the conditions for the conduct of armed Jihad

Having falsely concluded that armed Jihad is an Individual Religious Obligation continuously "until every piece of land that was once Islamic is regained," the next logical move in Violent Islamist Extremism is to abandon both the conditions for and regulations of a legitimate armed Islamic Jihad.

'Leaderless' Jihad

The most obvious condition of Jihad that is abandoned by VIE ideologues is the Mainstream Islamic stipulation that an armed Jihad must be declared and prosecuted under the authority of an internationally recognized ruler (i.e. recognized both by a consensus of a range of Muslim scholars and in international law), when under illegitimate attack from an aggressive power.

Thus, for example, both the Al-Qaeda magazine *Inspire* and the aforementioned *Dabiq* magazine of ISG routinely encourage the prosecution of 'leaderless' *Jihad*. That is to say the *ad hoc* violent targeting of civilian 'wrong' Muslim or non-Muslim populations by individuals or small collective cells embedded within them.

Crucially, the above-mentioned publications not only justify leaderless *Jihad* ideologically, but also contain copious articles in the form of instruction manuals in the making of Improvised Explosive Devices, with tantalizing titles such as 'How to wage Jihad from your kitchen'. This type of 'Leaderless' Jihad was propagated most recently and effectively by the spokesman of ISG, Abu Muhammad al-Adnani (1977–2016 CE), in his '*fatwa*' entitled, 'Indeed Your Lord is Ever Watchful' of August 2014, which we will return to in more detail in Chapter 7. This 'fatwa' is ideologically responsible for *ad hoc* 'leaderless' shootings and stabbings in Canada, Australia and London and hit-and-run attacks in Berlin, Nice and Manchester between 2014 and 2017. Those attacks in turn lead to the similar reprisal Islamophobic attack on the Finsbury Park Mosque in June 2017, which is what VIE ideologues intend to happen in the cause of polarizing society. Such leaderless attacks on non-Muslim citizens are cited as a proof of the 'true' Islamic 'disavowal 'of non-Muslims by the perpetrators.

The suspension of the regulations for the conduct of armed Jihad

Once the basic conditions for the declaration of an armed Jihad, in particular authorized leadership, are removed, it is a small step to the abandonment in Violent Islamist Extremism of the regulations for its conduct. This VIE abandonment of the regulations of *Qital* includes:

1 the authorization (indeed the encouragement and targeting) of the destruction of civic infrastructure and agriculture;

2   the execution of prisoners of war. One of the most sickening elements of the prosecution of terrorism by ISG has been the execution of thousands of prisoners of war and the dumping of their bodies in rivers and ditches;
3   the use of human shields;
4   the justification of collateral human damage in the form of the mass indiscriminate carnage of suicide killing.

These actions are usually justified,[144] again, by decontextualized recourse to obscure early medieval texts, such as *'Mashari al-Ashwaq ila Masari al-Ushaaq'* known as the Book of Jihad by a Mamluk scholar called Ibn Nuhas (d. c.1411 CE).

This de-contextualised *fatwa*, which has been extensively reproduced and commented on by such VIE luminaries such as the late Al-Qaeda spokesman, Anwar al-Awlaki (1971–2011 CE), includes chapters such as, *The Virtues of Killing a Non-Believer for the Sake of Allah* and *The Virtue of an Individual or a Small Group Immersing Themselves Within a Large Army of Non-Believers in Search of Martyrdom and Causing Damage to The Enemy*, which have been appropriated to justify the suicide bombing of civilian populations.

This de-contextualised *fatwa* of Ibn Nuhas also contains a chapter on the *Virtues of Martyrdom*, which for Violent Islamist Extremists is the ultimate prize.

The celestial carrot: the act of seeking martyrdom (Istishad*)*

In recent years, events such as the capture of the Bank of Mosul in July 2014 with $5 billion and vast black-market oil revenues, have given VIE groups large revenues and the ability to pay recruits 'proper' salaries.[145] Until such time, the rewards of Violent Islamist Extremism were almost all deferred to the Next World and came packaged in the form of the celestial rewards for becoming a martyr for the faith – *shaheed*.

Martyrdom in original Islam

Shaheed means a 'martyr for the faith of Islam', someone who has undergone *istishad* – martyrdom. It literally means 'a witness to the truth of Islam' by suffering martyrdom.

The value of those who are martyred legitimately for their faith is mentioned in famous Qur'anic verses, e.g. 3:169–170, and the word appears in the Qur'an itself on three occasions: 50:20, 4:71, 39:60.[146]

The idea behind the word *Shaheed* in the Qur'an and the *Sunna* of the Prophet Muhammad is that the Muslim who dies defending or protecting Islam goes directly to witness the presence of God without having to pass through the rigors of the Day of Judgment. This idea is narrated in the earliest Muslim traditions.

---

144   Increasingly, with the so-called Islamic State group no theological justification is offered.
145   $400 per month for fighters in 2014.
146   Ali (2000).

However, while those who died fighting in the way of God (*fiy sabilillah*) were celebrated as martyrs to the faith in the original Muslim community, and the idea of martyrdom was a motivating factor that relieved the fear of death, in the days of original Islam there never existed a cult with a concomitant ideology of martyrdom, whereby martyrdom was specifically a combat objective. None of the famous early martyrs of Islam intended to be killed in battle or elsewhere. For example, the uncle of the Prophet Muhammad, Hamza ibn Abdul Muttalib (570–645 CE), was ambushed by a spear-thrower called Wahshi ibn Harb (d.660 CE) in the Battle of Uhud (624 CE) and the Caliphs Uthman and Ali were both unexpectedly assassinated.

The Prophet Muhammad himself fought in the front-line of the battle and was wounded badly on one occasion, but did not actively seek his own death. In fact, to the contrary, he sought to preserve the lives of his Companions wherever and however possible. This is because the object of armed struggle (*Qital*) in Mainstream Islam was and is not death in the way of God but that God be worshipped and that human well-being be established (Qur'an 4:74–76).

Martyrdom in Violent Islamist Extremism

In contrast to Original, Mainstream Islam, in which martyrdom in defense of Islam was the by-product (albeit blessed) of the necessary preservation of Muslim life and faith, martyrdom in Violent Islamist Extremism and gaining the rewards of martyrdom, such as direct intercession with God, becomes itself the goal of combat. Thus, ISG and other VIE groups have rightly been called a death-cult.

In Violent Islamist Extremist sources, *istishad* – martyrdom – more often than not refers to suicide bombing attacks and suicide bombers. A high proportion of violently extreme texts are dedicated to the celebration and/or theological 'justification' of suicide bombing as a tactic for waging armed Jihad. This discourse of 'martyrdom' is supported by a gruesome online martyriology with photos of dead smiling martyrs posted online in huge numbers along with details of the circumstances of their death by VIE groups.

As we will see in Chapter 7, when we examine the 'contribution' to Violent Islamist Extremism by the Palestinian ideologue, Abdullah Azzam, and by those who have followed his lead, such as Abu Hamza al-Misri (Born 1958 CE) (the Egyptian Father of Hamza) and Abu Qatada al-Philistini (Born 1960 CE) (the Palestinian Father of Qatada), the cult of 'martyrdom' performs two key functions for VIE exponents:

1 It acts as confirmation of the absolute truth of the twin aims of Violent Islamist Extremists to destroy the infidel (*kuffar*), the apostates (*murtad*) and the religious hypocrites (*munafiqeen*) while establishing a pure Islamic, global state; and
2 It acts *in lieu* of material reward for fighters which has often been only scantily available in the types of insurrectionist circumstances in which

extremists have found themselves. Abu Qatada, for example, while recruiting for the Bosnian 'Jihad' in the 1990s published talks and videos in which he eulogized about the smell of musk emanating from the bodies of the martyrs and other visible manifestations that those who die in Jihad are fulfilling the Qur'anic promise of eternal life in the Presence of God.

(Qur'an 3:169).

The prospect of martyrdom is also deployed online as a key recruiting device. Some recruiters, particularly female ones (e.g. Runa Khan in 2014), bring considerable emotional pressure to bear on males to sign up as *ishtishadee* – a martyrdom exponent, i.e. as a suicide bomber. Thus, curiously for an ideological position that boasts of its religious 'purity', sexual pressure and the promise of sex is often used by VIE ideologues as part and parcel of the attraction of martyrdom with women used to appeal to the manhood of the 'martyr'. This sex appeal of martyrdom includes the promise of the so-called Virgins of Paradise (*houris*) that some Prophetic traditions record as the reward of the true martyr.

If sex is intermingled with the prospect of martyrdom, so is fame. As part of the appeal of 'martyrdom', the martyrdom videos of those about to conduct martyrdom operations have become a key VIE genre. These, for example the martyrdom video of the 7/7 bomber Shezhad Tanveer (1982–2005 CE), are often slick high-production outputs in which the words of the 'martyr' justifying his actions and encouraging others to follow in their footsteps are interspersed with snippets of Violent Islamist Extremist leaders. For example, in the case of Tanveer's video, footage of Ayman Al-Zawahiri (Born 1951 CE), the leader of Al-Qaeda, was interspersed offering hagiographic eulogies to the 'martyr' and thereby offering the promise of fame and respect for those who followed suit.

The Absolute Difference of the Martyr

In these propaganda videos, the act of seeking death through suicide is presented as the act of absolute, essential difference between the blessed Muslim and the damned *Kafir* victim. Phrases such as "We love death as you love life" are common in 'martyrdom' videos as statements of two entirely different types of human being whose attitudes to life and death are irreconcilable.

Thus, 'martyrdom' becomes a central feature of the absolutely, eternally divided Worldview of Violent Islamist Extremism which emphasizes how the 'true' 'Jihad-oriented' Muslim, by loving death, is *essentially* different and opposite in Worldview to every other type of human being.

5 Mainstream Islam
The people, texts and contexts

In the previous chapter we have examined the core practical, thematic and ethical characteristics and differences between Mainstream Islam (both Traditional and Activist), Islamism, both Ideological Islamism and Non-Violent Islamist Extremism, and Violent Islamist Extremism. In the following three chapters we will examine the people and the texts that have substantiated the Worldviews of Mainstream Islam, Ideological Islamism and Islamist Extremism and the contexts in which they occurred.

This is important, of course, since ideas, except those that are believed by people of faith to be transmitted in a transcendent manner by God (or equivalent[s]), are only ever born and communicated by human agents. Moreover, religiously or ideologically-charged individuals have often exhibited particularly potent – whether attractive or repulsive (or both) – human agency. Mainstream Islam, Islamism and Islamist Extremism are all populated by charismatic individuals of potent human agency together with the groups that they gather around them to propagate their ideas.

Hermeneutical health warning: people and their ideas are 'shifters'

The following three chapters, however, come with a number of 'health warnings'. First, people, especially religiously or ideologically-charged people, are not easily categorized or pigeonholed. People and their ideas are 'shifters': their ideas develop and change and are different at different stages and in different contexts of their lives. In our story, we will encounter huge shifts with, for example, the Al-Qaeda ideologue and spokesman Anwar Al-Awlaki shifting from left to right of our spectrum from a position in Mainstream Islam to a position at the forefront of Violent Islamist Extremism, and with others, such as the Saudi advocate of Activist Islam Salman al-Awda, shifting from a position at the fringes of Violent Islamist Extremism, to become one of the most mature Salafi advocates of Activist Islam.

Moreover, and this is especially the case with Extremisms, the ideas of the people that we will encounter here have often been used and abused by others in different circumstances after they are dead.

Most obviously in our story, Violent Islamist Extremists have repeatedly abused the work of a thirteenth-century Damascene jurist called Ibn Taymiyya (1263–1328 CE). Ibn Taymiyya's political-legal work focused on legitimizing Muslims fighting other Muslims when those Muslims being fought were aggressors who aimed to destroy legitimate centers of Muslim political authority, as the Mongols of his day were doing to the Mamluk Caliphate. Violent Islamist Extremists use bits and pieces of Ibn Taymiyya's legal judgments (*fatawa*) to legitimize exactly the opposite phenomenon – Muslims fighting and destroying legitimate centers of Muslim authority because they are not – in the Extremists' opinion – Muslim enough.

The character of any given text is also likely to be variegated and can shift. It is axiomatic to the science of textual interpretation (hermeneutics) that a text which has one meaning to a reader in one time and place can mean something else entirely to a different reader in another time and place. Also, what an author intended his/her text to mean can differ from the meaning drawn from it by its audience. The question, "Whose meaning is the meaning of the meaning?" needs to be borne in mind.

Having said this, and notwithstanding often absent sub-texts and contexts, meanings do have a trans-contextual ability to make themselves known, and the intentions of authors can communicate certain meanings accurately across time, place, language and culture. For example, Hamlet – a play written in English in the early seventeenth century by a middle-aged, Protestant English male is intelligible and illuminating, in Spanish translation, to a twenty-first-century young female, Catholic Spanish student.[1]

Health-warnings apart, this chapter will cite a few people and their texts – some 'ancient' and some 'contemporary' – that represent, indicate and illustrate the nature and general characteristics of the Worldview of Mainstream Islam.

Mainstream Islam: the people and the texts

The Worldview of Mainstream Islam – characterized as we have seen by an ontology of unity-in-diversity, 'serious' belief-practice consistency, the aspiration for ethical balance and moderation and, when necessary, agentic and structural change – has, of course, over its fourteen centuries of existence and development been substantiated, refined and illustrated by tens of thousands of thinkers, writers, activists and scholars. The task of selection of an indicative representation of people and texts is therefore nigh on impossible. I will therefore aim to highlight a small selection of people and texts which are

---

[1] Moreover, meanings can also be illuminated by historical research. The basic meanings of many texts can be ascertained centuries, as in the case of Anglo-Saxon or pre-Islamic Arab poetry, or even millenia after their production, as in the case of the Jewish Torah or the Bhagavad Gita.

representative of a number of the major varieties of Mainstream Islam, who are recognized as authoritative by significant numbers of Muslims today.

The Book of God – *Al-Qur'an* (the recitation)

I have already explained the theological nature and general worldview explicated by the Qur'an in Chapter 5, including its particular themes and tropes. I have indicated that, and how, the Qur'an in its General verses mandates the essential unity of humankind as creatures of God with real, though secondary, differences of ethnicity, faith, language and gender and, indeed, differences of wealth and class.

We have discovered that its core theological doctrine – the doctrine of *Tawhid* which states the Unity of God in his Names, Attributes and Essence – is at the heart of Islam and obliges the concomitant monotheistic worship of God without partners. This is coupled by an ethic of universal human well-being brought about and protected by justice and the rule of law.

Although the entirety of the Qur'an, taken as a whole, is considered by Mainstream Muslims to delineate the nature of the Divine-human covenant (*deen*), there are some Qur'anic chapters and verses that are considered to characterize the nature of God and His relationship with humanity with particular power, clarity and importance in terms of the daily matter of the Muslim religious transaction (*deen*).

The Opening Chapter (*Al-Fatiha*)

The first of these chapters is Chapter One, *Al-Fatiha*. *Al-Fatiha* means 'The Opening Chapter'. This is the first chapter of the Qur'an, which Muslims recite in every cycle (*raka'*) of the Obligatory Prayer so that observant Muslims will recite it at least 19 times per day.

In a similar way that the Lord's Prayer in Christianity can be considered to sum up the entirety of the Christian's basic relationship with God, *Al-Fatiha* delineates the basic contours of the Muslim's relationship with God. The Opening Chapter was described by the Prophet Muhammad as the 'Greatest Chapter' and was also referred to by him as the 'Mother of the Qur'an' (*Umm al-Qur'an*).[2] In other words, the Opening Chapter gives thematic birth to the rest of the Qur'an. The Opening Chapter runs:

1   *In the name of God, the Generally Compassionate, the Intensely Merciful*
2   *Praise belongs to God, Lord of All the Worlds;*
3   *The Generally Compassionate, the Intensely Merciful;*
4   *King of the Day of Reckoning;*
5   *You alone we worship; And to You alone we appeal for help;*
6   *Guide us on the Straight Path;*
7   *The Path of those whom you have blessed, not of those who have incurred your anger; nor of those who have gone astray.*

2   Bin Baz, *Explanation of Important Lessons (for Every Muslim)*.

The meanings of Al-Fatiha

Al-Fatiha starts:

Verse 1: *Bismillahi Rahman, ir-rahim*

"In the name of God, the Generally Merciful, the Intensely Merciful"

The names of God, *Ar-rahman* and *ar-rahim* being intensive forms of the root verb R-H-M to be merciful. These are the names by which God characterizes Himself most regularly and which Muslims repeat, not only in order to recite the Qur'an but also to sanctify everyday actions such as eating food, performing a task at work and marital sexual relations.

Verse 2: *Al-hamdulillahi Rabbil 'Alameen*

"Praise belongs to God, Lord of All the Worlds"

The basic characteristic of the entirety of the created Universe (All the Worlds) according to *Al-Fatiha* is to render praise to the Praiseworthy One (Al-Mahmud[3]) – God – whose character in return is to be Lord. The Arabic word *Rabb*, translated as 'Lord', as well as meaning a 'Master who is to be obeyed', has connotations of a Nurturer and Protector since it is derived from a verb meaning to protect, nurture and educate.[4] This idea of God as the Nurturer fits with His description of Himself as Merciful as in the nurturing of a womb (See Chapter 4).[5]

"All the Worlds" has in mainstream classical Islamic commentaries been said to refer to the worlds of the Earth and the Seven Heavens, the worlds of four communities – human beings, Jinn (invisible beings of smokeless fire), Angels and Devils – and even in some more rationalist commentaries (e.g. the commentary of Fakhr al-Deen al-Razi (1150–1210 CE) refer to the worlds – both seen and unseen – that God may choose or not choose to realize. This reference to the Angels and *Jinn* as unseen creatures identifies Islam as having an 'enchanted'[6] ontology, and belief in the existence of Unseen Realms – which in modern parlance includes sub-molecular worlds – is axiomatic to basic Islamic belief (Qur'an 2:3).

The aggregate force of these meanings given in the mainstream commentaries is that God is Sovereign Master of everything that is, has been, will or possibly could be. All being exists, either knowingly (as in the case with human beings) or unknowingly (as in the case with other created matter), voluntarily (as in

---

3 Qurtubi cited in Nasr et al., *The Study Qur'an*.
4 Ibid.
5 The notion of Rabbabiya – Lordship – has been developed by the contemporary commentator Tariq Ramadan into the notion of God as the Ultimate Educator since the Arabic word for education – Tarbiyya – is also derived from this root.
6 Taylor, *A Secular Age*.

the case with human beings) or involuntarily (as is the case with Angels) in a condition of the praise of God.

Verse 3: *Ar-rahman, ir-rahim*

"The Generally Merciful, the Intensely Merciful"

Ar-rahman is said by commentators to refer to the Generally Merciful character of God in His bestowing on all creatures their very existence. The name *Ar-Rahim*, another intensive nominal form of the verb 'to be merciful', is said to refer to the more particular Mercy of God in sustaining creatures according to their needs and bestowing other particular blessings on account of His other names of Mercy, such as the Subtly Aware (*Al-Latif*) and the Clement (*Al-Halim*).[7] These two names are the names of God that precede every single chapter of the Qur'an except one – *Al-Tawba* (Repentance, 9).

Verse 4: *Maliki Yawm i-deen*

"King (or Master) of the Day of Judgment"

It is foundational to Islam that all human beings will account for their actions in this world before God on a universal Day of Reckoning or Judgment when each soul will be presented with the Balance of our Good and Bad deeds and judged by God accordingly. There are two slight variants of this verse – either *Måliki Yawm iDeen* with the elongated *Alif* (a) meaning "Owner of the Day of Judgment" or *Maliki Yawm iDeen* the shortened a-sound meaning "King of the Day of Judgment". Both these variants can be traced to Muhammad and both indicate the complete Sovereignty of God over the destination of the human soul after the death.[8]

Verse 5: *Iyyaka Na'budu*

"You alone we worship"

This verse is a statement using the emphatic form of the Arabic for 'You' – *Iyyaka* – to express the uncompromising monotheism of Islam and the reality of the fact that *only* God is worthy of worship, as His name *Allah* – the One Worthy

---

7 Abdul-Rahman, *The Meaning and Explanation of the Glorious Qur'an* (Vol 9).
8 Mainstream Muslims believe in the reality of Heaven – called The Garden (*Al-Janna*) – and Hell – called The Fire (*An-Nar*). They also believe that God alone has the power and knowledge to consign a person either to one or the other and, according to the *Sunna*, only the most heinous wrong-doers will be confined eternally to Hell. The nature of eternity and the Next Life (*Akhira*) is of course unknown to us in the time-space reality of this World (*Dunya*).

of Worship – suggests. This practical commitment to the doctrine of *Tawhid* (Divine Unity) is sometimes called *Tawhid al-ululiyya* (the Oneness of Worship).

The fact that God expresses Himself using the second person 'You' pronoun is suggestive of the direct I-You nature of the relationship between God and the human being which does not require any priestly intermediary.

Wa Iyyaka Nasta'een

"And to You alone we appeal for help"

Again, the emphatic form of 'You' – *Iyyaka* – is used to express the reality that, ultimately, only God Almighty can hinder or help the human being and that secondary causes of help or hindrance are merely effecting the Ultimate Cause of His Will. It is also another expression of worship in the recognition of God's Ultimate and All-compassing Power over human affairs.

Verse 6: *Ihdina Sirat al-Mustaqeem*

"Guide us on the Straight Path".

This is recognition of a theme that is repeated throughout the Qur'an that God guides to the Path of Righteousness only those whom He wills and that, ultimately, guidance or its opposite is the preserve of God.[9]

The 'Straight Path' is interpreted by commentators not only as the Path with no moral crookedness or corruption, but also, crucially as we saw in Chapter 3, as the Middle Path between two possible extremes.[10] The Straight Path is the Path at the mid-point between indulgence and asceticism; it is the Path at the mid-point between excessive wealth and extreme poverty; it is the Path at the mid-point between ostentatious behavior and self-neglect; it is a Path at the mid-point between endless acts of worship and total neglect of God. The ethos of the Middle Path means that 'moderation' is not a 'nice-to-have' in Mainstream Islam; it is intrinsic to the essence of the Qur'anic message.

Verse 7: *Sirat al-dhina an'amta 'alayhim*

"The Path of Those whom you have blessed"

Moreover, the Straight Path is the Path traveled throughout history by the righteous. These are considered to be the Prophets, the Messengers, the true Martyrs and the Righteous, those who uphold and defend God's Law, and those who are endowed with virtuous moral characteristics such as truthfulness, kindness to God's creatures and just action.

---

9 Qur'an 24:46; 35:8; 28:56 etc.
10 Michot, *Ibn Taymiyya*.

Ghayr al-mughdubi 'alayhim

"Not of those who have incurred Your anger"

Islam posits the possibility that the actions of the human being, including actions fueled by unbelief, unkindness, hypocrisy, jealousy and vicious attitudes, may anger God and that those who persist in these activities or attitudes may tread a Path that earns God's perpetual displeasure. Nevertheless, it is also axiomatic to Islam that sincere repentance – that is to say asking God's forgiveness, coupled with a determination not to repeat the wrong action and to return to obedience – is always acceptable to God.[11,12]

Wa la Daleen

"Nor of those who have gone astray"

It is also possible to stray permanently from the Straight Path of virtuous, God-fearing action through persistent misdeeds or persistent neglect of recognition of God and the ethical imperatives that He places on humanity for leading the Good Life.[13]

Therefore, similar to the Lord's Prayer, the Opening Chapter either directly alludes to or implicitly suggests the entirety of the human's covenantal relationship with God in the cosmological circumstances of Divine Unity (*Tawhid*).

It describes the key elements of the nature of God as Singular, Uniquely Worthy of Worship, Absolutely and Intensely Merciful, Absolutely Powerful, Supreme Judge and Lord of All Existence, both actual and potential, and the nature of human beings as worshipful of Him alone and absolutely dependent on Him alone for life, sustenance, guidance and repeated forgiveness.

Thus, it describes the basic spiritual conditions in which the human being dwells in the world in a covenantal *I-You* relationship with his/her Creator that are elaborated throughout the text of the Qur'an and of which this Opening Chapter is both introduction and summation.

Other seminal chapters

Others of the many chapters of the Qur'an that articulate the foundational doctrinal elements of Mainstream Islam and that are loved by Muslims and

---

11 Qur'an 24:31; 66:8; 2:222; 4:17–18 etc.
12 According to some commentators, those with God's anger upon them refers to the Jews in that they habitually ignored and, indeed, killed their Prophets, although this is not a majority position. Nasr et al., *The Study Qur'an*.
13 Some commentators say that 'those who have gone astray refers to the Christians' in their setting up partners in the Trinity to worship alongside God, although this is not the majority position. Nasr et al, *The Study Qur'an*.

138 *Mainstream Islam: the people, texts and contexts*

seminal to the life of the Muslim believer include the Chapter of Sincerity (112) and the Verse of the Throne (2:255).

The Chapter of Sincerity (Surat al-Ikhlas)

The Chapter of Sincerity (Surat al-Ikhlas) translates as:

> *Say [Muhammad]: He, God is Absolutely Singular; God is eternally Self-sufficient; He did not give birth; nor was He begotten and there is nothing like Him.*

The Prophet Muhammad described this chapter as being equivalent in a spiritual value to one third of the whole Qur'an. It was described by the commentator Al-Razi as the pearl of the Qur'an. Like the Opening Chapter, it is a statement of uncompromising and primarily transcendent monotheism (*Tawhid*) and has the obvious effect of distancing Islamic Abrahamic beliefs from Christian doctrines of the incarnation of Jesus, literally, as the Son of God and non-Abrahamic doctrines of incarnation, as well as from idol-worship.[14]

The Verse of the Throne (Ayat al-Kursi)

God Almighty as transcendent and without partner

The Verse of the Throne (*Ayat al-Kursi* [2:255]) is another verse that delineates succinctly the essence of the difference between Creator and creature as understood in traditional Islamic monotheism (*Tawhid*). Its Arabic cadences and rhythm are often particularly pleasing to Muslims, and it typically adorns the walls of both living rooms and mosques.

> *God: there is no god but Him, the Ever Living, the Ever Watchful. Neither slumber nor sleep overtakes Him. All that is in the heavens and in the earth belongs to Him. Who is there who can intercede with Him except by His leave? He knows what lies before them and what is behind them, but they do not comprehend any of his knowledge except what He wills. His throne extends over the heavens and the earth; it does not weary Him to preserve them both. He is the Most High, the Tremendous.*

The verse declares the absolute transcendent difference between the Creator and the creature in that God, the Creator, does not share the characteristic of all sentient life, namely the need for sleep. Everything belongs to God; everything is determined by God; everything is known by God; and all knowledge is His only to be shared amongst humanity by His Leave. Likewise, admission to the Presence of His Majesty to ask for favors only occurs by His Leave.[15]

---

14 Nasr et al., *The Study Quran*.
15 In traditional Islam, following this verse and the sayings of Muhammad related to it, intercession with God is only granted to Prophets (*anbiyya*), the genuine martyrs for the

God Almighty as immanent and intimately aware

Seminal Qur'anic verses such as these substantiate the highly theocentric cosmology of Mainstream Islam. They describe the nature of God as Merciful, but also as predominantly Transcendent whose Presence is hard to access.

Nevertheless, other Qur'anic verses, which also describe the human-Divine Covenant (*deen*) within the basic terms of *Tawhid*, delineate the relationship between God and humanity in immanent and even intimate terms. These intimate verses indicate the immanence and presence of God and the accessibility of God's Mercy to His creatures. They include, for example, 2:186:

> And when My servants ask you about Me, [O Muhammad] – I am indeed near. I respond to those who call upon Me. So let them respond to Me and believe in Me that they may be guided.

This immanence of God and His intimate knowledge of and caring for His creatures is reflected in many of the repeated refrains of the Qur'an such as:

> Surely He is intimately aware of what is in human hearts[16]

and

> Surely He is All-Knowing and Subtly Aware[17]

Part of the persistence of Mainstream Islam as the faith of a fifth of humanity is surely accounted for by the fact that, for Mainstream Muslims, this Living and Knowing Presence of God as described in Qur'an is believed to be the most important active ingredient of their daily lived reality.

Commentaries on the Qur'an

The practice of giving interpretations of the Qur'an, such as my previous synthesis of commentaries on The Opening Chapter, can be traced back to the Prophet Muhammad himself who provided illustrations and clarifications of the verses of the Qur'an as they were revealed to him. The Qur'an informed the Prophet Muhammad's behavior to such a degree that he was described by his wife Aisha bint Abi Bakr (613–678 CE) as "the Qur'an in motion." In others words, as we have seen, the

---

faith of Islam (*shuhada*) and in some Sufi and Shia schools of thought, to those whose lives have been devoted to the worship of God, i.e. Saints, who in traditional Islam are called the 'Friends of God' (*Awliyya*). This latter possibility is strictly in the understanding, traditionally speaking, that it is only God who can effect the results of intercession in either Earth or Heaven.

16 Qur'an 42:24.
17 Qur'an 49:13.

Customary Behavior (*Sunna*) of the Prophet Muhammad illustrated the spirit and meanings of the Qur'an.

After the Prophet Muhammad's death, some of his Companions such as Abdullah ibn Abbas gained a reputation as explicators of the Qur'an and within a hundred years of the death of the Prophet Muhammad a class of scholar who were professional commentators (*mufassirun*) had arisen.

These scholars were necessary. While the meanings of much of the Qur'an are clear (the verses whose interpretations are obvious are called *qati'*), other verses are obscure (*zani'*) and require explaining and unpacking, often by the addition or insertion of words by commentators in order to complete their meanings (See Chapter 4).

These scholars were authorized exegetes, such as the great Al-Razi (d.1209 CE), Ibn Kathir (d.1373 CE), Al-Baydawi (d.1389 CE) and Al-Suyuti (d.1505 CE), whose qualifications, apart from a compendious knowledge of the Arabic language, included having memorized the text of the Qur'an. This was necessary so that they were able to comment on the Qur'an through the Qur'an itself and with reference to the *whole* of the Qur'an and the spirit of the Qur'anic message taken as a *whole*. This holistic approach was considered a bulwark against going to extremes and to literalism.

The existence over the centuries of a diverse range of commentators on the Qur'an gives the lie to the stereotype promoted by Islamists and Islamist Extremists that Islam is a pre-packaged God-made religion that has dropped from Heaven for humans to like or lump. Like any Worldview, Mainstream Islam, even if its source is in God, is mediated and interpreted by time-bound, limited and positioned humanity and therefore requires constant refreshing and updating according to the dictates of the times. Qur'anic commentary has formed an important part of that process of connecting eternal revealed principles with contingent, time-bound circumstances.

The canonical books of hadith

In Chapter 4, I have described the pivotal role of the Customary Behavior (*Sunna*) of Muhammad in determining Islamic practice, etiquette and law and how the *Sunna* has been recorded in and derived from the *hadith* material – the authenticated spoken events of Muhammad with his Companions. I refer the reader to pages 83–86.

The great works of Law (*Fiqh*), Jurisprudence (*Usul al-Fiqh*)

The development of law in the first three centuries of Islam, prompted, as I have suggested in Chapter 3, by the absence of the Prophet Muhammad and the need to address circumstances that had not happened during his lifetime, gave rise to many Schools of Law, which spread with their different jurisprudential flavors, tools and emphases across the Islamic world. These schools left copious texts of jurisprudence which harked back to the seminal texts of their eponymous founders – Malik ibn Anas, Ahmed Abu Hanifa, Muhammad Idris Ash-Shafi, Ahmad ibn Hanbal and Jafar as-Sadiq – who had taken responsibility for the formulation of a proto-legal understanding of the Prophetic message gleaned usually from reports of the followers (*tabi'in*) of the Companions of Muhammad.

The Maliki school arose as a commentary on the work The Well-Trodden Path (*Al-Muwatta*) by the Imam of Medina, Malik ibn Anas (711–795 CE). This work set the format for all classical books of law by dividing the sections of hadiths, both of the Prophet Muhammad and his Companions, and the legal judgments related to them into thematic legal sections on:

- Purity, mainly concerned with minor ablution (*wudu'*) and major ablution (*ghusl*) before prayer and the circumstances that break the state of ritual purity
- Prayer, when and how to perform it, including the more unusual Prayers such as the 'Eid Prayers, the Funeral Prayer and the Fear Prayer
- Poor Tax (*Zakat*)
- Hajj
- Warfare, in which its principles and practices began to be codified into established ethical-legal parameters
- Marriage
- Divorce
- Oaths
- Renting of Land
- Wills and Testaments

And so on.

In other words, *Al-Muwatta* laid out the basis of an entire Prophetically inspired jurisprudence and the basis for different specialisms of legal activity. It also articulated the important principle that the message of Islam was transmitted through the behavior of the Prophet Muhammad *and* his Companions – *Amal* – and that the principle of public good (*masala marsala*) lay at the heart of the Muhammadan message.

Al-Muwatta and the spread of pupils of Malik and his followers out of Medina led to the development of the other Schools of Law, each with their own jurisprudential flavors, tools and traditions.

Prominent among these, as we have seen, was the Hanafi School which established itself around the teaching of Abu Hanifa al-Numān ibn Thābit (699–767 CE) in Kufa in Iraq. The circumstances of Abu Hanifa were new. He lived at a long distance from Medina and the behavior (*amal*) of its inhabitants. Abu Hanifa also lived in a period in which Prophetic sayings were being fabricated *en masse* to justify the claims to authority of various rival Umayyad and The Party of Ali's political factions[18] (see Chapter 2). In these circumstances of the increasing unreliability of Prophetic *hadith*, Abu Hanifa advocated making analogous legal judgments (*qiyas*) using the dictates of reason by identifying shared legal causes for the promotion of the general interest (*istishan*) where no direct ruling could be found in the Qur'an or in authenticated Prophetic sayings.[19]

Although Abu Hanifa himself produced no written text of undisputed authorship, his book (possibly written by him or by students inspired by him) called *The Greatest Understanding* (*Al-Fiqh al-Akbar*) represents a sophisticated early codification of orthodox Islamic belief (*aqeeda*) and of the doctrines of the Unity of God (*Tawhid*) in a systematically theological way.

Importantly, in a Section called 'The Effects of Sin on a Person', Abu Hanifa comprehensively refutes the idea propagated by the *Khawarij* (see Chapter 2), as it is propagated by Islamist Extremists today, that sin (*dhanb; fisq* etc.), even grave sin, takes the believer outside the pale of Islam and restates the principle of the sanctity of the life of the Muslim believer using examples from the Customary Behavior (*Sunna*) of the Prophet Muhammad and his Companions. This shows how the early jurists were responding to the contextual issues of their day in their struggle to preserve and transmit the spirit as well as the letter of the Qur'anic and Muhammadan message.

Other seminal texts of the early period of the Schools of Law include 'The Book of the Communication on the Foundations of Legal Understanding' (*Kitab ar-Risala fiy Usul al-Fiqh*) usually known simply as Ar-Risala of Muhammad ibn Idris Ash-Shafi who studied with both Malik and Abu Hanifa. This text is considered by many[20] to be the most important work of Islamic jurisprudence because, in its efforts to synthesize and harmonize the methods of the Hanafi and Maliki Schools, Ash-Shafi articulated in this book three principles that have been absorbed into all Schools of Islamic jurisprudence:

1   The legal parity of the Sunna (Customary Behavior) of the Prophet Muhammad with the Revelation of the Qur'an;
2   A clear explication of the differences for the derivation of Law between the General (*Am*) and the Particular (*Khass*) verses of the Qur'an and the *Sunna*, as well as those verses and traditions which contain elements of both; and
3   An articulation of the principles of the Abrogated and Abrogating Verses of the Qur'an for the derivation of Law.

The influence of the *Risala* of Ash-Shafi is so seminal that when Mainstream Muslims of all denominational persuasions say that a Muslim must follow the

---

18   Brown, *Misquoting Muhammad*.
19   For example, since the Prophet Muhammad had not allowed the hand of the thief to be amputated for the theft of fruit because it was perishable, Abu Hanifa extended this ruling to the theft of all foodstuffs.
20   Kamali, *Principles of Islamic Jurisprudence*.

Qur'an and the *Sunna* taken together, they reveal their indebtedness to the *Risala* of Muhammad Idris Ash-Shafi. To some extent, therefore, all Sunni Muslim Schools of Law are, to some degree, Shafi'ite while retaining their own particular flavors and rulings. In this distinction of establishing the core legal framework of Mainstream Islam, Shia Muslims can also claim a share, since some of the jurisprudential roots of Ash-Shafi can be sourced in the teachings of the seminal Imam of Shia Islam, Jafar al-Sadiq, whose written teachings have otherwise been lost.[21]

We have already covered the fact, in Chapter 2, that some *Ulema*, especially scholars teaching without regular access to the emerging centers of jurisprudential development and scholarship such as Kufa and Cairo, lost trust with the plethora of jurisprudential tools being developed to derive and apply the *Sharia*. These scholars wanted a return to the simpler, more literal message that was closer in their eyes to the Islam of the *Salaf* – the pious three generations following the Prophet Muhammad.

Foremost among those whose tradition was to become the Salafi strand of Islam was the jurist Ahmed ibn Hanbal (780–855 CE) whose *Musnad* contained 27,700 narrations of *hadith* distilled, it is said, from 750,000 transmissions. These *hadith* cover every aspect of the believer's life, usually with multiple narrations around single events, in an effort to eradicate every scholarly error from the transmission of the Islam of the Prophet Muhammad and the *Salaf*. As Ibn Hanbal himself put it, "A flawed hadith is preferable to me than a scholar's opinion or an act of legal analogy (*qiyas*)."[22,23]

The Wahhabi reformation: the Book of Divine Unity (*Kitab al-Tawhid*)

This impulse to a literalist purity and to homogenous good Islamic practice through the eradication of 'impure' accretions to Islam, i.e. the Salafi project, came to a head a thousand years after Ahmad ibn Hanbal in the eighteenth century at the hands of a Najdi scholar from the North of the Arabian Peninsula called Muhammad ibn Abdal Wahhab (1703–1792 CE).

Ibn Abdal Wahhab was educated initially by his father, the Hanbali scholar, Abdal Wahhab, in the austere traditionalism of the Hanbali School. Ibn Abdal Wahhab was scandalized by some of the religious practices he encountered on the Arabian Peninsula, such as asking the intercession of Saints (*Awliya*) and even regarding objects as having mysterious power. Ibn Abdal Wahhab believed that these anomalies had stemmed from Ottoman-Hanafi hegemony over the

---

21 Salahi, *Pioneers of Islamic Scholarship*.
22 Abu Talib al-Makki, Qut al-qulub, 1:177.
23 However, as Brown (2014) has pointed out, his total reliance on *hadith* that were occasionally of dubious quality led to some strange legal opinions, such as allowing the Friday Prayer to be held in the mid-morning as opposed to when the sun passes its zenith. We have already seen in Chapter 2 (pp. 43–45) how this exclusive reliance of *hadiths* opened the door to literalists' interpretations of the Qur'an and the *Sunna*.

Sunni Muslim world and that they were religious innovations (*bida*) that had infected the purity of the Absolute Monotheism (*Tawhid*) of Original *Salafi* Islam.

In his seminal and revolutionary book 'The Book of Divine Unity' (*Kitab al-Tawhid*), Ibn Abdal Wahhab made copious use of hadiths, as a good Hanbalite, and Verses of Qur'an to restate the necessity and virtue of pure monotheistic Islamic belief in the Absolute Singularity of God (*Tawhid*) and highlighted the vices of practice and character that emanate from associating partners of God (*shirk*) and innovating religious practices (*bida*).

This teaching was accompanied with active protest in the Unayna Province of what is now Saudi Arabia, such as his calling for the destruction of venerated tombs of Saints (*'Awliya*) and the cutting down of supposedly sacred trees, that brought him vilification and expulsion by the rulers of that Province.

His active protest also brought him to the attention leader of the ruling tribe of the Province of Diriyah, Muhammad ibn Saud (1710–1765 CE). At a famous and seminally important meeting between the two men, Ibn Abdal Wahhab and Al-Saud entered into a religious-political pact that Al-Saud would combat the practices of the Ottoman regime that he regarded as idolatrous through political and military action and Ibn Al-Wahhab would support and substantiate his cause theologically. This Agreement of Diriyah (1744) became, and remains, the basis of the Saudi State and the *Wahhabi* strain of Salafi Islam that dominates the world of mainstream Sunni Islam today.

The Book of Divine Unity has been commentated upon and commentaries made of the commentaries, and so it remains one of the most influential source books of Mainstream Salafi Islam, calling as it does for a radical return to core Islamic monotheistic values and practices and (at the same time) mandating a shunning of those practices that detract or give lie to the Absolute Unity and Power of God.

Islam has already had its reformation

It needs to be noted, therefore, that although mainstream Wahhabi Islam today looks like conservative Islam in its obliging of long beards, robes (*thawab*) of a certain (shortened) length and a strict application of a literalist version of the Islamic penal code (*hudud*) and is often referred to as conservative or traditional Islam by the media, it is, in fact, radically *reformed* Hanbali Islam.[24]

---

24 Those commentators, both Muslim and ex-Muslim, who call for an Islamic Reformation seem oblivious to the fact that Islam has already had at least one Reformation – the Wahhabi Salafi Reformation. Moreover, it was, in essence, remarkably similar to the Protestant Reformation of Martin Luther and John Calvin in that it called for a return to the basic, scripturally determined essentials of the founder's faith, stripped of what were regarded as corrupt religious practices. Those who call for reform, if they call for anything, should, to my mind, be calling for the restoration, observation and prioritization of core Islamic principles and practices interpreted in light of novel contexts, which is not a reforming activity but a traditional Islamic activity done in a way that befits novel circumstances.

In addition to its inherent religious power, with the determined political backing by the Saudi regime of the Salafi-Wahhabi message, the collapse of Hanafi Ottoman Islam and the discovery of vast oil reserves in Arabia in the twentieth century, the doctrinal language of mainstream Wahhabism:

1   the different varieties of the doctrine of the Unity of God (*Tawhid*);
2   identifying and avoiding forms of religious innovation (*bida*); and
3   the detailed elaboration of what constitutes both *shirk* – associating partners with God

has become the dominant religious currency of mainstream Sunni Islam today.[25,26]

If the Wahhabi reforming impulse was to strip Islam down to what Muhammad ibn Abdal Wahhab and his followers regarded as its bare doctrinal and practical essentials, other famous Muslims throughout Islam's intellectual history have taken different routes to ensure the revival and survival of Mainstream Islam – all of them, like Muhammad ibn Abdal Wahhab, were both products of and agents of change in the context of their times.

To philosophize or not to philosophize? Al-Ghazali vs. Ibn Rushd

Most famous of these agents of Islamic revival are two scholars, who as were alluded to in Chapter 2, have become synonymous with the battle for the soul of Islam between traditionalism and rationalism.

These two scholars were

1   Abu Hamid Muhammad ibn Muhammad al-Ghazali (1058–1111 CE); and
2   Abu al-Walid ibn Rushd (1126–1198 CE).

---

25 Within the Worldview of many Salafi Muslims, for example *Albani* and *Madkhali* Salafi Muslims, these doctrines tend to retain the flavor and relatively moderate application that are suggested by their original sources. However, all of the above (see Chapter 3) have been co-opted in extreme ways by Non-Violent and Violent Islamist Extremists.
26 The undoubted piety and 'good' Islam of many Wahhabi-Salafi Muslims and its propagation by the Saudi state, have conferred many benefits on the Muslim world in terms of the preservation of Islam in a secularizing environment. However, methodologically the *Hanbalite-Wahhabite* demotion of the tools of legal reasoning and extreme elevation of the value of literal sayings has left the Muslim-majority world relatively bereft in terms of responding to the rationalized, secularized conditions of modernity and vulnerable to the Worldviews of Islamist Extremists. This literalism has, for example, generated the concept of short-Earth creationism and denial of some of the basic findings of natural science, such as the heliocentric nature of the universe. These attitudes render some Muslims open to the charge of anti-scientific religious fundamentalism that is more typical of some strains of evangelical Protestant Christianity than it is of classical, Mainstream Islam.

The first, known simply as Al-Ghazali and as Algazelus or Algazel in the Latin medieval world, was a Persian polymath – an adept of theology (*kalam*), Law (*fiqh*), philosophy (*falsafa*) and the science of inner purification (*tasawuf*), also known as Sufism.

Al-Ghazali has been referred to by some historians as the single most influential Muslim after the Prophet Muhammad. Within Islamic civilization he is considered to be a Reviver of the Faith (*Mujaddid*), who, according to tradition, appears once every century to restore the faith of the community. His works were so highly acclaimed by his contemporaries that Al-Ghazali was awarded the honorific title "Proof of Islam" (*Hujjat al-Islam*).

Al-Ghazali's career was shaped in 1095 CE by what we might call a nervous breakdown. This happened when he was at the zenith of his intellectual and political powers as the Dean of the *Nizamiyya* university in Abbasid Baghdad. He abandoned his glittering career as the darling of the Abbasid Vizier Nizam al-Mulk (1018–1092 CE) (who was later assassinated by the VIE Ismaili sect, the Assassins) and left Baghdad on the pretext of going on pilgrimage to Mecca, subsequently traveling to visit various of the teachers of *tasawwuf* (Sufism) in Jerusalem and elsewhere. He then underwent a ten-year period of spiritual seclusion and reflection in Tus in the Razavi Khorasan Province of modern Iran during which time he wrote his influential, revivalist text *The Revival of the Religious Sciences* (*Ihya' Ulum al-Din*).

Al-Ghazali's compendious work is laden with a dazzling array of spiritual insights about the nature of the good life and how to attain the Next World, such as a much-loved and still-read systematic theology of the duties of Islamic brotherhood. Nevertheless, in the round, Al-Ghazali left two lasting 'Big Picture' theological legacies.

First, he left a legacy of understanding that for the outward sciences and applications of the law (*Sharia*) and the science of theology (*kalam*) to be meaningful and useful, they needed to be reconnected with the third element of the Islamic rubric – inward sincerity (*ihsan*) – and the sciences of drawing close to the Presence of God. To this end, in *The Revival of the Religious Sciences*, he reintegrated the inward sciences of purifying the heart (*Ihsan*) with core Islamic belief (*Iman*) and the outward practice of faith (*Islam*). In other words, he restored Sufism into the core of Mainstream Islam.

Second, and contingent upon this first *raison d'être* of his work, Al-Ghazali opposed the rational philosophers (*falaysaf*) such as the polymath Ibn Sina because, in his eyes, they challenged the accepted doctrinal features of Islamic orthodoxy, such as the finite nature of the created Universe, which as a *Shafi'ite* jurist Al-Ghazali could not allow. Equally importantly, Al-Ghazali, as a Sufi, believed that an exaggerated reliance on Hellenistic philosophy had stripped believers from connection to the Living God.

Al-Ghazali, who was himself a great adept of Hellenistic philosophy and prone himself to using dialectical argument, launched a withering attack from the point of view of Asharite orthodoxy (see Chapter 2) on what he regarded as the incoherence of Hellenistic philosophy's insights in his other most famous text 'The Incoherence of the Philosophers' (*Tahāfut al-Falāsifa*).

In this text, he challenged what he regarded as 17 core claims (13 metaphysical and 4 physical) of Islamic Hellenistic Rationalism as, at best, incoherent and unable to furnish the believer with basic philosophical proofs about God and the physical world, and at worst as heretical and constituting unbelief (*kufr*) in some of its claims, such as the theory of an eternal universe and that bodily resurrection will not take place in the Hereafter.

He was particularly scathing of the Neo-Platonic idea of the universe emanating from its source in God as he viewed this as reducing the role of God in the universe to the equivalent of the deistic watchmaker winding up the Universe and letting it run without further interference.

Critically, Al-Ghazali also challenged the Hellenistic idea of the independent reality of secondary causes, e.g. that fire burns flammable substances such as cotton, had predictable outcomes due to the structures of the natural universe. In an 800-year prelude to David Hume, Al-Ghazali posited natural causes as merely constant conjunctions of events acting with, not by or through, each other. God could suspend the laws of nature, insofar they were laws, at any moment as he did in the Qur'anic example of fire not consuming the Prophet Abraham. He reasserted the traditional Asharite position (see Chapter 2) that nature is only predictable in its secondary causes because God, its Primary Cause, is willing its predictability and sustaining its secondary causes as an accident of His Mercy.

Thus, Al-Ghazali has, with some justification, been accused of undermining the philosophical basis – the presumption of the reality of secondary natural causes – for the explosion of natural scientific activity in the Muslim world (c. 800–1200 CE) and for the relative[27] 'closing of the Muslim mind' post 1200 CE. His religious opposition to the need to understand secondary causes in nature was undoubtedly detrimental to the cause of Islamic natural science, although this was almost certainly an entirely unintended consequence of his enlightened and brilliant attempt to protect and revive traditional, Islamic orthodoxy.

Al-Ghazali's great opponent, at the distance of one generation, was the great Andalucian polymath – jurist, philosopher, medic and mystic – Ibn Rushd, known to the medieval Latin West as Averroes. Ibn Rushd was a Maliki judge, commentator and translator of Aristotle who in his rebuttal of Al-Ghazali entitled 'The Incoherence of the Incoherence' (*Tuhafut at-Tuhafut*), reasserted the compatibility of revealed faith with dialectical reasoning. Ibn Rushd accused the traditionalists led by Al-Ghazali, by now a hero of the orthodox Sunni Muslim world, both of misunderstanding Aristotle and the fact that Aristotle had been misrepresented by the Neo-Platonists philosophers Al-Farabi and Ibn Sina (Avicenna). He also accused Al-Ghazali of not understanding the difference between the Unambiguous (*mukhamat*) verses of Qur'an, which were closed to philosophical reasoning, and the Obscure verses (*mutashabihat*) for which the Qur'an

---

27 To the explosion of Islamic intellectual innovation between 800 and 1200 CE.

itself mandated (2:29; 7:14) the use of reflection and interpretative rationality, of which the most advanced kind was Aristotelian dialectics.

Moreover, Ibn Rushd was scathing, not so much of the reasoning behind Al-Ghazali's denial of the reality of secondary causes, but of the fact that this type of reasoning effectively consigned the created order of nature to impotence, and, by ascribing Omnipotence to God in such a direct and absolute way, stripped it of any powers or initiative of its own.[28] This was debilitating and contrary to human experience. Ibn Rushd insisted that while God created the natural law, humans "could more usefully say that fire cause cotton to burn – because creation had a pattern that they could discern."[29]

Within the world of Sunni Islam, the argument between Al-Ghazali and Ibn Rushd was undoubtedly won by Al-Ghazali, and among large swathes of the Middle East and North Africa, the Asharite position on cause and effect was confirmed and has subsequently been reaffirmed as orthodoxy.

Ironically, Ibn Rushd's Commentaries on Aristotle and his views on causality in the natural world were enthusiastically absorbed by the Latin Christian Scholastics. Along with the contributions of Ibn Sina (Avicenna) and Al-Farabi, and other Muslim philosophers, his Commentaries became the major point of access to the intellectual world of the Ancients for Latin Western scholars that from the late thirteenth century became the humanistic basis of the European Renaissance.

So important were the translations and Arabic commentaries of Aristotle and the Neo-Platonists by these Muslim scholars to European humanistic learning that a knowledge of Arabic, along with Latin and Greek, was a standard accomplishment in European universities until the seventeenth century. Moreover, Ibn Rushd's philosophical assertion of recognizable and constituent structures and predictable patterns in the natural world has become the epistemological basis for all natural and medical science.[30]

---

28 Fakhry, *Averroes*.
29 Khalidi, ed. *Medieval Islamic Philosophical Writings*, p. 162.
30 The other great book by Ibn Rushd in his capacity of a classical Maliki jurist was the compendious *Distinguished Jurist's Primer* (Bidayat al-Mujtahid), in which Ibn Rushd systematically reviews a vast array of legal opinions on traditional Maliki themes as articulated, for example, in the Al-Muwatta as listed above and explains which opinion he thinks is best for whatever reason. The *Bidayat al-Mujtahid* represents in many respects the summit of classical Islamic law in its manifestation of Ibn Rushd's ability to select and decide between a complex set of legal judgments and opinions based on the Qur'an and the *Sunna*, the full gamut of jurisprudential tools developed in the Schools of Law over centuries in conversation with the context of his own time.

In this matter of context, it is also important to remember, however, that like the primary sources of Islam itself – the Qur'an and the *Sunna/hadith* material – the great legal and theological texts of Islam are also embedded in the context of their time and represent responses to the issues of their day.

For example, the Book of *Jihad* of the *Bidayat al-Mujtahid* represents circumstances of early medieval Europe when the territories governed by Muslims and Christians on the Iberian Peninsula were both in circumstances of both regular collaboration and cross-fertilization, e.g. in the use and translation of the texts of the Ancients, and of regular limited border skirmishing

Mainstream Islam in the modern and contemporary period

The period of classical Islam (800–1200 CE) was characterized by the contextual assumption of the intellectual, cultural and, more often than not, territorial and military superiority of Islam-led civilization over Latin Christendom. The Mainstream Islamic texts of the nineteenth, then twentieth century and now, indeed, the twenty-first century have been framed by a single political-theological problem: in the face of relative non-Muslim, Judeo-Christian and now secularist political, economic and intellectual ascendency and relative Muslim political, economic and intellectual decline,[31] what does it mean to be a Muslim and to follow Islam? The thinkers and texts that populate the Worldviews that I have termed Activist Islam, Ideological Islamism, Non-Violent and Violent Islamist Extremism have all presented responses to this basic theological and existential conundrum of apparent Divine abandonment of Islam, its followers and the territories of its law that are supposed by Divine Right to be pre-eminently blessed (Qur'an 5:3).

For those thinkers who can be characterized as exponents of Activist Islam in the modern and contemporary period, the solution to this conundrum has lain primarily in Muslims turning inwards to examine the quality of their own agency and to reappraise the way that Islam is interpreted and practiced, rather than in primarily turning outwards to blame the influence of pernicious non-Muslim forces outside of Islam.

Muhammad Abduh's both-and approach

For example, the great Egyptian Activist reformer and jurist Muhammad Abduh's (1849–1905 CE) response to the Western European ascendancy and relative Muslim decline was a 'both-and' approach to Islamic doctrine and Law. As a judge and intellectual of Al-Azhar University at the time of the British Protectorate of Egypt (1882–1913), Abduh witnessed the ascendancy of European technocratic empiricism over 'enchanted' Ottoman Islam close-up. He intuited that a mature, happy and healthy response to modernity needed to harness both the

---

and warfare. Therefore, in this context, Ibn Rushd notes that while juristically the categories of Struggle (Jihad) listed previously – of the heart, of the tongue, of the hand and of the sword – are most representative of the full gamut of the Islamic doctrine of Struggle for God (*Jihad*), the common man most normally thinks of *Jihad* as *Jihad* of the Sword.

These circumstances of warful coexistence in faith-based Spain are radically different from those of the contemporary period of International Treaties, Human Rights agreements and multinational trade and cooperation. This is why it is so important that the Islamic legal tradition remains a *living* tradition and also why the atrophy of the Islamic Schools of Law as living institutions of jurisprudence has been so detrimental to the spiritual and legal health of the Umma (global community) of Islam.

31 Most obviously represented by the collapse of the Ottoman Muslim Empire and abolition of the Islamic Caliphate in 1924.

progress and benefits of natural science and the values and virtues of faith. He also believed that the Islamic tradition with its mandate of seeking knowledge of all types and a centuries-old tradition of integrating natural science into the intellectual environment of faith was ideally positioned to take up the challenges of the post-Darwinian age.

Abduh took an inwards-out approach in that, although he was at times highly critical of Western Christianity, European colonialism and its materialism, he looked for both the causes and remedies for Muslim decline in the human agency and behavior of individual Muslims and in the intellectual procedures for determining law which meant that Islam had become stuck, quite unnecessarily, in the past.

In his Treatise on the Unity of God (*Risalat at-Tawhid*), Abduh takes a holistic and integrated view of humanity's spiritual, intellectual and emotional faculties, all of which have a place in determining the human being's trajectory in a divinely ordained universe. According to Abduh, human reason and Divine Revelation cannot, in principle, be in contradiction since God is the source of both. If there is an apparent contradiction between the findings of science and the descriptions and prescriptions of religion, then either one or the other has been misunderstood. Similarly, reason and the emotions or temperament are both, according to Abduh, "eyes" of the spirit which need to work in conjunction with each other in the apprehension of spiritual and temporal truth.

For Abduh "*religion may be counted the true friend of science, a stimulus for inquiry into the secrets of the universe and an appeal to respect established truths and rely upon them in cultivating our spirits and reforming our actions. All of this I have considered to be a single matter.*"[32]

In this phrase and in the title of *The Treatise on the Unity of God* we can observe in Muhammad Abduh's Worldview both strong echoes of Muslim Hellenistic philosophers' belief in the Unity of Truth (see Chapter 2) and a pragmatic and almost psychological approach to traditional Islamic conundrums such as the relationship between divine predestination and human free will. These are similar in feel to the existential approaches to Christianity pioneered by Søren Kierkegaard (1813–1855 CE) and picked up by the existentialist German theologian, Paul Tillich (1886–1965 CE). Abduh's approach is characteristically modern in its overt recognition that it is the whole human person that is engaged in the Divine-human transaction.

This modern existentialist approach is evidenced, for example, in Abduh's resolution of the apparent contradiction between Divine Omniscience and Predestination and the necessity for human free will and accountability that, as we have seen in Chapter 2, had baffled and been politicized in the Muslim-majority world since the struggles between the *Jabirites* and the *Qadirites* in the eighth century. Abduh takes a 'both-and' approach based upon both traditional Qur'anic teaching and the human experience of being-in-the-world.

---

32 Cited in Kerr, Islamic Reform, p. 108.

Abduh argues that, just as the Qur'an stipulates, we naturally apprehend that human beings freely will and are responsible for what we do on a choice-by-choice basis. Nevertheless, our free choices are also shaped by the "*natural disposition [to apprehend] that the human will is but one of the links of the chains [of causality]. Will itself is an effect of perception, which stems from sensory feelings; ultimately, all is to be traced back to the Supreme Being.*"[33]

Thus, human beings act freely under the circumstances of "an instinctive recognition" that all acts are ultimately attributable to God.[34]

Muhammad Abduh's intellectual and spiritual efforts (*jihad*) to integrate the spirit of Islam, including belief in the primacy of Divine Revelation, with the spirit of modern empirical scientific rationalism based on identifiable cause and effect can also be seen most clearly in his equation of the traditional notion of the Custom of God (*Sunnat Allah*) in ordering His Universe with the natural scientific laws of the universe.

Traditionalist *Asharite* and *Maturidite* theology, as we have seen, had taught that it was, for example, the Custom of God to raise the sun every morning and to set it every evening and that it was the Custom of God to ordain the necessary predictability of the universe for human and animal habitation. For Abduh this idea of the unchanging and predictable Custom of God was expressed by the laws of physics. He suggested that the Custom of God and the laws of physics corresponded to the same realities from different points of view. We might say that they were different epistemologies (ways of knowing) that reflected the same ontologies (ways of being).

Muhammad Abduh was advocating, therefore, 'both-and' thinking that is highly characteristic of the Worldview of Islam as unity-in-diversity and also critically realistic in its recognition of the multi-faith Egypt of his day, in which Abduh in his various legal roles advocated peace and respect between Sunni and Shia Muslims and Christian Copts. This attitude, as well as being mandated by the Qur'an as we have seen in Chapter 4, was also the expression of the same pragmatic realism of Abduh's theology that Islam as a praxis – the interpenetrated marriage of faith and behavior – is intended to serve the health and happiness of individual and collective human life in a way that respects the circumstances of the time.

The primacy of Muslim agency

For Abduh, it was pivotal to the Islamic message that every single Muslim was an agent of self-improvement through education, in which he was involved throughout his life, and through aspiring to righteous behavior. If Muslims

---

33 *Al 'Ur wal'Wuthqa*, Cairo, 1927', p. 107, cited in Kerr (1966: 113).
34 I have argued similarly elsewhere using the language of critical realist philosophy, that at the level of the empirical and the sensory we are freely responsible for our actions; at the level of the actual, we can perceive them as emanating from their source in God and at the level of the Real, they are, in reality, performed Uniquely by God (cf. Qur'an 8:17).

were in decline and the Muslim world was in a mess, it was neither because God's innate justice had departed this world, nor because Islam as a faith was not true, but because Muslims as individual human agents were not acting as responsible deputies of God and were not *doing* their Islam. Hence Abduh articulated his most famous saying:

> *I went to the West and saw Islam, but no Muslims; I got back to the East and saw Muslims, but not Islam.*

By this, he meant that the principles of Islam such as just governance, contractual agreements and the quest for innovative knowledge were more in evidence in his eyes in the West where people were clearly not religiously practicing Muslims than they were in traditionally Muslim lands.

To make his point and to the rage of some traditionalists of Al-Azhar University, he also developed the characteristically modern ideas about the necessary Stewardship (*Caliphate*) of God's creation that was the legacy of the deputyship described by the Qur'an (2:30) that we have examined as a key element of Activist Islam in Chapters 3 and 4.

While many commentators had traditionally taken this and other Qur'anic references to the Caliph to refer to the *political* succession of the Prophet Muhammad in leadership of the Muslim community, Abduh emphasized the theological role of *every* human being to be the deputy or representative of God and to act to further human health, happiness and civilization.

Abduh's views about Muslim-non-Muslim relations and his de-politicization of the idea of the Caliph at a sensitive moment in Muslim politics when the Caliphate itself in Istanbul was imperiled[35] brought Abduh many enemies and led to opposition in the form of the rise of either-or Ideological Islamist Worldviews.

Nevertheless, Abduh's 'both-and' Worldview:

1 Both natural science and revealed religion;
2 Both emotions and reason;
3 Both Muslim and part of the wider family of humanity;
4 Both rationalist modernity and enchanted spiritual tradition; and
5 Both acceptance of some of the tools of modern capital finance, which appeared to Abduh to have enabled the non-Muslim West to prosper materially and criticism of the materialism which they often engender.

has set the intellectual agenda for a diverse range of twentieth- and twenty-first-century Mainstream Islamic thinkers. These include the Kurdish revivalist scholar Said Nursi (1877–1960 CE), the Iranian philosopher Hossein Nasr (Born 1933 CE), the Egyptian exegete Muhammad Abu Zahra (1898–1974 CE) and the Pakistani liberal reformer Fazlur Rahman (1919–1988 CE).

---

35 Both by European colonial ambitions and internal Muslim political unrest.

Such Mainstream Muslim thinkers, from both the Sunni and Shia-dominated worlds, and of course many others, have built theologies based on the fundamental compatibility of natural science and revealed faith, the ideal of the Stewardship (*Calipha*) of Creation and the premise that the core principles of Islam can be interpreted to be followed authentically and provide core meaning for people who are full participants in the lived conditions of the contemporary world.[36]

---

36 For a list of some of the contemporary Basic Guides and websites that propagate these ideas from Mainstream Islam, please see Appendix 1.

6 Islamism
The people, texts and contexts

Maududi, Al-Banna and Khomeini: the Ideological Islamist shift from agency to structure

The primary locus of both religious practice and human change in Mainstream Islam, in both its Traditional and Activist forms, is the individual human agent. As we have seen in Chapters 3 and 4, in Ideological Islamism and for Ideological Islamists, as well as for Islamist Extremists, the accent of religious practice and human change shifts from individual agency to structure – state structure. Likewise, if for Muhammad Abduh, and those Activist Muslim thinkers who have followed his lead of critical reform, it was the revitalized individual Muslim as the Deputy of God (*Khalifatullah*) who was to be the agent of Islamic renewal, for the Islamists there exists only one possible remedy to the decline of the Muslim world – the establishment of the structure of a modern Islamic State.

In the subservience of the entirety of Islam to the political goal of the establishment of a modern Islamic state, the pre-eminent and first of the key Islamist thinkers, Abul Ala Maududi (1903–1979 CE) transformed the idea of Islam from a religious praxis based on the marriage of religious belief with righteous and appropriate behavior into a political ideology. Maududi believed that this Islamist political ideology would be a rival global force and deliver even greater seismic shifts in global geo-politics than those that were being effected in the early part of the twentieth century by the secular ideologies of Fascism and Communism.

Thus the language that Maududi borrowed to frame his ideologization of Islam – Islamic State, Islamic Revolution, Islamic Ideology and the religious categorization of the world as divided hermetically into the world of Islam and the world of *Kufr* (Unbelief) – were conscious borrowings from Fascism and Communism. The fascist and communist demonization of groups like 'the Bourgeoisie' and 'the Jews' became in Maududi's Islamist system the demonization of the out-groups of the *kafir* (infidel) and the *taghut* (irreligious tyrant).

If the master-narrative of Maududi's Islamist Worldview was the establishment of an Islamic State governed and functioning entirely and purely according to a pristine, revealed (and therefore fictitious) form of *Sharia* Law, then Maududi's analysis of how the Muslim world came to be in a fragmented, powerless condition was also one based heavily on the primacy of institutional structure over individual agency.

Maudaudi grew up in the context of the British Raj and participated as a journalist and then Founder of the *Jamiat e-Islami* (Party of Islam) in the deliberations and agitations of the Indian Nationalist movements. Maududi believed that Islam as a global force had been corrupted politically and legally and had been rendered 'impure' by the effects of European colonialism and by permitting the establishment of European, non-Muslim governmental and legal habits in previously 'pure' Muslim lands. Thus, in his efforts to rehabilitate ideologically the aspiration for a pure, unadulterated Islamic jurisdiction, Maududi in his sermons, speeches, pamphlets and books, e.g. *The Fundamentals of Islam*,[1] created a number of the ideological tropes that characterize Islamisms of all types today.

First, Maududi propagated the idea of the essential difference between the true political Muslim versus the impure and corrupt Infidel (*kafir*) who was part of what he regarded as a complete global System of Unbelief (*millat al-kufr*).

Brethren in Islam!

Every Muslim personally believes and you must believe alike that a Muslim's rank is higher than a kafir. God likes a Muslim and dislikes a kafir. A Muslim will get salvation from God while a kafir will not. A Muslim will go to Paradise and a Kafir will go to Hell. Today I want you to ponder on the reason why there should be so much difference between a Muslim and a Kafir.[2]

For Maududi, this fundamental difference also included the difference between the 'blessed' 'Full Muslim' and the 'Partial Muslim' who was tainted by involvement in systems and attitudes other-than-Islam which God did not intend.

If he obeys the directions of God in some matters and in others gives preference over these to selfish desires or customs or man-made laws, then he is involved in kufr to the extent that he has rebelled against the laws of God. Someone is half kafir, someone one-fourth, one-tenth or one-twentieth . . . Islam is nothing except man's exclusive subservience to God.[3]

Kinds of Muslim

Partial Muslims

One kind of Muslim are those who, having affirmed their faith in God and His Messenger, accept Islam as their religion but merely treat this religion as part of a section of their whole lives . . . Islam has suffered decay due to these people. As a result of the preponderance of such Muslims in the Muslim society, the control of the life-system of the world has passed into the hands of Kufr

---

1 Maududi, *Khutabat*.
2 Maududi Fundamentals in Islam, p. 9.
3 Ibid., p. 50.

156 *Islamism: the people, texts and contexts*

> [infidelity], *while Muslims are getting subjected to it, contented with the freedom to lead a limited religious life. God never desired to have such Muslims.*

Full Muslims

> *The second kind of Muslims are those who completely merge Islam into their full personality and their entire existence ... those Muslims who are desired by God fall into this second category.*[4]

The idea of the essential structural and moral difference of the System of Unbelief (*millat al-Kufr*) versus Islam was for Maududi played out in the incompatibility of 'non-Muslim' systems of governance, such as Monarchy and Democracy, together with those who adhere to them, with Islam. This incompatibility was coupled with the idea that it is impossible to be a fully realized Muslim without living under the jurisdiction of an Islamic State, functioning comprehensively according to a uncritically accepted, purified form of *Sharia* Law:

> *When you recite the Kalima* [utterance of faith] *la ilaha ilAllah* [there is no god except God], *it amounts to the simultaneous affirmation that the only law for you is the Law of God, your sovereign is only God, your Ruler is only God, you have to obey only God, and only that thing is true and right for you which is vouchsafed through God's Book and His Messenger. This means that you relinquished your independence in favour of God as soon as you became Muslim.*[5]

This was coupled with the notion, which, as we will see was to be strongly picked up in Egypt by the ideologue Sayyid Qutb, that entrance into Islam is an act of instant transformation, turning someone from being 'impure' to being 'pure', and providing a comprehensive, exclusive identity that trumps or eradicates all other allegiances and senses of belonging, including connection to family members:

> *On uttering these words of the Kalima, a man undergoes a remarkable transformation. From a Kafir he turns into a Muslim. He was impure, now he becomes pure. He was liable to the wrath of God; he is now beloved of God. He was destined for Hell but now the gates of Heaven are open for him. But the process does not end there. Due to this Kalima a great change takes place between man and man. Those who recite it are consolidated into one community, while those who reject it are consolidated into another community. If a father*

4 Ibid., pp. 69–70.
5 Ibid., p. 22.

recites it and the son rejects it, the father is no longer a father and the son is no longer a son.[6]

In his *The Concept of Jihad in Islam* (*Al-Jihad fiy al-Islam*),[7] Maududi explicitly expounds the idea that Jihad (Struggle in Islam) is a revolutionary force to overthrow the forces and structures that sustain the global system of Unbelief (*milla tul Kufr*) in order to impose a global, modern Islamic state.

> It must be evident to you from this discussion that the objective of the Islamic 'Jihād' is to eliminate the rule of an un-Islamic system and establish in its stead an Islamic system of state rule. Islam does not intend to confine this revolution to a single state or a few countries; the aim of Islam is to bring about a universal revolution. Although in the initial stages it is incumbent upon members of the party of Islam to carry out a revolution in the State system of the countries to which they belong, but their ultimate objective is no other than to effect a world revolution.[8]

This Islamic State, due to its ideological rather than territorial nature, was required 'by Islam' to cover the whole planet.

Maududi's basic Worldview of Islam as the comprehensive political ideology of an all-compassing state, with Jihad as the revolutionary means to accomplish it, manifested itself initially, unsurprisingly, as a political party based around the charismatic person of Maududi himself called *Jamat e-Islami* (the Islamic Party). The Islamic Party, although it has never actually gained power by itself, became, and is still, a highly effective power broker and balancer in the struggle between secular and more religious political parties that accompanied the creation of Pakistan in 1947. Echoes of Maududi's thinking can be heard even in the name Pakistan itself – meaning the Pure Land – and in some of its Islam-related legislation, such as retention of the highly controversial Blasphemy Laws inherited, somewhat ironically, from the days of the British Raj.

Maududi and his ideas of a global Islamic revolution to create a global Islamic state had been formed and mobilized as political action in the South Asian sub-continent in the maelstrom of the implosion of the British Empire and the murderous traumas of Indian Partition (1947). These traumatic and murderous civic disruptions created a social environment in which a chiastic and apocalyptic vision of the world strictly divided into the Pure vs. the Impure, the Faithful vs. Infidel, the Godly and the Godless was for many Muslims a convincing Worldview within which to make sense of a toxically divided political world.

At the same time that Maududi was calling for and mobilizing the Jamat e-Islami in India to work towards an idealized modern Islamic State, this sense of the

---

6 Ibid., p. 24.
7 Maududi, *Jihad in Islam*.
8 Ibid, p. 20.

Kafir-dominated, colonial world only being comprehensible in terms of strictly divided camps of the Pure vs. Impure, the Muslim vs. Infidel, the Partial Muslim vs. the True Comprehensive Muslim was also being mobilized, in the heartland of Arab Sunni Islam, Egypt.

In Egypt a teacher called Hassan al-Banna (1906–1949), who was from a scholarly Hanbali (see Chapter 3) and Sufi background, lived through the volatile political environment of the Egyptian Revolution against British governorship and occupation of Egypt of 1919, the Egyptian declaration of independence in 1922 and the subsequent jostling for power between the British-backed Monarchist and the Egyptian Nationalist factions.

Similar to Maududi, in his efforts to re-order ideologically a disintegrating and dangerous post-colonial political world, Al-Banna drew heavily on an Us (Muslim) vs. Them (*Kafir*) master-narrative. Al-Banna believed that the European presence in traditionally Muslim territories had been both politically oppressive and morally corrupting of the 'true' comprehensive spirit of Islam and that European 'materialism' had been responsible for the demise of Muslim lands by enslaving them to the tyranny of debt and to spiritual and moral decay. This European "Tyranny of Materialism" over Muslim lands consisted according to Al-Banna of:[9]

1. *Apostasy, doubt in God, denial of the soul, obliviousness to reward or punishment in the world to come and fixation with the material . . .*
2. *Licentiousness, unseemly dedication to pleasures, versatility in self-indulgence, unconditioned freedom for the lower instincts, gratification of the lusts of the belly and the genitals . . .*
3. *Individual selfishness . . .*
4. *Usury, granting it legal recognition . . .*

   These purely materialistic traits have produced in European society corruption of the spirit, the weakening of morality and flaccidity in the war against crime . . .[10]

According to Al-Banna:

> *The Europeans worked assiduously to enable the tide of this materialistic life, with its corrupting traits with its murderous germs, to overwhelm all the Islamic Lands toward which their hands were outstretched . . .*[11]

As a result of which:

> *We have sub-divided the Islamic countries, according the degrees to which they were affected by this materialistic civilisation and the domination of its materialism over them . . .*[12]

---

9 Al-Banna, *Five Tracts of Hassan Al-Banna (1906–1949) a Selection from the Majmu'at Rasa'il Al-Imam Al-Shahid Hasan Al-Banna*.
10 Ibid., pp. 26–27.
11 Ibid., p. 27.
12 Ibid., p. 29.

The answer for Al-Banna to the comprehensive *"demolition"* by European materialism of *"True Islam and the foundations of its culture"* lay in the comprehensive reconstitution of True Islam so that a . . .

> *free Islamic State may arise in this free fatherland, acting according to the precepts of Islam, applying its social regulations, proclaiming its sound principles and broadcasting its sage mission to all mankind . . .*[13]

Ideologically, Al-Banna, like Maududi, expressed the belief that this commitment to establish an Islamic state was itself an article and act of faith that signified the difference between the true Muslim and the partial, imperfect one, for:

> *As long as this* [Islamic] *state does not emerge, the Muslims in their totality are committing sin, and are responsible before God the Exalted for their failure to establish it and for their slackness in creating it.*[14]

In a parallel fashion to the way in which Maududi brought his ideas to bear on the lived experiences and political aspirations of Muslims through the foundation and activism of the *Jamat e-Islami* (the Islamic Party), Al-Banna applied his ideas socially by preaching in the cafés of the Suez Canal worker-districts of the canal-city of Ismayliyya in northeast Egypt. His energy, charisma and the message of emancipation from British colonialism and its material and spiritual effects won him followers among the workers, and in 1928 he founded The Society of Muslim Brothers (*Ikhwan al-Muslimeen*) according to the idea that

> *Islam is an all-embracing concept that regulates every aspect of life . . .*[15]

and that the Qur'an itself – despite its entire lack of mandating a constitution – provided the constitutional model for a modern Islamic State. A decade later, largely through the tireless traveling and preaching of Al-Banna himself, cells of the Muslim Brotherhood were to be found in 300 towns and cities in Egypt and beyond, and its members, who numbered over 500,000, were structurally embedded, like a state within a state, within every facet of Egyptian professional life. The Brotherhood's headquarters also moved to Cairo in 1932 signifying its now central role in shaping the political and social tone in Egyptian national life.

As well as the power of its ethos of personal Islamic piety and self-improvement advocated by Al-Banna, the Muslim Brotherhood gained a reputation for the grass-roots establishment and improvement of schools and hospitals and in general for caring for the poor and those who had been summarily neglected by both nationalist and monarchist elites.

13 Ibid., pp. 31–32.
14 Ibid., p. 32.
15 Ibid., p. 46.

However, in the face of the failure of the Egyptian state to rid itself in the 1940s of the symbols and institutions of the colonial British presence[16] and buoyed by its swelling membership and threatened by the appeal of Arab nationalism, the structures of The Muslim Brotherhood and Al-Banna's own teaching took a more extreme and aggressive turn. In his treatise *On Jihad*, Al-Banna stated that armed Jihad (*Qital*) was a

> *. . . religious duty on every Muslim, categorically and rigorously, from which there is neither evasion or escape. He [God] has rendered it a supreme object of desire and has made the reward of martyrs and fighters in his way a splendid one . . .*[17]
>
> *In this Tradition, there is a clear indication of the obligation to fight the people of the Book* [Christians and Jews], *and of the fact that God doubles the reward of those who fight them. Jihad is not against polytheists alone, but against all those who do not embrace Islam . . .*[18]

Simultaneously, Al-Banna authorized the creation of a paramilitary wing of the Muslim Brotherhood, one of whom was responsible for the assassination of a judge who had convicted the Brotherhood murderer of a British soldier. In an atmosphere of tension with both nationalist and monarchist parties, on 28 December 28 1948 Egypt's prime minister, Mahmoud an-Nukrashi Pasha, was assassinated by Brotherhood member and veterinary student Abdel Meguid Ahmed Hassan, in what is thought to have been retaliation for the nationalist government's crackdown on Muslim Brotherhood activities. A month and half later, Al-Banna himself was killed in Cairo by men who were either government agents and/or supporters of the murdered premier. Al-Banna was succeeded as head of the Brotherhood by Hassan Isma'il al-Hudaybi, a former judge.

The legacy of Hassan Al-Banna

The legacy of the thought and activism of Hassan al-Banna is complex and continues to be felt in many different directions throughout the Sunni Muslim world.

Moving from yellow to green in my diagram (See Plates 1 and 2 after Page 5), Al-Banna revived the salutary idea that the message of the Qur'an and the example of the Prophet Muhammad could provide the model for improving the social circumstances of the neglected and the oppressed and that it was an Islamic duty for Muslims to do so: a type of Muslim Liberation Theology. This type of commitment to social enterprise and Muslim-community self-improvement can be observed in hundreds if not thousands of Muslim-community groups and initiatives around the world. Thus, Al-Banna's thought can be considered

---

16 Such as army camps and the infrastructure of the Suez Canal.
17 Ibid., p. 133.
18 Ibid., p. 142.

in certain contexts to be an Islamist source of what I have delineated as the Worldview of Activist Islam.

Al-Banna was also, moving from yellow to red, responsible with Maududi for propagating the idea that was to be so fulsomely and viciously elaborated upon by Violent Islamist Extremists such as Muhammad Abd As-Salam Faraj (see next Chapter) that imperfect, corrupt or simply less obviously Islamic political regimes should be fought and toppled by the vanguard of 'pure' Muslim citizens *from within*, and that if democracy and the rule of law fail to deliver the desired result of the Islamization of society, a comprehensive Islamic State should be accomplished by force of arms.

This complex legacy is perhaps most obviously exemplified by the Palestinian offshoot of the Muslim Brotherhood, the Islamic Resistance Movement, known by its acronym HAMAS. The appeal of HAMAS lies in its commitment to the provision of local infrastructure of schools and hospitals in the brutalized Palestinian Gaza Strip. But HAMAS is also theologically and constitutionally[19] committed in the most savage and overt sense to the use of armed Jihad, including suicide killing, to destroy and eradicate the state of Israel.[20,21]

Finally, Al-Banna consolidated ideologically the core element of the Ideological Islamist Worldview introduced by Maududi that Europe and the West were, as a homogeneous monolithic unit, without differentiation, both the purveyor of rampant Godless 'materialism' and were, as an entity, an inherent enemy of True Islam. As we will see, this exaggerated, undifferentiated Us (true Muslim) vs. Them (*Kuffar infidels and partial Muslims*) Worldview was to sharpen into even more antagonistic and absolute duality in the Worldview of Non-Violent Islamist Extremism illustrated most enduringly and archetypically by the vision of Sayyid Qutb.

---

19 Donohue and Esposito, 'The Covenant of the Islamic Resistance Movement HAMAS'.
20 This inconsistent outcome of his ideas and activism was itself the product of the fact that Al-Banna did not make it clear in his teachings what the revitalized and purified Islam has as its ideal goal – a fully comprehensive one-party Islamic State ruling according to a 'purified' version of Islamic Law or a national democracy whose processes and institutions were, when an Islam-inspired party was elected, to be gradually and more gently Islamicized. His own teachings, influenced no doubt by the fluctuating political and intellectual context of his time, oscillated between a form of Islam-inspired Egyptian nationalism directed at uplifting the Muslim poor and full-blown global Islamism.
21 Indeed, the Arab-Israeli conflict (1948–present) is a running sore in the Muslim consciousness symbolizing as it does for many Muslims:

1 the apparent theological absence of God's blessing on Muslims, in the defeat of (relatively) united Arab Muslim armies in three major wars – 1948, 1967 and 1973;
2 that the UN and institutions of international justice are prepared to ratify at worst, and turn a blind eye, at least, to a land-grab of Muslim territory.

This reading of the Arab-Israeli conflict feeds viciously and decisively into the Islamist Us vs. Them meta-narrative that Muslims are *en masse* the victims of *Kafir*-dominated modern history.

The second phase of Islamism: Sayyid Qutb and the birth of Non-Violent Islamist Extremism

Sayyid Qutb (1906–1966 CE) was a complex and multi-disciplinary writer, academic, literary critic, amateur theologian, key member of the Muslim Brotherhood and a charismatic, brave and, I believe, fundamentally misguided Islamist Ideologue.

Qutb was born in Egypt in 1906 and, like Al-Banna, as a young man as an inspector in the Ministry of Education was growing into mature adulthood in a period of Egyptian history that saw the gradual and turbulent hand-over of power from the colonial British, who had effectively governed Egypt to protect Britain's access to Imperial India and the Egyptian cotton trade since the 1880s. This phase of the devolution of power saw nationalists compete with monarchists and with those who saw Egypt's Islamic heritage as key to its future, represented as we have seen, by the Society of Muslim Brothers.

As a writer and literary critic, Qutb played a key role in these intellectual debates that took place in a seesawing political environment that saw a constitutional British-backed monarchy eventually replaced by the Arab Republic of Egypt after the Free Officers' Revolution of 1952. Eventually, Qutb sided emphatically with the Islamist cause of the Muslim Brothers. Previous events in his own life, however, had shaped a more radical and troubled Worldview than that being propagated by the Muslim Brotherhood.

Prior to the Revolution of 1952 and its political denouement, in 1948 Qutb had been sent on secondment by the Ministry of Education to the United States. During this time, he worked and studied at Wilson Teachers' College in Washington, D.C. (one of the precursors to today's University of the District of Columbia), Colorado State College for Education in Greeley, and Stanford University in California. On this secondment, Qutb was troubled by his sense of the yawning gap between the US's standing as the pre-eminent advocate and global champion of democracy and the attitudes and behaviors that he observed among its citizens.

The America that I have seen: in the scale of human value – the birth of extreme Islamist anti-Americanism

Qutb recorded his traumatic exposure to small-town American culture in a text 'The America that I have seen: in the scale of human values' published in 1951 on his return from America. In this text, Qutb set the standard in the type of generalized anti-Americanism, which hitherto had *not* featured in Islamic discourse, since the West had primarily been represented by the British and the French. The young American Republic had hitherto tended to get a favorable write-up in Ottoman circles, but thereafter was to feature prominently as the object of Islamist ire.

The America That I Have Seen set the tone for the establishment of Universe that was strictly divided into a domain of un-Islamic Ignorance (which

Qutb was later to call *Jahiliyya*) that was cursed by God and inhabited by a sub-human type of person and the World of pure, pristine Islam established by those Muslims who had purified themselves of every kind of non-Muslim habit and disposition.

The basic thesis of *The America That I Have Seen*[22] was that, in its channeling of its genius into brutish productivity, America had eradicated the values that could have cultivated the intellectual, cultural and moral life of its citizens, who had been reduced to a purely bestial state.

The field of American innovation

It appears that all American ingenuity is concentrated in the field of work and production, so much so that no ability remains to advance in the field of human values [. . .] But man cannot maintain his balance before the machine and risks becoming a machine himself. He is unable to shoulder the burden of exhausting work and forge ahead on the path of humanity, he unleashes the animal within.[23]

This imbalance between work and the cultivation of humanity means that the US represented in Qutb's eyes both *The Peak of Advancement and the Depth of Primitiveness.*[24] [since] *They tackled nature with the weapons of science and the strength of the muscle, so nothing existed within them besides the crude power of the mind and the overwhelming lust for sensual pleasure.*[25]

In his own version of the founding myth of America, Qutb chose to ignore the religious Puritanism of the Founding Fathers and the creation of the US Constitution which do not fit his materialist thesis. Qutb proceeded to denounce the racism, superficiality, cultural tastes – he described Jazz music as bestial – manners, food, lack of any aesthetic sensibility and particularly what he perceived as the out-of-control sexual mores of American young people.

The appearance of the American temptress

The American girl is well acquainted with her body's seductive capacity. She knows it lies in the face, and in expressive eyes, and thirsty lips. She knows seductiveness lies in the round breasts, the full buttocks, and in the shapely thighs, sleek legs and she shows all this and does not hide it. She knows it lies in clothes: in bright colors that awaken primal sensations, and in designs that reveal the temptations of the body – and in American girls these are sometimes live, screaming temptations! Then she adds to all this the fetching laugh, the naked looks, and the bold moves, and she does not ignore this for one moment or forget it!

---

22 Qutb, *The America that I Have Seen*.
23 Ibid., p. 11.
24 Ibid.
25 Ibid., p. 13.

The American dream boy

The American boy knows well that the wide, strapping chest is the lure that cannot be denied by any girl, and that her dreams do not fall upon anyone as much as they fall upon the cowboys. A young nurse in a hospital told me very frankly, "I want nothing in the man of my dreams but two strong arms he can really squeeze me with!" And Look magazine ran a survey of several girls of different ages and levels of education and classes around what it called "ox muscles" and the overwhelming majority declared their open attraction for boys with ox muscles![26]

Qutb was also scandalized by the way that the 'empty' religious life of Americans was tainted by the raw, unfettered attraction of young men and women to each other:

The feelings of Americans toward religion are primitive

And what is said about their feelings toward death may also be said about their feelings toward religion.

Churches without life

There is no people who enjoys building churches more than the Americans [. . .] All this notwithstanding there is no one further than the American from appreciating the spirituality of religion and respect for its sacraments, and there is nothing farther from religion than the American's thinking and his feelings and manners.

Churches for carousal and enjoyment

If the church is a place for worship in the entire Christian world, in America it is for everything but worship. You will find it difficult to differentiate between it and any other place. They go to church for carousal and enjoyment, or, as they call it in their language "fun."[27]

This Qutbian horror of 'fun', perhaps tinged with a hint of an outsider's envy and fascination, reaches a climax in his description of a church dance.

A hot night at the church

[. . .] After the religious service in the church ended, boys and girls from among the members began taking part in chants, while others prayed, and we proceeded through a side door onto the dance floor that was connected to the prayer hall

---

26 Ibid., pp. 20–21.
27 Ibid., pp. 18–19.

by a door, and the Father jumped to his desk and every boy took the hand of a girl, including those who were chanting.

The dance floor was lit with red and yellow and blue lights, and with a few white lamps. And they danced to the tunes of the gramophone, and the dance floor was replete with tapping feet, enticing legs, arms wrapped around waists, lips pressed to lips, and chests pressed to chests. The atmosphere was full of desire. When the minister descended from his office, he looked intently around the place and at the people, and encouraged those men and women still sitting who had not yet participated in this circus to rise and take part.[28]

In short, *The America That I Have Seen* is the travelogue of a devout Muslim man brought up in a small provincial village in Upper Egypt, who has suffered a terrible culture-shock when encountering 'the Other', and who construes everything that he witnesses to fit his own prejudices. However, this type of generalized anti-Americanism, with the US as the Great Satan and as the global foil to 'pure' Islamic values, over the next decade was to become a key element in Non-Violent and Violent Islamist Extremism. The United States became the political object of demonization to be served up to the Muslim masses, as it shifted from post-colonial Europe to Cold War America.

Moreover, for Qutb this experience of 1950s America had the effect of confirming and intensifying the basic critical vision of Al-Banna and the Muslim Brotherhood of essential Islamic difference and superiority based on non-Muslim inferiority. It confirmed for him:

1 that the non-materialistic values and civilization of Islam were different and inherently superior to those of the materialistic West;
2 that the two sets of values were mutually exclusive, 'strange' and incommensurable one with the other; and, crucially,
3 that the values of Islam and the values of the West generated fundamentally different types of person – the human, value-bound civilized Muslim, and the bestial, immoral, sub-human non-Muslim, whose temporary global ascendency was grounded in a brutish, Godless, value-free materialistic productivity.

Qutb resigned from his work at the Ministry of Education and joined the Muslim Brotherhood. Shortly afterwards, following the 1952 coup of the Free Officers, Major General Muhammad Naguib (1901–1984 CE) and Gamal Abdel Nasser (1918–1970 CE) declared Egypt an Arab Republic, and King Farouk (1920–1965 CE) went into exile. Initially, Qutb and the Muslim

---

28 Ibid., pp. 19–20.

Brotherhood with whom, as an ex-government official and influential intellectual, he was now involved at the highest level were supportive of the Revolutionary Council of Free Officers. This was because they were confident that the Islamic ethos and law of Islam, as they envisioned them, would play a key role in Egypt's constitutional future. This confidence was in part due to intimate conversations between Qutb and Nasser who had been close confidants.

It soon became clear that Nasser's political and social model was Arab National Socialism in which Islam and the Muslim Brotherhood would play only a marginal role. Despite Nasser offering Qutb any place he wished in the government of the new republic, Qutb, the Muslim Brotherhood and the Free Officers quickly became mortal enemies with opposing, confrontational visions for the country's future. Nasser's vision for which he was idolized by many Arabs beyond Egypt was of an Arab nationalist and pan-African revival with Egypt at the head of united and resurgent Arab and African nations in a triumphant post-colonial world. Qutb's vision was of a pristine Islamic State ruled by Islamic law in which Egypt's Islamic heritage would be the defining feature of Egyptian national identity.

These different Worldviews soon manifested as violent confrontation. Upset that Nasser would not enforce a government based on Islamic ideology, Qutb and other Muslim Brotherhood members orchestrated a plot to assassinate Nasser in 1954. The attempt was foiled and Qutb was jailed. Soon afterwards the Egyptian government used the incident to justify a crackdown on various members of the Muslim Brotherhood for their vocal opposition towards the Nasser administration. During his first three years in prison, conditions were bad and Qutb was probably tortured. In later years he was allowed more mobility, including the opportunity to write.

Milestones (1964) – the 'ur-' text of Islamist Extremism

Out of this formative experience of a brutalized imprisonment, domestic political disenchantment and a revulsion at the West, represented by small-town United States, as well as a desire to restate, mythically, the essential and incommensurable superiority of Islamic civilization, Qutb wrote his major work of political ideology, *M'alim fiy Tariq* – Signs on the Way, which is usually translated simply as *Milestones* (1964).

Milestones is regarded by many as *the* seminal political manifesto of Violent Islamist Extremism. It gathered the momentum of influence from its cradle in the Muslim Brotherhood of Egypt through the school of Saudi *Wahhabism* where many of the most influential Brotherhood and Islamist figures fled persecution in their own country. However, I regard *Milestones* rather as the seminal text of Non-Violent Islamist Extremism – that is to say, the text that laid the foundations of the absolute, Manichean Us (pure Muslim) vs. Them (infidels and impure 'partial' and 'wrong' Muslims) Worldview that, as we will see, was later to motivate Violent Islamist Extremists. *Milestones* did not, however, foreground the use of violence to realize this divided vision.

The text of Milestones

The introduction of *Milestones*[29] sets out its revolutionary Maududi-style political stall by co-opting Islam as a tool of comprehensive, revolutionary change that will be inevitably and eternally opposed by those who represent the *status quo*:

> *Islam stands for change. It seeks to change the individual and the society. This change covers every aspect of human life: from personal morality to business, economics and politics. It is only natural that Islam should be fought by those who want to keep the status quo. This is the way it has always been throughout history: from Adam to Nuh, Ibrahim, Musa, Isa, and Muhammad (peace be on them). It will happen to anyone who wants to stand up and proclaim the true message of Islam to the world.*[30]

This theme, of the eternal confrontation of dichotomies such as change vs. the status quo, structures the whole book, which proposes a Worldview of *diametrically opposed* goods vs. evils, pure vs. impure intellectual and political systems, Muslim believers vs. *jahil* (ignorant) non-believers. By so doing, this work enormously exaggerates the Qur'anic warrant, which, as we have seen in Chapter 3, established the essential unity of all human life, by setting up these polar opposites for ideological ends.

Eternal recurrence of the same – ignorance (Jahiliyya)

Milestones achieves this division of the world into the unremittingly bad world of ignorance and impurity vs. the 'pure' world of Godly Islam by the rhetorical device of the endless repetition of the theme of *'Jahiliyya'* – Ignorance.

Jahiliyya is an Arabic Qur'anic word denoting the period of pre-Islamic 'ignorance' when most Arabs worshipped a pantheon of pagan gods before the Prophet Muhammad brought the message of the Unity and Singularity of the One God (Allah) and the need to worship Him.

This word, which appears a mere four times in the whole of the Qur'an, is repeated hundreds of times in this slim 168-page text. Following the lead of the Arabic translator of Maududi *Abu Hassan al-Nadwi*, Qutb reworked this idea of pre-Islamic ignorance to refer not only to those who had not heard or heeded the message of the Unity of God (*Tawhid*). He also, in a reworking of the Maududist concept of the 'partial' Muslim and the 'full' Muslim, reframed the concept to refer to those who were Muslim but who were not Muslim enough, and who were therefore ignorant of the pure, fully politicized Islam.

29 Qutb, *Milestones*.
30 Ibid., p. 3.

168 *Islamism: the people, texts and contexts*

Crucially, in Qutb's totalitarian vision of Islamist ideology there could be no intermingling between the ideas and peoples of *Jahiliyya* and the ideas and people of Islam since each represented a total, mutually exclusive vision of how to live the good life.

> *Islam cannot accept any mixing with Jahiliyya, either in its concept or in the modes of living which are derived from this concept. Either Islam will remain, or Jahiliyya: Islam cannot accept or agree to a situation which is half-Islam and half-Jahiliyya. In this respect Islam's stand is very clear. It says that the truth is one and cannot be divided; if it is not the truth, then it must be falsehood. The mixing and co-existence of the truth and falsehood is impossible. Command belongs to Allah Almighty, or otherwise to Jahiliyya; Allah's Sharia will prevail, or else people's desires.*[31]

Any resemblance of similarity between 'Islam' and '*Jahiliyya*' is denounced by Qutb as illusory:

> *Sometimes it appears that some parts of Islam resemble some aspects of the life of people in Jahiliyya; but these aspects are not Jahili nor are they from Jahiliyya. This apparent resemblance in some minor aspects is a mere coincidence; the roots of the two trees are entirely different. The tree of Islam has been sown and nurtured by the wisdom of Allah Almighty, while the tree of Jahiliyya is the product of the soil of human desires.*[32]
>
> *Indeed, Islam does not take its justifications from the Jahili system and its evil derivatives. And these 'civilizations', which have dazzled many and have defeated their spirits, are nothing but a Jahili system at heart, and this system is erroneous, hollow and worthless in comparison with Islam.*[33]

The rest of the book is, in effect, a fleshing-out and detailing of this principle of absolute, eternal separation between pure, 'Platonic' Islam vs. impure, corrupt *Jahiliyya* and how to put this ideological separation into concrete practice. In short, Qutbism is deduced in classic ideological fashion[34] from this one central motif of *Jahiliyya*.

The 'Pollution' of the West

True to the spirit of *The America that I have seen* and the anti-materialism of Al-Banna, *Milestones* presents a religio-sociological analysis of the West and the Muslim world that is also crude and simplistic, in order both to buttress and

---

31 Ibid., p. 146.
32 Ibid., p. 148.
33 Ibid., p. 153.
34 Arendt, *The Origins of Totalitarianism*.

reaffirm Qutb's premise of the world divided absolutely and neatly into 'pure' Islam and *Jahiliyya*. In this critique, he draws heavily on the language of Purity vs. Impurity that we have seen previously, mobilized by Maududi in which he descries the 'poisonous' influences of the West:

> *Thus, only Islamic values and morals, Islamic teachings and safeguards, are worthy of mankind, and from this unchanging and true measure of human progress, Islam is the real civilization and Islamic society is truly civilized.*[35]
>
> *The Western ways of thought and all the sciences started on the foundation of these poisonous influences with an enmity towards all religions, and in particular with greater hostility towards Islam [...] If, in spite of knowing this, we rely on Western ways of thought, even in teaching the Islamic sciences, it will be an unforgivable blindness on our part [...] A slight influence from them can pollute the clear spring of Islam.*[36]

Such a simplistic vision is understandable as a defense mechanism for someone in Qutb's position of imprisonment. Nevertheless, it contributed to the creation of a split Worldview of pure opposites that was to become the ideological basis of the Islamist doctrine of Loyalty and Disavowal (*Al-Wala' wal Bara'*) which, as we have seen in Chapter 4, is a doctrinal cornerstone of both Non-Violent and Violent Islamist Extremism.[37]

Absolute, radical separatism

This dynamic and encouragement to the complete and absolute separation of Islam and Muslims, and the people and ideas of Jahiliyya, extends even to Qutb's encouragement of separation from kith and kin in direct contravention of the Qur'an and the Normative Behavior (*Sunna*) of the Prophet Muhammad as articulated in Chapter 4.

> *A Muslim has no relationship with his mother, father, brother, wife and other family members except through their relationship with the Creator, and then they are also joined through blood.*[38]

This includes not only separation from the family, but also, in an extension of the ideas of Maududi and Al-Banna, means that identification with Islam eliminates all other identities. True Islam for Qutb entails the terminal separation

---

35 Ibid., p. 112.
36 Ibid., p. 131.
37 Brachman, *Global Jihadism*.
38 Ibid., p. 133.

from the nation and hostility towards any relationship that is not based on 'pure' Islam:

> *Islam came to establish only one relationship which binds men together in the sight of Allah, and if this relationship is firmly established, then all other relationships based on blood or other considerations become eliminated[. . .]*[39]

These are ideological pronouncements made with disregard for the Qur'anic generalized verses regarding both the essential unity of humanity as the Tribe of Adam and the particular unity of the blood family as the building block of society. Thus, Qutb clearly states the extreme Islamist case for a monolithic, exclusive, Muslim identity shorn of any complexity and inflection from other sources of belonging.

Jihad as the eternal struggle between Islam and Jahiliyya

For Maududi and Al-Banna the need and obligation for armed Jihad was primarily the product of a practical commitment to rid Muslims and the body politic of Islam of 'impure' kafir influences as a prelude to the establishment of an Islamic State. However, within this eternally Manichean Worldview, Qutb presents struggle in the path of God (*jihad fiy sabilillah*) as an *eternal cosmic condition* and an inevitable corollary of the way that the world is. By contrast, as we have seen, the Qur'an always presents Jihad as a temporary phase that precedes the cessation of hostilities and a return to the default position of peace.

> *Thus, this struggle is not a temporary phase but an eternal state – an eternal state, as truth and falsehood cannot co-exist on this earth.*[40]

This theme of the eternal need for armed *Jihad* as the outcome of the absolute uncompromising struggle between Islam and the Denial of Faith, as we will see next, was to become a defining feature of Violent Islamist Extremism. Thus, the Qutbian Worldview is the Worldview of someone with nowhere left to turn: of revulsion at the corrupt internal politics of the Muslim-majority world and revulsion and rejection of the moral standards – or lack of them – of the West. It is a Manichean Worldview of an embattled innocence: the entirely pristine purity of a mythic, 'total' Islam pitted eternally in struggle against the absolute and eternal degeneracy of *Jahiliyya*.

Ayatollah Khomeini: Shia Islamism succeeds where Sunni Islamism fails

By 1979, the divisive effects of Ideological Islamism (as well as other -isms) had been felt across the Sunni Muslim-majority Muslim world from contributing

---

39 Ibid., pp. 130–131.
40 Ibid., p. 7.

Islamism: the people, texts and contexts 171

to the Partition of India into Hindu-led India and Muslim-led Pakistan, to the assassination of Egypt's prime minister, Mahmoud an-Nukrashi Pasha, and the clampdown on the Muslim Brotherhood in Egypt. However, its creative impulse to create a 'pure' Islamic State had been unrealized. This realization was to come from the most unlikely of sources, Shia Revolutionary Islamism.

I say unlikely since, traditionally, Shia Islam (see Chapter 2) despite moments of great empowerment such as the mighty medieval Fatimid and early modern Safavid dynasties, and despite the contribution, for example of the great jurist Imam Jafar as-Sadiq to the development of the roots of Islamic jurisprudence, had often been pushed to the political margins of the Muslim community. Shia Muslims of various and complex denominational affiliations had often existed under Sunni regimes as a relatively hidden esoteric branch of the faith whose followers tended to eschew political governance, and the revolutionary impetus to grab it. Instead, Shia Muslims had tended to await the apocalyptic arrival of the 12th Hidden Imam (*Al-Mahdi*, The Guided One) to right the wrongs endured by the Prophetic House (*Ahl al-Bayt*) and usher in the end of times.

The late twentieth century was radically to reverse this normal Sunni-Shia order of things as, in common with Ideological Islamism of other sorts, a combination of unjust external intervention and internal political oppression laid the conditions for the Iranian Islamic Revolution of 1979. Outrage at the interventions of Western powers in the interest of protecting their access to oil, at the huge differentials of wealth between the ruling elite around the Shah[41] and the rest of the population, and at the government-backed secularization of the traditional centers of Twelver Shia learning[42] led to increasingly violent popular protests against Shah Muhammad Reza Shah Pahlavi, who went into exile in the United States on 31 December 1978.

This vacuum of power provided the opportunity for the exiled leader of the combined nationalist, Leftist and Islamist opposition, Ayatollah Ruhollah Khomeini (1902–1989), to return from exile in Paris to lead the Iranian Islamic Revolution in January 1979.

Khomeini – through a combination of force, his own personal charisma and popular support – implemented his core Revolutionary idea of the *Guardianship of the Jurist* (*Vilayet al-Faqih*) to establish a revolutionary state run by a cadre of empowered Shia clerics – Ayatollahs – that effected elements of *Sharia* Law without a democratic mandate. Simultaneously, he dismantled and executed the ruling elites of the previous regime.

Despite his diverse education in traditional Twelver Shia Islam, including a predilection to some of the most esoteric Sufi ideas about the Perfect Man and

---

41 Symbolized dramatically by a party in 1971 in which the Shah of Iran, the self-proclaimed 'king of kings', celebrated 2,500 years of Persian monarchy in a lavish tent city, using 37km of silk in a specially created oasis with a five-day banquet with the attendance of more than 60 Kings and Queens.
42 Including the clampdown on the power of the traditional Shia *Ulema* (called Ayatollahs, meaning 'Signs of God') over education and family law.

172   *Islamism: the people, texts and contexts*

philosophy, which was notably different from that of the literalist Sunni Muslim education of Maududi and Al-Banna, Khomeini's Worldview shared some markedly similar features to their Ideological Islamist Worldviews.

First, Khomeini shared with Al-Banna and Maududi the idea that only government according to 'pure' and fixed (and therefore fictitious) Islamic Law constituted a legitimate constitutional and legal process.

> *Government can only be legitimate when it accepts the rule of God and the rule of God means the implementation of the sharia'. All laws that are contrary to the sharia' must be abandoned because only the Law of God will stay valid and immutable in the face of changing times . . .*[43]

Second, Khomeini shared the view that the Islamization of Western political ideology, e.g. an Islamic Marxism, by which the land of powerful landowners was both reappropriated by the State and redistributed to the poor, was a legitimate part of the process of achieving that Islamic State.

Third, he shared a need to draw on a Worldview of the absolute Manichean difference between the goodness of Islam and the evil of the West and of those partial Muslim 'insiders' wishing to undermine pure *Sharia*-based Islam.

This fusion of Western style political ideology and Manichean dualism can be observed in the following quote, which was used as the justification for the post-revolutionary purging by the execution of senior functionaries of the Shah's regime:

> *We believe . . . that to destroy and kill evil is part of the truth and that the purging of society of these persons means paving the way for a unified society in which classes will not exist . . . To execute evildoers is the great mission of Muslims in order to realise the perfection of nature and society.*[44]

As part of this Manichean Worldview, Khomeini shared with Al-Banna and Maududi and, increasingly, as his own political power and the revolutionary fervor waned domestically, he shared with them *the need* to have his Worldview underpinned by the identification and vilification of a monstrously evil 'Other', as representative of the Godlessness of Unbelief *Kufr* juxtaposed against the Godliness of political Islam.

The repeated characterization of the United States by Khomeini as the 'Great Satan' in the 1980s and the infamous *fatwa* (legal judgment) in 1991 prescribing execution for the British-Indian writer Salman Rushdie for supposedly insulting the Prophet Muhammad and his wife Aisha in his book *The Satanic Verses* should not be understood as an expression of a genuine Islamic or even Islamist consciousness. The vast majority of the Muslim world rejected the legality of the *fatwa* and often have a begrudging admiration of the United States. Rather,

---

43 Cited in Rahnema, *Pioneers of Islamic Revival*, p. 80.
44 Cited in Ansari, *Modern Iran Since 1921*, p. 217.

these attitudes need to be understood more as part of the revolutionary Islamist need to create a Worldview strictly divided into Us vs. Them that we have seen characterizes Ideological Islamism of all types.

The ease with which the Iranian Revolution and its process of institutional Islamization was accomplished, with relatively little bloodshed, revolutionarily speaking, was and remains immensely influential in convincing other Ideological Islamists and Violent Islamist Extremists that their agenda of revolutionary political change might also be accomplished through force of arms with similar ease.

7 The Genealogy of Terror
The people, texts and contexts of Violent Islamist Extremism

Violent Islamist Extremism's 'pioneers': Abdullah Azzam and Muhammad Abd as-Salam Faraj

Violent Islamist Extremism is Non-Violent Islamist Extremism 'fought into existence'.

It is the visible manifestation of the Worldview of Maududi, Al-Banna and, pre-eminently, Sayyid Qutb propagated by those for whom the eternal and absolute incompatibility of 'pure' Islam with 'impure' *Kufr* (Unbelief) and corrupt 'partial' Islam means that a pure Islamic State must be fought into reality on the global stage.

The ideologues of Ideological Islamism and Non-Violent Islamist Extremism set up this Manichean Worldview of absolute, eternal division, but, on the whole, implied that the use of violence might be necessary to bring about the eradication of Unbelief (*Kufr*) as a precursor to the establishment of an Islamic State rather than explicitly calling for violence. However, each of the people examined in this Chapter made a distinct ideological contribution to the Worldview that explicitly foregrounds and prioritizes the violent task of realizing the total separation of Islam and *Kufr* (Unbelief) and all have intimately connected themselves to some type of conflict.

Muhammad Abd as-Salam Faraj: the opening salvo

The first explicitly violent text of modern Violent Islamist Extremism is arguably *Al-Jihad al-fareedah al-gha'ib*, best translated as *Jihad: the Absent Obligation* by Muhammad Abd as-Salam Faraj (1954–1982 CE), which was a series of lectures and pamphlets written in 1979.

Muhammad Abd as-Salam Faraj was an Egyptian Muslim Brotherhood member and an electrical engineer who became the chief ideologue of the violent splinter group of the Muslim Brotherhood, Islamic Jihad, one of whose cells, amongst other things, was led by the future and now current leader of Al-Qaeda, Ayman Al-Zawahiri (born 1951 CE). *The Absent Obligation* is attributed with inspiring the assassination of President Anwar Sadat by the army officer Khalid al-Islambouli in 1981, whose famous outcry, "We have killed Pharaoh", at what in Mainstream Islam would be considered both murder and treason, has become iconic in extremist circles.

In this pamphlet manifesto, Faraj also introduces some iconic VIE themes and makes explicit doctrinal shifts legitimizing violence which Qutb, Al-Banna and Maududi had often left implicit:

1   **The Obligation to fight the 'Near Jihad' to establish an Islamic State**

    The text begins with a statement of the religious 'obligation' to establish the Islamic state, if necessary, by force. No Qur'anic verse is adduced and four *hadiths* are indicated – none of which bear the force of a legal obligation in Mainstream Islam but are merely Prophetic statements of future states of affairs which involve Muslim rule.

    > *By the same token, if the state can only be established by fighting, then it is compulsory to fight.*[1]

2   **The 'Near Jihad' against 'apostate' Muslim rulers through the abuse of Ibn Taymiyya's writings**

    For Faraj, in this act of establishment of the Islamic State, the first struggle is a Near Jihad against what he called the 'apostate rulers' of Islam, i.e. contemporary governments of Muslim-majority countries. This obligatory 'Near Jihad' against 'Today's Rulers' is based on the failure of these governments to implement what he regards as comprehensive Sharia law:

    > *The present rulers have apostasised from Islam . . . What they carry they carry of Islam is nothing but names, even if they pray, fast and claim to be Muslims.*[2]

    In a manner that has become highly characteristic of Extremist abuse of a medieval jurist-theologian called Ibn Taymiyya (d. 1328), Faraj makes an analogy between 'Today's Rulers' and Ibn Taymiyya's medieval ruling that *Jihad* could be fought against the 'Tartar' (actually Mongol) invaders even though they were Muslims. This is, in fact, an inversion of Ibn Taymiyya's teaching since Ibn Tayymiyya was, in a medieval legal context, ruling that in certain circumstances Muslims could fight other Muslims as an act of authorized *resistance* against an attack *from outside* a governing Muslim regime.

---

1   Faraj, *The Absent Obligation*, p. 20.
2   Ibid., p. 24.

Faraj, by contrast, advocated armed insurrection within a state against an accepted leadership. He, in fact, advocated what the Qur'an expressly forbids, political insurrection (*fitna*) (see Chapter 4).[3]

3   Rejecting Routes to the Peaceful Establishment of Islam

In his foregrounding of the use of violence to establish the Islamic State, Faraj, in a move that has characterized the VIE Worldview ever since, specifically rejects the possibility that peaceful 'good deeds' might lead to its establishment and the creation of a more Islamic society.[4]

> But Salah, Zakah and good deeds are orders of God and we must not neglect them. However . . . would these good deeds and acts of worship establish the Islamic state? Immediately and without the first thought the answer would be NO.[5]

This includes in a manner that has become highly characteristic of VIE propaganda rejecting: (1) following Good Professions (p. 40) and (2) Giving Da'wah Alone, i.e. calling people to Islam (p. 40).

4   Fighting is an Individual Religious Obligation (*Fard al-Ayn*)

The rest of the main text (pp. 45–94) returns to a justification of the original theme that fighting is an individual obligation (*Fard al-Ayn*) on every believer. For example,

> It is also known that he who knows the obligations of the Salah must pray, and he who knows the obligations of the fasting in the month of Ramadhan must fast. Likewise he who knows the obligation of Jihad must fight in the cause of Allah.[6]

Abdullah Azzam (1941–1989): the 'Godfather of Jihad'

Faraj sketched out the Violent Islamist Extremist thematic blueprint of the Individual Religious Obligation of the Near Jihad and rejecting peaceful Activist means of structural change, and the group Islamic Jihad gave it its first expeditions of active violence in the assassination of President Anwar Sadat. The first

---

3   Ibn Taymiyya most definitely did not approve of 'fitnah' as is shown by this text:

> Among the fundamentals of the truth . . . is that people with a tyrannical and unjust leader are ordered to show patience in the face of his tyranny, his injustice and his oppression, and not to fight him. The Prophet . . . did not, absolutely, authorize pushing back of oppression by fighting.
> (Ibn Taymiyyah, al-Istiqama, i.32 cited in Michot, 2006: preface).

4   Ibid.
5   Ibid., p. 37.
6   Ibid., p. 45.

full-flowering of Violent Islamist Extremism came in the person of Abdullah Azzam (1941–1989 CE).

Abdullah Azzam was a Palestinian academic and scholar of jurisprudence at the University of Damascus, who fought in the 1967 Six-Day War of Israel against Egypt, Jordan and Syria. Like Qutb, Abdullah Azzam became disenchanted with the failure of the Muslim Brotherhood to restore Sunni Arab Muslim independence, the failure of the Arab Nation States to oust the State of Israel from Palestinian territories and more generally the failure of Arab nationalism to re-establish justice and Muslim power in the Arab World.[7] During a period of study in Al-Azhar University in Cairo, Abdullah Azzam met the family of the deceased Sayyid Qutb and was deeply impressed by Qutb's ideas.

After being expelled for his radical views from a teaching position at the University of Jordan, Abdullah Azzam migrated to Saudi Arabia and taught at the King Abdul Aziz University in Jeddah but was expelled from his position there during the crackdown on suspected Islamic Extremists after the occupation of the Grand Mosque of Mecca by terrorists in 1979.

It is thought that Abdullah Azzam first met his future mentee Osama bin Laden (1957–2011 CE) in the King Abdul Aziz University between 1976 and 1979. Abdullah Azzam moved to Peshawar in North Pakistan where he was ready to respond to the Soviet invasion of Afghanistan of 1979.

At the start of the Soviet-Afghan War (1979–1989), Azzam established the Service Office (*maktab al-khadamat*) for Arab recruits joining the war.

Defense of Muslim lands: the first obligation after faith (1979)

It was in the context of the US-backed resistance to the Soviet invasion of Afghanistan and his leadership of the Service Office that Azzam issued his fatwa (religious-legal judgment), *Defence of Muslim Lands: the first obligation after faith* (1979). This text, following Faraj, declared the Afghan struggle (Jihad) an Individual Religious Obligation (*Fard al-Ayn*), on a par with the Five Individual Obligations of Islam (see Chapter 3), on all Muslims wherever they were if any Muslim-controlled territory came under attack.[8]

Summary

1 *Jihad by one's person is an Individual Religious Obligation (Fard al-Ayn) upon every Muslim on the earth.*
2 *No permission is required for one from another and no permission is required from the parents for the child.* [i.e. the permission of parental and state authority – traditional mainstream stipulations, see Chapter 3]

---

7 Rogan, *The Arabs*.
8 Azzam, *Defence of Muslim Lands*, p. 27.

3   *Jihad by one's wealth is an Individual Religious Obligation (Fard al-Ayn) and it is forbidden (haram) to make savings while the Jihad is in need of the Muslims' wealth.*
4   *Neglecting the Jihad is like abandoning Fasting and Obligatory Prayer ...*

This declaration of armed *Jihad* as an Individual Religious Obligation on all adult Muslims everywhere and the abandonment of the traditional stipulations for statutory and parental permission to fight was clearly primarily a recruiting tactic. It was a successful one. By 1985 between 20,000 to 35,000 foreign Muslim fighters made their way to the North West Frontier Province in Pakistan to fight in Afghanistan. It also represented a radical shift from the position of classical Muslim scholars such as Ibn Rushd (1126–1198 CE) who, following the Qur'an and the *Sunna* (see pp. 101–109), had advocated Jihad as a Collective Religious Duty (*fard al-kifaya*) in defense of Muslim life and faith under specific circumstances, which became an Individual Obligation only if your person or direct vicinity was attacked.[9]

Buoyed by the success both of this theological sleight-of-hand and by the military success of the fighting itself, Azzam in a further Treatise *Join the Caravan [of martyrs]* (1981 CE) took the argument further. In this treatise, he argued that armed Jihad is an Individual Religious Obligation (*Fard al-Ayn*) on every adult Muslim in all places "until every piece of land that was once Muslim is regained" (p. 51) and that this included, for example, not only the usual suspect, his native Palestine, but also almost the entirety of the Iberian Peninsula, large tracts of China, the whole of India and so on.

In this treatise, Azzam also argued for the need for a Base (*Al-Qaeda*) from which to launch this program of 'Far Jihad' in the aggressive (re-)conquest of once Muslim lands. Thus, Azzam was instrumental in sowing the seeds of the Violent Islamist Extremist (VIE) idea that not only the direct enemy of Muslims should be fought defensively, but also the 'far' enemy of Islam in the form of non-Muslim powers in their own countries should be fought aggressively. This idea was to become a pillar of the VIE thinking of Al-Qaeda.

Together with the idea of the 'Far Jihad' as an Individual Religious Obligation, Azzam was also responsible for the propagation of a powerful ideology of martyrdom (*ishtishad*) for recruitment to the Soviet-Afghan Conflict (1979–1989). He recounted and made recruiting videos of often-fantastical tales surrounding those who fought and died in fighting armed '*Jihad*'. For example, in a literalist twist of a Qur'anic verse (2:154) which states that martyrs to faith are still spiritually alive, he told stories of the corpses of martyrs not rotting after a week in the open and heavenly hosts attending dying fighters.

---

9   Indeed, videos of the fiery demagogic speeches of Abdullah Azzam denouncing the position of classical jurists are prevalent on VIE social media networks. These videos are often snippets of Azzam and therefore can be fairly said not to represent the full force and nuance of his written texts and speeches. Nevertheless, they do represent what Azzam has powerfully come to mean for contemporary Violent Islamist Extremists.

These tales have now become stock VIE recruiting tools and were used as such in the Bosnian War (1991–1995), the First Chechen War (1994–1996) and the Second Chechen War (1999–2009). They were used, for example, in the most graphic way with highly charged rhetoric and imagery by the then London-based ideologues Abu Hamza Al-Masri (the Egyptian), infamous for his 'Captain Hook'-like claw, and Abu Qatada Al-Philistini (the Palestinian) with whom the UK government fought an extradition battle for many years. Most recently, the Azzam-inspired trope of martyrdom has been mobilized fulsomely in the context of the Syrian Civil War (2011–present) with pictures of the non-decomposing smiling corpses of 'martyrs' posted online in their hundreds on social media.

The glamour of Jihad

As well as his contribution to the theological architecture of Violent Islamist Extremism, Azzam provided glamorous, iconic images and catchy sound-bites that have been recycled *ad infinitum* ever since. With his trademark Afghan hat and Palestinian kefaya scarf, Azzam himself became a charismatic figurehead – a type of Che Guevara – of Violent Islamist Extremism and has rightly been called the Godfather of Global 'Jihad'.

Azzam's oft-repeated slogans and sound-bites,

> *"Jihad and the rifle alone. NO negotiations. NO conferences and NO dialogue."*
> *"The Jihad is in need of money, and the men are in need of Jihad."*
> *"We are the terrorists for God." (Nahnu muharibun fillah)*

have become the calling cards of Violent Islamist Extremism and are signifiers to others that someone is on the VIE page. They crop up repeatedly on Jihadist social media sites and blogs as the slogans of the Violent Islamist Revolution.

Azzam's two core ideas of armed 'Jihad' as an Individual Religious Obligation and of 'martyrdom' have been the doctrinal core of Violent Islamist Extremism ever since. Together with the powerful recruitment techniques and propaganda that Azzam pioneered, they were pivotal in shaping the ideology of Azzam's mentee, Osama bin Laden (1957–2011 CE), and the Al-Qaeda network.

The ideologues of Al-Qaeda: bin Laden, Al-Awlaki, Al-Zawahiri and As-Suri

Osama bin Laden: the eternal struggle against the Crusader-Zionist Alliance

The 'miraculous' defeat of the Soviet superpower in the ignominious Soviet withdrawal from Afghanistan in 1989 and the collapse of the Soviet-backed socialist Afghan government, at the hands of idealized bands of Muslim brothers, aided by angelic hosts and adorned by images of martyrs to God, provided an enduring founding myth for Violent Islamist Extremism.

The Afghan Jihad established the strong and still deeply entrenched VIE notion that, when individual Muslim fighters take matters into their own hands, by-passing the tyrant (*taghut*) 'partial' Muslim leaders of the Muslim-majority world, then God would inevitably give them success against a mighty foe. This was just as He had given victory to the Prophet Muhammad and his Companions against the overweening Meccan pagans at the Battle of Badr (624 CE) and later[10] against the arrogant Sassanid Persian Empire at al-Qādisiyyah and the mighty Byzantines at Yarmouk (both 636 CE).

In the global Islamic euphoria at a Muslim-led military triumph of the Afghan conflict after decades of debilitating colonialism and repeated military humiliation at the hands of Israel, some inconvenient counter-truths to the simplistic narrative of the triumph of Islam over *Kufr* (Unbelief) were overlooked. First, while one superpower, which was already imploding from within, had indeed been dealt a significant reverse, this had come with the considerable financial, moral and technological (for example portable anti-aircraft missiles) support of another 'infidel' superpower – the United States of America. In reality, notwithstanding the undoubted heroism and sacrifice of many of the *mujahideen* (people of armed Jihad) in the Afghan conflict, in ideological terms the struggle against the Soviets had been far from the struggle of 'pure' Islam against 'impure' Unbelief; it had been a messy Cold War conflict by proxy between the United States and the Soviet Union.

Second, the Soviet invasion was not, strictly speaking, an invasion since the Soviets had been invited in to deal with what was regarded as an Islamist insurrection by the Afghan Muslim (though socialist) government. Third, while the Muslim-street was euphoric and governments, including Saudi Arabia and the United States, were quick to bask – in David and Goliath mode – in the reflected glory of the triumph of the plucky *mujahideen* (people of armed Jihad), there were 20,000 to 35,000 foreign fighters, so-called Afghan-Arabs,[11] left after the conflict on the Northwest Frontier with no one to fight, except themselves, and no way to demobilize, since the vast majority of their countries of origin did not want them home.

Osama bin Laden (1957–2011 CE), a Saudi construction magnate from a prominent, well-connected Saudi family, turned Islamist financier and infrastructure-developer turned Arab-Afghan *Jihad* administrator and occasional fighter, had been anointed by Abdullah Azzam[12] as the leader of the Base (*Al-Qaeda*) for the global recovery of the lands of Islam. Bin Laden needed new enemies. In the turbulent 1990s he quickly found them.

The invasion of Kuwait in 1990 by the despotic ruler of Iraq, Saddam Hussain (1937–2006 CE), provided bin Laden with an opportunity to substantiate the

---

10 Under the Caliph Abu Bakr.
11 Recruited by Azzam from many different Muslim-majority countries.
12 Probably *posthumously* by his own faction.

ideological idea that the 'Far Enemy' had become the United States of America. In the face of the collapse of Kuwait to Iraqi forces and the failure of Saudi Arabia either the defend its ally or to persuade Saddam to withdraw, the Grand Mufti of Saudi Arabia, Sheikh Abdal Aziz bin Baz (1910–1999 CE), issued a religious-legal judgment (*fatwa*) permitting American non-Muslim troops to be stationed in Saudi Arabia as a base from which, as an ally, to defend Saudi Arabia and to expel the Iraqis from Kuwait. This *fatwa* was taken as proof by bin Laden both that the House of Saud was irrevocably an 'apostate regime' and also that the United States of America was the agent of destruction of the heartlands of Islam – the two Protected Areas (*Haramayn*) of Mecca and Medina – and had therefore become the legitimate object of the 'Far Jihad'.

The impact of the Bosnian War (1991–1995)

While events in Arabia in the early 1990s provided the ideological opportunity for bin Laden to begin to frame the United States of America as the eternal enemy of Islam, events in the Balkans in Europe provided the practical opportunity for the deployment of some of the men who were the VIE residue of the Afghan campaign.

The break-away of Slovenia and Croatia in 1991 from the disintegrating communist Russian-client state of Yugoslavia offered the nationalist Serbian President Slobodan Milošević, (1941–2006 CE), supported by Russia, the opportunity to annex ethnic-majority Serbian areas of multi-ethnic Bosnia by a policy of 'ethnic cleansing' of Muslim Bosniaks.[13]

Western governments dithered, unclear about Serbian War aims,[14] persisting in a prejudiced belief that all parties were equally to blame for a flare-up of 'ethnic tension' to which the Near East was supposedly perennially prone. As a result of this belief in the equal share of the blame for the conflict, the European powers decided that they would enforce an arms embargo on the region. Meanwhile, Serbian militias and the Army of Republika Srpska, i.e. of Serbian-dominated areas of Bosnia, set about the 1,425-day Siege of Sarajevo from 5 April 1992 to 29 February 1996, supplied with heavy Russian artillery, while the Bosnian National Army heroically defended its capital city, often with homemade weaponry.

Elsewhere, other Bosniak Muslims retreated in desperation to UN-protected enclaves such as the town of Srebrenica in the East of Bosnia. In Srebrenica on 11–12 July 1995 more than 8,000 Bosniak Muslim males were released from the 'protection' of the UN force of mainly Dutch soldiers into the murderous embrace of the Serb militias to be massacred in farm buildings and ditches

---

13 Often with the nationalist rhetorical pretext that he was liberating Greater Serbia from the Ottoman Turks, disregarding the fact that, ethnically speaking, Bosniak Muslims were no more Turkish than he was!
14 Silber and Little, *The Death of Yugoslavia*.

by units of the Bosnian Serb Army of Republika Srpska under the command of General Ratko Mladić.[15]

The West dithered; Al-Qaeda acted. Units of *mujahideen* fighters (called 'muj') were sent by Al-Qaeda, and came from elsewhere, including the UK, to support the Bosnian National Army. In fact, these fighters were both an embarrassment and a nuisance to the Bosnian government as, until the closing phases of the war, they operated outside official army control. Rumors soon emerged of extrajudicial killings by VIE Muslim groups that matched the atrocities carried out by Serbian militias. These rumors both played into the Western narrative that all the parties in the conflict were as bad as each other and Serbian nationalist mythology that what ethnic Christian Orthodox Serbs were facing was an international Islamist conspiracy to re-Islamize the Balkans.

Al-Qaeda was not concerned. Involvement in the Bosnian War gave 'career' Jihadists something to do and provided a new stock of grinning 'martyrs' with which to fill recruiting videos. The West's inaction, while Bosnian Muslims suffered, also fed conveniently into the core element of the VIE Worldview that *Dar al-Kufr* (the Abode of Unbelief) was eternally and inevitably committed to the eradication of Islam.

In terms of projecting this Worldview of the 'Far Jihad' against the eternal enemy of Islam to a potential global audience of Muslim recruits, the time was now ripe for bin Laden to force matters to a head in 1996 when, via Arab media outlets, he issued the first of two legal judgments declaring Al-Qaeda's war against the Americans

The first – *Declaration of War Against the Americans Occupying the Land of the Two Holy Places* – was a rambling tirade against the American presence in the *Hijaz* – the Land of the two Holy Places of Mecca and Medina – which was, in bin Laden's eyes, proof both of the apostasy of the House of Saud and the Saudi religious establishment, and of the destructive intent against Islam of what he repeatedly referred to as the Crusader-Zionist Alliance. For bin Laden, this Alliance, led by the United States of America, was responsible without differentiation for all the conflicts – Afghanistan, Bosnia-Herzegovina, Chechnya, Israel-Palestine and Iraq – besetting Muslims as a united and concerted effort of Jews and Christians to destroy Islam.

Bin Laden also picked up on the Azzam theme of 'legitimate' terrorism and, again alluding to the experience of Afghanistan, played on the idea that it was the youth of Islam in their absolute difference in Worldview to the soldiers of Unbelief who would respond to the call to armed *Jihad* and carry forward to the struggle.

> *Terrorising you, while you are carrying arms on our land, is a legitimate and morally demanded duty. It is a legitimate right well known to all humans*

---

15 The Bosnian War gave the world the term 'ethnic cleansing'. But for many Muslims, mainstream as well as extreme ones, it was not ethnic Bosniaks who had been cleansed, but European Muslims whose blood and the honor of whose women was less sacrosanct to the international community than that of their Christian neighbors. The true tragedy of the war became blatantly apparent when after NATO airstrikes on Serbian positions around Sarajevo, encouraged by President Bill Clinton, the siege of Sarajevo was lifted within a week after 1,425 days as suddenly and unexpectedly as it had started.

and other creatures. Your example and our example is like a snake which entered into a house of a man and got killed by him. The coward is the one who lets you walk, while carrying arms, freely on his land and provides you with peace and security. Those youths are different from your soldiers. Your problem will be how to convince your troops to fight, while our problem will be how to restrain our youths to wait for their turn in fighting and in operations. These youths are commendable and praiseworthy. They stood up tall to defend the religion; at the time when the government misled the prominent scholars and tricked them into issuing Fatwas (that have no basis neither in the book of Allah, nor in the Sunnah of His prophet (Allah's Blessings and Salutations may be on him)) of opening the land of the two Holy Places for the Christians' armies and handing the Al Aqsa Mosque to the Zionists.[16]

In his second *fatwa* of 1998 *Urging Jihad Against the Americans*, bin Laden ramped-up his demonic anti-Americanism using the Particular Qur'anic verse (2:191, see Chapter 3):

And slay them wherever ye find them, and drive them out of the places whence they drove you out, for persecution is worse than slaughter. And fight not with them at the Inviolable Place of Worship until they first attack you there, but if they attack you (there) then slay them. Such is the reward of disbelievers.

as a general encouragement for Muslims to

. . . comply with God's order to kill the Americans and plunder their money wherever and whenever they find it.

At the end of the 1990s, bin Laden's ideas of the Far Jihad against the Crusader-Zionist Alliance led by the United States of America 'bore fruit' in a number of 'raids' on US positions throughout the world. These included the bombings of the US embassies in Nairobi, Kenya, and Dar es Salaam, Tanzania, which killed more than 200 people and injured more than 5,000 others in August 1998.

However, Al-Qaeda's Violent Islamist Extremist Worldview and operational experience were to come spectacularly to a head in the attacks on the Twin Towers of the World Trade Center, New York and then the Pentagon building by planes hijacked by 19 Al-Qaeda affiliates on 11 September 2001. These attacks killed 2,996 people, injured over 6,000 others and caused at least $10 billion in property and infrastructure damage. The dead included all 19 hijackers and all 265 of the civilian passengers on the four airplanes.[17]

The hallucinating sight of the planes perpetrating these attacks, together with harrowing sight of people throwing themselves to their deaths out of multi-story skyscrapers to escape the towering infernos, meant that Al-Qaeda had

---

16 Bin Laden, 'Declaration of War Against the Americans,' p. 6.
17 18,000 further people suffered illnesses, many of them fatal, as a result of the 9/11 attacks due to the toxic dust released into New York City by the collapse of the Twin Towers.

given the twenty-first century its iconic images of terrorist destruction before the new century had barely begun.

Anwar Al-Awlaki: the globalization of Violent Islamist Extremism as a prelude to the Apocalypse

If vitriolic, lethal anti-Americanism classifying the US as the basis of the Crusader-Zionist Alliance to destroy Islam was bin Laden's most characteristic ideological contribution to the Worldview of Violent Islamist Extremism, it is an irony that it was an American citizen, Anwar al-Awlaki (1971–2011 CE), who was responsible for taking bin Laden's message to a global English-speaking, increasingly internet-inspired audience.

Al-Awlaki's journey into Violent Islamist Extremism is one from green through yellow to red in my diagram (see Plates 1 and 2 after Page 5); a journey of radicalization born of dislocation, restlessness and lack of educational fulfillment. Al-Awlaki was born in the US and had a piecemeal secular and Islamic education in the US and in Yemen during an 11-year period. As a restless young man in the early 1990s, he undertook but never completed a variety of technical and administrative academic courses in the US and was arrested for soliciting prostitution in 1997.

However, after fulfilling the role of Imam in a number of local community mosques in Denver and San Diego, Al-Awlaki established a reputation for himself as an engaging, popular Islamic speaker in the late 1990s. He traveled the US giving semi-formal Islamic lectures on the lives of the Prophet Muhammad and his Companions which he recorded on cassette and CD for which he gained the beginnings of a world-wide audience.

From 1996–2000, possibly after a trip to the training camps of Al-Qaeda built by bin Laden in Afghanistan, Al-Awlaki became imam of the Masjid Ar-Ribat al-Islami Mosque in San Diego, California where senior members of the community rebuked him for encouraging young congregants to join the insurrections against the Russian Federation in Chechnya. When he was an Imam in San Diego in 2000, Al-Awlaki is alleged by the US security agencies to have preached to and had behind doors conversations with two of the 9/11 hijackers who were both Al-Qaeda members, Nawaf al-Hazmi and Khalid al-Mihdhar. In 2001, Al-Awlaki is known to have preached regularly to four other 9/11 hijackers in Virginia, US. During this phase (2000–2001), Al-Awlaki's sermons became noticeably and violently anti-American.

For example, after the 9/11 attacks, Al-Awlaki wrote a blog piece on IslamOnline claiming that Israeli agents were behind the attacks – a view that gained wide credence in certain sectors of the Muslim community. Then in the following year, Al-Awlaki wrote a piece in support of suicide bombing called *Why Muslims Love Death* on the Islam Today website. In 2002–2003 Al-Awlaki conducted a much publicized and much criticized lecture tour of the UK in which he extolled the virtues of armed Jihad and martyrdom.

By 2006, Al-Awlaki had established himself as a key spokesman for Al-Qaeda in English due to his command of the English language and culture. Al-Awlaki was operating in Yemen when he was arrested by Yemeni authorities in 2006.

In 2007, Al-Awlaki was released from custody through tribal intercession and continued to propagate the Al-Qaeda message of global Jihad against the US and the West on the Internet and through other media. In September 2011, Al-Awlaki was, as a US citizen, controversially killed in a CIA drone strike in the Yemen by which time he was revered by global Islamist extremists as one of the most eloquent and convincing propagators of the message of Al-Qaeda.

The Battle for Hearts and Minds

One of Al-Awlaki's influential lectures written as part of Al-Qaeda in Yemen, *The Battle for Hearts and Minds* was delivered to a South African audience via live phone link on Sunday, 11 May 2008. In this talk, Awlaki used 'evidence' from the Rand Corporation to show that the United States, through its various agencies, was deliberately setting out to subvert and destroy Islam through the propagation of the idea of 'moderate' democratic Islam. Al-Awlaki repeated the bin Laden theme of the necessity to be 'wary' of, and to undertake Jihad against, the Americans.

This speech heralded the declaration of a Caliphate by an early incarnation of the so-called Islamic State group in Iraq at the behest of Al-Qaeda in Iraq as the apocalyptic presage to the 'final stage' of human history before the End of Time.

The Dust Will Never Settle Down

A second influential address, again issued from Yemen, in response to the 2005 Jyllands-Posten 'Muhammad Cartoons' controversy called *The Dust Will Never Settle Down* was more extreme and more influential.

The Jyllands-Posten 'Muhammad Cartoons' controversy arose as a result of the publication of 12 cartoons, most of which depicted the Prophet Muhammad in the Danish newspaper Jyllands-Posten on 30 September 2005.

The newspaper announced that their publication of the cartoons was an attempt to contribute to the debate about the criticism of Islam and of self-censorship. Muslim groups in Denmark complained that the cartoons were gratuitously insulting and their publication resulted in protests around the world, including violent demonstrations and riots in some Muslim countries and attacks on Danish embassies.

In 'The Dust Will Never Settle Down', Al-Awlaki recounts stories from the life (*Sira*) of the Prophet Muhammad such as an excerpt about the assassination of one Ka'ab ibn Ashraf (d. 624 CE), a Jewish poet and determined opponent of the Prophet Muhammad who wrote defamatory poetry in order to galvanize political and military support against Muhammad.

186   *The Genealogy of Terror*

'The Dust Will Never Settle Down' also narrates and celebrates the assassination of another inveterate opponent of the Prophet Muhammad, Abu Rafi' (d. 624 CE), and the execution of others who were implacable enemies of the Prophet Muhammad during his lifetime.

Al-Awlaki strips these stories of their military and political context in which, as we have seen in Chapter 2, the Prophet Muhammad and the Community of Medina were struggling for their survival. Instead, he builds a portmanteau case of literalist religious judgments from de-contextualized legal rulings – a classical piece of literalist abuse of text – including judgments from the medieval scholars Ibn Taymiyya (d. 328 CE) and from Qadi 'Iyad ibn Musa Al-Yahsubi (d. 1149 CE) that whoever insults the Prophet Muhammad should be executed.

For example, Al-Awlaki states, *"Whoever curses the Rasool* [the Messenger of God] *be he Muslim or* Kafir [Unbeliever] *must be killed"*, and, *"It is mandatory to kill anyone who curses Rasool Allah* [the Messenger of God]*"*.

Thus, *The Dust Will Never Settle Down* abuses respected Muslim authorities and jurisprudential method to call on Muslims to accomplish the extra-judicial murder of those who are believed to have insulted the Prophet Muhammad and to oppose Islam.

The Dust Will Never Settle Down went viral and snippets of it have been used ever since repeatedly to justify the murder of those – often publishers and authors – who are believed either to oppose Islam or to have in some way insulted the Prophet Muhammad.

For example, *The Dust Will Never Settle Down* is regularly quoted in videos and social media in celebration of the *Charlie Hebdo* attacks of 7 January 2015 in which 12 staff of the satirical magazine *Charlie Hebdo* were murdered by the two French-Algerian brothers, Saïd Kouachi and Chérif Kouachi. These videos often climax with the backdrop of the attackers 'finishing off' the wounded Muslim policeman, Ahmed Merabet, who is lying on the pavement, accompanied by the voice-over of Al-Awlaki speaking in the background. The murder of Ahmed Merabet in this attack is symptomatic of the fact that in their criminal activities VIE operatives, in reality, make no distinction between the Muslim and Non-believer.

44 Ways of Supporting Jihad

In January 2009, Al-Awlaki published and distributed both as hard copies and on the internet a book called '44 Ways of Supporting Jihad'. This was a practical, point-by-point guide to pursuing or supporting armed insurgency which has subsequently become a standard reference text for Al-Qaeda recruits.[18]

These and other Al-Awlaki publications and speeches have been endlessly reproduced and quoted on Violent Islamist Extremist websites and social media platforms and are one of the 'calling-cards' of people committed to violent

---

18 This publication also has appeared in updated edited versions such as '45 Ways of Supporting Jihad' and '46 Ways of Supporting Jihad'.

'Jihad'. Although the known affiliation of Al-Awlaki was with Al-Qaeda, the social media ideologues of ISG have also drawn extensively on quotes and snippets of his 'work'.

In summary, Anwar Al-Awlaki is a study in post-modern irony: a born and educated American citizen who propagated the most virulent and vicious anti-Americanism. Yet his appeal to VIE Muslims globally resided precisely in his ability to propagate the Worldview of Violent Islamist Extremism in dulcet American English tones.

Al-Zawahiri and As-Suri: Al-Qaeda's backroom boys

If Bin Laden and Al-Awlaki were Al-Qaeda's ideological frontmen, then it still needed a technically accomplished 'rhythm section': those who would convince the more scholarly of Salafist extremists that Al-Qaeda were the real theological deal.

The first of these technicians was Osama bin Laden's right-hand man, the current leader of Al-Qaeda, Ayman Al-Zawahiri (born 1951), who was a trained doctor and whose impeccable violent Islamist credentials stretched back to Islamic Jihad and the ideology of Faraj that lay behind the assassination of President Anwar Sadat in 1982 and to the Afghan Jihad.

Al-Zawahiri reached into the doctrinal toolbox and pulled out the essential spanner of all Islamist Extremism – the doctrine of Loyalty and Disavowal (*Al-Wala' wal Bara'*) –which had been significantly updated since Qutb's suggestion of it in his Milestones (1964) and Al-Qahtaani's seminal 1982 text on the doctrine (see pp. 117 ff). Al-Zawahiri extended the doctrine to make it available for use by VIE exponents, especially a vicious ideologue and mentor of the Leader of Al-Qaeda in Iraq, Abu Muhammad Al-Maqdisi (Born 1959 CE). In his own take on the tired theme of the apostasy of 'partial' Muslim rulers, Al-Zawahiri argued that when Muslim states collaborated or entered into alliances with non-Muslim states[19] then it became obligatory to declare them *kafir* (infidel) and to fight them.[20] Moreover, in a twist on the theme of spiraling acts of excommunication (*takfir*) (See pp. 123–124) anyone who failed to make this *takfir* of Muslim leaders and who failed to fight them, i.e. almost the entirety of the Muslim world, should also be declared *kafir* and themselves be fought.

By way of conclusion, Al-Zawahiri called upon the whole global community (*Umma*) of Islam to rise up in armed Jihad as a demonstration of its Loyalty (*Wala'*) to Islam and Disavowal (*Bara'*) of *Kufr* (Unbelief), advocating a kind of 'scorched Earth' policy in the Muslim-majority world.

> *We must re-double our action. Enough time has been lost. Let the Muslim youth not wait for anyone's permission, for Jihad against the Americans, Jews and*

---

19 Naturally ignoring the modern context of nation-states in which such 'pure' entities no longer exist.
20 Maher, *Salafi-Jihadism*.

their alliance of Hypocrites and Apostates is an Individual Religious Obligation . . . We must set our lands aflame beneath the feet of the raiders, they shall never depart otherwise.[21]

As well as extending the idea of Loyalty and Disavowal (*Al-Wala' wal Bara'*), Al-Zawahiri dedicated himself in various Al-Qaeda media outlets to producing colorful videos of revisionist history, 'proving' beyond all conceivable doubt using snazzy maps and graphics that the Crusader-Zionist Alliance was indeed the eternal enemy of Islam.

Although Bin Laden, Al-Awlaki and Al-Zawahiri provided the engine of the Al-Qaeda contribution to the development and perpetuation of the Worldview of Violent Islamist Extremism, a less well-known shadowy individual called Abu Musab as-Suri (Born 1958 CE) was to have a more lasting impact and take VIE into its next manifestation in a world saturated by use of the internet. Abu Musab as-Suri (the Father of Musab the Syrian), born Mustafa bin Abd al-Qadir Setmariam Nasar, argued in his 1600-page book *The Global Islamic Resistance Call* (*Da'wat al-muqawamah al-islamiyyah al-'alamiyyah*),[22] that cells waging war on multiple fronts embedded in the territories of the enemy and linked ideologically, but not necessarily territorially, to Al-Qaeda by the internet, was the best way to wear the enemy down. This wearing down the enemy in their own territories would be a prelude to the ultimate goal of *Jihad*, the final establishment of a full Islamic State. Essentially, As-Suri was, in a rambling way, announcing that the phase of The Base (*Al-Qaeda*) for the Far Jihad was over and presaging the era of the Islamic State.

The ideologues of the Islamic State: Abu Musab Az-Zarqawi, Naji, Abu Bakr Al-Baghdadi and Abu Muhammad Al-Adnani

Osama bin Laden provided a charismatic figurehead and 9/11 a singular triumph for the Worldview of Violent Islamist Extremism in its Al-Qaeda phase. But by 2006 'Al-Qaeda Central' had a number of great hurdles to surmount in order to sustain its ideological and operational leadership of the VIE faction.

First, the spectacular 'triumph' of 9/11, which they were never likely to repeat and certainly not 'improve', especially after Al-Qaeda's dispersal and degrading with the US-led Tora Bora campaign (2001), meant that their trump-card for the destruction of 'kufr and the kuffar'[23,24] – the ultimate act of Disavowal (*Bara'*) as theorized by Al-Zawahiri – had been played.

21 Al-Zawahiri, Ayman. Al-Wala' wal Bara': 'Aqidah Manqulah wa Waqi' Mafqud, p. 29 cited in Bin Ali (2015: 231).
22 Which appeared on the internet in January 2005.
23 Disregarding, naturally, that 31 Muslims were murdered in the 9/11 attacks, dismissed as human shields.
24 Kobeisi, 'Remembering the Muslims Who Were Killed in the 9/11 Attacks'.

Moreover, Al-Qaeda had never achieved the founding aim of Violent Islamist Extremism, to fight their way to the creation of an Islamic State, for three main reasons.

First and foremost, despite the chaos created by Western interference in Muslim affairs amplified and exploited by the actions of the VIE faction, the vast majority of the world's Muslims rejected and still reject the Manichean Worldview of Al-Qaeda and the violently extreme manner in which they propagate it.

Second, when its agents, commanders and affiliated groups, such as Al-Qaeda in the Arabian Peninsula (AQAP), Al-Qaeda in Iraq (AQI) and Al-Shabab (literally, The Youth) in Somalia did gain a local territorial foothold, their theological inflexibility and literalist and merciless application of corporal and capital punishments of the Penal Code (*hudud*) of what they took to be *Sharia* law, together with the imposition of *ad hoc* taxation, repelled local populations and leaders whose support was essential to consolidate their political claims.[25]

Third, whenever an opportunity, such as the anarchic chaos in Iraq post the American-led invasion of 2003, did present itself for territorial consolidation, in-fighting and factionalism prevented it from happening.[26]

Naji and Az-Zarqawi: the management of savagery

For one rogue Al-Qaeda affiliate, however, the reason for this lack of achieving a territorial Islamic State was different. For the leader of the Iraqi branch of Al-Qaeda, Al-Qaeda in Iraq, Abu Musab Az-Zarqawi (1966–2006 CE), who only eventually, begrudgingly offered Bin Laden his Oath of Allegiance (*Baya'*), the answer was simple: Al-Qaeda had not been ruthless enough and had not projected an image of sufficient brutality to scare people into accepting what was necessarily needed of *Sharia* Law and an Islamic State.

Abu Musab Az-Zarqawi was a petty Jordanian criminal for whom the dehumanization of brutal incarceration in Al-Suwaqah prison in Jordan in early 1990, like so many Islamist Extremists from Qutb to Faraj, had rendered him vulnerable to the VIE Worldview. By means of this absolute 'Us' vs. 'Them' Worldview it was easy for him to cast himself as the victim of a tyrannical (*taghut*) corrupt Muslim regime and to seek vengeance with a violent Islamist agenda. It is thought that Az-Zarqawi was groomed into the embrace of Violent Islamist Extremism while in Al-Suwaqah prison in under the influence of a key VIE individual who made a considerable contribution to extreme versions of the Doctrine of Loyalty and Disavowal, Abu Muhammad al-Maqdisi.

---

25 Burke, *Al-Qaeda*.
26 Such as a lack of support for the declaration of Caliphate by the progenitor of the so-called Islamic State in 2006 alluded to by Al-Awlaki in his lecture 'The Battle for Hearts and Minds'.

After release, through a commitment to violence, extreme 'piety' and brash physicality, Az-Zarqawi established himself at the core of like-minded individuals in Jordan and Iraq, in partnership with Al-Maqdisi, in VIE groups of various different names and permutations. He ended up in the late 1990s in the training camps of Al-Qaeda in the Tora Bora region of Afghanistan. After the clearance of Tora Bora, by the US-led (and deeply flawed[27]) operation in response to 9/11 in late 2001, Az-Zarqawi returned to gather support in order to create Al-Qaeda in Iraq where he was well-placed to orchestrate Al-Qaeda's contribution to the resistance to both the US invasion, but equally importantly, resistance to the Shia majority-led reconstitution of the governance of the country between 2003–2005.

At this point (possibly even before) he came under the influence of a key VIE ideologue called (by his Nom de Guerre/Plume) Abu Bakr Naji, who in 2004 published a treatise on the internet called *Management of Savagery: The Most Critical Stage Through Which the Islamic Nation Will Pass (Idārat at-Tawaḥus: Akhṭar marḥalah satamurru bihā l 'ummah)*. The *Management of Savagery* advocated the use of extreme orchestrated violence in Muslim-majority countries to generate the conditions of such chaos using "the power of vexation and exhaustion" that the only entities capable of restoring order would be Violent Islamist groups and those committed to Violent 'Jihad'.

This strategy of savage violence was designed to have a 'polarization effect' that would drive people into the embrace and protection of strongmen as a prelude to the establishment of a VIE Islamic State

> *. . . a kind of polarization begins to happen among the people who live in the region of chaos. The people, seeking security, rally around the great personages of the country or a party organization or a jihadi organization or a military organization composed of the remainders of the army or the police of the regimes of apostasy.*[28]

In 2004–2005 Az-Zarqawi set about creating the "region of chaos" and unleashed a wave of slaughter, in particular of Shia Muslims at shrines, such as Kerbala at the Ashura Festival in March 2004, which killed over 180 people, and the car bomb attacks in Najaf and Karbala in December 2004, which claimed over 60 lives[29], of such indiscriminate and alienating savagery that even Al-Qaeda Central, in the form of a letter by Al-Zawahiri, rebuked him that his barbarity was damaging their cause.

Undeterred, in 2005, Az-Zarqawi formalized his genocidal fury at Shia Muslims in the call for all-out war on Shia sectors of major Iraqi towns, which resulted in a wave of deadly suicide bombings across the country, as Iraq, from

---

27 Burke, *The 9/11 Wars*.
28 Naji, Abu Bakr. *The Management of Savagery*. p. 47, trans. McCants, William.
29 Gardiner, 'The Death of Zarqawi'.

the promise of its first democratic elections in January 2005, spiraled into a seemingly unstoppable vortex of Sunni-Shia sectarian violence. The US and the British in Basra were caught helplessly (until the US Surge of 2006) in the middle, wondering what on earth their lack of forward political planning and lack of religious-cultural awareness, after dismantling a 33-year-old, single-party dictatorship without a Plan B, had unleashed.

Az-Zarqawi himself was killed in a US operation called Operation Death in 2006. But in the American prison camps in Iraq, such as Camp Bucca, embittered, disenfranchised, unemployable former high and middle-ranking members of the Ba'ath Party, which had been disbanded *en bloc*, and Iraqi soldiers and army officers, who had also been demobilized *en bloc*, mingled with Violent Islamists. From this intermingling of Ba'ath Party managers and Violent Islamist Extremists, the particular ideological contribution of Az-Zarqawi of vitriolic anti-Shi'ism and the *Management of Savagery* was given a fresh and more organized impetus.

The result of this fusion of the disbanded state institutional apparatus of Saddam Hussain and the ideology of *The Management of Savagery* was that a terrifying of hybrid of National Socialism and Violent Islamist Extremism, combining of one-party state institutional know-how and the most vicious form of Violent Islamist Extremism yet known, was incubating under the noses of the (largely non-Arab speaking) occupying power. This hybrid ideological grouping was soon to declare itself, initially, as the Islamic State in Iraq.

Nine members of what eventually became the Islamic State Group's top command did time at Bucca. The emerging (but not yet enthroned) leader of the grouping, a man relatively unknown outside VIE circles, but increasingly infamous within it, called Abu Bakr al-Baghdadi (Born 1971 CE) spent five years in Camp Bucca, as did his deputy, Abu Muslim al-Turkmani (1959–2015 CE), as well as ISG's senior military leader Haji Bakr (1958–2014 CE).[30]

The Arab Spring reaches Syria

The US military completed its withdrawal from Iraq in December 2011. In early 2011 the so-called Arab Spring, a wave of mainly peaceful democratic protests which had unleashed dominoes-style toppling of hitherto un-shiftable (often Western-backed or established) autocratic regimes from Tunisia, Libya through Egypt arrived in the cities of Syria. Alienated by the empty promises of political reform from President Bashar Al-Assad (Born 1965 CE) and his one-party state, and aggravated by years of failing harvests and droughts which had seen mass rural-urban migration, protesters took to the streets in Homs in March 2011 and then in Damascus to voice their grievances against the Assad regime.

It is a matter of debate who shot first – the regime or the opposition – but by late 2011 the official opposition to Assad, the Turkish-protected, Western-backed Syrian National Council and its military wing of mainly Syrian Army

---

[30] McCoy, 'The American Prison That Became the Birthplace of Isis'.

defectors, the so-called Free Syrian Army, had failed to topple Assad. Instead, a dizzying collection of Violent Islamist militias armed and financed by various regional powers, all vying for influence both over the outcome of the conflict and for Islamist credentials on the Arab Muslim street,[31] had entered the fray. These Violent Islamist militias were united only by their desire to topple Assad, to establish some type of unarticulated Islamic State and by their hatred for the ruling Alawite Shia minority from which the Assad dynasty hailed.

Among these groups, the Al-Qaeda affiliate, the Al-Nusra Front (*Jabhat an-Nusra*), by mid-2013 had staked a claim for leadership of the VIE faction. It achieved this through the success of its military strategy of dislodging regime forces from key military bases, through a wave of suicide attacks on regime figures and their associates. It attracted recruits both from the local Sunni population and from across the Arab Sunni world using slick video productions that highlighted the effectiveness of its training in guerrilla warfare. These recruitment videos, in tried and trusted Al-Qaeda fashion, highlighted the deep bonds of Islamic brotherhood and masculine prowess that resulted from joining the 'Jihad'.

The Al-Nusra Front's main rival for VIE authority in the civil war was turning out to be neither the Assad regime nor other relatively 'moderate', but still genocidally anti-Shia, VIE groups such as the Army of Islam (*Jaysh al-Islam*) founded and funded by Saudi Arabia. It turned out to be its loosely affiliated Al-Qaeda partner, the Islamic State of Iraq, which due to incursions from Iraq into the areas of Northeast Syria, which were ungovernable for the embattled Assad regime, had re-named itself the Islamic State of Iraq and Sham.[32]

The anarchy of the Syrian Civil War specifically suited the VIE Worldview particular to *Islamic State of Iraq and Sham* or ISIS as ISG was known until June 2014. The ungoverned chaos enabled them to put fully in practice the ideas of the *Management of Savagery* by fighting to destroy any group that was not themselves and to enact the policy, played out in recruiting videos, of 'unmaking' the border between Syria and Iraq. This border had been specifically singled out by Naji as the evil colonial product of the Sykes-Picot agreement and the colonial carve-up of the Ottoman Caliphate at the end of the First World War (1918).

The second half of 2013 saw a series of tit-for-tat assassinations and skirmishes between the Al-Nusra Front and ISG in and around the towns of Deir Az-Zour and Raqqa in the Northeast of Syria, which were accompanied theologically online with mutual accusations of *takfir* (calling each other 'infidel') which became the stock-in-trade doctrine for VIE groups when fighting each other. Finally, in mid-2013, ISIS took control of the city of Raqqa as its HQ and achieved a significant territorial foothold in a major Syrian city for its expansion and *Management of Savagery*-style state-building ambitions declared under its motto, "Enduring and Expanding".

In the confusing melee of the war, the rise of ISG had gone relatively un-noticed. In June 2014 all that was to change. In columns of armed jeeps, ISG fighters

---

31 Phillips, *The Battle for Syria*.
32 Sham being the Prophetic and medieval name for the territory of the Levant.

swept back across the border into Iraq and captured the second Iraqi city of Mosul from the Iraqi National Army, which fled en masse, driven by the stories of the unbridled savagery that ISIS meted out on its Shia Muslim captives, who indeed had been butchered as POWs in their hundreds with their bodies often dumped in mass graves or rivers. Notable ISIS atrocities had included the murder on 10 June 2014 of 670 Shia inmates of Badush prison in Mosul and, on 12 June 2014, the murder of between 1,095–1,700 prisoners from the Iraqi army, including many cadets, after an engagement in the Saladin Province of northern Iraq. ISIS was now in charge of Iraq's second city and with it captured the Bank of Mosul containing $500m and considerable quantities of US-supplied military hardware.

The contribution of Al-Baghdadi: the declaration of Caliphate and the Oath of Allegiance (Baya)

Worse was to come when on 19 June 2014 the leader of ISIS, the shadowy figure of Abu Bakr al-Baghdadi, whose claim to leadership resided in his belonging to the Prophet Muhammad's tribe of Quraysh and the levels of violence that he was prepared to sanction in the name of Islam, declared himself Caliph Ibrahim and the Commander of the Faithful from the pulpit of the Central Mosque of Mosul. Wearing the black robes and turban that once symbolized the powerful Abbasid dynasty, Al-Baghdadi, now styled as Caliph Ibrahim, promised to restore the honor and dignity of Muslims by defeating "the *taghut*", i.e. Tyrant regimes, apostates, the "herds of *Rafidhi* cattle", i.e. Shia Muslims, the Jews, the atheist Chinese and the Crusader-Zionist Alliance. The spokesman of ISIS, Abu Muhammad Al-Adnani (1977–2016 CE), announced simultaneously that the group responsible for the 'Caliphate' was no longer to be called the Islamic State of Iraq and Sham (*ad-dawlat al-islamiyya fiy Iraq wa Sham*) but simply the Islamic State (*ad-dawlat al-islamiyya*) indicating its new claims to global authority over all Muslims.

Al-Baghdadi's declaration of the 'Caliphate' was overtly a declaration of his Supreme Authority over all Muslims taking on the mantle of the Prophet Muhammad and did send shockwaves around the Muslim world that even caused a degree of soul-searching among some Mainstream Muslims. The declaration needs, however, more to be understood as a claim to supreme authority amongst VIE groups and in particular as an act of wresting authority from Al-Qaeda. As was to be expected, credible Muslim scholars from authorized centers of learning in the Sunni and Shia worlds were unanimous in their rejection of the claims to Caliphate of so-called Islamic State and of Abu Bakr al-Baghdadi as a 'Caliph' for two main reasons:[33]

1. It is not possible for someone to self-declare as Caliph as the person must be chosen by and agreeable to a consensus of different elements of the Muslim community.[34]

---

33 Cockburn, *The Rise of Islamic State*.
34 Middle East Monitor, 'Prominent Scholars Declare ISIS Caliphate "Null and Void"'.

2   The task of the Caliph is to uphold the Law (*Sharia*) of Islam. ISG had willfully and viciously ignored the rulings of the *Sharia* on a host of matters, most obviously the strict rules and conditions of armed combat (*Qital*). The actions of the ISG and their claims to Caliphate have been condemned as spurious and repugnant across the Islamic world.[35]

More critically, however, Al-Qaeda in the form of the Al-Nusra Front rejected it, or at least rejected ISG's authority over them. This led to further bouts of in-fighting and the defection of a number of Al-Nusra battalions and commanders to ISG and, in particular, splits and confusion within the ranks of foreign fighter battalions.

The state-building of Islamic State

The declaration of Caliphate accompanied by claims to the establishment of the infrastructure of a global Islamic State was also a powerful recruiting device in the Muslim-majority and Muslim-minority worlds.

For example, the ISG English-language media-production unit Al-Hayat produced slick video productions 'showing' the full institutional infrastructure of a functioning state with:

- civilian border checkpoints;
- an education system that issued 'authorized' certificates and had classrooms illuminated by celestial light;
- a welfare system of sweets and toys delivered to grateful children;
- courts of law outside of which the corporal penalties of chopping off the hands of thieves and executing homosexuals were carried out; and
- borders patrolled by well-paid, uniformed fighters flying the iconic *Shahadah* flag of the Prophet Muhammad.

Many of these productions were brought to a climax with images of local Sunni tribesmen making the Islamic Oath of Allegiance (*Bayah*) to representatives of Caliph Ibrahim as a resplendent re-enactment of the Oath of Allegiance given by the Companions to the Prophet Muhammad. This re-enactment of the Prophetic Oath of Allegiance was an ultimate proof that Caliph Ibrahim really was a leader on the Prophetic model (*manhaj an-nabawiy*) and was recognized as such by the *Umma* (Global Community) of Islam. It was also the symbolic, political enactment of 'Loyalty and Disavowal' – Loyalty to Islamic State and Disavowal of citizenship rights and responsibilities of nation-states.

35 Hassaballa, 'Think Muslims Haven't Condemned ISIS?'.

Abdullah al-Feisal, Musa Cerantonio and Anjem Choudhary: the 'theology' of migration

This state-building aspect of ISG Loyalty (*Wala'*) with the reinstitution of the Muhamadan Oath of Allegiance (*Baya*) was accompanied by a 'theology' of migration – *'Hijra'* – promoted in the ISG monthly magazine *Dabiq*.

'Hijra' is an Arabic-Islamic term which means 'migration'. It has come in most Islamic contexts to mean 'migration in the path of God' and is modeled on the migration of the Prophet Muhammad with some 100 members of the early Muslim community in 622 CE from conditions of persecution in Mecca to conditions in which they could practice Islam freely and live without persecution in Yathrib about 200 miles North of Mecca (see Chapter 2).

VIE supporters and sympathizers of ISG worldwidec such as the Australian VIE ideologue Musa Cerantino, and the Jamaican Abdullah al-Feisalc seized on this theme and made the case for the Individual Religious Obligation (*Fard al-Ayn*) of migration to the Islamic State on the Prophetic model as a necessary precursor to participation in armed Jihad. The founder member of the UK-based *Al-Muhajirun* – meaning The Migrants – Anjem Choudhary (Born 1967 CE), behind closed doors but recorded by UK police, pledged allegiance to Al-Baghdadi and also encouraged his followers to migrate to ISG, which led to his conviction for terrorist offences after years of preaching hate for non-Muslims and 'non-Muslim' states.

Moreover, in this act of Loyalty (*Wala'*) of building an Islamic State, ISG also offered an uniquely appealing set of a VIE version of Bloom's taxonomy of human needs:[36]

1 **Sex,** with the infamous phenomenon of 'Jihadi' wives. These were both taken from local populations and from migrants persuaded to travel to Syria from abroad such as the Glaswegian Aqsa Mahmood and three school girls from Tower Hamlets – Kadiza Sultana, Amira Abase and Shamima Begum – who left for Syria in July 2015. They also came from captured Yazidi slave girls whom ISG fighters took from the area around Mount Sinjar in Iraq in August 2014;[37]
2 **Salary.** After the capture of the Bank of Mosul, ISG were offering local fighters $400 per month and foreign fighters as much as $1,000 per month;[38]
3 **Respect,** offered in online and social media eulogies to fighters and martyrs;
4 **Certainty,** in the absolutism of the VIE versions of the Doctrines of the Unity of God (*Tawhid*) and Loyalty and Disavowal (*Wala' wal Bara'*) and

---

36 While Al-Qaeda and other VIE groups had hitherto only offered fighters basic subsistence, weapons training, the joys of male Muslim brotherhood and the promise of Paradise for martyrs, suicide 'martyrs' in particular.
37 Pasha-Robinson, 'This Girl Was Captured by Isis When She Was 14 Years Old'.
38 McClam, 'ISIS Pays Foreign Fighters $1,000 a Month'.

excommunication (*takfir*) of all other Muslims which left no room for uncomfortable existential doubt;

5   **Paradise,** for martyrs, with the benefits of the virgins (*houris*) of the Garden and intercession with God for 72 family members.

However, its media strategy, "*To develop the media strategy such that it reaches and targets the heart of the middle leadership of the armies of apostasy in order to push them to join the jihad*"[39], also proved to be the eventual territorial undoing of ISG.

In the second half of 2014, Coalition US-led airstrikes began to bite, not least by limiting the capability of IS to operate in convoys of armed jeeps above ground. In response, ISG orchestrated and publicized the execution of Western hostages, dressed in the orange jumpsuits that had become synonymous with the US Guantanamo Bay Detention Center. This included gruesome beheadings with a knife conducted by the ISG executioner, the Londoner Muhammad Emwazi.

Those publicly executed were:

1   James Foley, an American journalist (19 August 2014);
2   Steven Sotloff, an Israeli-American journalist (2 September 2014);
3   David Haines, a British Aid Worker (13 September 2014);
4   Alan Henning, a British Aid Worker (3 October 2014);
5   Peter Abdul Rahman Kassig, an American Aid Worker who was a convert to Islam (16 November 2014);
6   The beheading of Kassig was accompanied by the mass beheading online of 18 Syrian Army prisoners of war (16 November 2014).

This managed and orchestrated savagery, which was designed to impress other extremists of the brutality of ISG revenge, reached its apogee in early January 2015, when ISG released a video of the immolation by fire in a cage of captured Jordanian pilot Muath Al-Kasasbeh (1988–2015), surrounded by ranks of hooded ISG fighters.

These acts of managed and orchestrated savagery added steel to the determination of the Coalition against ISG. They also eradicated any lingering doubts among normal Muslim citizens in Muslim-majority countries such as Jordan that ISG – or Da'ish as the Arab world calls it – was not only an enemy of the West, but also an enemy of Islam, in its flagrant violation of Islam's most basic laws of humane conduct for captives, which was common knowledge to have been part of the appeal of Original Islam. Every right-minded Muslim and non-Muslim could see that ISG represented a threat to civilization itself and, in particular, Islamic civilization.

39 Naji, 'Management of Savagery', p. 120.

Abu Muhammad Al-Adnani: lone wolf 'Jihad'

The context of the intensified Coalition effort since late 2014/early 2015 to degrade, destroy and de-territorialize ISG ushered in next final ideological phase of ISG's commitment to managed savagery, the period of the lone wolf.

This phase saw the emergence of our final ideologue of so-called Islamic State, its late spokesman Abu Muhammad al-Adnani, born Taha Falaha (1977– 2016 CE), who was ISG Chief of External Operations.

In an internet-propagated speech of high rhetorical bravado and intensity called *Indeed Your Lord is Ever-Watchful* issued on 22 September 2014, which was reminiscent of the speeches of Anwar Al-Awlaki (see above), Al-Adnani called on the People of Tawhid (*muwahhidin*) to enact their Disavowal (*Bara'*) of Kufr by rising up to attack in as savage and an *ad hoc* way as possible the military personnel, officials and civilians of the Coalition against ISG in their own countries.

> O muwahhidīn in Europe, America, Australia, and Canada . . . O muwahhidīn in Morocco and Algeria . . . O muwahhidīn in Khorasan, the Caucasus, and Iran . . . O muwahhidīn everywhere upon the face of the earth . . . O brothers in creed . . . O people of walā' [Loyalty to Islam] and barā' [Disavowal of Unbelief] . . . O patrons of the Islamic State . . . O you who have given bay'ah (pledge of allegiance) to the Caliph Ibrāhīm everywhere . . . O you who have loved the Islamic State . . . O you who support the Caliphate . . . O you who consider yourselves from amongst its soldiers and patrons . . .
>
> [...] So O muwahhid, do not let this battle pass you by wherever you may be. You must strike the soldiers, patrons, and troops of the tawāghīt. Strike their police, security, and intelligence members, as well as their treacherous agents. Destroy their beds. Embitter their lives for them and busy them with themselves. If you can kill a disbelieving American or European – especially the spiteful and filthy French – or an Australian, or a Canadian, or any other disbeliever from the disbelievers waging war, including the citizens of the countries that entered into a coalition against the Islamic State, then rely upon Allah, and kill him in any manner or way however it may be. Do not ask for anyone's advice and do not seek anyone's verdict. Kill the disbeliever whether he is civilian or military, for they have the same ruling. Both of them are disbelievers. Both of them are considered to be waging war [the civilian by belonging to a state waging war against the Muslims]. Both of their blood and wealth is legal for you to destroy, for blood does not become illegal or legal to spill by the clothes being worn. The civilian outfit does not make blood illegal to spill, and the military uniform does not make blood legal to spill. The only things that make blood illegal and legal to spill are Islam and a covenant (peace treaty, dhimma, etc.). Blood becomes legal to spill through disbelief. So whoever is a Muslim, his blood and wealth are sanctified. And whoever is a disbeliever, his wealth is legal for a Muslim to take and his blood is legal to

spill. His blood is like the blood of a dog; there is no sin for him [the Muslim] in spilling it nor is there any blood money to be paid for doing such.[40]

In a reminder of the real causative effects of powerfully articulated ideas, especially on those with fragile mental health, within weeks of the issue of this *'fatwa'* Europe, America, Australia and Canada had all witnessed spontaneous, lone-wolf attacks on its official personnel and citizenry by people with sympathies for ISG.

Canada, on 20 October and 22 October 2014, witnessed two lone-wolf attacks both by Muslim converts, one with known ISG sympathies, the first on two Canadian soldiers and the second on the Parliament building. An attack with hostage-taking on a Sydney café followed in Australia on December 15, 2014, whose perpetrator used the symbols of ISG to characterize his criminality. Between 2015 and 2017 *ad hoc* attacks usually with knives or vehicles driven at crowds of citizens took place in Australia, Nice, France, Berlin, Germany, Westminster Bridge and London Bridge, London and the Manchester Arena, so that by the time of writing, the type of attack called for by Al-Adnani in September 2014 has become the most typical terrorist attack in cities in the West. These attacks are made all the more terrorizing by their often complete unpredictability for the Security Services and the fact that, while the link to the Worldview and edicts of ISG is usually so clear as to be undeniable, the fragile mental health of such attackers is often another decisive contributory factor.

With the combination of the declaration of a VIE Caliphate, *takfir* of all other Muslim groups, the prosecution of a Shia Muslim genocide and the promotion of leaderless Jihad among the Infidel, ISG exploited the idea of Loyalty and Disavowal (*Al wala' wal bara'*) to its absolute ideological limit. While it is now clear that, territorially speaking, the so-called Islamic State is unlikely to re-constitute itself fully; in terms of the Worldview itself, ISG is likely to "endure and expand" in the prisons of Europe and the Middle East and in disaffected, war-ravaged, brutalized communities of young men and women, for whom the rewards of global capitalism are seemingly out of reach and for whom the promise of democracy offers little hope of life-improving change.

The tremendous 'success' and appalling effects of Violent Islamist Extremism

In the first two decades of the twenty-first century, the Worldview of Violent Islamist Extremism and its ideologues and followers have been spectacularly successful in terms in the three Rs that motivate terrorism:

---

40 Al-Adnani, 'Indeed Your Lord is Ever-Watchful'.

1. Revenge,
2. Renown and
3. Reaction.[41]

The 'awe-inspiring' '9/11' attacks by 19 Al-Qaeda affiliates on 11 September 2001, backed up slightly more 'prosaically' by the attacks of 7 July 2005 by four Al-Qaeda-inspired British extremists on the London Transport Network at rush-hour, established Al-Qaeda, in particular, and Violent Islamist Extremist groups more generally, as the greatest security threat to world peace and the stability of the West, replacing the former Soviet Union and other communist powers.[42]

Both attacks and the martyrdom of 'the Blessed 19' of 9/11 are still endlessly celebrated in VIE online circles as 'revenge' on the *Kafir* superpower that caused misery in Muslim lands. In the improbability of its success against the odds, 9/11 brought huge renown to Al-Qaeda as 'proof' of its strategic leadership of Islamist Extremists and of the blessings conferred on the mission by God.

As for Reaction, it could not have been more significant. Exponents of the Worldview of Violent Islamist Extremism have dramatically changed the foreign policy of three superpowers[43] and, in their current contribution to prolonging and undermining the genuine Muslim opposition to Bashar Al-Assad the President of Syria in the Syrian Civil War (2011–present), have altered the balance of *Sunni-Shia* power decisively in the Middle East in favor of the Shia branch of Islam, represented by the Islamic Republic of Iran. This is, of course, hugely ironic given the commitment of the Islamic State Group to eradicate Shia Islam.

It is a Worldview that has indirectly toppled at least one non-Muslim[44] government and many Muslim ones. It has triggered the Biblical-style Exodus of hundreds of thousands of migrant Muslims from the Middle East towards the conditions of peace in the West with which we started this book. It has contributed hugely to a climate of political and social fear of the non-white, non-Christian 'other' without which, surely, we would not have seen the seismic political anomalies of the election of President Donald Trump (Born 1946 CE) on the basis of a raft of overtly xenophobic policies (2016) or, perhaps, the departure from the European Union of one of its major constituent powers, the United Kingdom, driven by fear of migration.

---

41 Richardson, *What Terrorists Want*.
42 Grey, *The New Spymasters*.
43 The United States of America, the Russian Federation and the European Union.
44 e.g. the Spanish government in the elections that followed shortly after the Madrid train bombings in March 2004

As a partner in crime to unwise and often unlawful Western intervention in Muslim-majority affairs, Violent Islamist Extremism has directly caused the civic disruption, violence and the deaths of tens of thousands of Muslims from Kandahar to Timbuktu, whose names and faces we will never know, because they are not news-worthy Westerners. These VIE victims have usually been ignominiously butchered "as human shields to apostate regimes" while going about their daily lives.[45] In short, in its powerfully dichotomizing effects, Violent Islamist Extremist ideologues and exponents seek to create such an unstable world that the only possibility for human life left is that its complete 'Us vs. Them Worldview' of absolute and violent Manichean separation is actually realized.[46]

---

[45] Perhaps as many as 97% of all victims of Islamist terrorism have been Muslim. National Counterrorism Center, *Report on Terrorism*.

[46] Like Nazism the Worldview of Violent Islamist Extremism is an archetype of the 'demi-reality' (Bhaskar, 1993). That is to say that in and of itself has no alethic truth and little or no representation of the realities of the world but it has very real toxic effects in the world. Therefore, lest we forget in the relative safety and comfort of the well-protected West, it is the Worldview from which normal Mainstream Muslims have suffered most both in terms of civic disruption and violence in the Muslim-majority world and in terms of the climate of political and social suspicion that pervades the Muslim-minority contexts of Europe, the Americas and Australasia.

8 A second Age of Extremes or a second Age of Enlightenment?

Summary

This book has put forward the argument that Islam, Islamism and Islamist Extremism are Worldviews that have all been generated out of the various tendencies of the Islamic tradition, but which have become fundamentally different bodies of belief and practice with different concomitant outlooks on the world. The book has explored the substance of these Worldviews and why they have come to pass.

Mainstream Islam, in all its multifarious denominational forms, is characterized philosophically as a Worldview of unity-in-diversity, the integration of belief and practice and the balance between the rights of God Almighty to worship and the rights of humankind to well-being and respect, including just governance. Mainstream Islam is a unifying Worldview which provides the ethical and legal conditions for peace as the basic premise of just and worshipful human life. Mainstream Islam sanctions self-defensive, openly declared and regulated warfare as a *temporary phase* so that the conditions of peace between peoples of all types may be recovered as quickly as possible.

Islamism is characterized as a Worldview of exaggerated difference between the Muslim and the non-Muslim, and the inversion of the traditional relationship between religion and politics in Islam, so that for Ideological Islamists the establishment of an Islamic State becomes an article of faith and a *sine qua non* of genuine Islamic belief.

Non-Violent Islamist Extremism is characterized by the absolute, eternal separation and non-identity of the Muslim and non-Muslim and the Disavowal (*Bara'*) and the sub-humanization of the Infidel (*kafir*) (including the 'wrong' and 'partial' Muslim).

The Worldview of Violent Islamist Extremism (VIE) is characterized by the absolute, eternal separation and non-identity of the Muslim and non-Muslim (including the 'wrong' and 'partial' Muslim) with lethal consequences for non-VIE out-groups. The proof of a VIE Muslim's loyalty (*Wala'*) to Islam becomes the commitment to annihilate violently all aspects of *Kufr* (Unbelief) and the system (*milla*) of the Infidel (*kafir*) as the precursor to establishment of a violent, legally literalist Islamic State. Violent Islamist Extremism justifies savage, de-regulated *ad hoc* violence as an *eternal corollary* of the supposedly divided nature of the Cosmos.[1]

The political conditions of Extremism

The previous considerations are matters of theology and ideology which have been the principal focus of the book. Although I have alluded to the oppressive political conditions in which Ideological Islamism and Islamist Extremism are particularly prone to thrive, so far the focus of the book has not been the contemporary political conditions in which Islamist Extremism and, indeed, the other extremisms such as Far Right Extremism, which is its mirror image and foil, can flourish. In this summary chapter, I will embed the book's argument briefly in this Bigger Social and Political Picture.

The first Age of Extremes

In his book the *Age of Extremes* (1994), the historian Eric Hobsbawm (1917–2012 CE) explained that the 'short' twentieth century (1914–1991 CE) from the First World War to the fall of the USSR was the age both of nation-states and the ideological extremes of Communism, Fascism and Nationalism. These, in turn, were the statist legacy of the demise of the Empires which had thrived in the 'long' nineteenth century (1789–1914 CE) which ran from the French Revolution to the commencement of the First World War.

Islamism in all the various forms described in this book is, I suggest, the product of the same dynamic. It is the ideological outcome of the political demise of Imperial Ottoman Islam and the reconfiguration of the Muslim-majority world into nation-states, wedded to the master counter-narrative of the re-establishment of a pristine, pure Islamic State.

Hobsbawm's other insight about the changing nature of human political and social behavior over the course of the twentieth century also holds true both for Mainstream Islam and, dangerously, for the various forms of Islamist Extremism that we have examined. The power of real, live human collectives of all types and their cultures to shape, to give texture and to moderate human behavior has radically waned in the last part of the 'long' twentieth century (1991–present); at the same time as the power of the individual to shape, modify and powerfully project his/her own ideas about the nature of the world and

---

1 As a by-product, the book has argued that in the sincerity of their affirmation of the Unity of God and the finality of the Prophethood of Muhammad all the people that, in their own individual ways, have substantiated these Worldviews are undeniably Muslim. However, in the ways that this affirmation plays out in their religious beliefs, attitudes to others and behaviors in the world, they are profoundly and fundamentally different.

indeed the Next World and the theological World, un-moderated and un-mediated, has radically increased.[2]

The explosion in the use and power of social media of proliferating types is both an expression of this force of individualism and the means of its reproduction and amplification throughout the world. It is also an expression of the increase in tension in the individualized environment of knowledge and information between non-professional individuals and professional, collectivized actors such as a journalists and civil servants. From one point of view, fake news is just facts about events that are not true and therefore that are not facts at all; from another one point of view, fake news is the news about non-events that are believed to exist by thousands of individuals, regardless of the will of professional journalistic collectives. Therefore, fake news wields power as a demi-reality – something without truth or real existence, but which causes real effects in the world.

The individualization of Islamism

As far as religious Worldviews are concerned, therefore, the secularization thesis has undoubtedly been proved wrong by the 'long' twenty-first century: the religion of Islam and others, notably evangelical Christianity, are as important worldwide as ever before; the individualization thesis, however, holds true. In common with those of other faiths and political affiliations, Mainstream Muslims, Islamist Muslims and Islamist Extremists are likely to hold and mediate their Worldviews on a more individual basis with less contact with mosques, associations and large groups than ever before.

This is why it is so important to understand the differences as Worldviews between Islam, Islamism and Islamist Extremism, since individuals espousing extreme Islamist Worldviews are less and less likely, especially since the relative demise of Al-Qaeda, the killing of Osama bin Laden and the territorial collapse of ISG, to be part of a real, physical ideological mass movement, and more and more likely to be individuals whose extremism is projected into and by social media, with digital Islamisms, as the currency of their communication.

Why? The root causes of Islamist Extremism

In the twenty-first century, we have shifted from mass ideological movements to masses of individualized Worldviews that are the potent catalysts to a range of the root causes of extremism. These root causes, that only require the match of ideology to be ignited into full-blown extremism, include noxious determinate absences[3] and malign presences in some peoples' lives. Noxious absences at the root of Islamist Extremism include:

---

2   The power of President Donald Trump's Tweeting, both before and after his election, show us the power of the individualized Worldview.
3   Bhaskar, *Dialectic*.

1. **A *relative* lack of employment, status and wealth that is commensurate with a person's talent or qualifications;**

   As Wilkinson and Pickett[4] have shown, it is *relative* lack of employment, wealth and status, when people do not feel that they are achieving their just deserts relative to different types of other people that can be most alienating. It should be noted, for example, that the key 9/11 suicide bombers came from relatively affluent, educated backgrounds from societies in which it is notoriously difficult for the straightforwardly talented to make progress. Globalized media has amplified dreams of success for millions of educated people in the developing Muslim-majority world who are often then denied access to it.

2. **Lack of civic belonging and empowerment;**

   An absence of civic belonging in a *minority* of young Muslims in Western and Muslim nation-states makes them vulnerable to the extremist narrative of Disavowal (*bara'*) of all ties of national and local citizenship in favor of a monolithic Islamist sense of exclusive belonging to the Global Community (*Umma*) of Islam.[5]

3. **An absence of effective Islamic education and educational attainment;**

   An absence of a basic Islamic education and poor outcomes of mainstream schooling are regular features of all types of Islamist Extremism, especially among VIE footsoldiers. Moreover, madrasa-style Islamic education has often left children reflectively unprepared to deal with the complex issues of being a Muslim in a secularizing society. This absence of basic Islamic education and educational attainment leaves some people vulnerable to ideological recruitment and to the simplistic 'Us vs. Them' Worldview of Islamist Extremism. This lack of Islamic religious literacy also accounts in part for the over-representation of converts to Islam among extremists.

4. **An absence of engaged parenting.**

   Moreover, it is also a regular feature of VIE terrorism that parents of those convicted of terrorist charges have lost touch with the activities and development of their children, often mediated by the internet and social media, as they enter young adulthood.

These root causes of extremism also include 'vicious presences' such as:

1. **Political oppression and corruption;**

   This is related to the relative un- and under-employment cited above, since political oppression and corruption prevent the talent of the young from gaining its just recognition and desserts;

---

4 Wilkinson and Pickett, *The Spirit Level*.
5 It should be remembered in this regard that repeated surveys show that Muslims in general in the UK evince significantly high levels of civic loyalty and connection to Britain. Such findings are entirely commensurate with the Mainstream Islamic Worldview of unity-in-diversity.

2   **Anti-Muslim prejudice and invisible 'glass-ceilings';**

The testimony of job interviewees wearing the *hijab* or with an obviously Muslim name, as well as anti-Muslim Hate Crimes statistics,[6] suggest strongly that anti-Muslim prejudice is a determinate factor that prevents many young Muslims in Europe gaining fair access to the employment market and more generally prevents Muslims, as part of a 'suspect community', from gaining a fair social hearing in a whole range of different quarters.[7,8]

3   **The easy availability of arms and people prepared to fund violence in the Middle East;**

The responsibility of Qatari, Iranian and Saudi business people in keeping the Syrian Civil War active is an immense source of shame to the Muslim-majority world.[9] Mainstream Muslim-majority governments have often been prepared not to clamp down on VIE activity since they fear the damage to their credibility in Islamist quarters.

4   **The presence and actions of Western armies and governments in Muslim-majority states.**

The radicalizing effects of recent ill-judged Western policy and military interventions, even if they have been basically well-intentioned, including post-intervention policy that appears to have a sectarian either pro-Shia or pro-Sunni bias and drone-strikes aimed at militants that kill civilians, have been well documented.[10]

In the Middle East, it is common knowledge that a uniquely potent combination of a population explosion since the 1950s, an improvement in basic levels of technical education, relatively diminishing numbers of jobs and oppressive, corrupt, often Western-backed political regimes have created a uniquely 'suitable' environment for the ideologues of Islamist Extremism to thrive and find large numbers of willing recruits.

Within this cluster of 'root causes', Worldviews are not necessarily one of the root causes of Extremism – when adult human beings are prosperous, recognized by society and personally fulfilled, they overwhelmingly do not turn to violence against their fellow civilians to achieve political ends.

Nevertheless, the root causes cited previously[11] feed into, generate and then endlessly confirm the absolutely divided 'Us vs. Them', 'pure Muslim victimized by corrupt Infidel (*Kafir*)' Worldviews of Non-Violent and Violent Islamist Extremism. As such, these Worldviews certainly are undoubtedly potent catalysts to Islamist separatism and violence and the currency and the medium by which terrorism

---

6   TellMAMA, 'Anti-Muslim Hatred, Terrorism, Media Sources, Far Right Networks & Spike Points'.
7   Alexandra, 'Muslim Women at "Disadvantage" in Workplace'.
8   'Discrimination Against Muslim Women – Fact Sheet'.
9   Phillips, *The Battle for Syria*.
10 Burke, *Al-Qaeda*; Burke, *The 9/11 Wars*.
11 And doubtless others.

is communicated, justified and replicated by people suffering from a whole range of malign generative mechanisms of disaffection.

The second Age of Extremes

However, it is not only alienated, marginalized individuals propagating extreme ideological Worldviews through social media who are driving Non-Violent and Violent Islamist Extremism. We are now living in a period when powerful, global interest groups, both state actors and quasi-state actors, are premised on perpetuation of polarized extremes or the polarization of near-extremes.

Obviously, for example, the Israel-Palestine (1947-present) conflict is premised for many of its actors on the denial of the basic rights to self-determination and humanity of both parties and a mutual demonization and commitment to destruction of the 'out-group'. For some in HAMAS, 'the Jews' are the 'out-group' from God's Mercy who have been in eternal rebellion against God and His commands and are destined to be driven out of Israel and slaughtered as a presage to the End of Times.

For some Israeli Jews, Palestinian Muslims are an obstacle to their God-given inheritance of the Land of Greater Israel and therefore can only ever be, at best, second-class citizens and, at worst, need to be eradicated. These two polarized narratives are, for some, comfortable because, despite the endless cycle of bloodshed and attendant misery that they justify, they are clear explanatory Worldviews that provide a coherent world-ordering idea which is easy to sell to willing recruits and pass on to the next benighted generation.

Extremists need each other

In a fast-polarizing atmosphere of Western liberal politics, Islamist Extremists, as we have seen, find it relatively easy and convincing to explain the plight of the Muslim world in terms of the eternal enmity of the Crusading-Zionist forces of global Unbelief (*Kufr*) ranged against the pure, embattled, Godly community of pristine Islam.

This is mirrored by Far-right Extremists who blame the apparent decline of Western global hegemony and their own individual inability to come to terms emotionally and economically with changes brought about by globalization on a global Islamist conspiracy to Islamize Europe and the whole world.

It is obvious that in this polarized dynamic that both extreme sides 'need' each other as evidence that their extreme Worldview is true and that their *raison d'être* holds good. In this respect, it is common to find videos of Far-right, Islamophobic rallies embedded in Violent Islamist Extremist propaganda – for example in videos of the so-called Blasphemy Movement in Pakistan which encourage the extra-judicial lynching of those who are deemed to have insulted either Islam or the Prophet Muhammad-as 'evidence' of the eternal and essential enmity of Islam and the West.

The cultural hinterlands of Extremism

What is less obvious than the overt mutual 'othering' of extremists are the covert, cultural hinterlands that incubate these extremisms that many citizens of different types allow or even quietly encourage.

Far Right Extremism can only actively persist because many citizens of European countries believe or at least are not prepared to challenge the idea that Muslims, who may not accept prima facie *all* the premises of secular liberalism, do not fit into life in Europe. Such people do not realize how deeply alienating to Muslim young people their insulting attitudes are and how much they feed into extremist narratives.

Islamist Extremism can only persist because significant pockets of the Muslim community are prepared to stereotype non-Muslims as inherently Godless and lacking in morality and exist and operate as if the world were divided into the 'Us' world of the Muslim and the 'Them' world of the Infidel (*kuffar*).

In this new cultural Cold War of low-level mutual Muslim/non-Muslim 'othering', elements of the media in its obsession to 'find stories' based on polarized dialectics are also not without blame – generating the feeling for many people of faith that faith itself is now a marginal social activity and the views of the orthodox faithful on important matters such as abortion or homosexual marriage are barely tolerated and fast becoming 'taboo'.

"Those who go to extremes are bound to be destroyed"

In bemoaning the increasing proliferation of extremes or near-extremes, one should not be utopian. Individuals and groups always have and always will define themselves to some degree against and by not-being something/someone else: a basic characteristic of the 'I' is that I am not 'You'; a basic characteristic of any 'Us' is that we are not 'Them'. However, the mainstream political environment that has developed in the past ten years and accelerated with the Brexit vote (23 June 2016 CE) and the election of President Donald Trump (November 8 2016 CE) with vociferous support from the alt-right has recently introduced a regressive ugliness that had previously been restrained by, for example, a relatively tolerant pan-European Christian culture and multiculturalism.

This is not the place to discuss supposed realities and effects of the decline, if not fall, of institutional European Christianity. As for multiculturalism, the Civil Rights movement in the United States of America in the 1960s and the race riots in Britain of the 1970s inspired the grass-roots movement in education and politics of multiculturalism that ushered in three decades of relative civil/civic restraint in Europe and America when talking about and dealing with the 'Other', especially the ethnic and religiously minor, non-white Christian 'Other'.

However, this movement for a more universal equality, flourishing and respect has all but collapsed under the stultifying effects of its own political correctness, and the fact that the fruits of the globalized economy that the multicultural ethos heralded and facilitated have not been in any way evenly spread through society. Globalization has been accompanied by an increasing of the income and cultural gap within liberal democracies such as the UK and the US and between the globalized rich and the localized, relatively and sometimes absolutely poor.[12]

Increasingly, as a result of the almost constant discrediting of the multicultural center,[13] we are witnessing the emergence of two civil society ethical-rhetorical extremes. At one 'free-speech' extreme, it is now no longer taboo to surrender to the rhetoric of the extreme demonizing and insulting of out-groups, even in the most crass and populist terms. As we saw in Donald Trump's presidential campaign in his blanket threat to outlaw Muslims from entering America and his promise to build the US-Mexico Border Wall, it has even become a marker of political authenticity for politicians to 'other' non-white Europeans in general, and Muslims in particular, as a threat to the security of civilization. As we have seen, in a similar way it has long been a marker of Islamists since Sayyid Qutb to 'other' liberal democrats and especially American liberal democrats as prurient, Godless and an essential threat to Islam.

At the other rhetorical extreme, 'no-platforming' of anyone and any idea that a group or person does not like to hear in the public space by students, universities and governments, as happened recently to the feminist thinker Germaine Greer for expressing her views on transgendering, has created a dangerous tyranny of political correctness in which the direction of legal and normative travel of secular liberal society cannot in any way be openly challenged. This drives legitimate, critical alternative views underground and even to violent extremes.

In this cultural and political environment in which the extremes and the near-extremes have gobbled up so much of the center-ground, I would argue that the new Struggle for Muslims and those of other faiths alike is resisting and combatting extremisms of all types, including climate-change denial.[14] Our Struggle is to ensure the survival of civilized human and, relatedly, diverse and rich natural life and not to let the critical, rational voice of faith be silenced. Part of this Struggle will involve creating and protecting a public space in which rational debate, conducted in full sentences and not sound-bites, is possible and in which all types of rational voices, including rational religious voices, that do not advocate violence or the type of hatred that leads to violence, are included and respected.

---

12 Goodhart, *The Road to Somewhere*.
13 Triggered, or perhaps reflected, by the former Chair of the Commission for Racial Equality, Trevor Phillip's, comment that Britain was "sleepwalking into segregation". Casciani, 'Analysis'.
14 In the face of overwhelming empirical scientific evidence for it.

In this urgent imperative for society to pull back from the extremes and re-engage with the ideal of universal human and natural flourishing, everyone would, I believe, do well to heed the words of a seventh-century religious reformer called Muhammad, son of Abdullah, if you are not Muslim; Muhammad, the Prophet of God, if you are.

It is reported by Muslim on the authority of Ibn Mas'ud that the Prophet Muhammad said, *"Those who go to extremes are bound to be destroyed." And he repeated it three times.*

Appendix 1
Basic Guides to Mainstream Islam

In the contemporary period, the notion that Islam can be practiced fully and properly in the circumstances of everyday life[1] is shared by the authors of hundreds of Basic Guides to Islam written by local community or international scholars who are keen to distill and transmit the basic Religious Obligations and practices of Islam (*'ibadat*) that Muslims in their communities are likely to need on a daily basis.

Books in this Basic Guide genre include:

Islam – The Natural Way

(Hamid, 2004/1989)[2]

The Five Pillars of Islam

(Hussain, 2012)[3]

An Explanation of Important Lessons

(Bin Baz, 2003)[4]

What unites this type of book, which are sourced from a diverse range of legal and theological Islamic traditions, is the (often implicit) conviction that Islam can be practiced in its basic entirety within the social conditions of modernity, often in Muslim-minority contexts which are not overtly Islamic. They are also premised on the idea that the basic essentials of the Mainstream Islamic Worldview can be grasped by the individual Muslim relatively easily without violating the basic conditions of 'normal' life.

---

1 I.e. that it is a philosophically 'serious' faith.
2 Hamid, *Islam the Natural Way*.
3 Hussain, *The Five Pillars of Islam*.
4 Baz, *Explanation of Important Lessons for Every Muslim*.

Appendix 2
Digital Islam

A critical medium for communicating Mainstream Islam that needs to be considered is the medium of the Internet. Through this, the phenomenon of 'digital' Islam is transforming the way that Muslims understand, communicate and debate the meaning of Islam. The digital Islamic space is, of course, populated by a plethora of websites and blogs. These websites often have a Salafi Muslim flavor, identifiable by the extensive use of hadith material to illustrate rulings and the doubling of vowel sounds – as in Islaam or *hadeeth* – to provide what is regarded as an accurate transliteration of Islamic Arabic.

As is to be expected, they range enormously in the quality of the depth and information that they provide from the highly rigorous and useful to the sketchy and suspect. They fall into a number of genres (far from) exclusively:

A. General information, including basic beliefs and practices of Islam and Islamic history

There are hundreds, if not thousands, of these. Three of the most useful are:

1 Understand Islaam: www.understand-islam.net
2 Islaam.com: www.islaam.com
3 Sunnah Online: www.sunnahonline.com/main.htm

B. Islam-related heritage and current affairs, of which a prominent one is:

Muslim Heritage.com: www.muslimheritage.com

C. Informal legal judgments (*fatawa*) on a host of daily matters, given by online muftis

Two excellent ones in this category are:

Islam QA. com: www.islam-qa.com – which offers well-evidenced and balanced legal rulings handled by Sheikh Muhammad Salih al-Munajjid, and
Islamtoday.com: http://islamtoday.com/ – a site run under the general supervision of Salman al Awdah which also offers (mainly) balanced legal rulings.

D. **Websites directed at Muslim women**, often with links to providers of modest clothes such as:
   http://www.islamswomen.com/index.php

E. **Websites containing translations and commentaries of Qur'an and the hadith material**

   Some of the most influential ones are:
   https://quran.com/
   Tafsir.com: www.tafsir.com which offers a comparative line-up of all the major Sunni and Shia commentaries side-by-side.

These and other websites show that Mainstream Muslims have embraced the digital age and have tended not to be religiously 'Luddite'. As is to be expected from the exponents of a faith which has specifically foregrounded scientific progress since the ninth century, many Muslims have regarded the internet and technological progress more generally as an opportunity to discuss, update, revive, criticize and spread their faith and to renew the ties of a transnational global faith community.

Glossary of key terms and names

Abbasid – the dynasty of Successors (Caliphs) to the Prophet Muhammad in leadership of the Muslim community who were descendants of the Prophet's uncle Al-Abbas ibn Abd al-Muttalib (566–653 CE). They ruled the heartlands of Islam from 750-1258 CE.

Abduh, Muhammad (1849–1905) – a highly influential Egyptian Muslim reformist theologian. See Chapter 5.

Abdullah Azzam (1941–1989) – a Palestinian VIE ideologue, nicknamed 'The Godfather of Jihad'. See Chapter 7.

Abu Bakr as-Siddiq (573–634) – the intimate Companion of Muhammad and the first Successor (Caliph) to him in leadership of the Muslim community. See Chapter 2.

Abu Hamza Al-Masri (born 1958) – an Egyptian VIE ideologue and long-term resident of the UK who preached at the Finsbury Park Mosque. He is currently serving a life sentence in the United States for terrorism offences.

Abu Hanifa, al-Numan ibn Thabit (699–767) – the early Kufan jurist and teacher whose followers founded the Hanafi School of Law.

Abu Muhammad al-Adnani (1977–2016) – the spokesman and ideologue of the Islamic State Group responsible for the issue to two influential 'fatwas' calling for 'Jihad' against civilians in the West. See Chapter 7.

Abu Musab Az-Zarqawi (1966–2006) – the leader of Al-Qaeda in Iraq who exploited the ideas of 'The Management of Savagery' and genocide of Shia Muslims during the Iraqi insurgency of 2003–2006. This laid the ideological blueprint for the Islamic State Group. See Chapter 7.

Ada – the custom or pattern of God when acting in His creation.

Ahl al-Bayt – the People of the House, i.e. the Prophet Muhammad's family.

Ahl al-Hadith – 'People of Prophetic Sayings' who were early jurists who avoided jurisprudential tools and attempted to adhere strictly to Prophetic Sayings to make judgments of law.

Ahl al-Kitab – 'People of the Book' who are a Qur'anic and legal category of people who have been given Scripture by God prior to Islam. This usually refers exclusively to Christians and Jews, but in some rulings applies also to the non-Abrahamic faithful such as Hindus. People of the Book have particular rights in Islamic Law.

Ahl al-Rayi – 'People of Opinion' were people who exercised their own judgment and reason to arrive at legal judgments and who were opposed by Ahl al-Hadith.

Ahl as-Sunna wal Jama – 'People of Prophetic Example and Consensus,' i.e. Sunni Muslims. See Chapter 2.

Aisha bint Abi Bakr (613–678) – a wife of the Prophet Muhammad, who was the daughter of the close Companion and first Successor to Muhammad, Abu Bakr as-Siddiq. She is revered in Sunni Islam as the transmitter of thousands of Prophetic sayings.

Akhira – the Next World, i.e. life-after-death.

Al-Ashari, Abu al-Hassan (874–936) – founder of the orthodox Asharite School of Belief, whose ideas are explored in Chapter 2.

Al-Awlaki, Anwar (1971–2011) – the late influential spokesman and ideologue for Al-Qaeda, who, as an American citizen, was controversially killed in Yemen in 2011 in an American drone strike. See Chapter 7.

Al-Banna, Hassan (1906–1949) – an influential Ideological Islamist thinker whose ideas have influenced both Activist Islam and Islamist Extremism. His contribution is explored in Chapter 6.

Al-Farabi, Abu Nasr (d.951) – an early Muslim Hellenistic philosopher and polymath, who wrote an influential treatise on the ideal city.

Al-Fitnat ul-Kubra – the 'Great Split' between Sunni and Shia Muslims examined in Chapter 2.

Al-Ghazali, Abu Hamid (1058–1111) – a Persian jurist and Reviver of Islam who re-integrated Sufism into Mainstream Islam. His contribution is explored in Chapter 5.

Al-Islambouli, Khalid (1955–1982) – an Egyptian army officer and member of the Islamic Jihad VIE group who assassinated President Anwar Sadat in 1982.

Al-Mahdi – 'the Guided One', the Imam of the Muslims who will usher in the End of Times according to Muslim eschatology.

Al-Kindi, Abu Yusuf (801–873) – an early Muslim Hellenistic philosopher, jurist and polymath.

Al-Malhama – the Battle of Armageddon when it is believed in some forms of Muslim eschatology that the armies of Islam will defeat the armies of the Anti-Christ (Dajjal).

Al-Mamun (786–833) – the Abbasid Caliph who established the proto-university, the House of Wisdom, in Baghdad.

Al-Muwatta – 'The Well-Trodden Path' – the earliest codified, thematized text of Islamic legal rulings derived from hadiths compiled by Malik ibn Anas. See Chapters 2 and 5.

Al-Shabab – literally The Youth, a Somali VIE group that pledged allegiance to Al-Qaeda in 2012, which it retains, despite some defections to the Islamic State Group.

al-Wala' wal Bara' – 'Loyalty and Disavowal': a Salafi Muslim doctrine that is deployed by Islamist Extremists to divide the Universe into pure Muslims with Loyalty to an Islamic State together with total rejection (Disavowal)

Glossary of key terms and names 215

of anyone or anything that is not sourced in 'pure' Islam. See Chapters 4, 6 and 7.

Ali ibn Abi Talib (599–661) – the cousin and son-in-law of Muhammad who was the fourth Successor (Caliph) to Muhammad in leadership of the Muslim Community until his assassination in Kufa, Iraq. See Chapter 2.

Allah – the One God, literally the One Worthy of Worship. This word had been used in Arabic to denote God Almighty long before the coming of Islam in 610 CE.

Amal – a legal term for 'behavior', which refers to the habitual behavior of the Companions of Muhammad.

Amir – a leader of a community or a commander of troops.

Am – a legal term meaning 'general', which refers to Qur'anic verses which articulate principles that are applicable to all times and places.

Ansar – 'helpers' which refers to the inhabitants of the town of Yathrib, which is now named Medina in modern Saudi Arabia, who welcomed the Prophet Muhammad and his Companions after their migration from Mecca and helped them settle.

Aqeeda – 'belief', i.e. the science of what Muslims believe about God, Prophethood and related religious matters.

Aql – intellect, reason.

Asbab an-Nuzul – 'Reasons of the Revelation', i.e. the context and the purposes for which Muslim commentators believe that the verses of the Qur'an were revealed to the Prophet Muhammad.

Ash-Shafi, Muhammad ibn Idris (767–820) – a Gazzan jurist who founded the influential Shafi School of Law. See Chapters 2 and 5.

Awra – an Islamic legal term referring to the private parts of the body which must be covered in public.

Ayat – verse of Qur'an, literally 'a sign'.

Azza wa Jall – 'May He may exalted and glorified', an honorific for God.

Badr, Battle of (17 March 624) – the first major military engagement of the Islamic period which was fought between c. 300 Muslims commanded by the Prophet Muhammad and a pagan Qurayshi army of c.1000 at the wells of Badr in modern Saudi Arabia. It resulted in a crushing victory for the outnumbered Muslim force and established the Prophet Muhammad's reputation as a leader.

Baya – the traditional Oath of Allegiance between a Muslim and a Muslim leader. It was taken by Muhammad from his Companions following pre-Islamic custom.

Bida – religious innovation.

bin Laden, Osama (1957–2011) – the VIE ideologue, financier and leader of Al-Qaeda. His contribution is explored in Chapter 7.

Cerantino, Musa (b.1986) – an Australian VIE ideologue who has encouraged migration to the territory held by the so-called Islamic State group.

Dar al-Harb – 'The territory of War' in medieval Muslim times referred to territories or kingdoms with which a Muslim polity was at war. The concept

216 *Glossary of key terms and names*

has been revived and changed by Islamist Extremists to refer to any country that does not govern by what they regard as pure *Sharia* Law.

Dar al-Kufr – 'The territory of Unbelief' in medieval Muslim times referred variously to territories in which Muslims were in the minority and/or which did not govern themselves according to *Sharia* Law. The concept has been revived by Islamist Extremists to refer to any country that does not govern by what they regard as pure *Sharia* Law, even where Muslims can fulfill the obligations of their faith.

Dawa – literally means 'calling', i.e. calling people to accept Islam; proselytizing.

Deen – means a 'religion or religious Life-Transaction or Covenant with God'. Islam is usually referred to as *Deen al-Islam*.

Falsafa – Islamic Hellenistic philosophy. See Chapters 2 and 5.

Faqih – someone who is adept in *fiqh*, the rulings of Sharia Law, i.e. a religious jurist.

Faraj, Muhammad Abd as-Salam (1954–1982) – an Egyptian VIE ideologue of Islamic Jihad whose ideas are explored in Chapter 7.

Fard al-Ayn – an Individual Religious Obligation which every adult Muslim must do in all times and places. See Chapters 4 and 7.

Fard al-Kifaya – a Collective Religious Obligation which only one part of the Muslim community needs to perform in order for the duty to be fulfilled by all. See Chapters 4 and 7.

Fiqh – the rulings of *Sharia* Law, literally means 'understanding'.

Fitra – the natural state of submission to and awareness of God into which Muslims believe all babies are born.

Fiy Sabilillah – 'in the Path of God', usually connected with 'Jihad Fiy Sabilillah' meaning 'Struggle in the Path of God.'

Hafidh – 'protector', i.e. someone who has memorized the whole Qur'an.

Hajj – Pilgrimage. The Obligatory Pilgrimage to worship God in Mecca that the Muslim must perform once in a lifetime if s/he is able financially and physically to do so.

Hanafi – someone who adheres to the Sunni School of Law founded by Imam Abu Hanifa.

Hanbali – someone who adheres to the Sunni School of Law founded by Imam Ahmed ibn Hanbal.

Hijra – 'migration', which usually refers to the migration of the Prophet Muhammad and about 100 Companions from conditions of severe persecution in the town of Mecca to conditions of peace and recognition in the town of Yathrib, 200 miles to the North of Mecca, in July 622 CE. The Hijra marks the beginning of the Islamic Calendar. The concept has been abused by VIE ideologues such as Musa Cerantino and Anjem Choudhary to encourage migration of Western Muslims to the territory controlled by the Islamic State Group. See Chapter 7.

Hisb ut-Tahrir – an Ideological Islamist group committed to the re-establishment of a global Islamic Caliphate.

Hudud – literally means 'limits' and refers to the penal code of *Sharia* Law.

Ibn Abdal Wahhab, Muhammad (1703–1792) – the eighteenth-century religious reformer and founder of Wahhabi Islam. See Chapters 2 and 5.

Ibn Abi Sufyan, Muawiya (602–680) – the first Umayyad Successor to the Prophet Muhammad. See Chapter 2.

Ibn Affan, Uthman (577–656) – the third Rightly-Guided Successor to the Prophet Muhammad who was murdered in controversial circumstances. See Chapter 2.

Ibn Al-Arabi, Muhyi udeen (1165–1240) – an influential Andalusian Sufi adept whose ideas on the Unity of Being came close to monism. See Chapter 2.

Ibn Al-Khattab, Umar (579–644) – the second Rightly-Guided Successor to the Prophet Muhammad, who is revered by Muslims as a great statesman and lawmaker.

Ibn Hanbal, Ahmed (780–855) – the founder of the hadith-based Sunni Hanbali School of Law.

Ibn Rushd, Abu al-Walid (1126–1198) – an Andalusian judge and polymath from the Maliki School of Law whose commentaries on the philosophy of Aristotle were hugely influential on the Latin Christian Scholastics. See Chapter 5.

Ibn Taymiyya, Taqi ud-Deen Ahmed (1263–1328) – a thirteenth–fourteenth-century Hanbali jurist whose theological and jurisprudential views became influential on the Salafi strain of Wahhabi Islam. His ideas have been distorted beyond recognition to support VIE ideology. See Chapters 4 and 7.

Ihsan – 'sincerity of worship', defined by the Prophet Muhammad as worshipping God as if you see Him in the knowledge that, although you do not see Him, He sees you. It is the aspect of Islam that developed into Sufism.

Ijma – 'consensus' of the jurists of the Muslim community about a legal ruling according to the Qur'an and the *Sunna*. There are different varieties of legal consensus in *Sharia* Law.

Ikhwan al-Muslimeen – 'The Muslim Brothers', the originally Egyptian, now international, network of Ideological Islamist group 'The Muslim Brotherhood' founded in 1929 by Hassan al-Banna. See Chapters 3, 4 and 6.

Iman – traditional Islamic faith in God, His Books, His Prophets, His Angels, His Decree and His Final Judgment.

Irtidad – 'apostasy', which traditionally refers to the act of someone both leaving and then opposing or betraying Islam to its enemies. In Islamist Extremist circles it refers to the acts of governments and their citizens that are seen to compromise aspects of *Sharia* Law and which enter into agreements with 'infidel' States.

Islah – 'reform': one of the aspirations of Activist Islam. See Chapter 4.

Islam – means 'submission to God in way that brings peace'. A Life-Transaction (*deen*) described by the Qur'an and the *Sunna* of the Prophet Muhammad that is traditionally constituted by the outer religious aspects of the worship of One God (*Islam*), inner belief (*iman*) and sincerity of worship (*ihsan*).

Istishad – 'seeking martyrdom'. The act of seeking to die for the faith of Islam. Usually in VIE texts and circles this refers to murder by suicide.

Istishan – 'preference in the public good': an aspiration of Mainstream Islamic jurisprudence to seek judgments that further the public good.

Jafar as-Sadiq, Imam (702–765) – an early teacher of Islam and jurist whose followers founded the Shia Jafari School of Law.

Jahiliyya – pre-Islamic ignorance. This concept was re-defined by the Islamist Ideologue Sayyid Qutb to refer to anything or anyone that was not purified, political Islam. See Chapter 6.

Jamat e-Islami – the Islamic Party. The Pakistani Islamist Party founded by Abul Ala Maududi. See Chapter 6.

Jihad – Struggle. It is short for 'Jihad Fiy Sabilillah' meaning 'Struggle in the Path of God'. Doctrines of different dimensions of 'Struggle in the Path of God', including armed struggle in defense of Islam, were developed after the death of the Prophet Muhammad. See Chapters 3 and 4.

Ka'aba – the Cube. The House of God in Mecca which Muslims believe was first erected by the Prophet Abraham to worship God. It is the focal point of the Hajj pilgrimage and the direction (*qiblah*) of the Five Obligatory Daily Prayers.

Kafir, pl. Kuffar/Kafirun – an infidel, literally someone who covers up the reality of God's existence, i.e. a proactive atheist. It is used by Islamists to refer any non-Muslim, including believing Christians and Jews, and by Islamist Extremists to refer to anyone – Muslim or non-Muslim – who does not fight to establish an Islamic State. See Chapters 4, 6 and 7.

Kalam – speculative theology.

Khalifa – a Caliph. Either a political Successor to the Prophet Muhammad, or, in the theological sense, someone who deputizes for God on Earth. See Chapters 3 and 4.

Kharijite, pl. Khawarij – 'those who departed', i.e. rebels who abandoned the army of the Caliph Ali ibn Abi Talib. See Chapter 2.

Khass – particular. A legal term for a verse of the Qur'an whose meaning is particular to the circumstances of the Prophet Muhammad and his Companions.

Khilafa – Caliphate. A territory that is governed by a Caliph.

Khomeini, Ayatollah Ruhollah (1902–1989) – the revolutionary Islamist founder of the Islamic Republic of Iran. See Chapter 6.

Lawh – a writing board used traditionally for memorizing the Qur'an.

Malik ibn Anas (711–795) – the Medinan Imam, author of Al-Muwatta and founder of the Maliki School of Law. See Chapters 2 and 5.

Maqasid as-Sharia – the *Objectives* of the *Sharia*. These are the purposes underpinning Islamic Law such as the protection of human life, property, intellect, lineage and reputation.

Maududi, Abul Ala (1903–1979) – a key Pakistani Ideological Islamist writer and activist. See Chapter 6.

Medina – is short for 'Medinat an-Nabawiyya', which was called 'Yathrib' – the town in modern Saudi Arabia which welcomed Muhammad and his

Companions after migration in 622 CE and was re-named 'Medinat an-Nabawiyya', the Prophetic City.

Mufassirun – a person of tafsir; a commentator on the Qur'an. See Chapter 5.

Muhajirun – a person of Hijra; a religious migrant. 'Muhajirun' usually refers to the Meccan Companions who migrated with Muhammad from Mecca to Yathrib in 622 CE. It is also the name of a contemporary VIE group who have encouraged young people to migrate to the so-called Islamic State.

Mujahid, pl.Mujahideen – someone who struggles in the path of God, who makes Jihad, often with the meaning of armed Jihad.

Munafiqeen – a religious hypocrite; someone who says that s/he believes and follows the message of Islam when s/he does not. The concept has been abused by Islamist Extremists to refer to Muslims who are not prepared to fight non-Muslims or who enter into collaboration with non-Muslims.

Murtad – an apostate; someone who commits irtidad. See Irtidad above.

Mushrik – someone who associates divine partners with God, for example by worshipping idols.

Muslim – someone who has submitted to God by following Islam.

Mutakallimun – a speculative theologian; a person of 'kalam'.

Mutazilite – a rationalist. Someone who foregrounds the role of human reason in approaching Revelation. See Chapter 2.

Nabi, pl. Anbiyya – a Prophet. A person sent by God to humanity to remind us to worship and obey Him. See Chapter 4.

Qital – killing. The dimension of Struggle in the Path of God (*Jihad Fiy Sabilil-lah*) that refers to armed combat, under strict conditions and regulations. See Chapters 3, 4, 6 and 7.

Qiyas – analogy. A jurisprudential method for deriving Islamic legal rulings about matters on which the Qur'an and the *Sunna* are silent. See Chapters 2 and 5.

Qur'an – literally means 'The Recitation'. It is the book of Islam that Muslims believe was revealed from the Presence of God by the Archangel Gabriel to the Prophet Muhammad between 610 and 632 CE. See Chapters 4 and 5.

Quraysh – the powerful Meccan Arab tribe to which the Prophet Muhammad belonged.

Qutb, Sayyid (1906–1966) – a Egyptian Islamist ideologue who was key in the development of both Non-Violent and Violent Islamist Extremism. See Chapter 6.

Rafidha – Rejectors. A derogatory term used by Sunni extremists for Shia Muslims for supposedly rejecting the authority of the Rightly-Guided Successors. See Chapter 2.

Rasoolullah – the Messenger of God. The title that the Prophet Muhammad most normally used.

Sahaba – Companions of the Prophet Muhammad, who are defined legally as anyone who heard or saw him alive and believed in his message. Some of the closest Companions of Muhammad have a status in Islam that is analogous to that of the disciples of Jesus in Christianity.

Salaf as-Salih – the Pious Predecessors, who were the first three generations of Muslims, that is the generations of the Prophet Muhammad and his Companions (the Sahabah), their Successors (the Tabi'un) and the Successors of the Successors (the Taba Tabi'in).

Salah – the Obligatory Prayer, which Muslims must perform five times every day: before sunrise, at midday, in the mid-afternoon, at sunset and in the first part of the night.

Salafi – followers of the Pious Predecessors. Salafi usually refers to those who follow the stripped-down reformed Hanbalism of Muhammad ibn Abal Wahhab in their aspiration to copy the Pious Predecessors as closely as possible in every detail.

Salal Allahu alayhi wa salim – 'God bless him and grant him peace'. An honorific used in religious circumstances when the name of the Prophet Muhammad is mentioned.

Sawm – the Obligatory Fast of the month of Ramadan, the 9th month of the Islamic lunar calendar, when adult Muslims abstain from food, drink and sexual activity between dawn and dusk for 29–30 days.

Shahada – the Witnessing. The first Individual Religious Obligation of Islam to witness that there is no god except the One God (*Allah*) and Muhammad is the Messenger of God.

Shaheed, pl. Shuhada – 'martyr', literally 'a witness' [to the truth of Islam]. Anyone who dies in the defense of Islam legitimately is a martyr in Islam. The concept has been abused by VIE exponents to justify suicide warfare. See Chapters 4 and 7.

Sham – the Levant or Greater Syria.

Sharia – the Legal Pathway of Islam derived from the Qur'an and the Normative Prophetic Example of the Prophet Muhammad (*Sunna*).

Sheikh – a religious teacher or tribal leader.

Shia t'ul Ali – The Party of Ali ibn Abi Talib. The faction which was loyal to the claims of Ali to be the first Successor to the Prophet Muhammad which over generations developed into distinctively Shia Islam. See Chapter 2.

Shirk – associating and/or worshipping partners with God in his Divinity.

Shura – Counsel, usually in the political sense of taking counsel.

Sunna – the Normative Prophetic Example of Muhammad, which is the primary source of Islam with the Qur'an. See Chapters 3 and 4.

Surah – a chapter of Qur'an, which is comprised of 114 Surahs.

Tafsir – commentary on Qur'an.

Takfir – 'excommunication', to call a Muslim an Infidel (*Kafir*). It is a characteristic of VIE groups to make 'takfir' of each other as a prelude to fighting each other. See Chapters 4 and 7.

Tasawwuf – 'Sufism', the sciences of purifying the heart to approach the Presence of God.

Tawhid – the doctrine of the Unity of God: a core doctrine of Mainstream Islam that is politicized and abused by Islamist Extremists.

Uhud, the Battle of (625 CE) – the second battle of the Islamic period fought between the Muslims and their pagan Qurayshi opponents on the plain and foothills of Mount Uhud outside Medina. The Muslim army suffered a significant defeat after a detachment of their archers protecting their rear abandoned their positions in search of booty.

Ulema, sing. *Alim* – literally 'those who know', i.e. those who know how to make legal judgments, i.e. jurists. Often in the past, the Ulema were adept in a whole range of knowledges, including law, philosophy, mathematics, poetry and music theory.

Umayyad – the early Islamic ruling dynasty descended from the Caliph Uthman ibn Affan whose capital was in Damascus, Syria.

Umma – the global faith-community of Muslim believers. This is believed by Ideological Islamists to have the necessarily political dimension of an Islamic State.

Urf – 'custom', a category of legal decision-making in *Sharia* which takes account of the customs of a particular place.

Usul al-Fiqh – jurisprudence, literally 'the roots of legal understanding.'

Yathrib – the town in modern Saudi Arabia which welcomed the Prophet Muhammad and his Companions after migration in 622 CE and was renamed 'Medinat an-Nabawiyya', the Prophetic City, usually referred to simply as Medina.

Zakah – the 'Poor Tax': an obligatory payment of 2.5% of a Muslim's annual savings above a certain threshold for the upkeep of the poor and others in need.

References

Abdel Haleem, M. A. S. (trans.) *The Qur'an: English translation with parallel Arabic text*. Bilingual, Revised edition. OUP Oxford, 2010.

Abdul-Rahman, Muhammad Saed. *The Meaning and Explanation of the Glorious Qur'an* (Vol 9). London: MSA Publication Limited, 2009.

Abu Hanifa, Nu'mān ibn Thābit et al. *Iman Abu Hanifa's Al-Fiqh Al-Akbar Explained By Abu I-Muntaha Ai-Maghnisawi*. 1st edition. London: White Thread Press, 2007.

Abu Zahra, Muhammad. *The Four Imans Their Lives, Works and Their Schools of Thought*. Edited by Abdalhaqq Bewley and M. I. Waley. Translated by Aisha Abdurrahman Bewley. London: Dar Al Taqwa Ltd, 2000.

Adamson, Peter. *Al-Kindi*. Oxford: Oxford University Press, 2006.

Afsaruddin, Asma. *Striving in the Path of God: Jihad and Martyrdom in Islamic Thought*. New York, USA: Oxford University Press, 2013.

Al-Adnani, Abu Muhammad. 'Indeed Your Lord Is Ever Watchful'. Jihad Watch. Accessed 8 August 2017. www.jihadwatch.org/2014/09/islamic-state-we-will-conquer-your-rome-break-your-crosses-and-enslave-your-women-by-the-permission-of-allah.

Al-Banna, Hassan. *Five Tracts of Hassan Al-Banna (1906–1949) a Selection from the Majmu'at Rasa'il Al-Imam Al-Shahid Hasan Al-Banna*. Translated by Charles Wendell. Berkeley, CA: University of California Press, 1975.

Al-Bukhari, Muhammad. *Sahih al-Bukhari - Sunnah.com - Sayings and Teachings of Prophet Muhammad* (صلى الله عليه و سلم). Available at: https://sunnah.com/bukhari (Accessed: 23 May 2018).

Al-Dawoody, Ahmed. *The Islamic Law of War*. New York: Palgrave Macmillan US, 2011.

Alexandra, Kerry. 'Muslim Women at "Disadvantage" in Workplace'. BBC News, 11 August 2016, sec. UK. www.bbc.co.uk/news/uk-37042942.

Al-Hassani, Salim T. S., ed. *1001 Inventions: The Enduring Legacy of Muslim Civilization*. Washington, DC: National Geographic, 2012.

Ali, Yusuf. *The Holy Qur'an: Arabic Text with English Translation*. New Delhi: Kitab Bhavan, 2000.

Al-Khalili, Jim. *Pathfinders: The Golden Age of Arabic Science*. London: Penguin, 2012.

Al-Makki, Abu Talib. *Qut al-qulub fi mu'amalat al-mahbub wa wasf tariq al-murid ila maqam al-tawhid* (The nourishment of hearts in dealing with the Beloved and the description of the seeker's way to the station of declaring oneness). ed. Basil 'ayun al-sud, Dar al-kutub al-'ilmiyah, Beirut, 1997.

Al-Qahtaani, Muhammad Saed. *Al-Wala' Wa-L Bara': According to the 'Aqeedah of the Salaf.* London: Al-Firdaus, 1981.

Al-Qaradawi, Yusuf. *General Characteristics of Islam.* Cairo: Islamic Inc., 1972.

Al-Shafi', Muhammad I. *Al-Shafi'i's Risala: Treatise on the Foundations of Islamic Jurisprudence.* 2nd Revised edition. Translated by M. Khadduri. Cambridge: The Islamic Texts Society, 1987.

Al-Yaqoubi, Muhammad. *Refuting ISIS: A Rebuttal of Its Religious and Ideological Foundations.* Hayes: Sacred Knowledge, 2015.

Ansari, Ali M. *Modern Iran since 1921: The Pahlavis and After.* 1 edition. London: Longman, 2003

Arendt, Hannah. *The Origins of Totalitarianism.* Place of publication not identified: Benediction Books, 2009.

Awlaki, Anwar. *Allah Is Preparing Us for Victory*, 2006. Ummah.com. Accessed 24 April 2018. https://www.ummah.com/forum/forum/general/the-lounge/94056-anwar-al-awlaki-allah-is-preparing-us-for-victory-2006

Azzam, Abdullah Yusuf. *Defence of Muslim Lands.* London: Azzam Publications, 1979/2002.

Azzam, Abdullah Yusuf. *Join the Caravan.* London: Azzam Publication, 1981/2001.

Baderin, Mashood. 'Sharia Law and Secular Democracy'. In *Islam and English Law*, edited by Robin Griffith-Jones. Cambridge: Cambridge University Press, 2013.

BBC Europe. 'Cologne Attackers "Were Migrant Men"'. BBC News, 11 January 2016, sec. Europe. www.bbc.co.uk/news/world-europe-35280386.

Bin Ali, Mohamed, *The Roots of Religious Extremism: Understanding The Salafi Doctrine of Al-Wala' Wal Bara'.* London: Imperial College Press, 2015.

Bin Baz, Abdul-Aziz . *Explanation of Important Lessons* (for Every Muslim). Riyadh: Darussalam, 2002.

Bin Laden, Osama. *A Declaration of War Against the Americans.* London: Azzam Publications, 1996.

———. (1998) Urging Jihad Against the Americans. Available at: https://fas.org/irp/ world/para/docs/980223-fatwa.htm.

Bhaskar, Roy. *Dialectic: The Pulse of Freedom.* London: Verso, 1993.

———. *Dialectic: The Pulse of Freedom.* 2nd edition. Abingdon: Routledge, 2008.

Brice, Kevin. *A Minority within a Minority: A Report on Converts to Islam in the United Kingdom.* Swansea: University of Swansea & Faith Matters, 2010.

Brachman, Jarret M. *Global Jihadism.* London: Routledge, 2009.

Brockwell, Joshua, and CAIR. 'What's the Role of Mothers in Islam?'. ThoughtCo. Accessed 19 December 2017. www.thoughtco.com/paradise-is-at-the-feet-of-mothers-2004265.

Brown, Jonathan A. C. *Hadith: Muhammad's Legacy in the Medieval and Modern World.* London: Oneworld Publications, 2009.

———. *Misquoting Muhammad: The Challenge and Choices of Interpreting the Prophet's Legacy.* London: Oneworld Publications, 2014.

Brown, Katherine E. 'Contesting the Securitization of British Muslims'. *Interventions* 12, no. 2 (1 July 2010): 171–182. https://doi.org/10.1080/1369801X.2010.489690.

Burke, Jason. *Al-Qaeda.* London: Penguin, 2003.

———. *The 9/11 Wars.* 1st Edition 2011 edition. London: Allen Lane, 2011.

References

Casciani, Dominic. 'Analysis: Segregated Britain?', 22 September 2005. http://news.bbc.co.uk/1/hi/technology/4270010.stm.

Clarence-Smith, William Gervase. *Islam and the Abolition of Slavery*. Oxford; New York: Oxford University Press, USA, 2005.

Cockburn, Patrick. *The Rise of Islamic State*. London: Verso, 2015.

———. 'We Visited the Site of Isis's Worst-Ever Atrocity'. *The Independent*, 6 November 2017. www.independent.co.uk/news/world/middle-east/camp-speicher-massacre-isis-islamic-state-tikrit-air-academy-iraq-a8040576.html.

Connolly, Kate. '"I've Never Experienced Anything Like That": Cologne in Deep Shock over Attacks'. *The Guardian*, 8 January 2016, sec. World News. www.theguardian.com/world/2016/jan/08/ive-never-experienced-anything-like-that-cologne-in-deep-shock-over-attacks.

Crone, Patricia, and Martin Hinds. *God's Caliph: Religious Authority in the First Centuries of Islam*. New edition. Cambridge: Cambridge University Press, 2008.

Croucher, Shane. 'Refugees Crisis: Angela Merkel Leads Germany's Rebirth as a Promised Land for the Persecuted'. International Business Times UK, 8 September 2015. www.ibtimes.co.uk/refugees-crisis-angela-merkel-leads-germanys-rebirth-promised-land-persecuted-1518965.

'Discrimination against Muslim Women – Fact Sheet'. American Civil Liberties Union. Accessed 19 December 2017. www.aclu.org/other/discrimination-against-muslim-women-fact-sheet.

Donohue, John J., and John L. Esposito, eds. 'The Covenant of the Islamic Resistance Movement HAMAS'. In *Islam in Transition*. Oxford, UK: Oxford University Press, 2007.

Duderija, Adis. 'Islamic Law Reform and Maqasid al-Sharia' in *Maqasid al-Sharia and Contemporary Reformist Muslim Thought* edited by Adis Duderija, 13–37. New York: Palgrave Macmillan, 2014.

Fakhry, Majid. *Averroes: His Life, Work and Influence*. Oxford: Oneworld Publications, 2001.

Faraj, Mohammed Abdus Salam. *The Absent Obligation*. Edited by Abu Umamah. Birmingham: Maktabah al-Ansar, 2000.

Feldman, Noah. *After Jihad*. New York: Farrar, Straus and Giroux, 2003.

———. *The Fall and Rise of the Islamic State*. Princeton, NJ: Princeton University Press, 2008.

Gardham, Duncan. 'ISIL Issued Warning to "Filthy French"'. Politico, 17 November 2015. www.politico.eu/article/paris-terrorist-attacks-isil-issued-warning-to-filthy-french/.

Gardiner, Nile. 'The Death of Zarqawi: A Major Victory in the War on Terrorism'. The Heritage Foundation. Accessed 7 August 2017. https://web.archive.org/web/20100311083517/www.heritage.org/Research/MiddleEast/wm1118.cfm.

Gomaa, Sheikh Ali. 'A Fatwa on Jihad'. In *War and Peace in Islam*, edited by Prince Ghazi Bin Muhammad, Ibrahim Kalin, and Mohammed Hashim Kamali. Cambridge: Islamic Texts Society, 2013.

Goodhart, David. *The Road to Somewhere: The Populist Revolt and the Future of Politics*. London: C. Hurst & Co. Publishers, 2017.

Grey, Stephen. *The New Spymasters: Inside Espionage from the Cold War to Global Terror*. 1st edition. London: Viking, 2015.

Hakim, Catherine. *Honey Money: The Power of Erotic Capital*. London: Penguin Books Ltd., 2011.

Hallaq, Wael. *The Impossible State: Islam, Politics, and Modernity's Moral Predicament.* New York: Columbia University Press, 2012.
Hamid, Abdul Wahid. *Islam The Natural Way.* 2nd edition. London: MELS, 2004.
Hassaballa, Hesham A. 'Think Muslims Haven't Condemned ISIS? Think again'. Common Word, Common Lord, 22 August 2014. www.beliefnet.com/columnists/commonwordcommonlord/2014/08/think-muslims-havent-condemned-isis-think-again.html.
Hawting, Gerald R. *The First Dynasty of Islam: The Umayyad Caliphate AD 661–750.* 2nd edition. Abingdon, UK: Routledge, 2000.
Hizb ut-Tahrir. 'Hizb Ut Tahrir', 2015. www.hizb-ut-tahrir.org/index.php/EN/nshow/2919/.
———. 'Hizb Ut Tahrir', 2016. www.hizb-ut-tahrir.org/index.php/EN/def.
Hourani, Albert. *A History of the Arab Peoples.* New edition. London: Faber & Faber, 2005.
Hourani, George F. *Reason and Tradition in Islamic Ethics.* Cambridge: Cambridge University Press, 1985.
Hussain, Musharraf. *The Five Pillars of Islam: Laying the Foundations of Divine Love and Service to Humanity.* Markfield: Kube Publishing Ltd, 2012.
Ibn Ishaq. *The Life of Muhammad.* Translated by A. Guillaume. Oxford: Oxford University Press, 1955.
Ibn Khaldun, Al Muqaddimah: Prolegomena. Bletchley: JiaHu Books, 1377/2014.
Ibn Rushd. *The Distinguished Jurist's Primer: a translation of Bidayat al-Mujtahid.* Translated by Imran Ahsan Khan Nyazee. Reading: Garnet Publishing Limited, 1188/2000.
Ibrahim, E. and Johnson-Davies, D. (eds) *An-Nawawi's Forty Hadith.* Beirut: The Holy Koran Publishing House, 1976.
'ICM Unlimited | ICM Muslims Survey for Channel 4'. *ICM Unlimited* (blog), 11 April 2016. Accessed 23 September 2017. www.icmunlimited.com/polls/icm-muslims-survey-for-channel-4/.
Ipgrave, Julia. 'Multiculturalism, Communitarianism, Cohesion, and Security: The Impact of Changing Responses to British Islam on the Nature of English Religious Education'. In *Civic Enculturation and Citizenship in North America and Western Europe*, edited by Robert Heffner and Adam Seligman, 2014.
'Iyad, Qadi. *Foundations of Islam.* Norwich: Diwan Press, 1982.
Johnston, David L. 'Yusuf al-Qaradawi's Purposive Fiqh' in *Maqasid al-Sharia and Contemporary Reformist Muslim Thought* edited by Adis Duderija, 39–71. New York: Palgrave Macmillan, 2014.
Kamali, Mohammed Hashim. *Principles of Islamic Jurisprudence.* Cambridge: Cambridge University Press, 2003.
———. *Maqasid Al-Sharia'ah Made Simple.* International Institute of Islamic Thought, London: 2008
———. 'Introduction'. In *War and Peace in Islam*, edited by Prince Ghazi Bin Muhammad, Ibrahim Kalin, and Mohammed Hashim Kamali. Cambridge: The Islamic Texts Society, 2013.
Kennedy, Hugh N. *The Court of the Caliphs.* London, UK: Weidenfeld & Nicholson, 2004.
Kennedy, Hugh N. *The Caliphate.* London: Pelican, 2016.
Kerr, Malcolm H. *Islamic Reform: The Political and Legal Theories of Muhammad 'Abduh and Rashid Rida.* 1st edition. University of California Press, 1966.

———. *The Caliphate*. London: Pelican, 2016.
Brice, Kevin. *A Minority within a Minority: A Report on Converts to Islam in the United Kingdom*. Swansea: University of Swansea & Faith Matters, 2010.
Khalidi, Muhammad A. (ed.) *Medieval Islamic Philosophical Writings*. Cambridge: Cambridge University Press, 2005.
Kobeisi, Kamal. 'Remembering the Muslims Who Were Killed in the 9/11 Attacks'. Alarabiya News. Accessed 4 August 2017. https://english.alarabiya.net/articles/2011/09/11/166286.html.
Lewis, Bernard. *The Crisis of Islam: Holy War and Unholy Terror*. Reprint edition. London: Random House Trade Paperbacks, 2004.
Lewis, Phillip. *Islamic Britain: Religion, Politics and Identity among British Muslims*. London: I. B. Tauris & Co Ltd, 2002.
Lovat, Terence. *Saving Islam from Jihadism: A Theological Analysis*. Oxford: Oxford University Press, 2017.
Lumbard, Joseph E. B. *Islam, Fundamentalism, and the Betrayal of Tradition, Revised and Expanded: Essays by Western Muslim Scholars*. Rev Exp edition. Bloomington, Indiana: World Wisdom Books, 2009.
Lyons, Jonathan. *The House of Wisdom*. London: Bloomsbury Publishing Plc, 2009.
Madden, Imran. "Why Muslims Donate So Much To Charity, Particularly During Ramadan." HuffPost UK. May 17, 2018. http://www.huffingtonpost.co.uk/entry/why-muslims-donate-so-much-to-charity-particularly_uk_5afd799fe4b0cf33e9beafe2.
Maher, Shiraz. *Salafi-Jihadism: The History of an Idea*. London: C. Hurst & Co, 2016.
Mahmutćehajić, Rusmir. *On the Other: A Muslim View*. New York: Fordham University Press, 2011.
Malik, Ibn Anas. *Al-Muwatta of Imam Malik – Arabic-English*. 4 edition. Translated by A. Bewley. Diwan Press, 2014.
Martin, Richard C., Mark Woodward, and Dwi S. Atmaja. *Defenders of Reason in Islam: Mu'tazililism from Medieval School to Modern Symbol*. London: Oneworld Publications, 1997.
Maududi, Abul Ala. 'Political Theory of Islam'. In *Islam: Its Meaning and Message*, 147–171. Leicester, UK: The Islamic Foundation, 1939/1975.
———. *Jihad in Islam*. Beirut: The Holy Koran Publishing House, 1939/1980.
———. *Khutabat: Fundamentals of Islam*. 2nd edition. Chicago: Kazi Publications, 1988.
McCants, William. *The ISIS Apocalypse: The History, Strategy, and Doomsday Vision of the Islamic State*. New York: St. Martin's Press, 2015.
McCarthy, Vincent A. *The Phenomenology of Moods in Kierkegaard*. Boston: Martinus Nijhoff, 1978.
McClam, Erin. 'ISIS Pays Foreign Fighters $1,000 a Month: Jordan King'. NBC News, 22 September 2014. www.nbcnews.com/storyline/isis-terror/isis-pays-foreign-fighters-1-000-month-jordan-king-n209026.
McCoy, Terence. 'The American Prison That Became the Birthplace of Isis'. *The Independent*, 2014. www.independent.co.uk/news/world/middle-east/camp-bucca-the-us-prison-that-became-the-birthplace-of-isis-9838905.html.
Michot, Yahya. *Muslims Under Non-Muslim Rule Ibn Taymiyya*. Oxford: Interface Publications, 2006.
———. *Ibn Taymiyya*. London: Birkbeck College, University of London, 2015.
Middle East Monitor. 'Prominent Scholars Declare ISIS Caliphate "Null and Void"'. *Middle East Monitor* (blog), 5 July 2015. www.middleeastmonitor.com/news/middle-east/12567-prominent-scholars-declare-isis-caliphate-null-and-void.

Milani, Sayyid Fadhel Hosseini. *The Core of Islam*. Edited by Amar Hegedus. London: Islam in English Press, 2011.

Mosley, Michael. 'Eat, Fast and Live Longer, 2012–2013, Horizon'. BBC, 9 May 2012. www.bbc.co.uk/programmes/b01lxyzc.

Muslim, ibn Al-Hajjaj. *Sahih Muslim – Sunnah.com – Sayings and Teachings of Prophet Muhammad* Available at: https://sunnah.com/muslim (Accessed: 12 July 2018).

Muslim Council of Britain. 'Muslims Make Joint Declaration to Fight Climate Change | Muslim Council of Britain (MCB)', 18 August 2015. www.mcb.org.uk/muslims-make-joint-declaration-to-fight-climate-change/.

Muslim Women's Network UK. 'Banning of Burkinis on Beaches – Standing against Patriarchy in All Its Forms', 24 August 2016. www.mwnuk.co.uk/mediaStatmentDetail.php?id=166.

Naji, Abu Bakr *The Management of Savagery: The Most Critical Stage Through Which the Umma Will Pass*. Translated by W. McCants. John M. Olin Institute for Strategic Studies: Harvard University Press, 2006.

Nasr, Seyyed Hossein, Caner K. Dagli, Maria Massi Dakake, Joseph E. B. Lumbard, and Mohammed Rustom. *The Study Quran: A New Translation and Commentary*. Tra edition. New York: HarperOne, 2015.

National Counterrorism Centre. *Report on Terrorism*. Washington, DC: United States Government, 12 March 2012.

Naugle, David K., Jr. *Worldview: The History of a Concept*. 1st edition. Grand Rapids, Michigan: Eerdmans, 2002.

Nichols, Joel A. *Marriage and Divorce in a Multi-Cultural Context: Multi-Tiered Marriage and the Boundaries of Civil Law and Religion*. Cambridge: Cambridge University Press, 2011.

Norton, Claire. 'Blurring the Boundaries: Intellectual and Cultural Interactions between the Eastern and Western; Christian and Muslim Worlds'. In *The Renaissance and the Ottoman World*, edited by Anna Contadini and Claire Norton, 3–22. Farnham: Ashgate, 2013.

'November 2015 Paris Attacks'. Wikipedia, the Free Encyclopedia, 26 November 2015. https://en.wikipedia.org/w/index.php?title=November_2015_Paris_attacks&oldid=692537643.

Orr, James. *The Christian View of God and the World*. London: Regent College Publishing, 2001.

Pasha-Robinson, Lucy. 'This Girl Was Captured by Isis When She Was 14 Years Old: They Raped Her Every Day for Six Months'. *The Independent*, 24 July 2017. www.independent.co.uk/news/world/middle-east/isis-sex-slave-yazidi-girl-northern-iraq-rape-sexual-abuse-experiences-a7857246.html.

Peck, Tom. 'Theresa May to Set up Commission for Countering Extremism'. *The Independent*, 27 May 2017. www.independent.co.uk/news/uk/politics/theresa-may-conservative-manchester-attack-general-election-2017-commission-countering-extremism-a7759486.html.

Phillips, Christopher. *The Battle for Syria: International Rivalry in the New Middle East*. New Haven: Yale University Press, 2016.

Pizzi, Michael. 'In Wake of Attacks, Parisians Ask, Why Here?', 14 November 2015. http://america.aljazeera.com/articles/2015/11/14/after-worst-terror-attack-in-decade-parisians-ask-why-us.html.

Qutb, Sayyid. *The America That I Have Seen: In the Scale of Human Values* Al-Risala Vol. 19; no. 957, 959, 961; pp. 1245–7, 1301–6, 1357–1360. Cairo: 1951

———. *Milestones*. Karachi: International Islamic, 1964.

Rahnema, Ali. (ed.) *Pioneers of Islamic Revival*. London ; Atlantic Highlands, N.J: Zed Books Ltd., 1994.

Rapoport, Yossef, and Ahmed, Shahab. *Ibn Taymiyya and His Times*. Oxford: Oxford University Press, 2010.

Razeq, Abdel Ali. *Islam and the Foundations of Political Power*. Edited by Abdou Filali-Ansary and Maryam Loutfi. Edinburgh: Edinburgh University Press, 2012.

Reilly, Robert R. *The Closing of the Muslim Mind: How Intellectual Suicide Created the Modern Islamist Crisis*. Wilmington: Delaware: ISI Books, 2011.

Richardson, Louise. *What Terrorists Want: Understanding the Enemy, Containing the Threat*. New York: Random HouseTrade Paperbacks, 2007.

Rogan, Eugene. *The Arabs: A History*. 1st Trade Paper edition. New York: Basic Books, 2011.

Rogin, Josh. 'CIA Director: Attacks on Europe No Surprise, More Expected'. Bloomberg View, 16 November 2015. www.bloombergview.com/articles/2015-11-16/cia-director-attacks-on-europe-no-surprise-more-expected.

Ross, Alice. 'Academics Criticise Anti-Radicalisation Strategy in Open Letter'. *The Guardian*, 29 September 2016, sec. UK News. www.theguardian.com/uk-news/2016/sep/29/academics-criticise-prevent-anti-radicalisation-strategy-open-letter.

Salahi, Adil. *Pioneers of Islamic Scholarship*. Leicester: Islamic Foundation, 2006.

Sardar, Ziauddin. *Reading the Qur'an*. London: C. Hurst & Co Publishers Ltd, 2011.

Shaltut, Mahmoud. 'The Qur'an and Combat'. In *War and Peace in Islam*, edited by Prince Ghazi Bin Muhammad, Ibrahim Kalin, and Mohammed Hashim Kamali. Cambridge: Islamic Texts Society, 2013.

Sherif, Faruq. *A Guide to the Contents of the Qur'an*. Reading: Garnet Publishing Ltd., 1995.

Silber, Laura, and Alan Little. *The Death of Yugoslavia*. 2nd edition. London: BBC Books; Penguin, 1996.

Stone, Mark. 'Germans Worry about Growing Migrant Numbers'. Sky News, 8 October 2015. http://news.sky.com/story/1565925/germans-worry-about-growing-migrant-numbers.

Tajfel, Henri. *Human Groups & Social Categories*. Cambridge: Cambridge University Press, 1981.

Takim, Liyakat. '*Maqasid al-Sharia* in Contemporary Shi'i Jurisprudence' in *Maqasid al-Sharia and Contemporary Reformist Muslim Thought* edited by Adis Duderija, 101–125. New York: Palgrave Macmillan, 2014.

Taylor, Richard C. 'Averroes'. In *The Cambridge Companion to Arabic Philosophy*, edited by Richard C. Taylor and Peter Adamson, 180–200. Cambridge: Cambridge University Press, 2005.

Taylor, Charles Margrave. *A Secular Age*. Cambridge, MA: The Belknap Press of Harvard University Press, 2007.

TellMAMA. 'Anti-Muslim Hatred, Terrorism, Media Sources, Far Right Networks & Spike Points'. *TELL MAMA* (blog), 13 October 2017. https://tellmamauk.org/anti-muslim-hatred-terrorism-media-sources-far-right-networks-spike-points/.

TellMAMA. 'How Could Bob Blackman MP Host an Anti-Muslim Extremist in Parliament?' *TELL MAMA* (blog). October 25, 2017. https://tellmamauk.org/how-could-bob-blackman-mp-host-an-anti-muslim-extremist-in-parliament/.

Vidal, Clement. 'What Is a Worldview?'. In *Nieuwheid Denken. De Wetenschappen En Het Creatieve Aspect van de Werkelijkheid*, edited by H. Van Belle and J. Van der Veken. Leuven: Acco, 2008.

Wilkinson, Matthew L. N. 'Introducing Islamic Critical Realism'. *Journal of Critical Realism* 12, no. 4 (2013): 419–442.

———. *A Fresh Look at Islam in a Multi-Faith World: A Philosophy for Success through Education*. Abingdon: Routledge, 2015.

———. 'The Metaphysics of a Contemporary Islamic Sharia: A MetaRealist Perspective'. *Journal of Critical Realism* 14, no. 4 (1 August 2015): 350–365.

Wilkinson, Richard, and Kate Pickett. *The Spirit Level: Why Equality Is Better for Everyone*. London: Penguin, 2009.

Winter, Tim. 'Introduction'. In *The Cambridge Companion to Classical Islamic Theology*, edited by Tim Winter. Cambridge Companions to Religion. Cambridge: Cambridge University Press, 2008.

Index

'44 Ways of Supporting Jihad' (al-Awlaki) 186–187

ibn Abbas, Abdullah 140
Abbasid Executive 33
Abdal Jabbar, Qadi 39
Abd al Malik, Umayyad, Caliph 39
ibn Abdal Wahhab, Muhammad 45, 47, 143–145
Abduh, Muhammad 46, 66, 99, 149–153
ibn Abi Sufyan, Muawiya 25, 26
Abode of Islam (Dar al-Islam) 75–76
Abode of Unbelief (Dar al-Kufr) 75–76, 77
Abraham 18
Abu Bakr as-Siddiq 18, 22, 23, 80, 107–108
Abu Hanifa, al-Numan ibn Thabit 32–33, 141–142
Activist Islam: reform 112–113; sincere counsel 111–112; Struggle in the Path of God 113–114; themes and ethical praxis of 109–114; theological Caliphate 110; Worldview of 52, 61–66
al-Adnani, Abu Muhammad 74, 127, 197–198
ibn Affan, Uthman 23, 24, 25, 80
al-Afghani, Jamal al-Din 46
Age of Extremes (Hobsbawm) 202
Ahl as-Sunna wal Jama ['People of Prophetic Example and Consensus'] (Sunni Muslims) *see* Sunni Muslims
Ali ibn Abi Talib 22, 23, 24–25, 85
allowed (halal) 89–91
Al-Nusra Front (Jabhat an-Nusra) 191, 194
Al-Qaeda 29, 36, 74, 77, 123, 127, 174, 182, 188, 194, 199

Al-Qaeda in Iraq (AQI) 124, 187, 189, 191
Al-Qaeda in the Arabian Peninsula (AQAP) 189
Al-Shabab 77
Angels 92
animals 101–102
anti-Ahmadi Movement 47
anti-Americanism 162–166
Apocalypse 74–75, 77
apostasy (irtidad) 26
apostate (murtad) 71, 123
Apostel, Leo 51
Arab Spring 191
Arendt, Hannah 76
Aristotle 40, 41
Armageddon, Battle of 124
armed struggle (Qital): Ideological Islamism 114, 161, 170–171; Mainstream Islam 105–106; Non-Violent Islamist Extremism 121–122; Normative Prophetic Example 107–109; Violent Islamist Extremism 125–128, 174, 176, 179
al-Ashari, Abu al-Hassan 43
Asharite School of Belief 43
Ash-Shafi, Muhammad Idris 43, 141, 142–143
al-Assad, Bashar 35, 36, 191
al-Assad, Hafiz 35
al-Awda, Salman 66, 112
al-Awlaki, Anwar 73, 74, 128, 184–187
Azrael (Malak al-Maut/the Angel of Death) 92
Azzam, Abdullah 73, 176–179, 182
az-Zarqawi, Abu Musab 124, 189–191

Badr, Battle of 21, 180
Baghdad 27

Index

al-Baghdadi, Abu Bakr 191, 193–194
al-Banna, Hassan 36, 68, 69, 115, 158–161, 174
Barelwi movements 47
The Battle for Hearts and Minds (al-Awlaki) 185
al-Baydawi, Nasir al-Din 140
Becket, Thomas 34
Behavior of the People of Medina (amal ahl al-Medina) 32
belief (Iman) 71
bin Baz, Abdal Aziz 181
bin Idris ash-Shafi', Muhammad 33
bin Laden, Osama 36, 48, 73, 179–184
Bismillahi Al-Rahman Al-Raheem 116–117
Blackman, Bob 64–65
Blasphemy Movement 47, 206
Boko Haram 77
'The Book of Divine Unity' [Kitab al-Tawhid] (ibn Abdal Wahhab) 143–145
Bosnian War 181–185

Cairo 27
Caliphate (Khalifa) 110, 193–194
Caliphs (Successor): divisions over succession to Muhammad 18, 22–23; Rightly-guided Caliphs 23–24; theological Caliphate 110–111
Cerantino, Musa 73
Chapter of Sincerity (Surat al-Ikhlas) 138
Charlie Hebdo attacks 186
Collective Obligation (Fard al-Kifaya) 126
Companions (Sahaba) 18, 21, 22, 24, 32, 80, 96, 100
compassion 94–95
'The Compendium' (al-Mudawwana) 108
The Concept of Jihad in Islam [*Al-Jihad fiy al-Islam*] (Maududi) 157
counsel (shura) 21, 22
Covenant (Deen) 87
Crusader-Zionist Alliance 179–184
Custom of God (Sunnat Allah) 151

Damascus 26, 28, 40
al-Dawoody, Ahmed 103
Day of Resurrection and Judgment 93
Decree 93
Defence of Muslim Lands (Azzam) 177–179

Deobandi Movement 35, 47
Deputies of God (Khalifat Allah) 24
Deputizing for God (Khilafa) 66
Deputy of God (Khalifatullah) 154
diversity-in-unity 61–66
Divine books 92–93
'The Dust Will Never Settle Down' (al-Awlaki) 185–186

Empedocles 40
Euclid 40
excellent conduct 95–96
excommunication (takfir) 26, 45, 123–124
Extremism: cultural hinterlands of 207; ethical-rhetorical 208–209; first Age of Extremes 202–203; polarized dynamic of 206–207; political conditions of 202–203; root causes of Islamist 203–209; second age of extremes 206

al-Farabi, Abu Nasr Muhammad ibn Muhammad 41
Faraj, Muhammad Abd as-Salam 36, 123, 174–176
Fast (Sawm) 88, 126
Fatima (daughter of the Prophet) 22, 23, 25, 27, 85
Fatimid Ismaili Dynasty 27
female infanticide 101
Five Pillars of Islam 87–89
freedom of religion 102–103

Gabriel the Archangel, Saint 17, 80, 92
Galen of Pergamon 40
al-Ghazali, Abu Hamid 42–43, 145–148
The Global Islamic Resistance Call (as-Suri) 188
God (Allah) 24, 54, 56, 83–84, 87, 92, 116–120, 136, 167–168
Gospels 93
governance 26
Great Divide (Al-Fitnat al-Kubra) 19
Guided One (Al-Mahdi) 28, 74

Hajj (Pilgrimage) 88, 102, 126, 141
Hanafi School of Law 35, 79, 141–142
ibn Hanbal, Ahmed 33, 36, 43–44, 141, 143
Hanbali School of Law 34, 35, 43–44, 45, 79, 143, 158
Hasan ibn Ali 23, 25
Hasan of Basra (Hasan al-Basri) 38

headscarf (hijab) 98
Hegel, G.W.F. 50
Helpers (Ansar) 22
Henry II, King of England 34
Hezbollah 74
Hobsbawm, Eric 202
House of Wisdom (Bayt al-Hikma) 40
al-Hudaybi, Hassan Isma'il 160
Hussain ibn Ali 23, 25, 26–27, 28
Hussain, Saddam 35, 191

Ibn Taymiyya, Taqi ud-Deen Ahmed 175
Ideological Islamism: establishment of Islamic State 68–70; inversion of agency and structure 68–69; inversion of religion and politics 67–68; Islamist manifesto of Party of Liberation 115–117; key themes 116; kinds of Muslim 155–157; people and texts 154–173; political Caliphate 114–115; themes and ethical praxis of 114–117; Worldview of 52–54, 66–70; Worldview of separation and exaggerated difference between the Muslims and the non-Muslim 69–70; 'wrong' or deficient Muslim 70
ignorance (Jahiliyya) 122, 167
Indian Partition 157
individual obligation (Fard al-Ayn) 176, 177
infidel (kafir) 71, 123
Inquisition (Al-Mihna) 34, 39
Iranian Islamic Revolution of 1979 171–173
Iraq 192–193
Iraq War 36, 190–191
Islam: Activist 61–66; age of Islamic Enlightenment 29–31; allowed and prohibited in 89–91; basic beliefs of 92–93; collapse of the intellectual vibrancy of 36; contemporary Basic Guides 210; digital 211–212; fault lines of civilization 19–20; as governing political ethos 21; greatness of civilization 18–19; Ideological Islamism 52–54, 66–70; Islamism 66–70; joint declaration to fight climate change 62; Mainstream 52; martyrdom 128–129; Original 17; as religious practice 21; sources of the Worldview of 79–109; Sunni-Shia divide 20–29; Traditional 54–60; Violent Islamist Extremism (VIE) 53–54, 73–77; Worldviews 52–54

al-Islambouli, Khalid 175
Islamic Awakening (Sahwa) 111
Islamic Climate Declaration 62
Islamic Law (sharia) 30, 67, 70, 79, 86–87, 89, 194
Islamic Party (Jamat e-Islami) 157, 159
Islamic penal code (hudud) 112
Islamic Resistance Movement (HAMAS) 161
Islamic State Group (ISG) 29, 75–77, 123, 127, 194–198
Islamic State in Iraq and Syria (ISIS) 192–193
Islamism: Activist Islam 52, 61–66; contingent separation and exaggerated difference 66–70; Ideological Islamism 52–54, 66–70; individualization of 203; Non-Violent Islamist Extremism 53–54, 66–67; Worldview of 66–70
Islamist Extremism: Hanbali-Wahhabi traits of 45; Non-Violent Islamist Extremism 53–54, 117–122; sub-human treatment of women 98–99; Violent Islamist Extremism (VIE) 53–54

Jabarites 27
Jabhat al-Nusra 74
Jafar as-Sadiq, Imam 33, 44, 85
Jafar ibn Sulayman 34
Jafari School of Law 33, 35, 79
Jamat e-Islami 69
Jihad: the Absent Obligation (Faraj) 174
John, Gospel According to 40
al-Jubba'i, Abu 39
July 7 terrorist attacks 199
justice 95–96
Jyllands-Posten 'Muhammad Cartoons' controversy 185

Ka'aba ('the Cube') 18
Karbala: Battle of 26–27, 28; massacre of Shia Muslims 45
ibn Kathir, Ismail 140
Kharijite Muslims 25, 28
ibn al-Khattab, Umar 23, 24, 25, 80, 102
Khomeini, Ruhollah, Ayatollah 171–173
Kierkegaard, Søren 50
al-Kindi, Abu Yusuf 40–41
Kouachi, Chérif 186
Kouachi, Saïd 186

'leaderless' armed struggle 127
legally-binding judgments (ijtihad) 81–82

literalists: Hanbalism gives birth to Wahhabism 45; Salafi 47–48, 120–121; school of 43–44
lone-wolf attacks 197–198
Loyalty and Disavowal doctrine (Al-Wala' wal-Bara') 118–121, 122–123, 187–188, 198

Madhabist traditionalists 47
Mainstream Islam: Activist Islam 52, 54, 61–66, 109–114, 131; armed struggle 105–106; fair treatment and equal status of women 96–98; freedom of religion 102–103; general and particular verses that permit fighting 106–107; headscarf 98; justice and excellent conduct 95–96; legal conditions of armed struggle in Sunna 107–109; mercy and compassion 94–95; misogyny and crimes against women 98–99; in the modern and contemporary period 149–153; people and texts 132–153; reform 112–113; religious seriousness in 57; sanctity of life 101–102; sincere counsel 111–112; solidarity 99–101; Struggle in the Path of God 103–104, 113–114; themes and ethical praxis of 94–109; theological Caliphate 110; Traditional Islam 52, 54–60, 131; Unity of God in 55–56; Worldview of 52, 54–60, 94
Malik ibn Anas 32–33, 34, 36, 85, 104–105, 141
Maliki School of Law 32–33, 79, 104, 108, 141–142
al-Ma'mun, Caliph 34, 39, 40
Management of Savagery (an-Naji) 190, 191
Manichean Islamist narrative 37
Manichean Worldview 71–72, 172
al-Maqdisi, Abu Muhammad 187
martyrdom: in original Islam 128–130; in Violent Islamist Extremism 129–130, 178
al-Maturidi, Muhammad Abu Mansur 43
Maturidi School of Belief 43
Maududi, Abu Ala 69–70, 115, 154–158, 167
Mecca 17, 20, 22, 33, 45, 67, 80, 105, 181
Meccelle 35
Medina 17, 21, 25, 26, 32–33, 45, 67, 80, 81, 181

Merabet, Ahmed 186
mercy 94–95
messengers 93
Michael the Archangel, Saint 92
Migrants (Muhajirun) 22
migration (hijra) 17, 20, 22, 80, 81
Milestones [*M'alim fiy Tariq*] (Qutb): theme of text 167; 'ur' text of Islamist Extremism 167–168
Millennialism 124
Mladic, Radko 181
Mubarak, Hosni 35
Muhammad, Prophet of Islam: death of 18; divisions over succession 22–23; fault lines of Islamic civilization and absence of 19–20; greatness of Islamic civilization and absence of 18–19; Normative Prophetic Example 22, 42, 56–57, 72, 83–86, 95, 97, 102–103, 107–109; Original Islam and 17–18; Qur'an and 17–18, 80; succession of 21–22; united leadership of 20–21
ibn al-Mundhir, Hubab 21
Muslim executive: division of powers between religious judiciary and 29–37; schools of law 32–37; separation of powers between religious judiciary and 31–32; tension between religious judiciary and 19
Muslim Pious Generations (Salaf as-Salih) 47
Muslim scholars 19
Muslim Women's Network UK (MWNUK) 63–64
al-Mutasim, Caliph 39
Mutazilite (rationalist) 34, 38–39, 43
mystic (Sufi) 42

al-Nadwi, Abu Hassan 167
an-Naji, Abu Bakr 190, 192
Nasser, Gamal Abdul 122
Neoplatonists 40–41
Nietzsche, Friedrich 50
Non-Violent Islamist Extremism: armed struggle 121–122; birth of 162–166; contingent separation and exaggerated difference 66–67; dehumanizing of the 'other' as characteristic of extremism 71–72; doctrine of Loyalty and Disavowal 118–121; Madhabist traditionalists and 47; Manichean Worldview 71–72; themes and ethical praxis of 117–122; Worldview of 53–54

Normative Prophetic Example (Sunna): dehumanizing of the 'other' as characteristic of extremism 72; derivation of 84–86; divisions over succession to Muhammad and 22; fair treatment and equal status of 97; freedom of religion 102–103; legal conditions of armed struggle in 107–109; martyrdom 128–129; mercy and compassion 95; in praxis of the Worldview of Mainstream Islam 83–84; Traditional Islam 42, 56–57

Oath of Allegiance (Baya) 194–195
Obligatory Prayer (Salah) 18, 87–88, 126
al-Omar, Nasser 112
opening chapter (Al-Fatiha) 133–137
Original Islam 17–18

Pahlavi, Muhammad Reza Shah 171
Pakistan 47, 157, 171, 206
Paradise 88
Party of Ali (Shia't ul 'Ali) *see* Shia Muslims
Party of Liberation (Hisb ut-Tahrir) 70, 115–116
People of Book (Ahl al-Kitab), 71
People of Hadith (Ahl al-Hadith) 44
People of Opinion (Ahl al-Rayi) 44
People of the Prophetic House (Ahl al-Bayt) 22–23, 27, 86, 171
Pilgrimage (Hajj) 88, 126
political Caliphate (Khilafa) 114–115
Poor Tax (zakah) 21, 88, 101, 126
prohibited (haram) 89–91
prophetic sayings (hadith) 32, 84–85, 140–143
Psalms 93
Pythagoras 40

Qadafi, Muammar 35
Qadarites 27, 38
al-Qaradawi, Yusuf 36
Qasim, Abu 191
Qur'an: armed struggle 105–106; belief in 93; Chapter of Sincerity 138; commentaries on 139–140; commitment to personal and structural change 61; content of 80–81; diversity in 56; essential unity in 55; freedom of religion 102–103; general and particular verses that permit fighting 106–107; interpretation of 81–83; literalist view of 43–45, 47–48; martyrdom 128–129; Muhammad and 17–18; nature of 79–80; opening chapter 133–137; other seminal chapters 137–139; rationalist view of 37–42, 46; traditionalist view of 42–43, 47; use to justify political allegiances and actions 27; Verse of the Throne 138–139; written record of 80
Qutb, Sayyid 36, 69, 71, 174; anti-Americanism 162–166; *Milestones* 166–170

Rabiah ibn Abdurrahman 32
rationalist modernists 46
rationalists: Islamic rationalist Hellenism 40–41; modernists 46; schools of 37–39; theistic and original nature of philosophy 41–42
al-Razi, Fakhr al-Din 140
reform (islah) 66, 112–113
rejectors (rafidha) 29
religious judiciary (Ulema): division of powers between Muslim executive and 29–37; Rightly-guided Caliphs and 24; schools of law 32–37; separation of powers between Executive and 31–32; tension between Muslim executive and 19, 143
Righteous Predecessors (Salaf as-Salih) 28
Rightly-guided Caliphs 21–24, 29
rulers (nasiha) 66
ibn Rushd (Averroes) 41, 104, 145–148

al-Sadr, Muqtadar 36
Sadat, Anwar 174
Safavid dynasty 27
Saladin (Salah Uddin al-Ayyubi) 25
Salafi literalists 47–48, 120–121
sanctity of life 101–102
ibn Saud, Muhammad 48
Saudi Arabia 45, 48, 180
scholars (mujtahid) 81–82
School of Authentic Reports (akhbari) 44
schools of law (madhahib) 32–37, 79
September 11 terrorist attacks 183–184, 199
Shafi'i School of Law 35, 79
Shia Muslims: attacks 190–191; Great Divide 19, 20–29; irrevocable split 26–29; literalist and compendious

approach to the use of Prophetic sayings 44; millennial eschatology of 28; prophetic sayings and 141–142; rationalist approach to the use of Prophetic sayings 44; rebellion 24–26; success of 170–173; vilification of 76
Siffin, Battle of 25
sincere counsel (nasiha) 111–112
Society of Muslim Brothers (Muslim Brotherhood/Ikhwan al-Muslimin) 69, 70, 159–161, 174
solidarity 99–101
Struggle in the Path of God (Jihad fiy sabilillah) 103–104, 113–114
struggle (jihad) 36, 103–105, 121–122, 125
Struggle with the Sword (jihad bis saif) 105
succession (Calipha) 18, 21–22
Successor to the Messenger of God (khalifa rasul Allah) 24
Sunni Muslims: failure of 170–173; Great Divide 19, 20–29; irrevocable split 26–29; rebellion 24–26
as-Suri, Abu Musab 188
al-Suyuti, Jalal al-Din 140
Syria 26, 28
Syrian Civil War 29, 74, 76, 191–193

Talbi, Mohammed 46
Territory of Islam (Dar al-Islam) 39
theological Caliphate 110
Torah 92
Traditional Islam: Customary Prophetic Behavior 56–57; diversity and 56; Divine Unity in 55–56; ethics 59–60; human relationships 58–59; praxis 57; religious seriousness in 57–58; Worldview of 54–60
traditionalists 42–43, 47
Translation Movement 40
Trump, Donald 199, 207
al-Turkmani, Abu Muslim 191

Umayyad dynasty 28
unbelief (kufr) 71, 72, 117, 123
unity-in-diversity 54–60
Unity of God (Tawhid) 55–56, 119, 123, 124–125, 133, 167

Verse of the Throne (Ayat al-Kursi) 138–139
verses (ayats) 81

Violent Islamist Extremism (VIE): Abode of Islam (Dar al-Islam) vs. The Abode of Unbelief (Dar al-Kufr) 75–76; apocalyptic eschatology 74–75; armed struggle 124–128, 179; context 174–200; declaration of the 'Caliphate' 193–194; defense of Muslim lands 177–179; doctrinal shifts legitimizing violence 175–176; doctrine of Loyalty and Disavowal 122–123, 125–126; excommunication (takfir) 123–124; impact of Bosnian War 181–185; Madhabist traditionalists and 47; martyrdom 129–130, 178; Millennialism 124; nihilism of 76–77; people and texts 174–200; praxeology of 73–74; revisions of armed struggle in 125–128; seminal political manifesto of 166–171; shared basic Worldview with Non-Violent Islamist Extremism 73; state-building of Islamic State 194–198; Syrian Civil War 191–193; themes and ethical praxis of 122–130; tremendous 'success' and appalling effects of 198–200; use of doctrine of excommunication 26; use of doctrine of irtidad 26, 29; Worldview of 53–54
Voluntary Acts of Charity (Sadaqa) 101

Wahhabi Islam 45, 47, 144–145
well-being 59–60
The Well-Trodden Path [*Al-Muwatta*] (Malik ibn Anas) 85, 104, 141
Witnessing (Shahada), 87, 126
women: fair treatment and equal status of 96–98; misogyny and crimes against 98–99
Worldviews: components 50–52; Islam as 52–54; Islamism as 52–54; Islamist Extremism as 52–54
worship 59–60

Yazid I, (caliph of the Umayyad caliphate) 26
The Youth (Al-Shabab) 189

Zainabiyoun Brigade 74
al-Zawahiri, Ayman 36, 123, 174, 187–188